HIGH STREET, WREXHAM.

HISTORY

OF THE

Town of Wrexham,

ITS HOUSES, STREETS, FIELDS, AND OLD FAMILIES.

Being the Fourth Part of " A History of the Town and Parish of Wrexham."

BY

ALFRED NEOBARD PALMER, F.C.S.,

AUTHOR OF

Town, Fields, and Folk of Wrexham in the Time of James the First."

WREXHAM:

WOODALL, MINSHALL, AND THOMAS.

1893.

First published in 1893
2nd edition published in 1982

This edition published in Wales in 1997 by
BRIDGE BOOKS
61 Park Avenue, Wrexham, LL12 7AW

A CIP entry for this book is available from the British Library

ISBN 1-872424-59-7

Printed by
MFP, Manchester

PREFACE.

I PRESENT herewith the fourth of the five volumes which are to make up my *History of the Town and Parish of Wrexham*. No one is more sensible than I am of the defects which have characterised the volumes that have already appeared ; but I need not hesitate to say that there is present therein an enormous mass of interesting details relating to the history of the town which we could ill afford to have lost.

The reader who wishes to become acquainted with all that is written herein concerning any particular family or person, is respectfully referred to the Index.

This, and my other books, have been written in the intervals of a relaxing calling, and during uninterrupted ill health, and been subject to other casualties, so that I hope the indulgent reader will forgive the defects in them, of which I am myself painfully conscious. One thing I may venture to say, that I have spared no pains to secure accuracy and fulness of detail.

ALFRED NEOBARD PALMER.

WREXHAM,
August, 1890.

NOTE. The long period that has elapsed between the time the manuscript of this book left my hands and the time when the last pages of it were printed, has resulted in some portions of it being now out of date. The recent construction of the Wrexham and Ellesmere Railway, in particular, has completely altered the appearance of some quarters of the town, and swept away many of its old land marks. Many houses, and even streets, mentioned in this book as existing, are now gone.

The reader is requested to make in the text the corrections indicated on pages 291-3.

ALFRED NEOBARD PALMER.

1893.

CONTENTS.

LIST OF ILLUSTRATIONS.

INDEX.

—

NOTE :- When the figures are in ordinary type the reference is to the text
when in Italics the reference is to the notes. The figures refer always
to the pages of the History.

—

INDEX.

THE HISTORY OF THE
TOWN OF WREXHAM.

Introduction.

1. Wrexham lies in that district, east of Offa's Dyke, which, in the 7th and 9th centuries, was almost completely settled by Englishmen. One indication of this settlement is found in the fact that the district itself (Bromfield) bears a very ancient English name, and that the names of most of the townships in it are also English. We may venture to say that the name of the town itself (of which "Gwrecsam" is merely a late Welsh form) is undoubtedly English, though we may not be able to explain its meaning. The second part of this name needs no explanation at all, and as to the first, this stands probably for some personal name, or contains a reference to the Wrocansætan, the people around the Wrekin, from which district almost certainly Bromfield was in great part settled.

2. Before the time of the Norman Conquest, the Welsh, taking advantage of the weakness of the English government, began to advance eastward, and recapture the land of which they had been deprived so long, and at the time of the taking of the Domesday Survey had already in their possession the western and middle portions of Bromfield (including Wrexham, it would appear), and soon after, all the remaining part of the district fell into their hands and became thoroughly Cymricized, the English inhabitants being either slain, expelled, or absorbed. The greater part of Bromfield was now made into a Welsh commote (*cymwd*) or rhaglotry of which Wrexham was the head or "maerdref," while Merford (now called Marford) became the head of another commote which also included lands outside Bromfield. These two commotes with Maelor Saesneg were included in a cantref the name of which is not given in the oldest lists, but which is called in the untrustworthy Myfyrian list "Cantrev Uwch Nant." In the oldest lists the commote of which Wrexham was the head is called "unknan" "vuknan" and "wnknan," names which require explanation and have probably been wrongly copied. In later times this commote came to be called "Maelor Gymraeg," or "Welsh Maelor."

3. As in 1202 Wrexham is called "Wrechessam," it is plain that the town was then called by the same name as it is now. "Wrexham" and "Wrixham" are the two oldest forms of the name.

The other forms, found in 13th and 14th century charters, are evidently due to errors of transcribers who mistook " c " for " t." Inasmuch as, during the thick of what I call the *second Welsh* period, this town had an English name, it is plain that it was settled by Englishmen before that period began, and received its name during the *first English* period, at some time between the time of King Offa and the Norman Conquest and probably during the early part of that first English period.

4 In the year 1200 Madoc ap Gruffydd Maelor, prince of Powys Fadog (the princedom to which the rhaglotry of Wrexham belonged), granted his demesne lands, or a part of them, in Wrexham to the new abbey of Valle Crucis, and these lands with a part of the township of Stansty, formed henceforth the manor of Wrexham Abbot, the rest of the maerdref constituting the manor of Wrexham Regis.

5. In 1277 when Madoc ap Gruffydd ap Madoc (grandson of the aforesaid Madoc ap Gruffydd Maelor), died, Bromfield still belonged to Powys Fadog, but immediately after his death Edward I. nominated Roger Mortimer to be guardian of Llewelyn and Gruffydd, the two infant sons of Madoc ap Gruffydd, and appointed Gruffydd ap Iorwerth to be justiciary of the territories late of the said Madoc ap Gruffydd, and to collect the issues of those territories and deliver them to Margaret his widow for the maintenance of her two infant sons, and directed that what was over and above necessary for their maintenance should be laid by for the future use of those sons, according to what the Bishop of St. Asaph, the aforesaid Magaret and the aforesaid Gruffydd ap Iorwerth, acting for the king, should think best.   In the year 1281 Llewelyn and Gruffydd, the sons of Madoc ap Gruffydd died : it is said they were drowned by John Earl of Warren and Roger Mortimer, but I have not yet seen any evidence that this really happened.   It is certain, however, that on the 7th October, 1282, Edward I. granted the rhaglotries of Wrexham, Marford, and Yale, part of the inheritance of the two boys, to John Earl of Warren, and from that time to this Bromfield has always been under English lords.

6. Although John Earl of Warren began to build the castle of Lyons or Holt, which was intended to be the head of his new lordship of Bromfield and Yale, and although English customs were gradually introduced, nevertheless the courts of the three rhaglotries were still held, and also the courts of the various manors within them, which manors as I have elsewhere shown, evidently represented old Welsh divisions.   In the " customs " of these rhaglotries and manors also, many of the old Welsh regulations and forms of plea were preserved.

7. In 1339 and 1340 courts were held at Wrexham, in which cognizance was taken of civil and criminal offences committed within all the townships comprised in the rhaglotry or " bailiwick " as

well as of transfers of land within the same. These courts were really the "turns" which took place twice in the year, and that turn which was convened at Michalemas 1339, was held in the open air on Mons Tumba in Wrexham. Where " Mons Tumba " was I do not know. The under given names[1] of the jurors sworn at the time indicated will show how predominantly Welsh the district in 1339 was. And among the names of the plaintiffs and defendants (which were very numerous) at the same court, the English names can be almost counted on the fingers.

8. In the time of Edward IV. the courts of the three rhaglotries of Wrexham, Marford, and Yale were still held separately, although no longer at their ancient places of meeting, but at Holt, the head of the lordship. Of course, however, the court of the *manor* of Wrexham Regis was still kept at Wrexham, and from a record of that time (October 8th, 1466) it appears that the English tenants of Wrexham were now become numerous enough to present for appointment a bailiff of their own, while the Welsh tenants also presented another bailiff, as well as an escheator, whom they called " y shettwr."

9. At one of the rhaglotry courts of Wrexham in the year 1467, although three of the twelve jurors had adopted surnames, these were members of famous Welsh families, while another of them, who was descended from the family of Puleston, had actually discarded his English surname and called himself Edward ap Madoc.[2] Here we have very strong evidence of the over-whelmingly Welsh character of the district, and when we remember that these jurors were landed gentlemen, who would be the first to succumb to English influence, we get additional evidence of the fact how very little, by the middle of the 15th century, Bromfield had become Anglicized. How little the Anglification of the *parish* of Wrexham progressed during the next century is shown by an examination of the names of the churchwardens from 1506 to 1592 given on pages 117-119 of my *History of the Parish Church of Wrexham.*

10. The church of Wrexham must have been in existence before 1220, but that is the year in which I first find it mentioned, and in the second volume of this series I have given all those particulars of the history of the town which cluster round the church.

1 Ieuaf ap Hwfa; Iorwerth ap Gruffydd; Llewelyn ap Madoc; Iorwerth Goch ap Madoc; Dafydd Foel; Iorwerth Goch ap Ednyfed; Howel ap Dafydd; Griffri ap Llewelyn; Madoc Foel ap Ieuaf; Madoc ap Ednyfed Goch; Einion ap Iorwerth ap Einion; and Llewelyn ap Dafydd ap Howel. I have altered the spelling of these names to that by which they would now be represented.

2 The following is a complete list of the jurors at this court :—John Eyton; Robert ap Howel; Edward ap Madoc; David Eyton; Howel ap Ieuan ap Gruffydd; David Bromfield; Edward ap Howel; David ap Iorwerth ap Madoc Ddu; Robert ap Gruffydd ap Bleddyn; David ap Llewelyn ap Ednyfed Lloyd; and Rhys ap Llewelyn ap Ednyfed.

11. A market and fair were held at Wrexham from very early times. The market I first find specifically mentioned in the year 1467, in which year Alson ferch Gruffydd, widow, was presented for selling salmon, cocks, etc., before they came to Wrexham market, but as *the tolls* of Wrexham are referred to in 1439 as worth £6 a year we may conclude that the market was already then in existence, and was of some importance.

12. John, Earl of Warren, the first English lord of Bromfield and of the maerdref or provostry[3] of Wrexham appears to have resigned in 1284 Bromfield and Yale to his son William de Warren, who however, died the year following, leaving, as his heir, his son, John, Earl of Warren, whose heir was his sister Alice, the widow of Edmund Fitzalan, fourth Earl of Arundel, whose son Richard Fitzalan, fifth Earl of Arundel, then became lord of Bromfield: the latter was succeeded, in 1375, by his son of the same name, the sixth Earl of Arundel, who was beheaded in 1398 by Richard II. Bromfield, with other of his estates, being conferred on William de Scrope, Lord Scrope, Earl of Wiltshire, and King of Man, who, however, enjoyed his grants for a single year only. Thos. Fitzalan, son of the sixth Earl of Arundel, was restored to his father's estates in the first year of Henry IV. (1399):he died in 1421 without heirs male, leaving three sisters namely ; Elizabeth, wife of Thomas Mowbray, first Duke of Norfolk ; Joan, wife of William de Beauchamp, Lord Abergavenny ; and Margaret, wife of Sir Rowland Lenthall. The eldest sons of these three sisters came into possession, each of a third part, or rather of a third part of two parts, of Bromfield and Yale, the remaining third part being alloted as dower to Beatrix, widow of Thomas, Earl of Arundel.

13 Of the first of these three parts, the first holder was John Mowbray, second Duke of Norfolk, (son of the first Duke), who was succeeded in 1432 by his son John, third Duke of Norfolk, who died in 1461, and was followed by his son, John Mowbray, fourth Duke of Norfolk. The last named died in 1475 leaving an only daughter, who died young, this portion of Bromfield then reverting to the Crown.

14 William de Beauchamp, Lord Abergavenny, the holder of the second of the three parts of Bromfield and Yale, died in 1410, and was succeeded by his son Richard, Lord Abergavenny, and Earl of Worcester, who died in 1421, leaving an only daughter, Elizabeth, who married Sir Edward Neville, afterwards Lord Abergavenny, who was succeeded by his son, Sir George Neville, Lord Abergavenny, but it is doubtful whether the son of this last, Sir Edward Neville of Adlington, possessed at the time of his beheadal, his father's portion of Bromfield and Yale.

---

3. "Provostry" appears to have been the word commonly used to translate not merely the Welsh "Maerdref" but the word which may be best expressed in English as "servile township."

15. As to the third part of the lordship it descended from Sir Rowland Lenthall to his son Edmund Lenthall, Esq., who still held it in 1444, but by 1467 this third part was extinguished, and the lordship of Bromfield and Yale was held in two undivided moieties by the Duke of Norfolk and the above named Lord Abergavenny.

16. Before 1489 both these moieties had reverted to the crown, for in that year Henry VII. granted the lordship to Sir William Stanley, second son of Thomas, Lord Stanley, but resumed it in 1495 on Sir William Stanley's execution, for his share in Perkin Warbeck's conspiracy.

17. In 1534 Henry VIII. granted Bromfield and Yale to his natural son Henry Fitzroy, Duke of Richmond and Surrey, but the latter died in 1536 and the lordship then reverted to the king. According to Pennant, the lordship in the time of Edward VI. was in the possession of Thomas Seymour, Admiral of England, but after his execution must have reverted to the crown. It was in the hands of the crown during the reign of Philip and Mary, and during the early part of the reign of Queen Elizabeth, I have met with a statement which makes me suspect that in 1588 and 1589 Robert, Earl of Leicester, was lord of Bromfield and Yale, but I cannot say certainly that this was so. In the reign of James I. however, the lordship belonged to the crown, and so has continued without interruption, except during the Commonwealth period, to our own times.[4]

18. In the Chancery Inquisition taken in 1439, after the death of Beatrix the above-named Countess of Arundel, the following description of the manor or provostry of Wrexham (Regis) occurs : " In the town Wryxham is a certain pu'ostr' valued at vjs viiid ; also an esceator, valued at xs ; rents of assise x li, XL acres of arable land, valued at 1d per acre ; x acres of meadow, at vid per acre ; cxx acres of pasture, at ½d per acre ; court baron every three weeks, xLs ; view of frankpledge, xs ; tolls vi li ; courthouse of no value." (*Powys Fadog, Vol I. p. 387.*)

19. In 1620 Norden's jury of survey of Wrexham Regis returned: " that upon Mundays and Thursdays, marketts are kept within the towne of Wrexham ; and that there are three ffayers kept in the said towne yerely, viz: upon the xııth of March, fifte of June, and the viii of September," " the toule, pickage, and stallage " of the same being then leased by the Crown to Roger Bellot, gent ; and that there were " presented and made at the Mich'as Leete yerely, by the jurie of this mannor, two cunstables w'ch doe serue the yeare following." By the omission of the eleven days on the rectification of the calendar, the 12th of March became the 23rd, the

4. On the 13th May, 1640, Charles I. granted for 23 years in consideration of £4,000 to Sir Thomas Trevor, Knt., fifth son of John Trever, Esq., of Trefalyn, a lease of the lordship.

first day of the great March fair, which still goes on, while the 8th
of September became the 19th, on which day the Honey Fair is
still held.   The fair on the 5th (which would become the 16th) of
June, I cannot afterwards trace.   On Buck's View of Wrexham,
dated 1748, the annual fairs are said to be held on the 24th of
March, (doubtless a mistake for the 23rd,) Holy Thursday, 6th of
June and 19th of September.   In Nicholas Carlisle's *"Topographical
Dictionary of the Dominion of Wales,"* published in 1811, the same
dates are given for the annual fairs, as also in the second edition of
" Nicholson's Cambrian Traveller's Guide" published in 1813.   The
middle Monday of the March fair always has been, and still is,
most resorted to, and is called "Dydd Llun Pawb" or *Everybody's
Monday*.   By the addition of eleven days, the 5th of June and the
8th of September became the 16th of June and 19th of September,
and these were still fair days in the middle of this century.   Before
the Corporation began to meddle with the old arrangements, the
annual fairs held in Wrexham were the third Thursday in January;
March the 23rd, and the days following ; Holy Thursday ; June
16th ; August 7th ; September 19th ; October 29th ; and the third
Thursday in December.

20. In 1623 the tolls of Wrexham fairs and markets were held by
lease of the Crown, at an annual rent of £10 6 8, by Roger Bellot,
gent, of Bersham.   Ultimately they were purchased by the Erddig
Hall family from whom the Market Hall Company at first leased
them, and in 1886 purchased them outright.   The Market Hall
Company, in turn, leased the tolls on September 25th, 1877, to the
Corporation, which still hold them at £10 a year.

21. So much for the yearly fairs, now as to the weekly markets.
In 1620, as we have seen, these were held on Mondays and Thursdays.   In Carlisle's *" Topographical Dictionary"* published in 1811,
Monday and Thursday are also given as the market days.   This is
the more curious as until 1889, when Monday was fixed upon
as one of the market days by the Corporation, the markets have
always been held within the memory of man on Thursdays and
Saturdays only.

22. Coming back now again to Norden's survey of Wrexham
Regis in A.D. 1620, it is obvious that the town was at that time
predominantly Welsh.   This appears not merely from the names of
the inhabitants mentioned in the survey, but more especially
from the fact that every field except one within the manor bore in
1620, a Welsh or semi-Welsh name.   By 1661, the English
element, as appears from the church rate lists of that year, had
largely increased, but there was still a very large number of people
without surnames, and who had such names as John ap Edward,
Elizabeth ferch Richard and the like.   Even during the middle of
last century such names were not absent, while many persons had
nicknames which had no meaning except in Welsh.

23. The rateable value of the town at different times presents several points of interest. In 1661, the total assessment on the whole parish being £150, Wrexham Regis was assessed at £32 10 and Wrexham Abbot at £10. In 1705 £80 as church rate were levied on the parish, of which £72 1 3¾ were actually collected; of this sum £17 3 4 were collected in Wrexham Regis, and £4 12 3½ in Wrexham Abbot. In 1725, an assessment of 4d in the £ on the whole parish was made, of which £104 5 6½ were actually collected, £29 4 7 being taken in Wrexham Regis, and £7 3 11 in Wrexham Abbot. In 1742, an assessment of 1/- in the £ was made on the whole parish, whereof £167 5 2¾ were actually collected, £49 10 2 being taken in Wrexham Regis, and £10 18 6½ in Wrexham Abbot, there being £5 16 5 left unpaid in the former manor, and £1 12 4½ in the latter. In 1808 a poor rate of 4/- in the £ for the whole year was levied, £419 14 0 being obtained from Wrexham Regis, and £145 13 0 from Wrexham Abbot, and as near as I can make out, £1741 10 6 from the whole parish. In 1841 a church rate of 3d in the £ produced from Wrexham Regis £136 15 10, and from Wrexham Abbot £41 13 4½ ; a total of £178 9 2½. In 1857 a church rate of 2d in the £ produced from Wrexham Regis £80 18 6½, and from Wrexham Abbot £19 5 10 ; the whole parish producing £294 7 6. The rateable value of Wrexham Regis at this time was £9,711 10 1 ; of Wrexham Abbot £2375 3 10; and of the whole parish, (which then included the two small townships of Erlas and Erddig), £35,328 8 6. In 1890 a borough rate of 7d in the in the £ produced £1289 4 0.

24. As to the population of the town, the first return of which I have any note relates to the year 1801, when there were 2,575 inhabitants living in 580 houses. In 1841 there were 5,854 inhabitants, of whom there were 3,745 in Wrexham Regis, 2,073 in Wrexham Abbot, and 36 in Esclusham Detached, the population of the parish at the same time being 12,921. At the census of 1871, there were in the municipal borough, 8,576 persons. But the total of 10,903 in 1881, gives a very inadequate idea of the size and importance of the place, for continuous with Wrexham, but outside the municipal borough, has in recent years grown up the populous suburb of Rhosddu. The latter, however, is included in the parliamentary borough, the population of which in 1881 was 12,333, and is now very much more. Wrexham, moreover, is the centre of a group of populous villages, several of which contain more inhabitants than the town itself did fifty years ago.

25. Here it may be well to say that the area of Wrexham Regis is 952.948 acres, of Wrexham Abbot 351.161 acres, and of the two detached portions of Esclusham within it, 1.603 acres ; the total area of the municipal borough being 1,305 acres, and that of the parliamentary borough about 1791 acres.

26. I now have to speak of the history of Wrexham during the

Commonwealth period. And here a curious point has to be noticed. Although Charles I. was lord of the manor of Wrexham
Regis, and of the lordship of Bromfield, nowhere in North Wales
was the parliamentary party so numerous as here, and I have given in
my *History of the Older Nonconformity of Wrexham*, (pp 3-10) an
account of some of those who were strong on that side, as
well as of those who were of the King's party. Denbighshire, in
general, however, rallied to the King, giving the latter, at the out-
break of the civil war a complete regiment of volunteers and 1000li
The petition of the county against the orders and ordinances of
parliament was presented to the King at York, August 4th, 1642,
and the commission of array put in force throughout the county.
(Note Book of William Maurice Esq., of Cefnybraich.)

27. Later in the year, on the 27th of September, the King, on
his way from Chester to Shrewsbury, reviewed at Wrexham the
train bands of Bromfield and Chirk. On the 3rd of the October
following, according to the same note book, " the King came again
from Salop to Wrexam . . . and vywed the traine bands of the hole
county who weare to marche the morrowe after to Shrewsbury, for a
gard to the Prince." It was probably upon this occasion that the incident took place which is described in the following extract from
Ormerod's *History of Cheshire*, although the date therein assigned to
it differs slightly from the date given by Mr. Maurice for the
King's second visit to Wrexham.

"Upon October 7th, 1642, the King, having come over from Shrewsbury
to Wrexham, to meet a commission from the city of Chester, and intending
to return the same day, appears to have taken up his quarters at Sir
Richard Lloyd's house[5] who is said to have urged the length of the day's
journey and the unseasonableness of the weather, and to have pressed his
royal guest to stay till the next day at Wrexham, and the King to have
dismissed him and the other gentlemen with these pathetic and simple
words : " Gentlemen, go you and take to your rests, for you have homes
and houses to go to, and beds of your own to lodge in, and God grant that
you may long enjoy them, I am deprived of these comforts, I must attend
my present affairs, and return this night to the place whence I came."

28. According to Maurice's note book, on the 9th of November,
1643, the parliamentary leaders, Sir Thomas Myddelton and Sir
William Brereton captured Holt bridge and " presently entered
Wrexam." It was on this occasion the soldiers broke down "the or-
gans " in Wrexham church, and destroyed the tomb of Robert ap
Iorwerth, and are said to have been actually quartered in the church.
But they did not do nearly so much damage to the building as was
done under the name of " restoration " when the King " came to
his own again " and in later times. And they abstained from
plundering, and much increased their force, through many persons

5. Sir Richard Lloyd lived at this time either at Esclusham Hall, or at
Brynyffynnon House, Wrexham, probably at the former.

in the neighbourhood joining them.   They took also at Holt,
" Captain Price, Captain Jones and Lieutenant Salisbury prisoners,"
Mr. Burghall, the minister of Acton in Cheshire, from whose
" Providence Improved " the last given particulars are taken, tells
us also that in the October preceding " some of Sir Thomas
Myddleton's troops went into Wales and fetched Sir Edmund
Broughton, (probably Sir Edward Broughton of Marchwiel) from
his own house at Broughton, and two of his sons, and brought
them prisoners to Nantwich."

29. Spite of these proceedings the entries are continued in the
same handwriting in the parish register without a break, until the
beginning of the year 1645.

30. The commissioners appointed under the Act of 1649-50, *For
the better propagation and preaching of the Gospel in Wales* held
always their meetings for *North* Wales in Wrexham.

31. In the year 1647, [Thomas] Edwards, Esq., of Cilhendref,
was governor of Wrexham in the parliamentary interest.

32. Although the parliamentary party was very strong in Wrexham during the Commonwealth period, in little more than fifty
years afterwards the town had become furiously attached to the
Stuart interest and in 1715 the mob wrecked the two Dissenting
meeting houses, while the church bells were rung to celebrate the
escape of a Wrexham man who had been taken prisoner with the
rebels at Preston, and in July 1716, Ambrose Tanner, a soldier,
was " shot by the [Shire] Hall."

33. I will now say something about a very interesting subject—
the ancient industries of the town.   Wrexham, lying in the marches or " goror " and close to the hills, where large numbers of
Welsh black cattle and mountain sheep were reared, and being also
an ancient market town, became from very early times an empor-
ium for the sale of skins.   Thus it was that so many tanners, skinners, curriers and glovers, were established in Wrexham, from at
least the beginning of the 17th century.   Many of these were men
of considerable influence, and will be mentioned in the following
chapters.   Upon these trades others were dependent.   Thus consider-
ing the small size of the town, the number of leather breeches makers
and feltmakers[6] is quite astonishing.   I find also a few leather
dressers, parchment makers, and hair buyers mentioned.   The
horns which the tanners did not need were sold and worked up by
comb makers and button makers.   The wool from the sheep skins
was spun and woven in the cottages of the town and neighbour-

---

6. In felling, loose flocks of hair or wool were interlaid by hand into a
compact fabric, by dexterously compressing and working them on a table by
means of a piece of thick blanket, slightly moistened.   The hair or wool was obtained directly form the tanners, or through the " hair buyers " mentioned
above.

hood, and the number of weavers mentioned in the parish registers is almost incalculable[7]. The woollen cloth thus produced was then dealt with by another set of men called walkers or fullers, and in Welsh " panwyr." I find only one walk mill mentioned as being in the *town* of Wrexham, but there were several "*pandai*" (three at least) in the parish. At the walk mills or *pandai*, the cloth was put into troughs filled with soaped water, and there beaten with wooden stocks, which were worked by means of a water wheel. This treatment not only removed the oil and size introduced during the spinning and weaving, but also matted the fibres of the cloth together, so that afterwards it became much thicker, and at the same shrunk both in breadth and length. The cloth was then sometimes sent to the dyers, of whom there was a large number in the town, and was afterwards stretched to dry on tenter hooks. There were two fields called " Cae Denter " (Tenter field), which will be described in the subsequent chapters.

34. Not all the weavers of Wrexham, used however, spun *wool* as their material. I have noticed for example the names of ten silk-weavers between 1661 and 1710, of whom one was called John Sidan, " sidan " being the Welsh for " silk," and in 1741 the name of Elias Price, crape weaver, occurs, and in 1705 that of " Guiles Jones, stockine weaver." I copied also from the registers the names of thirteen persons who are variously described as " jersey weavers," " gargey weavers," and " gérgy weavers," the first of these names occurs in 1699, and the last in 1767. In 1803 and 1807, Benjamin Yates, *cotton* spinner is also mentioned.

35. Then there were the linen weavers, who of course, used the material called flax. In the 17th century, when nearly all the field names of Bromfield were Welsh, a large proportion of the few English-named fields were " flax yards " showing that flax was then grown in the neighbourhood. At a later date flax seems to have been brought from Liverpool, being probably imported from Ireland, but this circumstance does not seem to have at all diminished the number of flax dressers in Wrexham, who were very numerous far on into the present century. The flax dressers prepared the flax for the linen spinners and weavers, by " teasing " it, and combing it with " cards," and I find three Wrexham " card-makers " mentioned in the registers between the years 1693 and 1700.

36. Then there was an extraordinary number of hat-makers, or as they were commonly called " castor makers " in the town. Besides the hats that were known as " castors," straw hats were also made in Wrexham, and I find, besides, two persons described as " straw bathers."

37. The mineral wealth of the neighbourhood gave opportunity for the development of another class of handicrafts in the town.

---

7. Many of those weavers were known as " friezers " the cloth they wove being called " frieze."

This was especially the case with the iron ore smelted near Wrexham. At the end of the 15th century, Guto'r Glyn addressed to Dafydd ap Ieuan, the Abbot of Valle Crucis, a "cywydd" in which the abbot is thanked for the gift of a sword and buckler, "the pricksong of Wrexham's shop," *(prickswng y siop o Wrecsam)* and Leland, writing of Wrexham, in the time of Henry VIII. says that there were "sum ... good Bokeler makers" in it. Of the manufacture of these bucklers, which were certainly in part at least made of iron, I find no mention after Leland's time, but of nailors there was down to our own days a very large number indeed, not merely in the town but also in the villages which were included in the parish. Between 1714 and 1758 also I find three lockmakers or locksmiths mentioned, between 1738 and 1757 two spurriers or spurmakers, and in 1747 one scythe-smith. Again between 1671 and 1751 I have the names of six needle-makers. Pins were also made in the town, although to a small extent only, but five tin plate workers are mentioned in the parish registers between 1817 and 1831. In the beginning of this century a wire mill was erected on the Hafod y wern estate by Mr. Charles Evans, and was continued for many years.

38. At the beginning of the 17th century there was a *lead* smelting house in Wrexham Fechan.

39. Malting was also very extensively followed in the town, but from the beginning of this century, brewing gradually became the staple industry of the town.

40. Two other handicrafts, carried on in the cottages in Wrexham remain to be mentioned. The "body-makers" or "bodice-makers" and stay-makers were formerly so numerous, that after beginning to take the names of them in the parish register, I ceased to enumerate them.

41. Finally, I find mentioned one boss-maker (in 1740), one bell-founder (in 1714), two clog-makers, two engravers[8], one heckel-maker (in 1770), five heel-makers between 1727 and 1776), three soap-boilers, (between 1714 and 1765), one spectacle-maker (in 1717), and one toy-turner (in 1770).

42. I forget to say that in 1663 there was a paper mill in Wrexham Regis, and that in 1682 "Thomas Hynton, papper-man" is mentioned.

43. I have not referred in the foregoing account to those trades and handicrafts that were common in all towns that were of any importance.

---

8. Of these engravers one was "Will Gryce" living in February 1697-8. and the other Mr. Sylvanus Crue (see Chap. I. sec 20). and "History of the Older Nonconformity in Wrexham ' p. 132.) who has left memorials of his skill in the churches of Wrexham, Holt and Llangollen.

44. Untii the year 1857, Wrexham had no municipal organization, and it was not until 1832 that it was admitted along with Ruthin and Holt, as a contributory borough to the parliamentary borough of Denbigh.   Before its incorporation, Wrexham was solely governed through its manorial courts. But the town was divided into two manors, while a small part of it belonged, as a detached portion, to the manor of Esclusham.   Thus there was no single authority and no common action.   Besides this, by the beginning of the present century the powers of the manorial courts were fallen into desuetude.   The only real living authority lay in the parish vestry, but the town of Wrexham formed only a small portion (about a fourteenth part) of the whole parish, and it would have been neither just nor possible to levy a rate on the latter for the benefit of the town only.   The result of all this was that the local government was powerless for sanitary purposes.   The town was, for the most part unsewered and unpaved, the mortality was very high, and in many important respects, everyone did what was right in his own eyes.   As to the mortality of the town, I copy the following from the official report on the condition of Wrexham, made to the General Board of Health in the year 1849 :—

" It appears from the statements of Mr. Hughes, the registrar, that the deaths in the townships of Wrexham Abbot and Wrexham Regis, during the seven years ending 30th June, 1848, averaged 168 per annum. This compared with the population of 1841, the last official census, amounts to an annual mortality of 28.6 per 1,000.   In the years 1848-9, the deaths were 205 ; here the same comparison gives a mortality of 35 per 1,000, and if the present population be assumed at 7,000 the mortality will be 29.2 per 1,000, a very excessive rate even for a town.[9]

But this is not all.   In 14 of the streets, according to the same report, the mortality was over 30, and in 8 over 40 per thousand, while in Henblas and Abbot Street it was respectively 54, and 56.2 per 1,000.   The report continues :—

" The house drainage is what might be expected in a place without street sewers . . . In many cases there is not even a gutter · in others the gutter flows along a covered entry into the open street.   Sometimes, there is a trench cut beneath the floor, and covered with loose flags or bricks of the dwelling room.   The privies, where there are any, have cesspools, which are usually open, and without drains, so that when full, as they frequently are, from rain, the diluted and most offensive filth overflows into the yards and courts, and not unfrequently into the houses.   Wrexham is full of such places . . . These cesspools and the cottage pigstyes are among the chief evils of Wrexham.   Not only are the privy cesspools . . . very numerous but the people are in the habit of forming very large pits on their premises, and storing manure collected in the streets and elsewhere.   Into these places they put straw, with a view to its becoming rotten, and from the

----

9. In 1890, the death rate for the whole town had diminished to 17.98 in a 1,000, the death rate for the Wrexham Rural Sanitary District being much higher.

sale of the whole they derive a considerable revenue, selling the stuff at 3s to 4s 6d a ton. One man recently received £10 per annum from such a cesspool. In the Irish quarter such places are numerous. I saw one collection of about 20 tons on sale at 4s 6d a ton. The profit derived in this way is very considerable. I enquired very closely into the matter, and believe 7s 6d per house per annum on the whole town to be a very low average, although this amounts for the whole town, to a sum of £532. Of course this sum is gained by individuals at a great loss to the community, from the consequences of the pauperism, sickness and premature death directly attributable to such filthy practice."

The reporter then goes on to speak of the inadequate and often tainted water supply, and then describes the condition of the town as to " paving and scavinging," in the following words :—

" The main street of Wrexham is in good order, and the footways have been neatly flagged by subscription among the inhabitants. The flagging, however, extends to but few of the subordinate streets. The carriage ways in these are pitched with boulder stones of irregular size, shape, and hardness. The alleys are, for the most part, pitched with smaller boulders or pebbles, with a central gutter. This pitching is generally laid very badly, and full of holes. Of course, a gutter formed of such materials can never be clean. Very many of the courts and backyards are not pitched at all, and it is difficult to distinguish between the proper surface of the ground and the coating of dust and ordure upon it. In wet seasons the state of things is very bad . . . There is no scavenger, public or private in the town, £17 per annum is paid for watering the streets of Wrexham Regis during the summer season."

A statement is then quoted of Mr. E. Griffiths, Superintendent of police.[10]

" There are in the town of Wrexham 41 lodging houses: the majority of these houses are of the very worst description, and situate in the worst locality of the town. I have known upon certain occasions, such as at fairs and bands, as many as 200 extra lodgers taken in at these houses. What I mean by *extra* is that 200 persons have been admitted without suitable accommodation; and on these occasions I have seen as many as 12 dogs accommodated at one house, thereby increasing the nuisance."

Superintendent Griffiths also reported that-"Drunkenness among the lower classes, male and female, is very frequent, and difficult to check owing to the bad state of the lodging houses ; prostitution is also to be complained of: scarcely a lodging house in the town refuses to harbour for this purpose. Thefts are very numerous ; and altogether I consider the town as regards crime and immorality, among the worst in North Wales."

As to drunkenness, from what I have heard, it was almost as prevalent among the trading classes and resident gentry, as among the labouring population. There were in 1849 in the town, 60 licensed victuallers, 5 beer shops, and 4 spirit vaults, so that about one house in every twenty was licensed for the sale of beer, wine, or spirits. The reporter adds that there were " 11 slaughter houses

10. A superintendent and four men were allotted at this time to the town of Wrexham, out of the county police.

and about 600 pigstyes in the town," both "nuisances of a danger-
ous order, especially the latter, from their number, and their presence ordinarily in the most crowded and damp localities, in close
proximity to the dwelling rooms of the poor."

As to the provision against fire, Mr. Clark states that there
were "two fire engines in the town, one of which is efficient, but
the supply of water is not such as to allow of these engines being
employed with effect, unless the fire occured close to the brook, or
near the Brynyffynnon, so that practically, these engines are of
very little use."

45. For the correction of these evils the reporter recommended
the incorporation of the town, in which recommendation he was
strongly supported by some of the principal inhabitants, especially
by the resident medical men. The opposition to incorporation
was nevertheless so strong, that it did not take effect until September 23rd, 1857.   An annotated list of the mayors from that time
to the present day is given in Appendix I.   The late Mr. John
James[11] was appointed the first Town Clerk, and continued in
office until 1879, when he resigned, and Mr. Thomas Bury, the
present Town Clerk became his successor.

46. The new corporation had an enormous leeway to make up,
and have doubtless made many mistakes, but none can doubt,
looking to the vastly improved condition of the town, that they
have on the whole done their duty well,   They met at first in the
old Music Hall, (now the Advertiser Office), Henblas Street, but
rented of Mr. Edward Griffith soon after, for £15 a year, the ground
floor of Brynyffynnon House,[12] which they continued to occupy
until they purchased, in 1883, the old Grammar School, into the
possession of which, however, they did not enter until the next
year.

47. The town having been incorporated, application was made
to the Herald's College for a coat of arms.   A coat of arms was
granted them November 26th, 1857, which is thus described in the
grant from the College :—*Ermine*, two crosiers in saltire *or*, on a
chief dancette, per pale, *gules* and *or*, two Lions passant, guardant,
counterchanged, and for the crest, in a wreath of the colours upon
a mount *vert*, a Dragon *gules*, resting the dexter claw upon a shield
or charged with the character of Mars *sable*."

48. There were formerly annual races in Wrexham, held on the
racecourse behind the Turf Tavern, outside the town. I do not

---

11. Mr. John James died May 1st, 1888, at Plas Acton, which he built, and
was buried in Gwersyllt churchyard. He was thrice married, firstly, June 16th,
1829, to Mary Anne, daughter of Mr. John Painter of High Street, Wrexham ;
secondly, (at Rhuddlan, October 16th, 1838), to Catherine, daughter of Mr. Thomas
Hilditch, of Oswestry ; and thirdly, to Anne Elizabeth, daughter of Mr. John
Farrer, of Wrexham.

12. The first meeting of the Corporation was held at Brynyffynnon, December 16th, 1857.

know when they were begun, nor when they were discontinued, but I have found them mentioned in 1818 and 1830. They were resumed August 28th, 1890.

CHAPTER I

High Street.

1. In describing the various houses in this important street, I do not think I can do better than follow the existing numbering, beginning with No. 1 at the corner of Hope Street, and going to the bottom, round by the Wynnstay Arms and back on the other side to No. 43, at the corner of Church Street.

2. But first, I ought to mention the high cross, which I find referred to in an old deed dated the 3rd year of King Edward, probably Edward *the Fourth.* Norden also mentions it in 1620. It stood in front of the Shire Hall, now called " the Town Hall," and old people still speak of the space in front of the hall as " The Cross."

3. The name " High Street" was firmly established in the year 1590, but I am not sure that I have met with it earlier than that date.

4. The houses which represented Nos. 1, 2 and 3 belonged by lease in 1620, to Sir Henry Salusbury, Kt. and Bart., of Lleweni, and had been built upon a piece of land called " Tir Gwalchmai " *Gwalchmai's land.* This land is spoken of 48 years before (in 1572) under the same name, and as belonging to Sir Henry Salusbury Kt. but no mention is then made of any house upon it. I am not sure that this same Gwalchmai is not actually named in the deed just mentioned (dated 3rd year of King Edward), where " the half of a place of land " situated in High Street, is described as bounded on one side by the land of Gruffydd ap Gwalchmai. Sir Henry Salusbury had also in 1620, a shop and curtilage in Hope Street, adjoining the fore-named three houses. No. 3, which consisted until the beginning of the present century of two distinct tenements, was long the property of the Burtons, *see History of Older Nonconformity of Wrexham,* p. 83. note 30.

5. Nos. 4 and 5 which formed originally one house and shop, have a distinct history. They have belonged for about two centuries and a half to the Merediths of Pentrebychan, and were rebuilt in 1738 by Mr. Thomas Meredith. The following entry relating to this holding occurs in Norden's *Survey,* (A.D. 1620) :—

"Rent 12d [lease] 11 years expired. Hugh Meredith, Esquire, holds one messuage, shop, and curtilage on the north part of the street called the High Street, lately in the occupation of William Stilles adjacent upon the lands called "Tir Gwalchmaii" granted to Robert Puleston by lease dated 27th of May in the 10th year of Elizabeth [fine at renewal] 26s 8d."

According to a deed of 1572, there "pertained" to this house "four parcels or quillets in the fields of Wrexham."

When in 1738 this house was rebuilt, Mr. Meredith granted a lease of it for 20 years to the tenant, Mr. Joseph Jones, mercer, (successor to Mr. Robert Perrott, mercer,) at a rent of £20 a year. This Mr. Joseph Jones was a man of some importance. I think he must have been the Joseph Jones who was the son and heir of John Jones, gent, the owner of the Croes Eneurys estate in Acton. However this may be, it is certain from deeds that I have examined, that he married Elizabeth, one of the younger daughters of John Hughes, gent, of Heol Pwll y Kiln, Acton. He died in 1757 leaving his two sisters, Mary and Sarah, his heirs at law. Of these, Mary married Mr. Robert McCrea of the parish of St. Mary's Whitechapel, Middlesex, and Sarah married (June 7th, 1720), Mr. John Jackson, dyer, of Church Street, Wrexham. (see ch. III. sec. 4.) Mr. Jones was followed by Mr. John Bowen, whose family tenanted the house for nearly a hundred years. Mr. Charles Bowen, auctioneer, the last of the family to occupy it, is still very well remembered. Part of the building is now occupied by Mr. Yeaman Strachan, horticulturist and seedsman, mayor of the borough in 1882-3, who purchased the whole premises of H. Warter Meredith, Esq.

6. The house next on the east to that last described, and which is now represented by Nos. 6 and 7 (Mr. Albany Paddon's shop), was in 1742 in the occupation of Mr. William Samuel and in 1760, in that of his widow. In the last-named year it was sold by the Rev. Edward Hughes, of Radway, Warwickshire,[1] to Peter Taylor gent, of Llwyn y cnottié, and is then described as "commonly known as The Lamb." It was immediately after divided into two tenements, whereof that which we may call No. 6 was occupied by a series of surgeons and apothecaries. In 1780 it is described as owned by William Taylor, gent, who, it is nearly certain, was Mr. William Taylor, of Coed Aben, Abenbury, Mr. Robert Taylor's brother. Mr. Taylor of Coed Aben died in September 1784, and we find accordingly that in the rate books of 1784, No. 6 is still returned as belonging to him, but in those of the next year they are

---

1. From some deeds which Sir Robert A. Cunliffe has permitted me to examine, it appears that this Rev. Edward Hughes was descended from Edward Hughes, gent, of Wrexham, who lived in a house at the bottom of what is now York Street, on the east side of it, who possessed a great deal of property in this town, and who was living in 1682. His eldest son was Edward Hughes, gent of Brecon, (living in 1721), who either himself afterwards became the Rev. Edward Hughes, vicar of Shennington, Gloucestershire, or more probably, was the father of the latter, whose last will was dated March 3rd, 1734, and who was the father of the Rev. Edward Hughes of Radway. The last-named disposed of all the family property in Wrexham.

described as belonging to Mrs. Taylor, and in those of 1791, as belonging to Mr. William Taylor, *surgeon*, doubtless son of the Mr.
William Taylor first-named, who is known to have had a son of
that name.   Then, in, or a little before 1797, this and the adjoining
houses (Nos. 6 and 7) were purchased and made into one by Mr.
Richard Jones, ironmonger, who had hitherto lived lower down
the street, and here he (and his son Mr. John Jones after him), lived
for many years.   As this Mr. Richard Jones was a conspicuous
figure in the Wrexham of those days, it may be well to say something about him.   Mr. Jones came from Llanddyn, in the parish
of Llangollen, and went up to London, when young, with only
seventeen shillings in his pocket.   There he was attracted by the
preaching of Whitfield, Romaine, and others, and became deeply
religious after their fashion.   There also he met Miss Ann Jones,
elder daughter of John Jones, gent, of Coed y glyn, Wrexham,
a devoted Methodist, whom he afterwards married (see ch. xvii sec.
41.)   He ultimately established himself in business in Wrexham,
as an ironmonger, and became very prosperous.   Mr. Edward
Francis in his *Hanes Dechreuad a Chynydd y Methodistiaid Calfinaidd yn Ngwrecsam* gives reasons for believing that he was already
settled in this town in or before the year 1770, but the rate books
show indisputably that he was not established in business here,
on his own account, before the year 1784.   He married for his second
wife, Anne, the eldest daughter of Richard Phillips Esq., of Ty'n-
rhos, and had many children.   He was the backbone and steady
supporter of Calvinistic Methodism in this town, and further
notice of him will be found in the account given in Abbot Street
of the old chapel there.   But it is worthy of notice that spite of
this, all his children were baptized at the parish church.   So much
for the owners of the house now being described.   Now for the occupants :—In 1780 Mr. Prosser, surgeon, lived in the house, but
soon after removed further down the street, and was followed by
Mr. John Rowland, apothecary, who was living there in 1786 and
1788.   In 1788 or 1789, Mr. Thomas Griffith, surgeon, occupied it,
who came from what is now No. 29 Bridge Street, but who speedily removed to Hope Street, under the heading of which we shall
have much to say of him, and was followed in 1790 by Mr.
Wm. Taylor, surgeon, the owner of the house, whose name disappears from the rate books after 1794.   In or about 1797, as we
have already seen, Mr. Richard Jones came to live in the house,
and his widow was still living there in 1828.   After she left it, the
house was converted, in 1834, into a branch of the Northern and
Central Bank of England, with Mr. John Farrer for manager,
till then manager of Messrs. Kenrick and Bowman's Bank in
Hope Street.   He was an active Wesleyan, and superintendent of the
Green Chapel Sunday School.   His daughter, Anne Elizabeth, was
the third wife of the late John James, Esq., first town clerk of

Wrexham. Under his management the Wrexham branch bank was successful, but in 1836 the central bank failed, and he then left Wrexham, becoming ultimately manager of the Consolidated Bank, Manchester. He died December 23rd, 1882, aged 85, at Plas Acton, the residence of his son in law. After a considerable interval, the Hope Street premises were occupied by Mr. Robert Lloyd, draper, now of Rhyl, who was mayor of the borough in 1873-4 and 1874-5.

7. We now come to Nos. 8 and 9. Here was living in 1699 Mr. Richard Speed, a well-to-do ironmonger, who was buried October 23rd, 1711. After the death of his widow, Mrs. Mary Speed, in August 1734. the house was occupied by Mr. Griffith Speed, (who was Mr. Richard Speed's son), born December 14th, 1699. He removed about the year 1746 to what is now No. 58 Hope Street, where he lived until his death. He is variously described as "iron merchant" and "esquire." He was high-sheriff of the county in 1760. Further particulars relating to him will be found in note 2 j. p. 203 of *Hist. of Par. Church of Wrexham*. Mr. Griffith Speed was followed by Mr. Thomas Collins, glover. In 1760 the house was divided and occupied by Mr. Dean, ironmonger, and Mr. Edward Jones, flax-dresser. Then about 1794, what we may call No. 9, was taken by Mr. Joseph Tye, printer and bookseller, Mr. Tye and especially his widow, Mrs. Anna Tye, merit notice as having produced many important pieces of local printing. (see Appendix II.). In 1760, the house and shop are described as belonging to Adam Davies, gent, but were soon after acquired by the Robert Taylor, gent, mentioned in the last paragraph, and continued until quite recent years to share the fortunes, as to ownership, of Nos. 6 and 7.

8. The present Market Hall front was erected in 1848, from the design of Mr. Penson. Three half-timbered houses stood formerly on its site. The two westernmost of them are described in 1780 as belonging to Edward Rogers, gent, who appears to have lived at Chester. In the first of the three lived Mr. Richard Jones, ironmonger (see sec. 6.) from 1784 until he removed to Nos. 6 and 7, and he was succeeded by Mr. Thomas Jones, flaxdresser, whom many still remember, and who died December 8th, 1837, and was buried in the Dissenter's Graveyard. I think he was the last but one of the Wrexham flax-dressers, once so numerous. The second of the three houses was occupied in 1715, by Mr. Thomas Edgworth, hatter or castor-maker (see ch. xvii, sec. 46), and after the death of his widow in 1743, by Mr. Thomas Jones, who was also a hatter. Then in 1784, after Mrs. Jones' death, it was converted into a public house, and called "The Bear" or "The White Bear," and so continued until it was pulled down. It belonged in 1808 to Mr. Rogers, of Chester, and in 1810, and for many years after, to Mr. Dunbabin. The third and easternmost of the three houses was

occupied, between 1728 and 1748, by Mr. Thomas Hampson, clock-maker, and was known as "The Clock." Some clocks with Mr. Hampson's name upon them are still in existence, and very good they are. Mr. Hampson was buried April 12th, 1755. In 1756, I find this house described as an inn—"The Oak" or "Royal Oak" and so it remained until it was cleared away.[2] I think it must have been in one of these three houses, then occupied by Hugh Blanthorne, that the plague broke out in 1665, being brought thither by a traveller from London who lodged there.

9. The next house to the three mentioned in the last paragraph, now the Golden Lion (Nos. 12 and 13), was aforetime a very im-portant one. It belonged to the Pulfords of Wrexham, a family as to which I shall have something to say under a distinct heading at the close of this chapter (see sec. 42 and 45). In 1661, John Pulford, gent, was living there, and was followed after his death, by George Goldsmith, gent., who was somehow connected with him. In 1674, it was more highly assessed than any other house in the street, though there were only five hearths in it, while in the Red Lion there were fourteen. Afterwards, it was converted into a public house, and in 1700 is described specifically as "The Golden Lion," and in 1702 as consisting of "house, kilne and barne." Immediately after, it was converted into two shops, while in 1705, the whole house seems to have been occupied by another Mr. Pulford, probably Mr. John Pulford, prothonotary of North Wales, who was, I think, a son of the Mr. John Pulford first-named. Mr. Pulford died in 1738. After this, the house was again converted into an inn, and resumed its old name of "The Golden Lion." In January 1745-6, Robert Samuel married Ellen Pulford, widow, (relict perhaps of the prothonotary), and in 1780 is returned as the owner of the house as well as of the Pulford prop-erty in Henblas Street and of part of that in the Town Fields.[3] This is the Robert Samuel, the inscription on whose tomb I have given on page 207 of my *History of the Parish Church*, but I now see, contrary to what is there stated, that it was another Robert Samuel who married Elizabeth Wragg. The Robert Samuel who married Mrs Pulford was a son of Mr. William Samuel of The Lamb, (see sec. 6), and living close to the widow, was conveniently situated for courting her.

10. Of the house (No. 14) between the Golden Lion and the Red Lion, now occupied by Messrs. C. K. Benson & Co., I have already given some account in note 7, page 63 of my *History of the Older Nonconformity of Wrexham*. A kiln belonged to it down to quite late times. From before 1780 until his death in 1799 this house was occupied by Mr. Jonathan Brown, grocer, who bought it, and

2. This house belonged to Mr. Richard Marsh, and remained in the possess-ion of his family until the extinction of the latter here.

3. He only became entitled to an estate for life in this property.

it was afterwards occupied by his son Mr. Thos. Brown, grocer, and came ultimately into the possession of Mr. Thos. Stanton Eddowes, (see ch. xi. sec. 13) whose mother was Mr. Thos. Brown's sister.

11. "The Red Lion," now commonly called "The Lion," which comes next, was formerly the most important inn in the town. In 1670 it contained fourteen hearths, more than any other house in Wrexham except Bryn y ffynnon. In 1715 it was assessed more highly than any other house in the street, the occupier of it paying 26/9, while the occupier of the Eagles paid only 16/8, and the occupier of the Golden Lion 10/-. In 1742 there was a new assessment, and the Red Lion was then still rated higher than the others, being charged 19/8, while the Eagles was charged 13/10 and the Golden Lion 10/-. But at the time of the next assessment (in 1808), the Red Lion was only charged 12/-, and the Golden Lion 9/4, while the Eagles was charged 15/-. In 1663, Mr. Thomas Bostock was living here, and is not in that year only described as a "recusant" and "constantly absent from church," but also as an innkeeper, so that this house was already an inn at that time. It belonged in later times to the Myddeltons of Chirk Castle, and was at one time the great Whig "house" as the Eagles was the great Tory house for local politicians. It still belonged to the Hon. Frederick West in 1844. The Red Lion yard was entered from Chester Street. Part of the house is now used as a workshop by Mrs. Rogers, upholsterer, and includes a fine massive oak staircase. The house is definitely called "the Red Lion" in 1699.

12. Just as the Eagles(see sec. 15-17) was in some measure connected with bull-baiting, so was the Red Lion connected with cock-fighting, the landlords of it renting the cock-pit "or conveniency for ffighting of cocks" (as it is amusingly called in 1712), which belonged to the trustees of the poor of the Presbyterian Chapel, Chester Street, This was continued long on into the present century.

13. The predecessor of the house, now numbered 18 and 19, and occupied by Mr. Potter, was from before 1742, occupied by Mr. Daniel Payne, mercer,. After his death in 1770, a succession of surgeons and apothecaries lived in the house. The first of these was Mr. Richard Manning, apothecary, who was buried at Wrexham, September 28th, 1778,[4] He married Miss Margaret Pate, and was the father of the Richard Pate Manning, surgeon, of Whitchurch who, in October, 1799, shot in a duel Captain Thomas Jones or Willow House, Wrexham, and afterwards went into a lunatic asylum, and was buried in Wrexham churchyard, January, 1880, (not

---

4 An earlier Richard Manning, apothecary, of Wrexham, probably the father of the above-named is mentioned in the parish register as early as 1718, and was buried December 31st, 1763.

1883, as I have, by a misreading of the inscription on his tomb, stated in note 24, page 215 of my *History of the Parish Church*). Mr. Manning was followed, about 1783, by Mr. Prosser, surgeon, who removed hither from higher up the street, (see sec. 6), and he, about 1797, by Mr. Basnett, apothecary. who remained for two or three years only, and who then appears to have gone to live at the Dog Kennel. Whether or not this Mr. Basnett was a member of the family of Basnett of Eyton, in the parish of Bangor Isycoed, I do not know. There was buried at Wrexham on December 9th, 1752, a "Joseph Basnet, of W. R. gent," who was perhaps connected with him. Then about the beginning of the present century, Mr. John Painter, (see *History of Older Nonconformity of Wrexham*, note 33 page 86), took the house, removing thither from No. 42, and set up in it a printing, stationery and bookselling business, which has continued there ever since. Several important works were printed by him, among others, Yorke's *Royal Tribes*, and Edwards' edition of Browne Willis' *History of the Diocese of St. Asaph*. He was succeeded first by his elder son John, and then by his second son, the late Mr. Thomas Painter, J.P., who rebuilt the house, (the old shop had three steps leading to the door), and ultimately relinquished the business to the late Mr. Railton Potter.

14. Next to the house last-named, were two ancient half-timbered shops and houses (Nos. 20 and 21), which reached to Chester Street, and which, about the year 1887, were pulled down by the corporation so as to remove the sharp corner made by No. 21 between the two streets. When this was done, a long oaken beam in the gable of No. 21 facing Charles Street, was found to bear the date of 1625.

15. We now come to speak of the "Wynnstay Arms," formerly called "the Eagles," and at an earlier time still "the George." I stated in my *History of the Older Nonconformity of Wrexham* that Mr. Thomas Bostock was living at this house in 1663, and that it was then the largest inn in the town, but I have since found that I had mistaken "The George" for "The Red Lion," that Mr. Bostock lived at the house last named, and that it was this which was the largest inn in the town. The George was originally a very small affair, and was in 1704, charged only 2/6 in the rate books, while the Red Lion was charged 6/4. It is in 1702 that I first find it called "the George," and John Edwards, smith and publican, was then the occupier of it. It was still "the George" in 1721, but it was called "the Eagles" in 1730, and oftentimes afterwards "The Three Eagles" or "the Three Spread Eagles." We may be sure then that by that time that house had passed into the possession of the Williams-Wynn family, for it is certain that the "the three spread eagles" are "the three eagles displayed in fesse" which that family bears. In 1724, Mr. Daniel Porter, junr. was the tenant of the house, and here on the 1st May of that year, a general meeting was

held of the Cycle, a club which, at its formation, was Jacobite and secret, but afterwards developed into one which was merely maintained for social and festive purposes, and lasted at least as late as 1843. In 1724, doubtless, it was still occupied with schemes for bringing back the Stuarts to the throne. The following circular then issued to the members of the Cycle, is reprinted from the *Chester Courant* of May 30th, 1884. I have annotated the names of the signators :—

"We whose names are underwritten do promise [to meet] at ye time and place to our names respectively affixed, and to observe the rules following viz :—

"Imp's (Imprimis). Every member of this society shall, for default of his appearance, submit to be censured, and shall thereupon be censured by the judg'nt of the society.

2ndly. Every member y't cannot come shall be obliged to send notice of his non-appearance by 12 a'clock at noon, together with his reason in writing ; otherwise his plea shall not excuse him, if within the compass of fifteen miles from the place of meeting.

3rdly. Each member obliges himself to have dinner upon the table by 12 a'clock at noon from Michaelmas to Lady-day, and from Lady-day to Michaelmas at 1 of the clock.

4thly. The respective masters of the place of meeting oblige themselves to take down in writing each default, and to deliver the same at the general meeting.

5thly. Every member shall keep a copy of these articles by him to prevent plea of mistake.

6thly. It is agreed y't a general meeting shall be held by all ye subscribers at the house of Daniel Porter, junr., holden at Wrexham, on the 1st day of May, 1724, by 11 of ye clock in the forenoon, and there to dine and to determine upon all points relating to and according to the sense of these articles.

1723. Signed

Thomas Puleston, May 21st (of Emral),
Richard Clayton, June 11th, (of Brymbo Hall),
Eubule Lloyd, July 2nd, (of Penylan),
Robert Ellis, July 23rd, (of Croes Newydd),
W. Wms-Wynn, August 13th, (afterwards the first Sir Watkin Williams-Wynn, of Wynnstay),
John Puleston. September 3rd, (of Pickhill Hall),
Thomas Eyton, September 24th, (of Leeswood),
Wm. Edwards, October 15th, (? of Plas Newydd, Chirk),
Thomas Holland, November 6th.5
Ken. Eyton, November 26th, (of Eyton, Denbighshire),

5. Rev. Thomas Holland, of Marchwiel, and of Berw, in the county of Anglesea, the last of the Hollands of this place. He died October 12th, 1746, and was buried at Mold, where also was buried his wife, Mrs. Mary Holland, June 24th, 1740. Who the "Madam Trygarn" who lived at Bryn y ffynnon House for two or three years after 1746 was, I do not know, but there was buried at Mold, in the tomb of the Rev. Thomas Holland, a certain "Jane Trygarn, daughter of Elizabeth Trygarn, of Berw," who died July 24th, 1748. The Rev. Thomas Holland's sister, Jane, married the Rev. Ellis Anwyl, rector of Llaniestyn, whose daughter Elizabeth married Richard Trygarn, of Trygarn, attorney.

Phil. Egerton, December 17th, (of Acton Hall, near Wrexham, and of
Oulton, Cheshire),
Jno. Robinson, January 8th, 1723-4, (of Upper Gwersyllt),
Geo. Shackerly, January 29th, (of Lower Gwersyllt),
Robert Davies, February 19th, (of Gwysanney),
Jno. Puleston, March 13th, (of Hafod y wern),
Broughton Whitehall, April 3rd, (of Broughton Hall, in Maelor
Saesneg),
Wm. Hanmer, April 24th, 1724, (of The Fenns).

16. "The Parcau," (Nos. 81, 82, 83, 327 and 328 on the map),
or "Parkey"(*The Parks*), belonged to the Wynnstay family, and were
generally let to the tenant of the Eagles, and after the beginning of
the present century, when the same family acquired "the great
meadow" (since known as "the Eagles meadow,") the latter has
always been let along with the inn. The inn also has in recent years
absorbed not merely a house adjoining it in Charles Street, but also
one adjoining it in York Street. In 1817, it was still *officially* known
as "the Eagles." It is in the year 1822 that I first find it called
"the Wynnstay Arms," but the old name for many years held
its ground, and in the tithe schedule of 1844 it is still described as
"The Eagles Inn."

17. At the beginning of the present century, there stood in front
of the Eagles Inn, a stout post where a bull was regularly baited
(I think once a week), and gentlemen from the country used to
come to set their dogs at the poor beast, paying the bull-baiter a
customary fee. The bull, after it had been baited, was killed, and
its flesh was believed to be more tender to the teeth for the suffering it had undergone. The bull-baiter was at one time the champion prize-fighter of the town.

18. Nos. 23 and 24 High Street (at the corner of High Street
and York Street), are important because they were occupied for
more than a hundred years by a family—the Langfords—which has
descendants among us still, though they do not bear the name of
the stock from which they sprang. The first of these was Mr.
Arthur Langford, sadler, who established himself at the corner of
the two streets in the year 1729,[6] and was buried July 6th, 1769.
His son, Mr. Joseph Langford, succeeded him in business, and died
May 21st, 1834, at the advanced age of 91. I find him described
not merely as owner of his own house and of No. 25 High Street,
but also of several houses adjacent in York Street. His daughter,
Sarah, became the second wife of John Foulkes, Esq., the elder,
and mother of the late Wm. Langford Foulkes, Esq., barrister.
His son, Joseph, was a wine merchant and grocer, in partnership
with Mr. Peter Poole, at 32 High Street. Mr. Joseph Langford
the younger died September 9th, 1813, aged 31, leaving three

6. A sadler's business has been maintained without interruption on this site
from 1729 to the present time.

daughters, of whom one, Mary, married Mr. Hugh Hughes, surgeon, (see ch. iv, sec. 38), and another, Sarah, married (April 26th, 1825), Mr. Charles Poyser (see sec. 32.), bringing thus ultimately all the property before mentioned into the Poyser family.

19. No 25 belonged also to the Langfords, and was an inn—"The Coach and Horses,"—which is first mentioned as such in 1755, and which continued down to quite recent years.

20. No. 26, now the Conservative club, has a somewhat ancient history. Mr. Eustace Crue, apothecary, brother of Sylvanus Crue, the engraver, was living in the house and shop on this site in 1661, and here remained until his death in March, 1705, and was succeeded by his son Mr. Thomas Crue, who died May 3rd, 1707. Mrs. Anne Crue, widow of Mr. Eustace Crue, continued the business until her death November 1st, 1723, and it was carried on by various female members of the family until 1752. It afterwards fell into the possession of John Ellis, Esq., of whom we shall have to speak presently, and in 1808 belonged to Owen Ellis, Esq., his heir. A little before 1818, Mr. Richard Briscoe, druggist and wine merchant, bought it, and removed into it from Lichgate House, Church Street, and here remained for the greater part of his life. He was the father of the Rev. Thomas Briscoe, D.D., vicar of Holyhead, and chancellor of Bangor, (bapt. October 5th, 1813) ; of the Rev. Wm. Kyffyn Bostock Briscoe, M.A., rector of Nutfield, Surrey (bapt. September 24th, 1828); of the late Rev. Richard Briscoe, D.D., vicar of Whitford, Flintshire, and of Mr. Paul Giles Owen Briscoe who was a solicitor in London. His daughter, Mary Deborah, married at Wrexham, (November 23rd, 1841) Mr. Augustus Henry Churchill, surgeon, of Hawarden ; and his daughter Caroline Jane married(August 11th, 1841) Edward Pryce Griffiths, Esq., of London. Mr. Briscoe died in King Street, January 24th, 1848, aged 64, having relinquished, about the year 1837, his business at 26 High Street to the late Mr. Joshua Broughton, druggist, which latter was succeeded in 1880, by Mr. Edward Smith, draper, who was mayor of the borough in 1879-80.

21. Between this and the house west of it was an open passage leading from High Street into the north-east corner of the churchyard. It was called " the Nef:" there were formerly at least three houses in it, which were cleared away when the present Provincial Insurance offices were built, and the iron gates at each end were at the same time set up.

22. The site of the Provincial Insurance offices[7] and North and

7. The Provincial Insurance Company was founded in Wrexham in the year 1850 by Mr. Anthony Dillon, who was at that time manager of the National Provincial Bank, and who became Secretary of the new company, which had at first its offices in the rooms above Mr. Potter's shop, No. 19 High Street. Mr. Dillon was succeeded in 1869 by Mr. Robert Williams, who in his turn was succeeded 1875 by the present secretary, Mr. John Francis. In 1854, the company took

South Wales Bank (erected in 1860 and 1861), was formerly occupied by two houses. Of the easternmost of them I need only say
that it was owned by the same Robert Samuel who, by his marriage
with Mrs. Pulford (see sec. 9), acquired The Golden Lion and other
portions of the Pulford estate. In the other house was living in
1726, Edward Wickstead, (see *Hist. of the Par. Church*, page 152
note 63), who is mistakenly said to have produced the first printed
book in Wrexham, and who was followed in 1728 (1728 to about
1748), by Mr. Thomas Payne, stationer. Here lived afterwards until his death, the still-remembered Rowland Samuel (see *Hist. of the
Par. Church*, p. 107, note 274) who, as vicar's churchwarden and
general overseer, practically governed the town for so many years.
The house belonged as far back as I can trace, to the Hugheses of
Rhosddu, Stansty, as to whom I shall say something in ch. vi,
sec. 8.

23. No. 30, (now Messrs. Rogers and Jackson's ironmongers'
shop), is a very interesting house. The messuage which in 1699
stood on its site was then owned and occupied by Edward Jones,
glover. In 1710 it was sold by his son John Jones, yeoman, together with a garden in Wrexham Abbot, for £60 to Stephen
Stephenton, dyer, (see ch. ii, sec. 5). On the back of the
indentures of sale is the following curious agreement :—

"Memorandum, that I, the within-named John Jones doe assign over
forty boards, being in the backside of the messuage within-menc'oned, and
17 butcher's tresles, and 12 shoemakers standings."

These boards were for making up the stalls that used to stand in
the High Street on market days. Soon after the sale of the house in
1710, it was turned into an inn, and called " The Mitre," and before
1724, Mr. John Stephenton, only son of Mr. Stephen Stephenton was
living in it, and continued to do so until his death in 1731. He inherited also from his father, the Fawnog Fechan farm in Bersham,
No. 5 Church Street, and the house afterwards the King's Head, in
Penybryn. He married, December 5th, 1721, Elizabeth Pulford, and
thus obtained for his children the reversion of Willow House and
of that portion of the Pulford property which lay in Wrexham
Fechan. His daughter Elizabeth married (July 9th, 1750,) Mr.
Benjamin Parry, glover, of Wrexham, (see ch. xxi, sec. 11).
His eldest son Stephen (born March 9th, 1721-2), became afterwards an attorney in Wrexham, living at No. 5 Church Street, and
was buried March 28th, 1770. Mr. Stephen Stephenton must have
been a staunch Jacobite, for while the young Pretender was besieg-
ing Stirling Castle, he caused his first-born child to be baptized

up life insurance, their operations having hitherto been confined to insurance
against fire. But in 1874, their fire insurance business was made over to the
Alliance Company, whose offices, until 1887, were held on the same premises and
upon the same floor, the ground floor being occupied as the Wrexham branch
of the North and South Wales Bank. Since the foregoing sentences were written,
the Alliance Assurance Company has purchased out and out (February, 1890) the
business of the Provincial Insurance Company.

(January 21st, 1745-6) under the name of "Charles Edward." A Mr. Thomas Stephenton ultimately succeeded to Willow House, and there died December, 1825, aged 74. He was certainly a member of the same family as the last named Mr. Stephen Stephenton, and I believe he was his son. After the death of Mr. John Stephenton The Mitre was converted into a mercer's shop, and occupied by Mr. Thomas Lloyd until 1756, when he removed to a shop higher up the street, (Nos. 38 and 39), so that presently we shall have to say more about him. Mr. Lloyd was succeeded at No. 30 by Mr. Samuel Barber, draper and wine merchant, son of Mr. Samuel Barber, of "The Blue Posts," (see ch. xxi, sec. 6). He died December, 1773, and his widow, Penelope, married (October 12th, 1777), Mr. Charles Woollam, of 34 High Street (see below). He left two sons, Samuel and Watkin Robert. Between 1781 and 1814 (or thereabout), Mr. Joseph Wilkinson, surgeon, lived here, but afterwards removed to No 36 Chester Street, which he purchased. He married (September 9th, 1811), Miss Hannah Lewis, of Old Llwyn Onn, Abenbury, and lies buried in the old cemetery, with this inscription on his monument :—" Infra sepultus jacet Josephus Wilkinson, excessit 22nd Aug., A.D. 1818, natus annos 59." The house, which at that time belonged to John Rowland, Esq., was a little before 1818 bought by Mr. Wm. Overton, father of the present Mr. Overton, who had hitherto lived in Charles Street.

24. In the house where No. 31 now is, from 1750 to his death (December 9th, 1789), lived Mr. John Broadfoot, mercer, who was apparently son of the Mr. William Broadfoot who will be mentioned in connection with No. 40. Here he was succeeded by Mr. Samuel Roberts, mercer, who died December 12th, 1806, aged 42. Inasmuch as he was buried in the same tomb as the Broadfoots, he was probably connected in some way with them. His widow (Mrs. Ann Roberts, who died December, 1815, aged 59), left £100 to the poor of the parish. He was followed by Mr. Richard Lewis, whom many still remember. In 1780 the house and shop are described as belonging to Mrs. Lloyd, whom I believe to be Maria Charlotte, daughter of Rowland Pugh, Esq., of Mathafarn, and wife of the Rev. John Lloyd, and after her death they passed into the possession of Lieut.-Col. Edward Williams Vaughan, of the First Life Guards (second son of the first Sir Robert Howell Vaughan of Hengwrt), who afterwards assumed the name of Salusbury. and who about the end of the century sold the premises to Mr. Samuel Roberts, the occupier of them. This house was rebuilt and the Overton Arcade constructed in the year 1868.

25. In 1705, No. 34, (now containing cocoa rooms on the ground floor, and spirit vaults below), began to be occcupied by Mr. George Myddelton, apothecary, who remained here until his death, and was succeeded by his son, Mr. John Myddelton, apothecary, who removed about 1748 to the Henblas (see ch. v, sec. 3).

These Myddeltons were a branch of the Myddeltons of
Gwaunynog. As the members of this branch of the family were
not only important in themselves, but intermarried a great deal
with members of other local families, I have compiled the annexed
abbreviated pedigree of them, a pedigree[8] which has been kindly
supervised and corrected by Mr. Wm. M. Myddelton, of Saint
Albans, who is a grandson of the Rev. John Myddelton, of Bucknall mentioned in it.[9] Mrs. Dorothy Myddelton, widow of Mr.
George Myddelton, lived, from before 1742 until her death, in the
house in York Street which was immediately above The Bear, and
her two unmarried daughters, the Misses Eleanor and Martha
Myddelton, continued to live in the same house until their death.
This house indeed belonged to them, and was owned afterwards by
the Rev. Edward Davies, who had married one of their sisters, until
late on in the present century, while the Henblas, where Mr. John
Myddelton lived during the latter part of his life, passed in succession into the possession of two of his nieces, the wife of the Rev.
John Jones, and the wife of John Jones, Esq., of Coed y glyn. In
1775 the above-named Misses Eleanor and Martha Myddelton
bought of the churchwardens for £52 10 0, a vacant spot of ground
in Wrexham Church for a burial place, but no memorial of them
can now be found there.

26. When Mr. John Myddelton left No. 34 High Street, he was
succeeded by Mr. John Ellis, surgeon, who remained there until
about 1765, when he relinquished his practice, and went to live at
Eyton Villa, in the parish of Bangor Isycoed, becoming high-sheriff
of Denbighshire in 1784. In Wrexham he owned No. 26 High
Street, and the Bryn Gwiail lands to the east of the Beast Market.
He was twice married. By his first wife Jane, who died March 10th,
1748-9, and was buried at Wrexham, he had four children, Edward
and John, who died infants, and were buried at Wrexham on the
same day, May 3rd, 1745 ; Jane, (baptized at Wrexham, May 16th,
1746); and Edward (baptized there May 16th, 1747.) The last-
named I have fancied, perhaps without sufficient warrant, to be the
Edward Ellis mentioned in note 4, page 208 of the *Hist. of the Par.
Church of Wrexham.* Mr. John Ellis married secondly, at Bangor,
(September 20th, 1763), Mrs. Theophila Maurice, of the parish of

8. The Mr. John Morgan mentioned in the pedigree was a very important
man in the Wrexham of his time. Mr. Myddelton informs me that "he was
clerk of the peace for the county of Denbigh in 1691, and probably before and
after ; under-sheriff in 1683 and again in 1688 to Sir Richard Myddelton; and in
June 1693 his name appears as recorder of the lordship of Chirk and Chirkland."
He died in London in the parish of St. Martin in the Fields, and adminstration
was granted to his widow, Anne Morgan, 22nd September, 1694. As the rate
books for the whole period covering Morgan's residence in Wrexham are lost, I
have not been able to discover the house in which he lived.

9. Mr. W. M. Myddelton is the son of the Rev. Thomas Myddelton, who was
the son of the above-named Rev. John Myddelton.

Foulk Myddelton, Esq.,
of Gwaunynog : died Aug. 16, 1669. ==

Eldest son.

2nd son.

Annie, 1st wife, daughter of Dr. George Griffith, bishop of St. Asaph

John Myddelton, Esq., of Gwaunynog: bapt. at Wrexham, Jan. 28, 1639-40 : buried at Henllan, Jan. 3, 1687-8. =(2) Elizabeth, daughter of Richard Myddelton, Esq., of Bodlith.

(3) Jane, daughter of Major Holmes, of Bodelwyddan, and relict of John Foulkes, of Y Faenol, and of William Jeffreys, of Acton.

Richard Myddelton, baptized at Wrexham May 27, 1641, buried at Wrexham, May 28, 1641.

*

John, baptized, April 28, 1682.

Eldest son.

second son.

John Myddelton, Esq., of Gwaunynog : buried at Henllan, Feb. 14, 1754. =Anne, daughter of Robert Turbridge, Esq., of Llanbedr, near Ruthin.

George Myddelton, apothecary, of Wrexham: buried at Wrexham, June 18, 1725.

Wm. Myddelton, Esq., of Gwaunynog : died July 27, 1759: married Catherine, daughter of Thos. Shaw, Esq., of Denbigh.

Rev. Thos. Myddelton, rector of Ufton, Berks, and of Croes Newydd, near Wrexham : died Dec. 8, 1754, aged 47: buried at Wrexham. = Arabella, daughter of the Rev. Chas. Hacker, of Bridgeford, Notts : married Jan. 11, 1748-9 died April 10, 1756, aged 38 : buried at Wrexham.

four children : all died young.

*

John Myddelton, apothecary, of Wrexham, buried at Wrexham, Oct. 9, 1761. =Elizabeth Edwards, married at Wrexham, Jan. 21, 1734-5 : buried there Feb. 10, 1761.

Roger Myddelton, born, Nov. 11, 1706 : buried at Wrexham, Nov. 21, 1729.

Rev. Thomas Myddelton, M.A., vicar of Melton Mowbray, and of Twyby: died 1773, aged 58 : buried at Melton Mowbray.

(1)

= Sarah Edwards, of Croes Newydd: first wife: married Aug. 11, 1743: died July 3, 1759, aged 36.

Rev. Robt. Myddelton, D.D., of Gwaunynog, rector of Rotherhithe: died at Gwaunynog, 1815.

Rev. John Myddelton, B.D., born, Jan. 6, 1759, rector of Bucknall for 30 years : died, 1834.

George Myddelton, born Sept. 22, 1744 : died in India.

Mary Bennett, born 1745, married at Wrexham, Nov. 11, 1775.

= Rev. John Jones, A. rector of Knoc (1761 - 98), vi of Llansantffrai yn Mechain, (1783-98).

Rev. Robert Myddelton, of Gwaunynog (see under Coed y glyn).

Memorandum.—Those to whose names an asterisk is attached were baptized at Wrexham.

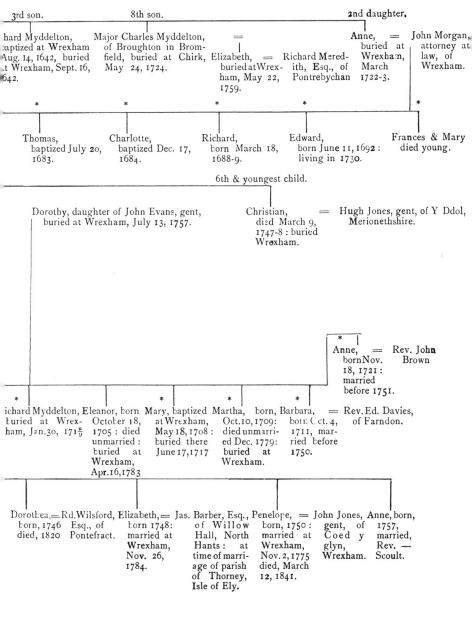

Elizabeth, daughter of Capt. Roger Myddelton,
of Plas Cadwgan : died March 23, 1675-6.

3rd son.

8th son.

2nd daughter.

Richard Myddelton,
baptized at Wrexham
Aug. 14, 1642, buried
at Wrexham, Sept. 16,
1642.

Major Charles Myddelton,
of Broughton in Brom-
field, buried at Chirk,
May 24, 1724.

=

Elizabeth,
buried at Wrex-
ham, May 22,
1759.

=

Richard Mered-
ith, Esq., of
Pontrebychan

Anne,
buried at
Wrexham,
March
1722-3.

=

John Morgan,
attorney at
law, of
Wrexham.

Thomas,
baptized July 20,
1683.

Charlotte,
baptized Dec. 17,
1684.

Richard,
born March 18,
1688-9.

Edward,
born June 11, 1692 :
living in 1730.

Frances & Mary
died young.

6th & youngest child.

Dorothy, daughter of John Evans, gent,
buried at Wrexham, July 13, 1757.

Christian,
died March 9,
1747-8 : buried
Wrexham.

=

Hugh Jones, gent, of Y Ddol,
Merionethshire.

Anne,
born Nov.
18, 1721 :
married
before 1751.

=

Rev. John
Brown

Richard Myddelton,
buried at Wrex-
ham, Jan. 30, 171 8/9

Eleanor, born
October 18,
1705 : died
unmarried :
buried at
Wrexham,
Apr. 16, 1783

Mary, baptized
at Wrexham,
May 18, 1708 :
buried there
June 17, 1717

Martha, born,
Oct. 10, 1709 :
died unmarri-
ed Dec. 1779:
buried at
Wrexham.

Barbara,
born Oct. 4,
1711, mar-
ried before
1750.

=

Rev. Ed. Davies,
of Farndon.

Dorothea,
born, 1746
died, 1820

=

Rd. Wilsford,
Esq., of
Pontefract.

Elizabeth,
born 1748:
married at
Wrexham,
Nov. 26,
1784.

=

Jas. Barber, Esq.,
of Willow
Hall, North
Hants : at
time of marri-
age of parish
of Thorney,
Isle of Ely.

Penelope,
born, 1750 :
married at
Wrexham,
Nov. 2, 1775
died, March
12, 1841.

=

John Jones,
gent, of
Coed y
glyn,
Wrexham.

Anne, born,
1757,
married,
Rev. —
Scoult.

Bangor, and had by her at least three children : William Edward who died an infant ; Theophila (baptized at Bangor, July 19th, 1766); and Mary (baptized at Bangor, September 15th, 1767). Mr. John Ellis who died April 13th, 1791, aged 77, and was buried at Marchwiel, was succeeded at Eyton by a Mr. Owen Ellis, who married at Bangor, (December 5th, 1791), Mary Ellis, spinster, perhaps one of the daughters of the above-named Mr John Ellis. Mr. Owen Ellis was high-sheriff of Flintshire in 1809-10. I find three children of his mentioned in the parish registers of Bangor : Thomas David, born August 22nd, 1792 ; Owen, born July 23rd, 1793 ; and John Cradoc, born August 31st, 1798. The eldest son was the Captain Ellis, of Bath, who died May 9th, 1858, and left £5,000 to the poor of Marchwiel. In 1808 all the property in Wrexham formerly belonging to John Ellis, Esq., is returned as belonging to Owen Ellis, Esq., and in 1844 Captain Henry Ellis is mentioned as the owner of the Bryn Gwiail lands there.

27. Mr. John Ellis was succeeded at No. 34 High Street, by Mr. Wm. Lloyd, surgeon, who remained there until after the year 1771. He afterwards lived elsewhere (see Index). Nimrod in his *Life and Times* gives a very unflattering picture of him, but Nimrod paints often with a very black brush, and is not always trustworthy. I think there is little doubt but this Mr. Lloyd is he who became, in 1793, the second William Lloyd, Esq., of Plaspower. Before the year 1780, the house had been acquired by Mr. Charles Woollam. mercer and wine merchant, a strange combination of trades which was long continued on the same premises and by successive tenants. Mr. Woollam died December 13th, 1797, and was succeeded by Messrs. Poole and Langford (Peter Poole and Joseph Langford) (see sec. 18), mercers and wine merchants, and they were followed in 1814, by Mr. Hugh Davies, draper, the premises being owned until 1825 by Mr. Watkin Robert Barber, step-son of Mr. Woollam (see sec. 23). Mr. Davies occupied the house and ground floor, but the vaults formed, from about 1823, the retail premises of Mr. Bartholomew Dillon, wine and spirit merchant, whose private residence was No. 10, Charles Street, and whose warehouse was at the bottom of Kenrick Street, near to the present entrance of the Market Hall. Mr. Dillon was the son of Thomas Dillon, tinplate-worker, and his mother's maiden name was Anne Wilbraham. I believe the famous Rowland Samuel, mentioned in sec. 22, was also somehow connected with the Wilbrahams, and he left, at his death in 1812, Mr. Bartholomew Dillon all his money (amounting as 'tis said to £8000). Mr. Dillon was a man of scientific tastes and had, among other things, a collection of fossils and minerals, all duly labelled. He was an excellent accountant, and was auditor to the Wrexham Union, and accountant to the Wrexham branch of the North and South Wales Bank. He was also for a time prosperous in his own business, but having, as I

am informed, in conjunction with the late Dr. George Lewis, made an attempt to regulate the Sunday traffic in public houses, the publicans, who were his chief customers, made a dead set at him and refused to deal with him, so that his business declined. However this may be, it is certain that he became involved in business difficulties. I find him described in the parish register under date January 1st, 1833, as schoolmaster, of King Street. In October, 1837, he was appointed actuary to the Savings Bank, his connection with which was terminated in a most painful manner in December, 1842. He subsequently went to Liverpool, and ultimately to Coventry, where he died at the residence of his eldest son.

28. No. 35 is the only house and shop in High Street which now retains its original aspect, very little modified. Here lived from 1751 until 1780, John Jones, a prosperous butcher, who was followed by Mr. Thomas Jones, the " old Tom Jones " of Nimrod's *Life and Times*. In 1780, it is first described as " The Royal Oak," and the place ever since, until quite lately, retained its double character of a public house and butcher's shop.

29. Nos 36 and 37, (now the shop of Mr. Scotcher and another shop), can be traced back as far as 1699, when they were the house and shop of Mrs Weld, the Welds being a local family of considerable importance. From 1700 to after 1708, they were occupied by the Mr. Edward Hanmer about whom I have said something under Charles Street. There used to be another house connected with the aforesaid house and shop, but facing the churchyard. From before 1721 until his death (April 19th, 1752, aged 61), Mr. Richard Jones, apothecary, lived at Nos. 36 and 37 High Street, having previously occupied No. 31. With this Mr. Jones was apprenticed, as a boy, the famous Dr. Thomas Henry, F.R.S., of Manchester (see ch. ix sec. 3). Mr. Jones was the representative of a very good family seated at Llai, in the parish of Gresford, and I believe at the house which from him was called " Apothecary's Hall." He married at Wrexham, (June 20th, 1760), Mrs. Mary Williams. His daughter Mary, (baptized at Wrexham, June 10th, 1717), married at Wrexham, (February 15th, 1756), William Lloyd, Esq. His daughter Ruth, (baptized at Wrexham, March 2nd, 1718-19,) married at Wrexham (February 18th, 1750-1), Mr. Griffith Speed, (see sec. 7). He had a son John, born January 14th, 1719-20, who died May 3rd, 1751, and was buried, as was his father after him, at Gresford. The later Joneses of Llai, to whom there is a monument in Gresford churchyard on the north side of the church, belonged almost certainly to the same family as Mr. Richard Jones, the apothecary, though in what precise way they were connected with him I cannot explain.

30. Although the premises described in the last paragraph were the property of Sir Watkin Williams Wynn, they were occupied from 1763 downwards by a long succession of prominent dissenters,

from 1763 to 1788 by Mr. John Evans, mercer, (see *Hist. of the Older Nonconformity of Wrexham*, p. 81, sec. 48), from 1789 to a little after 1805 by Mr. John Burton, mercer, (see the same, p. 86, note 31); from the date last-named to 1826 by Mr. John Jones, draper (see the same, p. 140, note 46), who was followed by Mr. William Bowker, (see the same, p. 85, sec. 62).

31. We now come to Nos 38 and 39, (the shop of Mr. John Rowlands and another shop). From about 1757 until his death, April 1793 (aged 82), these premises were occupied by Mr. Thomas Lloyd, mercer, who had (from before 1742), previously lived at No. 30. Mr. Thomas Lloyd was the second son of the Rev. Thomas Lloyd, of Plaspower, and the brother of the first William Lloyd, Esq., of Plaspower. He married, December 1740, Mary Shepherd, of Birmingham. Omitting the names of those who died young, I find the after-named children of his mentioned in the parish register :—William, born October 21st, 1742, afterwards of London ; Elizabeth, baptized May 31st, 1745 ; Charlotte, baptized February 3rd, 1746-7 ; John, baptized February 3rd, 1747-8, afterwards of Chester ; Richard Myddelton Massie, baptized May 10th, 1751, of whom I have given an account under Chester Street, (see ch. vii, sec. 4); and Anna Maria, baptized January 5th, 1753. Of the fore-named, Miss Charlotte Lloyd married at Wrexham, (November 2nd, 1767), Mr. Maurice Evans described in the register as of West Cheap. I wonder whether she was the mother of the Maurice Evans who in 1813 married Miss Maria Benedicta Massie (see ch. xiii, sec. 2).

32. After Mr. Thomas Lloyd's death, Mr. Charles Poyser, (see sec. 18), the elder, mercer, bought Nos. 38 and 39 of Mrs Lloyd, and occupied them as a house and shop, and was succeeded by his son Mr. Charles Poyser, the younger, mercer, who ultimately retired to Summer Hill, and was the father of the present Mr. Hampden A. Poyser, solicitor, of Wrexham.[10] A mercer's shop has been maintained continuously on this site since 1757.

33. Nos. 40, 41 and 42, were owned in 1780 by the same person —Mr. Richard Marsh, and when they were rebuilt, late in the present century, they were made to form one block.

34. Of No. 40 I need not say anything, but at No.41,(now the shop of Mr. R. O. Jones, ironmonger), lived from 1717 to his death in January, 1724, the Mr. Wm. Broadfoot, mercer, who was apparently the father of the Mr. John Broadfoot who is mentioned in connection with No. 31, and who was himself, I believe, the son of the Mr. John Broadfoot, who will be mentioned in connection with No. 42. In 1756, Mr. Walter Robinson, (see *Hist. of the Older Nonconformity of Wrexham*, p. 136, note 16), who, like the Broadfoots, was of

10. Mr. Poyser the elder died May 18th, 1844, aged 76, and Mr. Poyser the younger. March 23rd, 1871, aged 69.

Scotch origin, started here the business of a linen draper, which was continued until 1813 by his widow and daughters.

35. The house and shop now represented by No. 42, (the shop of Mr. A. W. Butt), were occupied from before 1699 by Mr. John Broadfoot, mercer, a Scotchman, who was settled in Wrexham at least as early as 1694. Here he remained until his death (October 27th, 1724, aged 68), and the business was conducted for some years afterwards by his widow. The Broadfoots were prominent men in the Wrexham of last century. Two of them (I believe his son and grandson) were also mercers in High Street, (see sec. 24 and 34). Omitting the names of the occupiers of the premises immediately following Mrs. Broadfoot, we come, in 1755, to the notable name of Richard Marsh, bookseller and printer. We first meet with him on February 12th, 1746-7, when he married Mary Hurst, of Wrexham. We then find him described as "writing master," and it was not until two years before he removed into the house now being described that he became a bookseller and printer. He was as far as I can make out, the first producer of printed books in Wrexham, and he printed a great many, a list of which will be found in Appendix II. He died May 24th, 1792, and was buried in Wrexham churchyard. He seems to have been prosperous, for he owned not merely his own house, but the two houses east of it, as well as The Royal Oak, High Street, which stood where the Market Hall front now is. His son Mr. John Marsh, (born January 8th, 1747), inherited the business, and printed at least two books, but died (October, 1795),three years after his father. Old Mr. Marsh was said to have haunted, after his death, the house he had left, and there were certainly, I have been told by one who was born in it, noises there that could not easily be accounted for. Mr. John Marsh was followed by Mr John Painter, printer and bookseller, who at the beginning of the present century removed to No. 18, and of whom, I have already given some account, (see sec. 13). Then came a succession of druggists, the last of which was Mr. Edward Rowland, father of the late Mr. Edward Rowland, of Bryn Offa.

36. The house at the corner of High Street and Church Street, (No. 43), has a history which dates a very long way back. It is clearly indicated in Norden's Survey, A.D. 1620, wherein the following entry relating to it occurs :—

"Thomas ap Richard holds one tenement (by right of Anne his wife), lying in the east corner of the street called Church Street, with shops and cellars, next the Cross, granted to John Robert, and Catherine his wife, by lease dated 21st March, 45th year of Elizabeth."

It will already have been noticed how many cadets and even heads of good country families were formerly engaged in retail trade in this town. Accordingly, we find that in 1699, Mr. Godfrey Lloyd, son of Mr. Robert Lloyd, of Rhydwrial, and descended from Owain Brogyntyn, was in business as a mercer in the house now being described, and here he continued to live until 1707, when he removed into Wrexham Abbot. He married November 5th, 1689, at Wrexham, Mary Critchley, who, I am nearly sure, was a daughter of Joseph Critchley, of "The Black Boy," (see *Hist. of the Par. Church of Wrexham*, p. 90, note 55). I give in a foot note[11] the names of his children baptized at Wrexham. His son Critchley, married Margaret Jones, sister and heiress of Dr. John Jones, of Bryn Banon, Penaner, and Penyfed, and had a son, Rev. John Lloyd, B.A., rector of Betwys Gwerfil Goch, who was the father of John Lloyd Salusbury, Esq., of Galltfaenan, Rhydwrial, etc. (see ch. iii, sec. 25).

37. From 1755 to some date after 1771, Mr. Joseph Jackson, a prosperous draper and clothier, occupied No. 43. He was the eldest son of Mr. John Jackson, dyer, (mentioned under ch. ii), was baptized March 3rd, 1722-3, and afterwards owned No. 5, Penybryn, and all the cottages between it and Tenters' Square. He married (at Wrexham), February 26th, 1746-7, Miss Judith Bruen, only child of Benjamin Bruen, Esq., of Trefalyn House, in the parish of Gresford, and of the family of Bruen, of Bruen Stapleford, Cheshire.[11a] His two sons, Joseph Bruen Jackson and John Langford Jackson, died young, and his eldest daughter, Judith, marrying Mr. John Mellor, carried the Penybryn property to her husband. Mr. Joseph Jackson died January 23rd, 1795, age 72, long surviving his wife, who was buried January 4th, 1774.

38. Mr. Joseph Jackson was followed by the Misses Mary and Anne Jenkins, drapers, sisters of the Rev. Joseph Jenkins, M.A., minister of the Baptist Chapel, and they bought the premises, which were afterwards occupied by their nephew, Mr. Wm. Fossey Jenkins, draper, son of the Rev. Joseph Jenkins, aforesaid.

39. By the year 1843, a branch of the North and South Wales Bank had been established at No. 43 High Street, and here it remained until, on the building of the Provincial Assurance office in 1860, it was removed to the ground floor of that building. This explains why No. 43 is now called "The Old Bank Buildings."

40. The frontispiece to this volume is a reproduction of an old sketch of High Street which I picked up in a print shop in London.

11. Critchley, baptized February 17th, 1690-1, born 7th; Ruth, baptized November 16th, 1694, born 9th; Robert baptized August 18th, 1696, born 7th; Joseph, baptized December 25th, 1697, born 18th; Elizabeth, baptized November 25th, 1699, born 20th; and Eleanor, baptized January 23, 1705-6, born 23rd. I omit the names of those who died young. There were also buried at Wrexham, his wife Mary, (June 15th, 1711), and his daughters : Katherine, (May 17th, 1711, and Anne, (July 16th, 1711). See also under Llwyn Isaf, Queen Street.

11a. Mr. Benjamin Bruen obtained Trefalyn House by his marriage with Dorothy, one of the two daughters of John Langford, Esq., and sisters of Richard Langford, Esq., and George Langford, Esq., the successive owners of the estate.

It is not dated, but it is evident from various signs that it must
have been made about the year 1830. Notice the entire absence
of foot pavements, and the tradesmen's stalls standing in the street.
The greater part of High Street and of Hope Street was furnished
with paved footpaths in 1846, under the direction of Mr. William
Overton and Mr. John Clark, the overseers of that year, at the
expense partly of the owners or tenants of the houses benefitted
by the operation, and partly by public subscription.

41. Norden, in his survey of 1620, mentions "The Crown" standing on the south side of High Street, as well as "The Red Lion" in
the same street next the High Cross. He mentions also a large
house on the south side of the street called "Ty Mawr," ("Big
House,") held by Valentine Tilston, (see *Hist. of Older Nonconformity of Wrexham*, p. 10). None of these houses have I been able to
identify.

THE PULFORD FAMILY OF WREXHAM.

42. The family of Pulford was not merely, for about a century
and a half, one of the chief families of Wrexham, but was also connected by marriage, with other of the principal families of the town
—the Goldsmiths, Wraggs, Stephentons, and others. The Pulfords
appear to have come hither from the neighbourhood of Holt, and
in 1638, I find Thomas Pulford, the younger, of Farndon, and
Thomas Pulford, of Wrexham, bracketed together.

43. By reason of the many gaps in the earlier registers of Wrexham, I have not found it possible to give a satisfactory account of
the succession of this family, or of the relations to one another of
the various members of it, and I have therefore merely copied from
the parish registers all the entries relating to them. The last of
the family, in the male line, was the Rev. Thomas Pulford, of
Willow House, who died in 1768. He was the owner of a great
deal of property in the town, namely :—Willow House, and the
lands belonging to it, (see ch. xvii, sec. 31 & 32); a house in Town Hill,
(see ch. iii, sec. 22); a house, stable, yard etc., where the Vegetable
Market in Henblas Street now is ; the Golden Lion in High Street;
a house in Beast Market Street ; another in the Beast Market; No.
40 High Street ; the Bryn Gwiail lands east of the Beast Market ;
many quillets in the Town Fields ; other property not worth mentioning ; and an " old dwelling house and piece of land thereto belonging, in the town of Holt," which probably represented the home
of the Pulfords before they came to Wrexham.

44. When the Rev. Thomas Pulford died, he left, as his heirs,
Thomas Wragg, gent, and Mrs. Elizabeth Stephenton, widow, both
of Wrexham, and these on the 4th December, 1770, agreed as to a
partition of the property.

45. I now give the extracts relating to the Pulfords, from the registers :—

Thomas, the sonne of Thomas Pulford[12] was bapt[d] the first daie October, 1626.

Catherine, the daughter of Thomas Pulford, was bapt[d] the viith daie, April 1631.

Randle, the sonne of Thomas Pulford, was bapt[d] the ixth daie, March 1632-3.

Randle, the sonne of Thomas Pulford, was buried the xith daie September 1634.

Randle, the sonne of Thomas Pulford, was bapt[d] the xvth daie March 1634-5.

Rondelus Pulford, 29th die Decembris, 1641, (sepultus fuit).

November 1663, Thomas, the son of John Pooford, of Wrexham Regis, gentn, baptized.

May 3rd, 1665, John, the son of John Pulford, of Wrexham Regis, baptized.

September 25th, 1665, Thomas, son of Mr. John Pulford, of Wrexh. Reg., buried.

May 1695, Ursulah da of Mr. Alexander Pulford, of Wrexh. Regis, born the 13th, baptized 28th.

August 14th, 1700, Katherine Pulford, died at Ireland (Green).

July 1705, Elinor,[13] Da of Mr. Alexander Pulford, born 11th of July and baptized the 13th, 1705.

August 22nd, 1706, George, son of Mr. Alexander Pulford, of Wrexham Regis, was Buryed.

August 1707, Richard, son of Mr. Alexander Pulford of w.r., born 13th of August, baptized 18th, [buried 31st.]

August 1708, Katherine,[14] Da: of Alexander Pulford, gent, of w.r. born ye 7th of August, baptized 9th, 1708.

January 1710-1, Alexander, son of Alexander Pulford, gent, of w.r. born 3rd, baptized 15th, [buried April 9th, 1711].

February 5th, 1710-1, Elizabeth, wife of Alexander Pulford, Gent, of w.r., was Buryed.

December 5th, 1721, John Stephenton, and Elizabeth Pulford, maryed.

April 30th, 1725, John Appleton and Eleanor Pulford, married. (See note 13).

12. This Mr. Thomas Pulford was fined during the parliamentary period, £69 for his adherance to the King's cause.

13. This Eleanor was probably afterwards the wife of the Rev. John Appleton, master of the Grammar School. The extract is taken from the Erbistock registers.

14. Catherine Pulford was probably afterwards the wife of Mr. Ralph Wragg. This Mr. Wragg was a son of Mr. Thomas Wragg, surveyor of excise, Wrexham. He had a son, Thomas Wragg, gent, of Wrexham, who was buried May 22nd, 1771, and whose only son, Thomas Wragg, gent, the younger, of Liverpool, I find mentioned in the year 1784. All the entries relating to the Wraggs will be given in Appendix iii. Of the Stephentons, I have said enough elsewhere.

June 12th, 1726, Mr. Alexander Pulford, Gent, buryed.

May 15th, 1728, Mr. Ralph Wragg, gent and Mrs Catherine Pulford, marryed.

May 3rd, 1738, John Pulford, Esq., Protonotary, buried.

November 4th, 1738, Elizabeth, daughter of John Pulford, gent, born ye 18th of 8br [Bapt.]

June 2nd, 1741, Eliza, daughter of John Pulford, late Protonotary, Buried.

June 1742, Mr. John Pulford and Mrs. Anne Jennings, both of this parish, married.

January 1745, Robert Samuel and Ellen Pulford, widow, both of ys Parish, by License, married.

February 23, 1762, Robert Taylor, of Llwyn y cnottiè, and Sarah Pulford, married.

December 30th, 1768, The Rev. Mr Thomas Pulford, buried.

Who the Elizabeth Pulford was who married Mr. John Stephenton (see ch. i, sec. 23), I cannot make out, but that she belonged to this family is certain.

CHAPTER II.

Church Street.

1. The name "Church Street" was firmly established and universally used in the year 1620.

2. We will begin with the houses (Nos. 1 to 4), on the east side of the street, and follow the existing numbering.

3. All the houses on the east side of Church Street belonged, during a great part of last century, to Mr. Samuel Edwards, of the Lichgate House, (of whom I shall again speak presently), and afterwards to Mr. John Price of the same place, (who will also be again mentioned). Nos. 1 and 2 were rebuilt in 1766 by Mr. Edwards, and this rebuilding is commemorated by the following inscription on No. 2:—

> E.
> S.   M.
> 1766.

the initials being those of Samuel Edwards and Margaret his wife.[1]

These two houses, (or one of them), were converted immediately afterwards into an inn: "The Coach and Horses," which was kept by Mr. Robert Jones, vintner, who appears to have been a person of some importance, and who died March 3rd, 1791, aged 53. About 1824, Mr. Richard Hughes, bookseller and printer, (see note 6, ch. xvii), occupied No. 2, and in 1843 was still there, and carried on in No. 3 adjoining, the Wrexham Post Office, using also No. 7, on the opposite side of the street, as a printing office. Mr. Richard Hughes was the father of the late Mr. Charles Hughes, J.P.

4. The house and shop where Nos. 3 and 4 now are, became known as "The Lichgate House" (being directly adjoining the Lichgate of the churchyard), and was occupied before 1721 and after 1732 by Mr. John Jackson, dyer. He married, June 7th, 1720, Sarah, one of the two sisters of Mr. Joseph Jones, of Nos. 4 and 5 High Street, and had, among other children, two sons, Mr. Joseph Jackson, mercer, and Mr. John Jackson, tanner, elsewhere mentioned in this book. In 1751, this house and shop came into the occupation of Mr. Samuel Edwards, clothier, who in 1757 rebuilt it, making two houses and shops, and inserting on the side of

---

1. Mr. Samuel Edwards married at Wrexham (December 1749), Margaret Price, and in this fact we may perhaps find the explanation of Mr. John Price succeeding to his property.

the building that faced the churchyard, the following inscription

which may still be seen there :—

```
    E.
S.      M.
   1757.
```

the initials standing, as before, for Samuel and Margaret Edwards.

The other houses on the same side of the street he also owned, and were rebuilt by him.Here he remained until 1781, when he retired from business. He died February 20th, 1788, aged 71, and was buried in Wrexham churchyard. He was succeeded at the Lichgate House by Mr. John Price, mercer, who was one of the Prices of Pentrefelin House. He acquired all the houses and shops on the east side of Church Stteet, and they were all in 1857 still in the possession of members of his family. He continued in business at the Lichgate House until a little after 1808, and died February 15th, 1813, aged 52. He was succeeded by Mr. Richard Briscoe, druggist, who removed, about 1817, to No. 26 High Street.

5. At No. 5, exactly opposite the Lichgate House, lived, from 1699 to his death (December 1716), Mr. Stephen Stephenton, dyer, the founder of the Stephenton family, and ultimately his grandson, Mr. Stephen Stephenton, attorney-at-law, (see ch. I, sec. 23). This house belonged to the Stephentons, but after the death of the last-named Mr. Stephenton, it passed into the possession of a certain "Thomas Jones, gent."

. 6. The only other house on the west side of the street that I need describe is No. 10, now the shop of Mr. H. J. Collens. Norden thus describes in 1620 the building that then stood here :—

"Rent 6s 8d (Lease) 23 yea' in being. Thomas ap John Robert holds one tenement with shops and cellars and other necessary offices, being the corner tenement on the west side of Church Street by lease granted 30th July, in the 6th year of James."

7. No. 10 Church Street absorbed, during the last century, a shop adjoining it on Town Hill, and about 1804 began to be occupied by Mr. John Williams, draper, who married at Wrexham, (February 14th, 1797), Elizabeth, daughter of Mr. Benjamin Gilpin, of Bersham, and sister of the well-known and versatile Gilbert Gilpin, of Coalport (afterwards of Dawley). Mr. Williams, about the year 1824, gave up the whole premises in Church Street to business, and went to live at the house in the churchyard, between Church Street and Cefn y Cwn. His daughter, Mary, married the present Mr. Tubal Cain Jones, J.P., who succeeded him in his shop and house, and who about 1887 relinquished his business to Mr. Collens.

CHAPTER III

The Town Hill.

1 The year 1801 is that in which I first find the street described in this chapter mentioned under the name "Town Hill." That name must have been in use before 1801, but it is certainly not an old name. During the last century Town Hill was sometimes regarded as a part of High Street, while in deeds of an earlier date it is periphrastically described as "the street leading towards Oswestry." In 1670 and 1671 I find it called "Bridge Street," but this is a name which did not last, and by "Bridge Street" we now mean the street between the Horns Bridge and Pen y bryn.

2. The most important building in this street is of course "the Shirehall," now always called "The Town Hall," a building which merits a long and particular notice. The first mention that I can find of the Shirehall occurs in the year 1562. It was then called "The Common Hall" and "Hall of Pleas." Nine shops beneath it, held at will by William ap Robert at a rent of 28s 8d, are at the same time mentioned, and there was also. besides the shops, an open space beneath the hall. The hall itself, or Grand Chamber above the shops and open space, was reserved to the Crown, and was used for the holding of the Great and Quarter Sessions, and of the courts of the manor of Wrexham Regis, as well as perhaps or the courts of other manors of the lordship of Bromfield and Yale. This building superseded the older court house of Wrexham Regis, which was also, it is probable, the the head of the lordship, and stood on the tract of land called "The Parkey," (see *Hist. of Ancient Tenures of Land* p. 71) and (*Hist. of Par. Church of Wrexham*, ch. i, sec. 6). According to a statement made in 1705, the Shirehall was erected on lands belonging to the Crown. This is what, not merely from the nature of the case, but from a consideration of the position of the building, might have been anticipated. I feel confident, moreover, that the whole block here standing, that is, not the court house only, but the building represented by "The Hand Inn" as well, belonged at first immediately to the Crown. On one of the beams of the Hand Inn is carved, in fact, the crowned portcullis—the badge of Henry VII. But the site of the last-named building must have been once appropriated, by gift of the lord, to the use of the church. I infer this not merely from the curious symbol of the Trinity carved on one of the

beams of the Hand Inn, but also from the fact that at the Quarter Sessions held at Wrexham, in October 1663, the grand jury presented that " some of this said court house or building standeth on the church land wch hath brought xxs p. ann., to the wardens for the p'ish use, as the books will make appear." The courthouse must at some time subsequent to the alienation of the site of " The Hand" have been extended westward, and land taken for which an acknowledgment was annually paid to the churchwardens. There is, however, no mention made in the books of the churchwardens of any such payment made to the latter, although these books begin two years before the date of the above-named presentment.

3. On April 15th, 21st year of Queen Elizabeth, (1578), the nine shops beneath the Shirehall were leased, apparently for forty years, to Robert Puleston (I suppose of Hafod y wern), and in or about the year 1619,were leased again, at 50s a year,to Thomas Goldsmith, gentleman of Wrexham, then living in " the street next the church "(a very vague description[1]) On the 28th of March,1628, they were once more leased at the same rent for 31 years, dating from the Michaelmas next preceeding, to John and David Edwards, who were to assign the lease to George Manley, gentleman. The lessees

---

1. The above-named Thomas Goldsmith, (or Gouldsmith, as he himself spelled his name), was a very important man in the Wrexham of his day. He possessed not merely considerable property in Wrexham, but also much freehold land in the country around, in Cacca Dutton, Bedwell, Moreton, Marchwiel, Bersham, and Esclusham. He is almost always described as " gentleman," but calls himself " mercer " in his will, which is dated November 22nd, 1623. He died before the 19th of March following the date just mentioned. His widow's name was Anne (daughter of Mr. Wells, of Holt), and he mentions in his will his mother-in-law, Mrs. Jane Warburton. He also mentions his brothers: George, probably of Wrexham Fechan (to whom he bequeathed a ring or signet and £10 to be divided among his three children), Arthur and John. He speaks also of his daughters Alice and Elizabeth, (to whom were to be paid £200 apiece, on attaining the age of 18 or on their marriage), of his daughter, Mary, the wife of Randle Jones, son of Roger Jones, Esq., of Llwynonn, and of Mary and Elizabeth, sisters of the said Randle Jones. He speaks also of his daughter Dorothy, married to David Edwards, son of John Edwards, Esq,, of Stansty, and of the three children of the said David and Dorothy Edwards. He mentions his sons, George, Edward, Michael, and John, who were to receive £100 each on attaining the age of 21. He makes provision for his son Arthur (" if it pleases God he comes home,") and his son Thomas " who hath lately married Jane, his now wife, dau. of Edward Puleston, Esq. [of Llwyn y cnottié], deceased, who by his will left her a portion of £300, which I have not yet received." In my " Hist. of the Par. Church of Wrexham" (p. 86, note 4), following Lloyd's " History of Powys Fadog," I have stated that Robert Bellot, gent, of Wrexham, married Jane, relict of Thomas Gouldsmith,gent, and daughter of Edward Puleston, of Llwyn y cnottié, gent, but from the above summary of Mr. Thomas Gouldsmith's will, and from a deed which I have since seen, it is evident that Mr. Bellot's wife was the relict of Mr. Thomas Gouldsmith, the " younger," and that the widow of Mr. Thomas Gouldsmith, the elder, became the second wife of the first John Roberts, Esq., of Hafod y bwch. Then (in my " Hist. of the Older Nonconformity of Wrexham" p. 63, note 7), I have spoken of Richard Benjamin, butcher, having married Ermine, daughter of Mr. Thomas Gouldsmith, but the latter does not mention a daughter of that name in his will, and that statement was really based on a formal statement, made in 1620, that Richard Benjamin held a certain tenement in Wrexham as the of heir Thomas Gouldsmith, by right of Ermine his wife.

were to keep not merely the shops, but also "the court house and houses for juries in good repair." The John Edwards just mentioned, was John Edwards, gent, of Stansty Issa, and David Edwards was his son. The latter married Dorothy, one of the daughters of the before-named Thomas Goldsmith, and had, among other children, a son, Peter Edwards, who will be mentioned presently. Mr. George Manley, who married (October 17th, 1638) Margaret Goldsmith, appears himself to have been a son-in-law of Mr. Thomas Goldsmith. When, after the execution of Charles I., a survey was made of his possessions, the nine shops were found to be still in the tenure of Mr. Manley, and were valued at £12 a year.

4. Mr. Manley's lease expired in 1658, and the whole building must then have been in a ruinous condition, for the grand jury soon after presented the want of a proper Shirehall in the town of Wrexham, and the justices at the sessions here held, on July 12th, 1659, ordered £450 to be levied throughout the county as a part of the sum of £650 required, for the erection of such a hall. A site different from that of the old building appears to have been selected. But after all, no new hall was at that time built here, and a part of the money raised for that purpose was ordered to be applied to build a new Shirehall in the town of Ruthin, the hall at Wrexham being I suppose repaired. The latter must have been repaired quite effectually, for on the 22nd February, 1661, it was leased to Mr. Peter Edwards for 31 years at the increased rent of £4. This Peter Edwards was grandson both of John Edwards and of Thomas Goldsmith, two of the former lessees.

5. Mr. Thomas Baker, grocer, must have been the subtenant, or one of the subtenants, of the shops beneath the hall, for in October 1663 the grand jury of the county made the following presentment relating to him :—"We present Mr. Thomas Baker for stopinge and blocking up the passages or Arches under this buildinge and refusing to suffer the towne people, or others to sell fish, lemons and other fruits, wch they bring from Chester, and other places,

---

The following entries in Wrexham parish registers relate to these Gouldsmiths :—

October 1625, Margaret, the daughter of Thomas Gouldsmith, [the younger] was bapt. the vith daie.
November 1633, Martha, the daughter of George Gouldsmith was bapt., the xxvith daie.
 Eduardus Gouldsmith 28 die Februarii 1636, [sepultus fuit].
 Georgius Manley et Margaretta Goldsmith, 17 Octobris 1638 [mariti fuere].
 November 14th, 1654, John Gouldsmith was buried.
 February 24th, 1668-9, Mrs. Mary Goldsmith was buried.
 August 14th, 1674, Mary Goldsmith buried.
 July 14th, 1683, Mary, da of John Goldsmith, of Wrexham, bapt.
 For an account of another branch of the Gouldsmiths, see under Wrexham Fechan. The arms of the Gouldsmiths are said to have been :-- *Ermine*, a chevron *gules* charged with three open crowns *or*, cn a canton of the second, a leopard's face of the third.

for the comoditye of the towne and country, unless the (y) pay extortion;'and as we are informed, he hath refused to suffer the stockes to be put under the shad (e), some of us having knowne people almost p'isht therin by reason cf a sudden storme." The jury wind up their presentments by the following declaration :—" We are requested to motion that while Justice is here above, yt extortion and opp'sion be not below upon the poorer sort yt Travell for ther Subsistance, and the towne's necessary use."

6. When in 1691, the lease granted to Peter Edwards expired, the Shirehall remained until 1705 in the hands of the Crown, in which year, upon a petition addressed to them by the justices of the county, a lease was granted for 50 years, at £4 a year to Peter Ellice, of Croes Newydd ; John Puleston, of Pickhill Hall ; John Puleston of Hafod y wern; and Thomas Pulford, of Wrexham, Esquires, who were authorised to rebuild the Hall. Under the powers of this lease, the present Hall was accordingly in 1713, at the expense of the county, and upon the site of the old building erected. The Hall stood on open arches resting on pillars, and there was entirely open spaces below, between the pillars where the shops had been. The building was extended westward on the northern side (so as to admit probably of the formation of a jury room), and an additional building of two stories was erected "at the south west end of the hall consisting of a few rooms which were occupied by Mr. Philip Cross, [corvisor], the treasurer for the county, who, it was reported paid the Crown lessees £8 per annum." These last recited particulars, as well as others hereafter given, are taken from an interesting memorandum obtained by Mr. Overton from the Crown authorities when he and Mr. Painter purchased the Hall from them in 1857.

7 This lease just mentioned expired in 1755, and the whole building remained for several years in the hands of the Crown, but in 1756 the vacant space between the pillars and the house part were leased for another fifty years, at the old rent of £4 a year, to Sir Lynch Salusbury Cotton, Bart., of Combermere and Lleweni. Sir Lynch subsequently (in 1778, according to the above-mentioned memorandum, but he died in 1775), sold his interest in the lease to Mr. Joseph Jackson, draper, (see ch. i, sec. 27), and to his son-in-law John Meller, merchant, both of Wrexham,[1a] for £300. Mr. Jackson died in 1795, so that when the lease expired in 1706, Mr. Meller was the sole lessee. According to Mr. Overton's memorandum : " It appears that, up to this time, the hall itself, although not included in the leases, was occasionally let by the Crown lessees

1a. In note 280, p. 109, of my "Hist. of Par. Church of Wrexham," I have given a rather long account of this Mr. Meller, but the name is there wrongly spelled, and it should have been added that he lived only a short time in Pen y-bryn, removing about 1791 to Gatewen, where he remained nearly 20 years, and ultimately occupying the house part of the Shirehall, where he died, (see under 35 Pen y bryn).

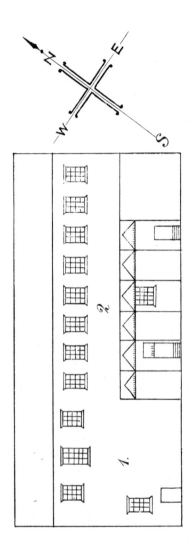

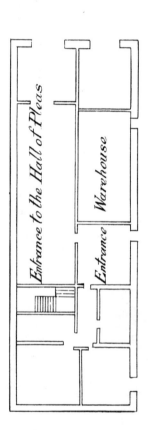

ELEVATION AND GROUND PLAN

Of the Town Hall, etc., in Wrexham belonging to the Crown, taken in 1820 by W Williams.

1. *House Part*
2. *Hall of Pleas*

Entrance to the Hall of Pleas

Entrance Warehouse

Scale of 8 yards to an Inch.

to strolling players, and for public entertainments, and meetings when not required for county purposes, and probably in return for this concession, the lessees bore the whole expense of keeping the building in repair, the county not contributing anything towards it. When Messrs. Jackson and Meller purchased the grant from Sir L. S. Cotton, the premises were also used as the Yorkshire Cloth Market " during the great March fair and yielded from that source about £30 a year. But about the year 1788, the dealers in Yorkshire cloth, apprehensive lest, through the suggested re-acquisition of the Shirehall by the county, they should be deprived of a place for the vending of their wares, arranged with Mr. William Edwards, tanner, (see *Hist. of Par. Church of Wrexham*, note 260, p. 106), for the erection on his property of a square of small shops (still called "Yorkshire Square,") for their yearly use and occupation. In 1788, however, through the transfer of the great Sessions or Assizes from Wrexham to Ruthin, the magistrates relinquished their project of purchasing Messrs. Jackson and Meller's lease, and a new Hall of Pleas and Record office was built at Ruthin. Mr. Meller is recorded to have raised the house part two stories higher and this must have been done before 1800, for in that year the whole premises are described as being under one roof. At this time about £24 a year were received by the lessee for the rent of the house, hall, and various standings in the vacant space below the great room.

8. When the lease originally granted to Sir Lynch Salusbury Cotton expired on September 5th, 1806, the whole building, including "the Hall of Pleas or Town Hall," was leased to Mr. John Meller for 50 years and 7 months, the latter agreeing to pay a fine of £112, and a yearly rent of £16 13 6. Mr. Overton's memorandum recites that "when the lease to Mr. Meller was granted, the hall was supported on gritstone pillars, but in 1812, some of these pillars having very much decayed, Mr. Meller enclosed a great portion of the underpart of the hall on the N.E. and S.W. sides with a brick wall, and made two convenient warehouses." The great room itself was also long used as a dèpot for the East Denbighshire Militia, their uniforms and muskets being ranged around the walls.

9. In 1820 the building is thus described :—" A Town Hall or Hall of Pleas, with convenient entrances thereto ; also, a dwelling house annexed, consisting of a good kitchen, parlour, scullery, pantry, and other convenient rooms above the same ; also a warehouse on the ground floor, and one other above the same."

10. Mr. Meller died in 1829, having previously assigned the lease of the Hall to Mr. Richard Roberts, of Y Felin Puleston, smith, whose widow made it over in 1841, to Mr. John Richards, who married Miss Elizabeth Parry, (see *Hist. of the Par. Church of Wrexham*, p. 111, note 288c), half-sister to Mr. William Overton. Mr.

Richards converted the lower part on the premises into "spirit vaults," and when he died in 1843, Mr. Overton carried on the business.   The lease expiring in 1857, Mr. Overton and Mr. Thomas Painter, his brother-in-law, purchased the Town Hall of the Crown.

11. It seems a pity that the Town Hall should not have been acquired in 1857 for the public use.

12. The clock at the east end of the hall was set up at the cost of various subscribers to commemorate the marriage of the late Sir Watkin Williams-Wynn, (April 28th, 1852).   The coat of arms of Charles II. beneath the clock, bearing the date 1663, is a relic of the former building, and was at first at the other end of the hall.

13. Although the carved beams in the Hand Inn, at the west end of the Town Hall, date certainly from the time of Henry VII, they undoubtedly belong to an earlier building, and must have been incorporated in the present building when it was erected, probably on the old site, at the beginning of last century.   This rebuilding must have taken place about 1715, for in that year the following entry, relating to the house now being described, occurs in the parish rate books :—" John Lloyd and *ye new house* at end of Hall."   Not merely are the main beams of this house covered with carved figures and designs, but there are very curious carvings on the under-sides of the sills of two of the windows.   On one of these are three rabbits so disposed that their ears form a triangle enclosing a circle—an emblem of the Trinity in Unity, while on the other is the crowned portcullis, the badge of Henry VII.   This house was held in 1620 by the same person who held the tenement in Hope Street on the north side of the hall, and this community of ownership still existed in 1780, when both houses belonged to to Roger Atcherly, Esq., and in 1808 and 1828, when they belonged to E. Atcherly, Esq.   Norden thus describes the building in which we are now interested :—" Edward Davies holds . . . . . one fair tenement with two shops and curtilage, at the west end of the Shirehall."   After it was rebuilt, a little before 1715, it was called " The Black Lion," and was still so called in 1771.   In 1788 it was known as "The Bull's Head," but in 1801 was already known as " The Hand," a name which it has retained ever since. It is proposed to clear away this house, so as to widen the entrance to Abbot Street.   It is hoped, if this should be ever done, that the carved beams which beautify its front will be presented to the town, and be preserved in the Municipal Buildings.

14. Having now dealt with the Hand Inn, we will describe some of the other houses in Town Hill, beginning at the top on the south side, going to the bottom, and returning on the other side, following thus the existing numbering.

15. No. 1, (Messrs. Phillips & Company's shop), represents a very old and important house which belonged, from the beginning

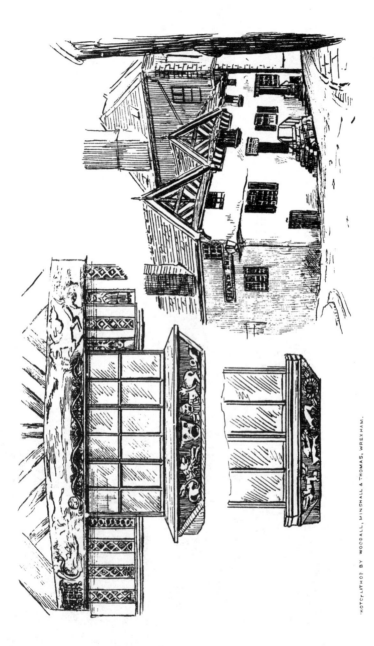

THE HAND INN.

Details from Photo. by J. Oswell Bury, Esq.

of the 17th to the beginning of the present century, to the Benjamin family, (see *Hist. of Older Nonconformity of Wrexham*, p. 63, note 7). It is thus described in Norden's survey, of A.D. 1620 :—

"(Chief) Rent 8d. Richard Benjamin, butcher, holds freely one messuage or tenement in which he himself dwells, lying opposite the Shirehall, and adjoining the tenement some time of John Gittins on the west side, and the tenement of Thomas ap John Robert (see ch. ii, sec. 6) on the east side, and two parcels of land in the Town Fields of Wrexham pertaining to the same messuage containing by estimation one (customary) acre."

Richard Benjamin obtained by right of his wife, Ermin, (see note 1), much of his property in Wrexham, but I am not sure, as I inadvertently stated in the note in *Hist. of the Older Nonconformity* above indicated), that he acquired the Town Hill property in this way. In 1663, Philip Benjamin, butcher, probably son of Richard Benjamin, lived in this house, and here remained until his death in February 1670-1. He was the father of Richard Benjamin, *butcher*, whose son, Richard Benjamin, *grocer*, is mentioned in the above cited note. The premises extended from Town Hill, to the churchyard, and upon the back part of them, facing the churchyard, was built a very good house (already in existence in 1699), in which many members of the Benjamin family lived, and which was ultimately sold to Mr. John Williams, draper, of Church Street. The Town Hill house and shop were purchased March 10th, 1800, when part of the Benjamin property was sold by auction, by Mr. Henry Ratcliffe, grocer, who thereupon set up in business there, and they thus ultimately passed into the possession of Mr. James Edisbury, who married (February 17th, 1829), Elizabeth Walker Ratcliffe, daughter of Mr. Ratcliffe.

16. The "house and shop" next below Mr. Benjamin's are described in 1671 as the property of Mr. Roger Mostyn, almost certainly Roger Mostyn, Esq., of Plas Mostyn, Brymbo, and in 1783, Nos. 2 and 3 Town Hill, and a malt-kiln at the back,[2] are returned as belonging to William Mostyn, Esq.,—Plas Mostyn, Brymbo, being returned the same year as belonging to the same person. At the beginning of the present century all this property was bought by Mr. Watkin Samuel, of Plas Coch, and to his son they still belonged in 1857. As to the occupiers of the houses. the only one that I shall mention is Mr, John Roberts, watchmaker, who lived at No. 3 from the year 1764 until after 1771. He was the father of the Rev. Peter Roberts, A.M., rector of Llanarmon Dyffryn Ceiriog, (1811-1819), and of Halkyn (1818-1819), and author of various religous ond antiquarian works. The Rev. Peter Roberts was born at Ruabon, in 1760, where his father was then living.

17. The house represented by Nos, 4 and 4a, was in 1755 called " The Bull and Dogs," and immediately afterwards became the

2. This malt-kiln is no doubt that which still stands in the Churchyard at the top of Camfa'r Cwn steps.

shop of Mr. West Humphreys, chandler.   Mr. Humphreys owned
not merely this shop and the shop adjoining (now No. 5), but also
the estate of Little Berse, and appears to have been the son of Mr.
John Humphreys of that place, who was the second son of Edward
Humphreys, gent, of Golftyn, in the parish of Northop.   Mr. West
Humphreys is therefore in the parish registers always invested
with his territorial name and described as "of Bersham."   He
must have been in some way connected with Gresford, for nearly
all the members of his family were buried there.   He himself was
buried at Gresford, January 29th, 1785.   He had seventeen children, of whom his daughter, Margaret, married (October 2nd, 1786)
at Wrexham, Josiah Lloyd of the parish of Northop, who succeeded his father-in-law in his business, and I think died about 1811,
the property then passing to Mary, the wife of Mr. Edward Jones,
of Croes Newydd, who was another daughter of Mr. West Humphreys.

18. Between the house and shop at the corner of Town Hill and
College Street and the river, are various houses, (Nos. 9 to 14), on
the same side of the street, which are now numbered as part of
Town Hill, but which seem to have been formerly regarded as in
College Street.   These houses unlike the rest of Town Hill, (which
is in Wrexham Regis) are in Wrexham Abbot, and I shall there-
fore follow the ancient arrangement and deal with them under
College Street, (see ch. xxi).

19. We now accordingly pass to the other or north side of Town
Hill, to the bottom house at the corner of Brook Street.   In 1780
all the houses in Town Hill, between Brook Street and Mr.
Williamson the pork butcher's (that is all the houses now numbered 15, 15a, 16, 17, 18, and 19), belonged to Robert Griffith, gent,
of Hafod y bwch, (see ch. viii, sec. 6 and 8), and in 1797 to Mr.
Thomas Griffith, his son, but soon afterwards were disposed of to
various persons, and then were all, almost immediately after, purchased by Mr. William Edisbury, maltster, of the Three Tuns (see
ch. xxi, sec. 10), who was buried at Wrexham, November 2nd,
1803.   Of only one of these houses need I speak.   In the house
where Nos. 16 and 17 now stand, David Price came to live about
1791, and this house he converted into an inn and called "The
Blue Bell," which, after the battle of Waterloo came to be known
as "The Waterloo Tavern."   This house, as well as that next adjoining, (now represented by No. 18), he bought of Mr. Thomas
Griffith, but it afterwards passed into the possession of Mrs. Edisbury, widow of the above-named William Edisbury, from whose
son, Mr. Thomas Edisbury, of Brook Street House, it came to Mr.
John Harrison, glazier, of Abbot Street, who put his son, Mr.
Benjamin Harrison, into possession of The Waterloo Tavern, where
he remained until his death in 1821, after which, I believe, it was

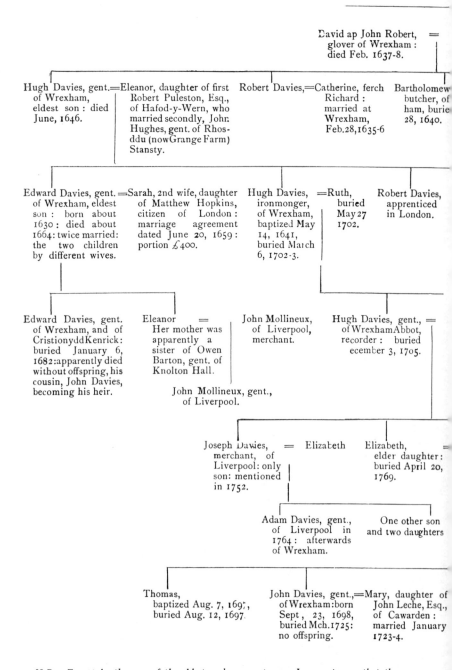

David ap John Robert, =
glover of Wrexham :
died Feb. 1637-8.

Hugh Davies, gent.=Eleanor, daughter of first
of Wrexham,   Robert Puleston, Esq.,
eldest son : died   of Hafod-y-Wern, who
June, 1646.   married secondly, John
  Hughes, gent. of Rhos-
  ddu (nowGrange Farm)
  Stansty.

Robert Davies,=Catherine, ferch
  Richard :
  married at
  Wrexham,
  Feb.28,1635-6

Bartholomew
butcher, of
ham, burie
28, 1640.

Edward Davies, gent. =Sarah, 2nd wife, daughter
of Wrexham, eldest   of Matthew Hopkins,
son : born about   citizen of London :
1630 : died about   marriage agreement
1664: twice married: dated June 20, 1659 :
the two children   portion £400.
by different wives.

Hugh Davies, =Ruth,
ironmonger,   buried
of Wrexham,   May 27
baptized May   1702.
14, 1641,
buried March
6, 1702-3.

Robert Davies,
apprenticed
in London.

Edward Davies, gent.
of Wrexham, and of
CristionyddKenrick:
buried January 6,
1682:apparently died
without offspring, his
cousin, John Davies,
becoming his heir.

Eleanor   =
Her mother was
apparently a
sister of Owen
Barton, gent. of
Knolton Hall.

John Mollineux,
of Liverpool,
merchant.

Hugh Davies, gent., =
of WrexhamAbbot,
recorder : buried
ecember 3, 1705.

John Mollineux, gent.,
of Liverpool.

Joseph Davies,   =   Elizabeth
merchant, of
Liverpool: only
son: mentioned
in 1752.

Elizabeth,
elder daughter:
buried April 20,
1769.

Adam Davies, gent.,
of Liverpool in
1764 : afterwards
of Wrexham.

One other son
and two daughters

Thomas,
baptized Aug. 7, 1697,
buried Aug. 12, 1697.

John Davies, gent.,=Mary, daughter of
of Wrexham:born   John Leche, Esq.,
Sept , 23, 1698,   of Cawarden :
buried Mch.1725:   married January
no offspring.   1723-4.

N.B.—*Except in the case of the eldest and youngest sons, I am not sure that the
children of David ap John Robert, and of Hugh Davies, the elder,
are arranged in the order of seniority.*

DAVIES of WREXHAM.

Elizabeth.

...avies,=Gwen Eyton, Wrex- married at Nov. Wrexham, July 17, 1636: buried there July 1, 1684.	Philip Davies, living in 1637.	Edward Davies, draper, of London, living in 1639.	John Davies, youngest son, baptized Dec. 25, 1623, probably John Davies, of Wrexham, mercer.	Other children.

...homas Davies, gent.=Mary, daughter of of Wrexham, bapt. April 24, 1644, youngest son : marriage settlement dated Sept. 1664 : buried Feb.5,1682-3	Rd. Presland, yeoman, of Ridley, Isycoed : buried May 1, 1696.	Elizabeth, living in 1655 : baptized June 26, 1635.	Other children.

John Davies, gent.,=Sarah Lewis, spinster,
of the Greyhound,   of Westminster :
Wrexham : bapt.   marriage agreement
July 1, 1673 : bur-   dated January 1694-5
ied Nov. 4, 1706.   buried Oct. 27, 1746.

Elizabeth Nicolls, married Dec. 7, 1692, living in 1732.

Rev. Stephen Davies,=Ann Presbyterian minister of Banbury : called by Dr. Daniel Williams,"my cousin," and residuary legatee under the Doctor's will: living in 1723.

John Dannald, surgeon of Wrexham.

Bridget = Edward Lloyd, attorney, of Wrexham.

Mary, Baptized Nov. 8, 1700: married Feb. 17, 1728-9 buried at Bryn Eglwys, Sept. 20, 1793.	=David Thelwall, apothecary of Wrexham, afterwards of Blaen Iâl.	Martha, Born, Nov. 24, 1706 : buried March 1714.

converted into a shop. Mr. Harrison rebuilt Nos. 16, 17 and 18, about the year 1825.

20. Nos. 20, 21, 22, 22a, and 23, occupy the site of, and in part incorporate, a large house which was formerly the house of the Davieses, an important Wrexham family, and afterwards, by marriage, of the Thelwalls, of Blaen Iâl. It had many gables and stood back a little from the street, having iron railings in front of it, and, though not a public house, was commonly called "The Greyhound." There was a great deal of carved oak about the place, and when, some years ago, (before 1852), the late Mr. Hugh Davies, contractor, brought the frontage forward to the street, and divided the whole into shops, nearly as we now see them, he presented a triplet composed of three panels in a line, to Mrs Townshend Mainwaring, (then of Marchwiel Hall), as the living representation of the old family to which it had belonged. The panels were of oak or Spanish chestnut, and beautifully carved, each panel being separated from the one adjoining it by a strip of oak carved with the "linen pattern." The first panel contained the carved head of a man with peaked beard, and pointed hat : the second was occupied wholly with the initials " R. D.," perhaps those of Robert Davies ; while on the third was carved the greater part of the figure of a woman, her hair seemingly confined in a net, and having a necklace or chain round her neck, a leather belt and strap round her waist, and a flower in her hand. There was no date on any of the panels. The Greyhound seems always to have included at least one shop which was often let apart from the house. The founder of the family of Davies was David ap John Robert, a prosperous glover, of Wrexham, of whom an account will be found under College Street. I annex a pedigree of this family, which I have compiled from entries in the parish registers and from various deeds in the possession of C. S. Mainwaring, Esq., which that gentleman has kindly permitted me to examine. Who built the Greyhound I do not know, but it could hardly have been in existence when on Oct. 16th, 1616, the fore-named David ap John Robert bought the buildings there for £72 of Hugh Meredith, gent. In the deed of sale bearing this date, the premises are described as consisting of a " messuage in the high streete there leading towards Oswestrie," sometime in the occupation of Robert ap David ap John Tona, afterwards of Hugh ap Robert ap David, and then (in 1616), of John Coytmore, leased to the said Hugh Meredith by Queen Elizabeth, on March 21st, in the 45th year of her reign, for forty years; and also of all that backside and garden, with all the buildings thereon standing, adjacent to the last-named messuage on the one end, and to a garden in the occupation of John Robert ap Edward on the other, and between the High Street on the one side, and the lands of the Right Honourable Lord Wotton on the other, which backside and garden (four years later described as a kiln, curtilage

and garden) were leased by the Queen on the 1st of August, in the 28th year of her reign, for forty years. The messuage was subject to a rent of 5s a year, and the backside and garden to a rent of 16d a year payable to the Crown.

21. In 1661 Edward Davies, gent, grandson of David ap John Robert, was living at the Greyhound, where he was succeeded by his widow, who let the house in 1669 to John Harvey, gent. Here also lived until his death in 1706 John Davies, gent, the elder, son of Thomas Davies, gent, youngest brother of the fore-named Mr. Edward Davies. John Davies, the younger, gent, son of Mr. John Davies, the elder, let the house to Mr. Hugh Moore, ironmonger, who was buried February 24th, 1709-10, and who probably belong-ed to the family of Moore, of Erddig Fechan. Then it was divided into two, the house, shop, and kiln, being occupied by Thomas Gough, grocer, and a shop by Robert Owens. Finally, Mr. David Thelwall, apothecary, who had married Miss Mary Davies, sister and heir of the last-named Mr. John Davies, occupied the whole house until the year when, by the death of his elder brother Simon Thelwall, Esq., he succeeded to the Blaen Iàl estate. I give under a separate heading, at the close of this chapter, a full account of the connection of the Thelwalls with Wrexham, and notices of them will be found in other parts of the book, for consulting which the Index may be used. When Mr. David Thelwall left The Grey-hound, Mr. Archibald Kenrick, apothecary, (see *Hist. of the Older Nonconformity of Wrexham*, p. 70), rented it of him, and there re-mained until his death in 1762. He was succeeded by various tenants, the only one of which that need be named was Thomas Jones, gunsmith, who came there about 1799, and therein remained until his death (December 12th, 1833, aged 65), having previously purchased the premises of the representatives of the Thelwalls. A little before 1818, a new " show shop," probably that now occupied by Mr. Ralph Williamson, pork butcher, was built on the premises. Two of Mr. Thomas Jones's sons were Mr. Edward Jones, iron-founder, (see *History of the Older Nonconformity*, p. 90, note 40,) and Thomas Jones, (see Appendix iii, sec. 17, April 23rd, 1806) who called himself Thomas Cambria Jones, and in 1837 published (through James Fraser, 215, Regent Street, London), a volume of poems entitled " Mortality, a Poem sung in Solitude, with Notes, to which are added Sonnets and Songs."[3] One of Mr. Thos. Jones's daughters Margaret Elizabeth, married (January 21st, 1831), Mr. William Rowe, civil engineer.

22. No. 24, at the corner of Town Hill and Abbot Street, need only be mentioned as being formerly a portion of the Pulford prop-erty, wherefrom it passed by descent to Thomas Wragg, the young-er, gent, of Liverpool, who still possessed it in 1783, but who sold

3. An edition of Thomas Cambria Jones' " Mortality " was published in Chester, in 1835, but not being revised by the author, was disavowed by him.

it soon after to John Jones, flax-dresser, in the possession of whom, and of whose descendants, it long remained.

23. Here I ought to say something of Back Chamber Street, a passage running along the north side of the Hand Inn and Town Hall. I find this street mentioned under that name for the first time in 1820, but in the previous century there are references (in 1712 and 1772), to two persons living in *Black* Chamber Street. It so happens, however, that the rate books for the two years named are lost, so that it is impossible to identify the houses in which they lived. Inasmuch, however, as the lord's prison during the 16th century was actually called " Y Siambr Ddu," or "The Black Chamber," a building which was probably included in the old Shirehall, and as I have been told that some old people still actually call the passage under discussion Black Chamber Street, I have fancied that " Black Chamber Street," and " Back Chamber Street," are merely the older and more recent names for the same lane.

THE THELWALLS OF WREXHAM.

24. Of the history of the earlier Thelwalls, of Blaen Iâl, I shall have much to say when in the next volume of this series I come to deal with the estate of Llwyn y cnottiê. The first of them to live in the *town* of Wrexham was Andrew Thelwall, Esq., of Blaen Iâl and Llwyn y cnottiê, generally called " Captain Thelwall," who, after living in Holt Street and Beast Market Street, went in 1803 to occupy the house in Lambpit Street, which afterwards was the residence of John Santhey, Esq., (see under ch. ix, sec 3). Here Captain Thelwall died, and was buried at Wrexham, August 29th, 1705. His elder son, Simon Thelwall, Esq., succeeded him at Blaen Iâl. His second son, David, (born 1692), established himself, as an apothecary, at the house in Farndon Street (see ch. xi, sec. 15), which had previously belonged to his father. He married February 17th, 1728, at Wrexham, Mary Davies, sister and heiress of John Davies, the younger, gent, and so came ultimately into possession of all the property of the Davieses, namely:—The Greyhound on Town Hill, Groft Tudor, and the other lands in the Fields of Wrexhem Fechan, (see ch. xvii sec. 23 & 28), the Tenters' Field in Pentre'r felin, and the dyehouse there (see ch. xxv, sec. 3), as well as the house, yard, and dye-house, which now form the Albion Brewery, and Nos. 14 and 15 Charles Street. During the latter part of his residence in Wrexham he occupied, still as an apothecary, The Greyhound, until by the death of his brother Simon, he inherited the Blaen Iâl estate. The after-named children of his were baptized at Wrexham:—Simon, (bapt. March 9th, 1722-30, "born ye 17th," afterwards Simon Thelwall, Esq., of Blaen Iâl; Mary, (bapt. May 22nd, 1731, " born ye 11th,") died January 16th, 1813, unmarried and was buried at Bryn Eglwys; Catherine, (bapt. 23rd Septem-

ber, 1732," born 8th "); Sara, (bapt. May 3rd, 1734, "born 24," buried
June 13th); Sydney, (bapt. July 21st, 1736, buried the 26th); Watkin,
(bapt. November 17th, 1738, "born 8br ye 14th)," living in 1813 ;
David, (bapt. May 1740, "born April 27th"); John, (bapt. July 11th,
1741), who attained mainhood and married; and Catherine, (bapt.
March 19th, 1744-5, "born 7th," buried April 28th, 1752).

25. When Mr. David Thelwall died in 1760,[4] he was succeeded
in his estates by his eldest son Simon, who died without issue, as
did also his other sons. The Blaen lâl and Wrexham properties
then devolved upon Mr. David Thelwall's daughter Ann, (who was
not baptized at Wrexham), the wife of Rev. John Lloyd, (see ch. i,
sec. 36, and Appendix iii, sec. 13, and note 4), of Rhydwrial, Penaner,
and Penyfed, who had a son, Colonel John Lloyd, of Rhydwrial.
And it was the Colonel Lloyd just mentioned, who, on his succeeding to the estates of the Salusburys, of Galltfaenan, assumed the
name of Salusbury, and this is how it came about, that the new
road which, some years ago, was carried across Groft Tudor, an old
possession of the Thelwalls in Wrexham, came to be called " Salusbury Road," or Salusbury Park." Colonel John Lloyd Salusbury
married Anna Maria, only daughter of John Mostyn, Esq., of,
Segrwyd and Llewesog, and had two daughters, between whom his
estates were divided. One of these, Anna Maria, married Townshend Mainwaring, Esq., formerly of Marchwiel Hall, and afterwards
of Galltfaenan, M.P. for the Denbighshire boroughs, and father of the
present Charles Salusbury Mainwaring, Esq., of Galltfaenan. Whatever property the late Colonel J. Lloyd Salusbury possessed in this
town came to him as the heir of the Thelwalls and Davieses of
Wrexham.

4. There is a monument in the chancel of Bryn Eglwys church, erected by
his son, Watkin Thelwall, Esq., to the memory of Mr. David Thelwall, and of his
widow, of which the following is a copy :- -"Y beddadail hwn a osodwyd gan
Watkin Thelwall, Yswain, er coffadwriaeth am ei dad Dafydd Thelwall, Yswain, o
Flaen Ial. yr hwn gladdwyd yr 21 dydd o fis Ebrill, 1760, ei oedran 69. Ac hefyd
am ei fam Mari Thelwall yr hon a gladdwyd yr 20 dydd o fis Medi 1793, ei hoedran
92. Y ddau a orweddant ym meddrod eu hynafiaid ynghafell, yr eglwys hon.

HOPE STREET, WREXHAM.

From an old print.

CHAPTER IV

Ibope Street.

1. In recent years the upper part of Hope Street, between Priory Lane and the Station Bridge (or rather Wat's Dyke, the boundary of the township), has come to be called " Regent Street," but formerly the whole Street between the Shirehall and Wat's Dyke was known as " Hope Street." And I have even found, in a deed dated 1553, the continuation of this street beyond the township boundary (now known as Mold Road), called "stryd yr hopp [hòb]," which is the Welsh form of the name " Hope Street." That name is thus very old, and as to the thoroughfare properly so called, the name Hope Street was already an old established one in the year 1590.

2. In describing the several houses, thought worthy of notice, in this ancient street, I shall follow the existing numbering, proceeding along its west side from the Town Hall towards the Great Western Station, and returning along the other side to High Street, and I shall deal separately, at the end of the chapter, with the various fields lying on each side of the street, where formerly there were no houses.

3. We begin, then, with Nos. 1 and 2, now the shops of Mr. E. Rhys Jones, hatter, and of the Household Stores Co., grocers. Where these houses now stand, immediately adjoining Back Chamber Street, was a quaint old house and shop, with its gable facing Hope Street, while immediately adjoining it, perhaps in Back Chamber Street, were three cottages, which formed part of the same property. This property is thus described in Norden's Survey of 1620 :—

" Edward Davies holds [by lease], one fair tenement, three shops, stable, and curtilage next the Cross, on the north side of The Shirehall, containing by estimation eight [customary] perches."

The same Edward Davies had also the Hand Inn, three cottages and garden at the corner of Back Chamber Street and Abbot Street, and a parcel of lands called " Yspytty," the whole subject to a crown rent of eleven shillings. In 1700, Mr. Thomas Atcherley, ironmonger, came to live at this house from No. 41 High Street, and here he remained until some time after 1721. He must have bought this property, for in 1780 it is returned as belonging to Roger Atcherley, Esq., who was probably Mr. Thomas Atcherley's son, Roger, baptized at Wrexham, November 1st, 1712, and in 1808 and again in 1828, it is described as belonging to E. Atcherley, Esq. In 1758, Mr. David Crue, surgeon, came to occupy these premises, where he remained until his death, March 30th, 1803, at the age of 73. His first wife was "Elizabeth Davies, of this parish," whom he married September 8th, 1761, and by whom he had several children. His second wife was Dorothy Morrall, apparently one of the Morralls, of Cilhendref, to whom he was married at Wrexham, February 14th, 1797, and who survived him, dying October, 1822, aged 84. Mr. Crewe, (see Index) was succeeded by Mr. Alexander Wylde Thornley, hatter (see *History of Older Nonconformity*, p. 116, note 6), previously in business at No. 3, who ultimately purchased the premises. His son, Mr. Robert Thornley, sold them in 1850, to the late Mr. Edward Jones, hatter, who in 1863, pulled down the whole of the old buildings, and erected on their site those which now stand there.

4. Where Nos. 3 and 4 now are, were during last century a house and warehouse belonging to the Kenricks, of Wynne Hall, who appear to have derived them from their ancestor Edward John Kenrick, of Gwersyllt, who died before 1693. Here lived many members of the Kenrick family—from 1727 until his death (about 1747), Mr. Daniel Kenrick, chandler, (grandson of the above-named Edward John Kenrick), who was succeeded by his widow, and afterwards, from 1769 to his death in 1793, by Mr. William Kenrick, brazier, one of the sons of the Rev. John Kenrick, (see *Hist. of Older Nonconformity*, p. 70, sec. 23). I believe that it was this house, then occupied by John Hughes, who appears to have been a bookseller (see *Hist. of Older Nonconformity*, p. 48, sec. 15), which was licensed in 1672, for Presbyterian worship. The Kenricks sold the property about the end of last or the beginning of the present century, and the house has been since rebuilt.

5 On the site of Nos. 7, 8, and 9—now the shops of Mr. J. C. Gittins, Mr. John Little, and Mr. Ernest Allmand,—stood in 1699, and for many years after, a large inn called "The Raven," or "The Old Raven." In 1715, the occupier of it paid 10s 4d as church rate, while the occupier of The Golden Lion, in High Street, paid 10s. About 1746, it came to be occupied by Mr. Rowland Samuel, who changed its name to "The King's Head." After Mr. Samuel's death, in October 1762, Mr. Edward Davies acquired the premises and converted them into a mercer's shop. I believe this is the "Edward Davies. of the parish of Llanfair, diocese of Bangor," who (September 7th, 1763), married "Jane Smith, of this parish," and it is certain that Thomas Smith, gent, of Minera, and Mr. Davies were buried in the same tomb. He appears also to have been connected with the Rev. Edward Davies, B.A., master of the Wrexham Grammar School, and his daughter, Jane, married the

Rev. John Walters, M.A., vicar of Efenechtyd, and master of Ruthin Grammar School. Mr. Davies died August 22nd, 1777, aged 44, but the business was carried on by his widow until after 1794, when the house was divided into two tenements, and the premises passed into the possession of Mr. John Edwards, the elder, farmer, of Stansty. One of the tenements was then occupied by Mr. Samuel Edwards, grocer, who married Mary, daughter of Richard Jones, Esq., of Llai, who became general overseer of the parish, and who was almost certainly a son of the before-named Mr. John Edwards. The other tenement was occupied until about 1812, by Thomas Griffith, Esq., surgeon, who came hither from Nos. 6 and 7 High Street, and who afterwards removed to Queen Street. Mr. Griffith was the eldest son and heir of Thomas Griffith, Esq., of Nant y Belan, and Cae Cyriog, in the parish of Ruabon, and married Mary, daughter of William Tandy, Esq., of South Littleton House, near Evesham, and had eleven children, all born at this house, and baptized at Wrexham church, namely :—

Theresa, bapt. September 5th, 1787, died January 26th, 1858
Harriet, born August 13th, 1789, died April 4th, 1875
Mary, born September 2nd, 1791, died April 1st, 1875
Elizabeth, born March 16th, 1793, died October 29th, 1842
Frances, born March 12th, 1794, died March 1st, 1870
Thomas Taylor, bapt. January 2nd, 1796, eldest son and heir, of whom a full account will be found under Chester Street.
John, bapt. September 23rd, 1799, afterwards a surgeon at Hereford
Emma, bapt. February 6th, 1800
Henry, bapt. August 15th, 1802
Henrietta Essex, bapt. June 5th, 1804, died July 13th, 1878
Charles, born August 29th, 1805

Mr. Thomas Griffith died September 10th, 1846, aged 93, his wife having predeceased him, January, 1845, at the age of 82.

6. The two tenements just described, now forming three shops, (Nos. 7, 8 and 9), were bought in 1828 , or a little before, by Mr. Joseph Jones, of "The Corner Shop," Hope Street, and were sold, (or at least No. 7 was sold), by his son-in-law Mr. Wm. Jones, to the late Mr. John Gittins, father of Mr. J. Colemere Gittins.

7. The house now represented by No. 10, the shop of Mr. Evan Richards, was in 1699, occupied by Thomas Morton, Esq., of Cristionydd, in the parish of Ruabon, a member of an important family, which I have nowhere seen any account given. Here Mr. Morton remained until his death.[1] Soon after, his son Thomas, (bapt. at Ruabon, March 8th, 1678-9), married at Gresford, (July 4th, 1706),

---

1. He was buried at Ruabon, January 4th, 1702-3.

Anne, daughter of Kenrick Eyton, Esq., of Wrexham and Eyton Isaf.[2] Mr. Eyton was at this time practising as an attorney, and occupied part of Bryn y ffynnon house, and Mr. Morton, his son-in-law, appears also for a time to have occupied another part of the same house, for although his elder son Thomas, was baptized at Ruabon, (August 6th, 1707), his younger son Edward, was baptized at Wrexham, (July 16th, 1708). and the rate books show clearly that Mr. Morton did live for a short time at Bryn y ffynnon. The following other entry relating to the Morton family occurs in the Wrexham registers :—" October 9th, 1724, Thomas Kenrick, gent, from Liverpool, and Mrs. Anne Morton, married."

8. About the year 1709, Mr. Robert Hughes, attorney-at-law, came to live at the house now being described. He married at Wrexham, (January 15th, 1706), Sarah Cawley, daughter, apparently, of Robert Cawley, Esq., of Gwersyllt Uchaf, who was at that time living at Croes Newydd,[3] and it was at Croes Newydd, that Mr. Hughes, for at least a year after his marriage, lived. But in 1709, he is described as of Wrexham Regis, and the rate books show that from before 1715 until after 1732, he was living at what we may call No. 10.[4] He appears to have married secondly, in 1721, Miss Jane Roydon, one of the Roydons, of Roydon Hall, Sutton Isycoed. I do not know to what family he belonged, when he died, nor what became of his sons. About 1783, this shop came to be occupied by Ralph Williamson, tinman, (see *History of Par. Church of Wrexham*, p. 107, note 264), who was ultimately succeeded by his son, Francis Williamson, tinman, (see the same, p. 111, note 291), and the premises were in 1857, still owned by Miss Williamson.

9. North of No. 10 were two houses, represented in part by Nos. 11 and 12. which seem always to have had a common ownership, and one of which stood up the yard next Mr. Weaver's shop. In

2. In Gresford register, there is the following entry:—July 14th, 1727, Anne Mooton, [Morton], of Wrexham, buried.

3. Thomas Humberstone, gent, of Holt, married, (July 9th, 1707), at Wrexham, Margaret, another daughter of the above-named Mr. Robert Cawley, who is also described as of Croes Newydd, and so founded the family of Humberstone, of Gwersyllt Park. By the death without issue, of John Cawley, Esq., of Gwersyllt, (buried at Wrexham, April 9th, 1712), son of Mr. Robert Cawley, his sisters became his heirs.

4. The following entries relating to the children of the above named Mr. Robert Hughes, by Sarah, his wife, occur :

Sept. 17, 1711, Robert, son of Mr. Robert Hughes, attorney at law, born 1st. bapt
" May 28, 1716, Will: „   „   „   „   born ye 24, „
" Jan. 15th, 1717-18, Richard, „   „   „   „   „   4, „
" Nov. 3, 1719, John,   „   „   „   „   „ 20 Oct „
I omit the names of those who died young.

one of these came to live in 1728, Thomas Beech,[5] gent, concerning whom the following notice occurs in *The Gentleman's Magazine* for 1737:—

"(Died) May 17th, Mr. Thomas Beech, Merchant at Wrexham in Denbighshire, suddenly. He was Master of a fine genius. Author of Eugenio, a poem just publish'd, and some other Poetical Pieces."

He hanged himself in a barn near Chester Road.[6] I have not seen "Eugenio," but Dr. Samuel Johnson once quoted a portion of it and treated it as fair subject for sport. And I have read several of his poems which appeared in *The Gentleman's Magazine* under the several signatures of "Fido," "E.C." and "Mrs. Manage." In all these he was ungallantly encountering Mrs. Jane Brereton, who supposed him to be her friend, who had shown him her "Letters to Fidelia," which she proposed sending to *The Gentleman's Magazine*, and upon which she asked his advice. In his poems in answer to Melissa (Mrs. Brereton), he gave utterance to expressions meant to wound her, and also let slip phrases which made her suspect the identity of her antagonist. On her taxing Mr. Beech with the insincere part he had taken, he flatly denied it, "not without the most shocking Imprecations." Mr. Beech does not shine in this relation, (given in "The Account" of Mrs. Brereton's Life, 1744), and Mrs. Brereton certainly got the better of him in the contest of wit waged between them in *The Gentleman's Magazine*. In the other house, from before 1742 until his death in December 1762, aged 70, lived Captain John Meredith, wine merchant, a younger son of the second Ellis Meredith, Esq., of Pentrebychan. In 1780, both these houses were owned, and the second of them occupied by Mr. Thomas Jones, flax-dresser, who was succeeded, about 1786, by Mr. Edward Jones, flax-dresser. The warehouse still standing in the yard or court above-mentioned was originally built as a flaxdresser's shop. In one of these two houses lived from about 1818 until his death, (September 1828, aged 78), Mr. John Hutchinson, attorney-at-law. I have been told that he came from Abergele, and was uncle to Mr. John Foulkes, senior, of Charles Street, and it is certain that these two houses did, from 1808 downwards, belong to Mr Foulkes.

10. No. 13, (Mr. Weaver's house and shop), is not mentioned in the rate books earlier than 1808.

5. In a deed which I have seen, this Mr. Beech is said to have himself built a house, (probably this very one), on a piece of land in Hope Street, belonging to the family of Hughes, represented in 1760 by the Rev. Edward Hughes, of Radway, (see the note to the description of Nos. 4 and 5 High Street).

6. This barn remained long on into the present century, and stood in a parcel of land called "Erw clai." As I have seen an old plan of Erw glai with the barn marked within it, I happen to know the exact position of what was called "Beech's Barn," which I have indicated by an asterisk in field No. 384 in the map of Wrexham, herewith given.

11. The house, No. 14, now the shop of Messrs. Wm. and Jno. Prichard, appears to have been built, soon after 1725, by Roger Griffith, gent, of Cefn, in the township of Abenbury Fawr, who in August of that year purchased the old house which then stood there, together with "the seat or pew in the parish church" appendent to it, for £60. The new house came to be occupied for a short time by Mr. John Jones, attorney, and then by Dr. Edward Weaver, son of Richard Weaver, Esq., of Abenbury Hall, who remained there for seventeen years, and who about the year 1746, removed to Chester.[7] Then from 1753 to about 1765, Mr. Danvers Gartside, attorney-at-law, of whom I shall have something to say later on in this chapter, (see sec. 41), occupied it, and was succeeded by Mrs. Kenrick, widow of the Rev. John Kenrick, (see *Hist. of Older Nonconformity of Wrexham*, p. 72, sec. 39). From 1786 for many years, Mr. Richard Meeson, the parish clerk, lived here, but afterwards removed to Queen Street.   Having said this much as to *tenancy* of the premises, it is now time to say something as to their *ownership*.   In 1766, Miss Catherine Griffith, daughter of the above-named Mr. Roger Griffith, and Mrs. Elizabeth Hughes, his granddaughter, wife of Mr. Benjamin Hughes, clothier, of Wrexham, sold the property for £500, to Bulkeley Hatchett, Esq., of Lea, in the parish of Ellesmere, who in 1798 sold it for £270, to Mr. John Meller, merchant, of Wrexham, by whom it was sold in 1811, to Mr. Thomas Evans, maltster, who resided here until his death. Mr. Evans in his will, dated August 31st, 1828, left his two messuages in Hope Street, and the stable, cowhouse and garden, to his wife Elizabeth Evans for life, and afterwards to his niece Jane Parsonage, and to the Parsonages they have belonged until quite recently.   In this house was first published by the late Mr. George Bayley, (who died January 12th, 1863, aged 42, and was buried in the Dissenters' graveyard), *The Wrexham Registrar*, of which seventeen monthly numbers were published. The first number appeared in August 1848, and the last in December 1849, being replaced immediately afterwards, as a weekly paper, also published by Mr. George Bayley on the same premises, by *The Wrexham Advertiser*. The offices of the latter were removed in 1857 to Bank Street, and thence in 1868 to the Music Hall, (see ch. v, sec 5).

12. In the will of the Mr. Thomas Evans mentioned in the last paragraph, the testator speaks of his *two* messuages in Hope Street The second of these directly adjoined the first, and was acquired at about the same time. It had hitherto been known as "The Ship Inn," but Mr. Evans gave it at once, in honour of Admiral Nelson, the new name of "The Nelson's Arms," a name which it still retains.

7. There is recorded in the parish register the burial of "Mrs. Weaver, wife of Doctor Weaver," (May 13th, 1757), and of "Miss Weaver from Chester, spinster," (December 23rd, 1765).

13. In or about the year 1786, Mr. Richard Williams, hatter, and "clerk of the old meeting," (see *Hist. of Older Nonconformity* p. 139, note 36), acquired Nos. 16 and 17, and laid down a weighing machine in front of his house which remained until recent years. Henceforth the house itself came to be called "The Machine."

14. No. 19, the shop of Messrs. Phillips & Co., teamen, belongs to the poor of the Congregational Chapel, Chester Street, (see *Hist. of Older Nonconformity*, p. 79, sec. 44).

15. The Fleece Inn, (No. 22), I first find called by that name in 1804. At the back of this Inn, and belonging to it, was formerly a bowling green, which is marked in Wood's map of Wrexham in 1833.

16. Turner's yard takes its name from Mr. Richard Haighton Turner, who formerly owned the houses on both sides of it.

17. No. 26, now the branch shop of Messrs. Thomas Williams & Co., Town Hall Vaults, was formerly "The Green Man." It was so called at least as early as 1788, and down to quite recent times.

18 I have not found No. 26B—the King's Head, called by that name earlier than 1808, but the Edward Read who entered into the occupation of the house in 1770, is described as an innkeeper. There was, and is, another King's Head, in Pen y bryn.

19. Next to the King's Head is "The Black Lion," (No. 27). In the parish register, under date June 17th, 1775, the burial of Edward Jones, of the Black Lion is recorded, and Edward Jones, as appears from the rate books, had been the occupant of this house from before 1742. In The Black Lion a somewhat exclusive club of tradesmen used to meet, which was called "The Senior Society" (see ch. xx, sec. 10).

20. In this part of Hope Street public houses are rather thick upon the ground, and adjoining the Black Lion is The Buck (Nos. 28 and 29), which I find mentioned for the first time in the year 1788.

21. Between the Buck and Priory Lane were, until 1889, three low thatched cottages. The first two of these were in the year just-named pulled down. The third, at the corner of Hope Street and Priory Lane, still stands.

22. Priory Lane is itself very old, though the name has only come into use within the last century. Until the year 1887, it was fairly broad until it reached The Priory on the one side and Bryn y ffynnon gatehouse on the other, after which it became a narrow steep footpath running past the back of The Old Vicarage, (now the offices of the Wrexham, Mold, and Connah's Quay Railway), into the open space in which the Town Well is situate, and so by another bit of narrow lane (Bath Street) to Pen y bont. In 1877, the narrow and lower part of Priory Lane was absorbed by the

railway, and the broader part was connected by a new curved road, made through the Old Vicarage gardens, with Abbot Street and Vicarage Hill.

23. As I have explained in *The History of the Parish Church*, (p. 58), I have never found the house now known as " The Priory " called by that name earlier than the end of last century. But from 1699 until 1783 (when Peter Edwards, Esq., the last of the race, died), it was the town house of the ancient and important family of Edwards, of Stansty Isaf. It probably belonged to them much earlier, for between 1661 and 1664, the house of Mrs. Dorothy Edwards, widow of David Edwards, gent, of Stansty, is mentioned in the rate books in close conjunction with the house called Bryn y ffynnon. About 1744, this house was let to Madam or Miss Yonge, evidently one of the Yonges, of Bryn Iorcyn, who remained there until after 1771, and who, towards the close of her occupancy, shared the house with Miss Barbara Speed, sister of Griffith Speed, Esq., (see ch. 1, sec. 7), who was buried at Wrexham, November 18th, 1772, aged 69. From before 1808 until her death in 1836, Miss Letitia Eyton, third daughter of the Rev. John Eyton, of Leeswood, lived here (see ch. xiv, sec. 10), and afterwards Mr. Charles Poyser, who bought the house about the beginning of the present century. It now forms the offices of Sir Evan Morris & Company, solicitors.

24. It is a subject of great regret to me that in the case of so important a house as Bryn y ffynnon (once the largest house in the town), I should not be able to give a confident account of its origin. The house itself is so covered with stucco that it is impossible to say more than that it belongs apparently to the 17th century. But the front portion of the gatehouse, which is of fine red brick and not stuccoed (and of which I give a sketch by Mr. Wm. Thomas), I judge, from the mouldings of its beams, to date from the first half of that century. The house, however, cannot be identified in Norden's survey of A.D. 1620, unless it be the house of Edward Jones, which, though mentioned, is not specifically described therein. But though in Norden's Survey Bryn y ffynnon House does not seem to be mentioned, its gardens, dovehouse, and perhaps the site on which it was shortly afterwards built, are quite clearly described in the following extracts :—

" (Chief) rent 4d. Thomas Trafford, Esq., holds freely one dove house, one parcel of land and . . . . . . containing by estimation half a (customary) acre, purchased of Edward Jones, (situate) in Wrexham, extending in length from the footway (that is Priory Lane) from " Streate yr hopp " (notice the Welsh form of the name Hope Street) to Bryn y ffynnon on the east side, to a quillet lying between the aforesaid parcel of land and the lands of Edward Phillips on the west side, and in breadth from the road leading towards Hope on the north side and the tenement of the aforesaid Edward Jones on the south side." . . . . . (Chief) rent 8d. The same holds one close

PHOTO-LITHOD BY WOODALL, MINSHALL & THOMAS, WREXHAM.

BRYNYFFYNNON IN 1890.

From a Photograph.

of land containing by estimation, three (customary) acres, lying in Eslomes in Wrexham, purchased of Richard ap Edward Philip, now converted into orchard, gardens and walks."

The Mr. Thomas Trafford mentioned in these extracts appears, so far as this parish is concerned, to have been the last of an important Welsh family which was seated at Esclus, and in the 16th century adopted the surname of "Trafford." He was buried at Wrexham, 13th January, 1644-5. A great part of his estates, including Esclus beyond doubt, and Bryn y ffynnon probably, passed into the possession of Richard Lloyd, Esq., of Dulasau, afterwards Sir Richard Lloyd, knight, who defended Holt Castle against the parliamentary troops. If the statement is true, made in Ormerod's Cheshire, that when Charles the First came to Wrexham, October 7th, 1642, Sir Richard Lloyd received the King at his house of Bryn y ffynnon, we might be led to imagine that Sir Richard Lloyd had acquired Bryn y ffynnon before Mr. Trafford's death. But Sir Richard may only have been the tenant of the house. My own impression is that Mr. Trafford built Bryn y ffynnon, and that Sir Richard Lloyd lived at Esclus. There belonged to the house a barn, kiln, and orchard: the gardens stretched between it and Hope Street; and the lands, which included two crofts and a large field, stretched along the street to a point opposite to King Street. In 1659 and again in 1674 I find Major John Manley, (see *Hist. of Older Nonconformity*, p. 3), mentioned as living, doubtless as tenant, at Bryn y ffynnon House, which in 1670 was taxed as containing fourteen hearths. All the rate books for the years between 1674 and 1699 have perished, but during this interval the house became the property of Sir William Williams, of Glascoed, and ultimately of his son, who adopted the surname of Wynn, and became the first Sir Watkin Williams-Wynn, of Wynnstay. In 1682, Thomas Lloyd, gent, was, we learn from the registers, living at Bryn y ffynnon, and on June 9th, 1682, his second son Roger was baptized at Wrexham. We may be sure that this Mr. Thomas Lloyd was of Plas Madoc in Llansannan, and the father of the Rev. Thomas Lloyd of Plaspower. He married, for his second wife, Elizabeth, daughter of Mr. John Myddelton, of London, son of Captain Roger Myddelton, of Plas Cadwgan. It is less certain that he lived in the large house now exclusively called "Bryn y ffynnon," for in former times that name was given, not merely to the house now being described, but to the area surrounding it, and to the other houses which stood within that area. By 1699 we find that the large house to which the name "Bryn y ffynnon" is now restricted had become divided into three separate tenements, and its gate-

---

8. "Eslome," probably a transcriber's mistake for "Estome," which is itself an abreviation of Maes Ystum," a large common field lying between Hope Street and the brook.

house into two, each inhabited by persons of consequence. The barn, kiln, and lands, were let separately. Of the three tenements into which, in 1699, Bryn y ffynnon was divided, the second Sir Henry Bunbury, bart., of Stanney, and Bunbury, Cheshire, occupied the first. His father, the first Sir Henry Bunbury, had lived for many years at Hafod y wern, having married Mary, half-sister of Mrs, Puleston of that place, and daughter of Sir Kenrick Eyton, of Eyton Isaf. In the Wrexham parish register there are no fewer than thirteen entries relating to the Bunburys, entries which I have copied, and give in a foot note.[9] The first Sir Henry Bunbury succeeded to the baronetcy in 1681, and it is therefore surprising that in the parish register on April 25th, 1682, he should be called " Henry Bunbury, *Esq.*" There was formerly a Bunbury monument in Wrexham Church, a copy of the inscription on which is given on page 186 of my *History of the Parish Church of Wrexham*, where, however, for "Ffrances" we should evidently read " Ffrancis."

25. Sir Henry Bunbury, the second, afterwards M.P. for City of Chester, apparently left Wrexham in 1699, and was succeeded at Bryn y ffynnon by Kenrick Eyton, Esq., who remained there until 1708 at least, and who was either the son or grandson of Sir Kenrick Eyton, of Eyton Isaf.

26. The second of the three tenements into which, in 1699, Bryn y ffynnon House was divided was at that time occupied by Lady Eyton, (see *Hist. of Older Nonconformity of Wrexham*, p 51, sec. 23), who remained there until her death in 1701, and was succeeded by Madam Morton (see sec. 7).

27. In the third of the three tenements lived in 1699 the Rev. John Evans, Independent minister (see *Hist. of Older Nonconformity of Wrexham*, pp 44—46, 50, 55), where he kept a school. This house, after his death in 1700, his widow continued to occupy

---

9. December 9, 1675, Thomas, son to henery BumBury, Esq., was Babtized.
December 6, 1676, Henery Bunbury, (afterwards the second Sir Henry) sonn to Henery Bunbury, of Havod y werne, Esq., Bapt.
November 9, 1678, William, (afterwards a barrister and attorney-general for the county of Chester), sonn to Henery Bunbery, of Havod y wern, Esq., Bapt.
March 9, 1679, Elizabeth, Daughter of Henry Bumbury, of Havod y wern, Esq. was Buryed.
August 11, 1680, John, son of Henry Bunbury, of Havod y wern, Esq., Baptized.
April 25, 1682, Joseph, son of Henry Bunbery, Esq. of Wrexham Regis, Bapt.
March 10, 1683-4, Richard, son of Sr Henry Bunbury, Baronett, of Wrexham Regis, Bapt.
June 30, 1685, Francis, son of Sir Henry Bunbury, Baronett, Bapt.
August 1, 1685, John, son of Sir Henry Bumbury, Baronett, of Wrexham Regis, Buryed.
April 10, 1686, Joseph, son of Sr Henry Bunbury, Barron, was Buryed.
March 26, 1686-7, Mary the wife of Sir Henry Bumbury, Baronett, was Buried.
May 10, 1687, Ffrancis, son of Sr Henry Bumbury, Bart., Buried.
July 27, 1687, Richd. son of Sir Henry Bumbury, buried.

until 1705 or 1706, when she was succeeded by Mr. Thomas Pulford (see ch. i, 42-45).

28. The rate books between 1708 and 1715 are missing, but those of the latter year show that the part of Bryn y ffynnon in which Sir Henry Bunbury and Kenrick Eyton, Esq. had lived was then in the occupation of Richard Weaver, Esq., who also had the kiln, and part of the barn, paying a yearly rent of £21 16 6, and who remained at Bryn y ffynnon until after 1732. This was doubtless Richard Weaver, Esq., of Abenbury Hall, about whom I shall have a great deal to say in the next volume of this series. He used, it is evident, part of Bryn y ffynnon as his town house. As to the other parts of Bryn y ffynnon, one formed in 1715 the house of Dr. John Davies, who had another part of the barn, paying a yearly rent of £21 5 0 ; and the other had been the house of a certain William Anwyl, gent, who was buried at Wrexham, April 29th, 1713. In 1716, these two tenements, together with the gatehouse, were occupied by Henry Conway, Esq., only son of Sir John Conway, Bart., of Bodrhyddan On September 30th, of the same year, he married, at Wrexham, Miss Honora Ravenscroft, daughter and co-heiress of Thomas Ravenscroft, Esq., of Bretton, Flintshire, and immediately afterwards left the town.[10] Mr. Henry Conway was followed at Bryn y ffynnon, by Watkin Williams, Esq., who, in the year 1718, on the death of Sir John Wynn, succeeeded to Wynnstay, and went to live there, and in 1740. on the death of his father, Sir William Williams, became the first Sir Watkin Williams Wynn. In 1730, Robert Williams, Esq., the second son of the Sir William Williams just named occupied *the whole house*, and remained there until 1746, and was followed by Madam Trygarn (see ch. i, note 5). Then, in 1751, George Warrington, Esq., came to occupy Bryn y ffynnon, and there continued until his death, July 22nd, 1770, at the age of 75. He was buried at Gresford, and his widow, Mrs. Elizabeth Warrington, went to live at The Cottage there, and was buried, September 22nd, 1788.[11] In what way this Mr. George Warring-

10. The following entries relating to the Conways occur in the parish registers :—

Feb. 6, 1712-3, Katharin Conway, of Pen y bryn, buryed.

Sept. 18, 1730, Mr. John Conway, Cler., of Evenechtyd, and Mrs. Sarah Morris marryd.

A Mr. Robert Conway, attorney at law, was living in a house below the church in 1712, but left in 1714 or 1715. With those members of the same family who lived at Esclus Hall, I shall deal in the next volume.

11. Mrs. Ann Hesketh, widow, second daughter of Geo. Warrington, Esq., who died September 26th, 1790, aged 52, was also buried at Gresford. The Eleanora Warrington who died March 9th, 1829, aged 89, and was buried at Gresford, was, I believe, his third daughter. And the Miss Elizabeth Warrington, who was married at Wrexham (November 11th, 1765), to William Simpson, Esq., of Hatfield, Yorkshire, was perhaps another daughter.

ton was related to the Rev. George Warrington, vicar of Hope, who also lived in Wrexham, and who will be mentioned under Queen Street, I do not know, but I suspect he was the father of the latter.   Mr. Warrington was succeeded at Bryn y ffynnon by Thomas Boycott, Esq., of Rudge, Boycott, and Hinton, Shropshire. He had married, Jane, youngest daughter of John Puleston, Esq., of Pickhill Hall, in the parish of Bangor Isycoed, and it was at Bangor that his daughters, Emma (bapt. December 14th, 1765), who married, in 1793, Edward Ravenscroft, Esq., (see ch. xiv, sec. 22), and Sophia (bapt. June 16th, 1768), were baptized.   Then he went live at Trefalyn, in the parish of Gresford, where (December 12th, 1769), his daughter Maria, was buried[12].   In Wrexham parish registers the following entries relating to the baptism of four of his children occur :—

> July 28, 1773, Richd., son of Thos. Boycott, of Brynn a funnon, Esq., was born the 23rd of May (afterwards a captain in the 34th Regiment).
>
> July 19, 1774, Charlotte, Dau. of Thos. Bycott, Esq., of Bryn a funnon, was born the 19 of May.
>
> March 11, 1776, Charles, Son of Thos. Bycot, of Bryn a funon, Esq., was born the 2nd of Feb. (afterwards a major in the 29th Regiment.
>
> Feb. 21, 1778, Louisa Victoria Foxhunter Sobieski Moll, Daur. of Thos. Bycott, of Bryn y ffynnon, was born the 31 of Dec. 1777.

29. Mr. Boycott left Bryn y ffynnon in the year 1790, and was followed by Mrs. Puleston, who remained there until 1797 or 1798.   Then in 1808, or a little before, Mr. John Parry rented it, and converted it into a school.   Mr. Parry married Catherine, one of the daughters of Mr. Edward Meredith, who was very famous as a baritone singer during the fourth quarter of the last century.   Mr. Meredith spent his last days at Bryn y ffynnon, and there died, December 1809, and was buried at Marchwiel.[13] In 1818, Mr Parry removed to Pen y gardden, in the parish of Ruabon, and Bryn y ffynnon then became a young ladies' school,

12. Mr. Boycott lived for a short time at one of the houses called "Parcau," in Pickhill. He probably came from Pickhill to Wrexham.

13. Mr. Edward Meredith, the singer, appears to have been the elder son of Edward Meredith, smith, of Y Felin Puleston, and was baptized at Wrexham, March 24th, 1740-1. His daughter Catherine, married, as has above been said, Mr. John Parry, of Bryn y ffynnon. Dorothy, another daughter, married (September 8th, 1808), at Wrexham, Mr. Thomas Henry Hindley, cotton merchant, of Manchester, afterwards of Liverpool, (brother of Mr. Wm. Hindley brewer, Stanhope Street, Liverpool). Mr. Hindley himself for a time lived at Bryn y ffynnon : he died Aug. 7th, 1830, aged 49, and was buried at Marchwiel. Elizabeth, another daughter of Mr. Edward Meredith, was the wife of Thomas Edgworth, Esq., of Bryn y grog, and the mother of the late Thomas Edgworth, Esq., the first mayor of Wrexham ; while a fourth daughter married Mr. George Hargreaves, of Liverpool. Mrs. Dorothy Meredith, the singer's widow, died January 19th, 1822, aged 77, and was buried at Marchwiel.

which was conducted for many years by the three Misses Kenrick, daughters of the third John Kenrick, Esq , of Wynne Hall.

30. The late Mr. Hugh Davies, sanitary inspector, has described Bryn y ffynnon as he remembered it about this time. The gate-house or Lodge, now Messrs. James & James's office, which has been in recent years enlarged, "had its front as at present, with a cumbrous oak door to the entrance, and a small door inserted in it for con-venience. The ground in front of the lodge was open to Priory Street After going through the opening through the lodge there was a broad gravel walk .... to the front door of the 'house,' and on the right a raised embankment, covered with grass, with clumps of trees and shrubs and flower beds : on the left hand was a flat glass lawn with a small fish pond in it: this lawn reached as as far as the lime trees. At the back of the embankment on t he right was the kitchen garden, covering the whole of the ground from the lodge to Regent Street and (what is now) Hill Street, in which (garden) was a large number of choice fruit trees, one or two of which still remain in Mr. Turner's garden." (This garden was built over and the trees cut down in 1889. A.N.P.) Sur-rounding the kitchen garden "from the lodge along Priory Street, and up Regent street as far as Hill Street, was a stone wall about 12 feet high and 2 feet thick. . . . At the end of Hill Street was the back entrance, and the whole of Hill Street was a common yard." There were a double coach house and stables where the Free Schools" on the south side of Well Street recently were. Bryn y ffynnon orchard (numbered 36 in the annexed map, and containing $5\frac{1}{4}$ acres) contained several large sycamore trees, grow-ing luxuriously, but so old that some of them were hollow. Here and there were some smaller trees growing on the land, but where is now Hill Street Chapel was a cluster of very tall trees of various kinds, and another cluster where Bryn Edwyn and the Wesleyan Chapel now are, and in the second cluster there was a colony of rooks. Below the wall which separated the orchard from Mold Road (now Regent Street) was a gravel promenade raised above the ground of the orchard and level from one end to the other.

31. Ultimately, Bryn y ffynnon House was sold (about 1844) to the Shrewsbury and Chester Railway Company (since absorbed in the Great Western Railway Company), which at that time enter-tained the project of having their Wrexham Station in the middle of the town. Then, after the incorporation of the borough, Bryn y ffynnon House formed the municipal buildings of the town, and so remained until 1883, when the corporation purchased the old Grammar School.

32. "Bryn y ffynnon" means "Hill of the Well," and takes its name from the "Town Well" at the foot of the hill on which Bryn y ffynnon House stands. The name, however, was formerly not restricted to the house just described, but was also applied to

the houses in Priory Lane, and to two or three houses on the opposite side of Hope Street. It was in fact not so much the name of a house as of an area.

33. The present Hill Street represents the old back way to Bryn y ffynnon House, or rather the drive to the stables and coach-house, all belonging to that house.

34. The English Calvinistic, or Presbyterian, Chapel in Hill Street, was built, in the years 1856 and 1857. The opening services were held on Good Friday, 1857, when the Rev. William Howells, of Liverpool, afterwards a tutor at Trefecca College, preached. Mr. Edward Francis says that the number of communicants at that time was 37, and there were 70 in the Sunday School. The English Calvinistic Methodist cause in this town, which was an offshoot from the Welsh Calvinistic church, in Abbot Street, had already been in existence for more than eleven years, having been started towards the end of 1845, in a hired room in a warehouse in Bank Street.[13a] Those most concerned in originating it were the Rev. William Edwards, of Town Hill; the Rev. William Hughes ; Mr. Isaac Jones, Hope Street ; and Mr. Richard Davies, Temperance Hotel, Bank Street. A Sunday School was connected with it from the beginning. The number of those who attended this room was for some time very small, and at one time it seemed on the point of extinction. But in 1855, the supporters of the cause, now incorporated into a distinct church, invited Mr. Joseph Jones, of Liverpool, to become their minister, an offer which he accepted, and it was during his ministry that the Hill Street Chapel was built. The churches at Crabtree Green, Glan yr afon, and at Summer Hill, were also placed under his care, but his ministerial labours were ultimately restricted to Wrexham and Glan yr afon. The late Mr. Charles Hughes, (see under No. 56 Hope Street) son of Mr. Richard Hughes, was elected the first deacon, and when the chapel in Hill Street was built, the Rev. Thomas Francis and Messrs. Thomas Phennah and W. H. Williams, hitherto connected with Abbot Street, attached themselves to the English cause. In 1865, the Rev. Joseph Jones left Wrexham for Oswestry, and was succeeded, after an interval of about twelve months, by the Rev. Edward Jerman, the present minister. In 1870 the number of communicants was 70, and of the congregation about 200, and there were 126 in the Sunday school. I owe most of these particulars to Mr. Edward Francis' book.

13a. On Sunday, March 30th, 1851, the number of persons present at the Bank Street rooms was counted. There were in attendance 65 in the afternoon, and 59 in the evening.

35. Until Hope Cottage was built, Bryn y ffynnon was the last house on that side of Hope Street. We accordingly now cross the street, and come to deal with the old house, now Aston's Auction Mart, which also belonged to the Wynnstay estate, and was also formerly called "Bryn y ffynnon" though in later years it came to be known for distinction as "Bryn y ffynnon Lodge." In 1808 the property is described as consisting of house and stable. In 1699, John Wynne, gent, was living in this house, and was still living there in 1704. I believe he was the Mr. John Wynne, of Wynne Hall, of whom I have spoken in *The History of Older Nonconformity of Wrexham*, p. 59. He was followed in 1705, by the Rev. Nathaniel Long, minister of the Presbyterian (now Congregational) Chapel, Chester Street (see the same, p. 60, sec. 4). Then in 1716 Richard Clayton, Esq., of Brymbo Hall, came to live here, making it his town house, and in 1727, Arthur Owen, Esq., who appears to have married Mr. Clayton's widow. Mr. Owen was succeeded by Mr. Wm. Henry, dancing master, who came hither from The Lampint (see ch. ix, sec. 3), and who left in 1751, and was followed by Mr. Thomas Payne, bookseller, who had hitherto lived in High Street (see ch. 1, sec. 22), and who remained here until his death in 1765 (buried November 4th). Mr. Payne was a man of some influence, and had a great deal of property in the town. Mrs. Payne lived on in the house until her death in February, 1774, and was followed by Mr. William Durack, dancing master, who held the house until his death (June 1799), and was followed by his son Mr. Thomas Durack, who ultimately rented the Lower Crispin, and is commemorated by "Durack's Pool," close to the Great Western Station. In 1844 the house still belonged to Sir Watkin Williams Wynn.

36. Southward of the house just described was another good old house, to which pertained a barn and croft (the croft measuring half an acre, and marked 41 on the annexed map), and which also belonged to the Wynnstay estate. Its site is now occupied by the surgery of Messrs. Williams & Evans, and the offices of Mr. J. Allington Hughes. Here was living in 1699, Mrs. Lloyd, of Y Fferm, in the parish of Mold, and here, in 1704, came to live Wm. Yonge, Esq , of Bryn Iorcyn, high sheriff of Flintshire in 1716. He was the son of Ellis Yonge, Esq., of Bryn Iorcyn, and the father of Ellis Yonge, Esq., of Bryn Iorcyn and Acton Hall. The two following entries in Wrexham parish registers relate to these Yonges, of Hope Street :—

Dorithy, da. of Mr. William Young, of W. Born the 21st of May, bapt. the 6th of June (1690), (buried at Hope, June 29th, 1692).

Ellis, the son of Mr. Ellis (? William) Young, of Hope Street, born the 14th of July, Baptized 21st, 1693.

July 2nd, 1746, Miss Mary Yonge, buried at Mold.

37. In 1715, Mrs. Williams was living in this house, and she continued to do so until her death February 20th, 1755. I believe

she was the widow of Mr. John Williams, attorney-at-law, and that her maiden name was Elizabeth Lloyd. She was married at Wrexham, June 1st, 1711, and her husband died the year after her marriage. She was followed by Mr. Thomas Jones, who lived here until 1784, and who was almost certainly the Mr. Thomas Jones, attorney at law, who died October 14th, 1784, aged 70. Then came a Mr. John Valentine, grazier, who went to live at The Cacau in 1793, and was succeeded in the Hope Street house by the Rev. Edward Davies, master of the Grammar School, who here remained until 1804. Then came the well known Thomas Jones, butcher, commemorated by Nimrod (see under No. 35 High Street) Finally, Mr. Thomas Hughes, solicitor, acquired the house, which was a half-timbered structure, and pulled it down, erecting the present building, which now forms Nos. 31 and 32 Regent Street. Mr. Thomas Hughes married at Wrexham, May 26th, 1835, Frances, daughter of Mr. John Humphreys, of Berse, and had several children, of whom the present Mr. John Allington Hughes is one of the sons. Mr. Thomas Hughes died at Bryn y groes, Gresford, December 12th, 1863, aged 60, and is buried in the Old Cemetery, Wrexham.

38. Next to the house last described, and occupying the site of the present Westminster Buildings, was another important old house, which in later times had a pillared front door, and to which pertained a croft. In 1699 and 1701, a Mr. John Lloyd was living here, who was succeeded in 1702 by Mr. Edward Maurice, of Cae Mor, in Hafod Gynfor (Glyn Ceiriog). He had been living the year before at the house in Lambpit Street, afterwards occupied by Mr. John Santhy. He was the son of Maurice ap Edward, of Cae Mor, and married (January 2nd, 1682-3), at Erbistock, Martha, daughter of Mr. John Jones, of Park Eyton.[14] In the year 1708, I find him described as "Edward Maurice, gent, of Eyton Park." Mr. Maurice was followed at the Hope Street house by Mr. Alexander Robinson, who lived there for many years. Then it was occupied in 1751, by Richard Surridge, Esq., who left it in 1760 to live at Ty Meredith (see under Chester Street), being followed by Mrs. Murrall, perhaps Mrs. Morrall, of Cilhendre, Shropshire. Several of the Morralls were connected with Wrexham. On March 25th, 1781, Charles Gartside, Esq., of the parish of Holt, and Rebecca Essex Morrall, of the parish of Wrexham, were married, those who signed the register being Dorothy Morrall, Eliz-

14. At Erbistock, the following children of his were baptized :—Humphrey, (bapt. February 5, 1680-1); Robert, (bapt. February 17, 1682-3); Edward, (died an infant); Margaret, (born April 17, bapt. April 21, 1690, married at Erbistock, October 22, 1708, to David Yale, gent, of Plas yn Ial) ; Elizabeth, (born February 10, bapt. March 1, 1694, afterwards the wife of John Wynn, of Abercynlleth); and Martha, (bapt. June 2,1699), buried at Wrexham, May 14, 1700, Mr. Edward Maurice being then described in the Register as of Park Eyton and "W.R." (Wrexham Regis).

abeth Ravenscroft, Harriet Constantia Ravenscroft, and David Crewe. On February 14th, 1797, two of the abovenamed witnesses —Dorothy Morrall and Mr. David Crewe, surgeon (see under No. 1 Hope Street), were themselves married. On June 17th, 1844, Mary Elizabeth Morrall, aged 27, was buried at Wrexham. Francis Esther, the wife of Thomas Jones, Esq., of Plas Grono, was also a Morrall, a daughter of Charles Morrall, Esq., of Cilhendre.

39. By 1766, Mrs. Morrall had left the house now being described, and in the following year, one Madam Lloyd was living in it, and was still there in 1771. In 1769 it appears to have been owned by Mr. Crewe, doubtless the abovenamed Mr. David Crewe, and was certainly owned by him from 1780 until his death. Then some time between 1811 and 1818, Mr. Hugh Hughes, surgeon, bought the house, and there remained until his death (March 1838, aged 50). He was somehow related (I believe uncle), to Mr. Thomas Hughes, solicitor, mentioned in connection with the house last described. He married at Wrexham (June 25th, 1833), Mary, second daughter of Mr. Joseph Langford (see under Nos. 23 and 24 High Street). Mr. Hughes was followed by Mr. John Kenrick Lewis, surgeon, son of Mr. George Lewis, surgeon (see later in the chapter), who ultimately emigrated to Australia, and was succeeded by the present Dr. Edward Davies. The old house was pulled down, and the present Westminster Buildings erected by the late Mr. William Low, of Roseneath, Wrexham.

40. The next house on the same side of Hope Street that I need speak of is "The Talbot," which I first find called by that name in the year 1721. It is a picturesque old building, and occupies the corners of Hope and Queen Streets. It belonged in 1712, to Mr. Samuel Kenrick, of Bersham (see *Hist. of Nonconformity of Wrexham*, p. 52, sec. 27), as it had apparently belonged in 1665, to his father, Edward John Kenrick (see the same, p. 47, sec. 13), and as it belonged until late on in the present century to his descendents, the Kenricks of Wynne Hall. A barn belonging to it, situate in Queen Street, was for nearly a hundred years (until 1762), used as a meeting house for the Independents and Baptists, and was called "The Old Meeting House."

41. We now cross the street to No. 50, the Rainbow Inn. The first time I find this inn mentioned under that name is in the parish registers under date May 2nd, 1774, when "Samuel Edwards Cooper, of the Rainbow," was buried, but from the rate books it appears that this Samuel Edwards began his occupancy of the house in the year 1756. The Rainbow was part of a group of houses which extended down Queen Street, and all along on one side of Henblas Street (see under Henblas Street), and which, until about 1818, continued in the ownership of the representatives of the Myddeltons, of Wrexham, a branch of the Myddeltons, of

Gwaunynog. The weighing machine in front of the Rainbow is
mentioned specifically in 1841, and apparently in 1819. The premises belonging to the old Rainbow, included not merely the site of
the present Rainbow, but also that of No. 51, now the shop of
Messrs. Bayley and Company.

42 Between the old Rainbow and the shop at the corner of Bank
Street, where Nos. 52, 53, and 53a now are, was until late on in
the present century a very good old house, with a garden behind,
which can be traced in the rate books as far back as 1742, in
which year it is described as the late house of Arthur Owens, Esq.,
(see above, sec. 35). In 1744 and 1746 Lady Longueville was rated for
it, and in 1753 and 1754 George Hope, Esq., of Hope Hall, who
married Elizabeth Charlotte Longueville. Then, in 1755, Sir
Thomas Longueville himself came to live at the house, removing
in 1758 to the Upper Yspytty, now the Vicarage, (see under ch. vi,
sec. 10 and 11). Sir Thomas was followed in 1760, by Mr. Humberstone, probably John Cawley Humberstone, Esq , of Gwersyllt, for
on September 11th, 1764, Frances, daughter of the latter, was baptiz
ed at Wrexham. Then, about 1766, Mr. Danvers Gartside, attorney,
removed hither from No. 14 Hope Street, and having bought
the house, remained there until his death, (April 7th, 1803, aged
81). I believe he belonged to a Manchester, or at least a Lancashire family. He was often called " Adjutant Gartside," and was
deputy-steward of one of the two Wrexham manors. He married
Eleanor, daughter of Mr. William Peters, of Platt Bridge, Lancashire, who survived her husband, and continued to live at the
house now being described until her death (August 19th, 1822,
aged 92). The house was then bought by Mr. George Lewis,
surgeon (see *History of Older Nonconformity of Wrexham,* p. 118),
who was living there in 1824, and still occupying it in 1843. He
was, in 1849, one of the surgeons to the Wrexham Infirmary, and
died in February 1854, being, I believe, buried in the Dissenters'
Graveyard. He made a determined stand against church rates.
Mr. J. Kenrick Lewis, surgeon, already mentioned in this chapter
(see sec. 38), was his son. In 1857 the premises belonged to
Richard Thompson, Esq., of Stansty Hall.

43. Between the house just described and Messrs. Hughes & Sons'
shop, including the mouth of Bank Street and the site of the
National Provincial Bank, were during the last century several
houses and shops all belonging to the Traverses, of Trefalyn House
(see *Hist. of Older Nonconformity of Wrexham,* p. 66, note 8), who
had derived them from Mr. Edward Mainwaring

44. What is now called " Bank Street (a name established at
least as early as 1849), was formerly known as " Kenrick Street,"
having been laid out by James Kenrick, Esq., banker. It is first
mentioned in the rate books in the year 1818, when it contained
five houses and three warehouses, all belonging to Mr. Kenrick,

but for many years after it continued to be treated as a private street, and at the bottom of it was a chain supported by posts intending to preserve its character as such.

45. The site of the present National Provincial Bank was purchased from the representatives of the Traverses by Mr. James Kenrick, who had hitherto been in business in the adjoining premises (now No. 56), and who erected thereupon a bank, house, and coach-house which he continued to occupy until his death (September 26th, 1824, aged 67). He left his property to his nephew, Mr. Samuel Kenrick, son of his brother, the Rev. Timothy Kenrick, who carried on here the business of a banker for many years, subsequently taking into partnership John Eddowes Bowman, Esq., F.L.S , F G.S.,[15] the firm being then called "Kenrick and Bowman," but in 1849 became bankrupt, paying 14s 6d in the pound, and the premises became afterwards those of the National Provincial Bank, as they still are, but have been since rebuilt.

46. The history of No. 56 adjoining, can be traced back as far as 1699. In 1702 it is described as belonging to the Benjamins (see *Hist. of Older Nonconformity of Wrexham*, p. 63, note 7). In 1715 it appears to have been an inn—The Crown, but soon after 1732 came to be occupied by Mr. John Brereton, first tinman, afterwards tallow chandler, the premises being described in 1742 as consisting of house, kiln, and brew-house. Mr. Brereton appears, for a great part of his life at any rate, to have been a Dissenter (Presbyterian), and was a man of some standing. He married first (August 19th, 1736), at Wrexham "Mrs. Catherine Key," (query whether not Keay, one of the Keays of Newmarket, see *Hist. of Older Nonconformity of Wrexham*, p. 77, note 20) and, secondly, Miss Margaret Benjamin, a daughter of his landlord (see the same, p. 134, note 4). Here he remained all his life, and was buried in the churchyard, September 12th, 1776. He was followed by Mr. James Kenrick, grocer and tallow chandler (see *Hist. of Older Nonconformity of Wrexham*, p. 75, sec. 75, (3)], who gradually added to his business that of banking On March 10th, 1800, the the greater part of the property of the Benjamins was sold by auction, this house among them, which Mr. Kenrick then bought.

---

15. This Mr. J. E. Bowman was a very distinguished amateur botanist and man of science. There is in one of the Gresford parish registers a long and interesting note by him on the yew trees in Gresford churchyard. While in Wrexham, he lived at The Court. He was a Unitarian, and there is a tablet to his memory in Upper Brook Street Free Church, Manchester. He was born at Nantwich, October 30th, 1785, and died at Manchester, December 4th, 1841. He was connected with the Eddoweses of Shrewsbury, the proprietors of *The Salopian Journal*. Sir Wm. Bowman, Bart., M.D., L.L.D., etc., a distinguished London physician, and the author of various medical books and essays, is one of his sons, and Mr. John Eddowes Bowman, formerly Professor of Chemistry at King's College, London, was another.

In the particulars of sale the property is described as consisting of dwelling house and shop, with valuable and very extensive warehouses, building ground, yard, stable, etc., communicating with Chester Street. Subsequently, as I have said in the previous paragraph, Mr. Kenrick relinquished his business as a grocer, and built the bank adjoining. Most circumstantial stories have been told me of his ghost revisiting, after his death, Kenrick Street and the places with which in his life time he had so long been associated. Indeed all sorts of odd tales about the man himself during his life have reached me. It is evident that he possessed great energy and force of character, but also various weaknesses, of which it would be unbecoming now to speak. Between 1843 and 1857 the premises were purchased by Mr. Richard Hughes, who removed hither from Church Street (see ch. ii, sec. 3), and who founded the firm of Hughes & Son, booksellers, stationers, and printers, especially to be remembered as publishers of Welsh books. Mr. Richard Hughes died January 13th, 1871, aged 77. He was succeeded by his son, the late Charles Hughes, Esq., J.P., of Brynhyfryd, who died March 24th, 1886, aged 63.

47. No. 57, now the Lion Stores, was until two or three years ago an inn, and called "The Lion." This latter name, however is of quite recent origin, its older name being "The Three Pigeons." It was so called as early as 1699, and at least as late as 1843 In 1780 it belonged to Mr. Joseph Griffith, and in 1827 to his descendant, Thomas Murhall Griffith, Esq. (see under Holt Street), who subsequently sold it

48. No. 58, until recently the shop of Mr. Charles Davies, tailor, and now the site of an arcade, was, for many years during last century, an inn, known as The King's Head. It was so called in 1711. In 1730 Mr. Rowland Samuel came to occupy it, and when he removed, about 1745, to The Old Raven, on the opposite side of the street, he transferred to his new house the name of his old one. From 1746 until his death, May 1773, the house was occupied by Griffith Speed, Esq., High Sheriff in 1760 (see under Nos. 8 and 9 High Street), and during the later years of his life at any rate, was owned also by him. He married Ruth, daughter of Mr. Richard Jones, apothecary (see under Nos. 36 and 37 High Street), who survived him, and continued to live in the same house until her death (April 1785). Then it became a grocer's shop, and finally the shop of Mr. John Clark, tailor, mayor of the borough in 1860-1, who ultimately removed to Chester, and became a wine merchant there

49. As to 59, Messrs. Summers & Fitch's Vaults, the house which stood on its site can be traced in the rate books as far back as 1699. In 1742 it was an inn, and called "The White Lion," being carried on by Mr. Rowland Samuel, who lived at The King's

Head next door. In 1757 it became the shop of Mr. Peter Hurst,[15a] brazier, and about 1810, that of Mr. William Ross, wine merchant, and liquor and porter dealer, who was succeeded in 1828, by his nephew, Mr. Joseph Aldersey, a Cumberland man, who died in 1832. Then the business was purchased by Mr. Joseph Clark, another Cumberland man, elder brother of Mr. John Clark, of No. 58. Mr. Joseph Clark became mayor of the borough in 1864-5, and at the conclusion of his year of office presented the corporation with £50, wherewith was purchased the silver mace. Further particulars relating to him will be found in sec. 15, ch. xx.

50. The next shop to 59, at the corner of Hope and High Street, commonly called "The Corner Shop," was occupied from about 1804 until after 1828,[15b] by Mr. Joseph Jones, a prosperous grocer and chandler. He bought Nos 7 to 9 Hope Street. His daughter married a Mr. William Jones, ultimately his heir, who lived for many years at 14 Gloucester Place, Low Hill, Liverpool, but during the latter part of his life, having retired from business, lodged at Rhyd Broughton, near Wrexham, being commonly called "Gentleman Jones" and died April 6th, 1881, aged 81.

51. Mr. Joseph Jones was followed in the occupation of the Corner Shop, by Mr. John Beale, druggist, a native of Worcester, who had previously been in business in York Street. He afterwards bought the premises, and ultimately retired from business. He was mayor of the borough in 1870, and put on the commission of the peace in 1879. He died at Egerton Lodge. January 16th, 1887, aged 77, and was buried in the Old Cemetery, Ruthin Road, He was thrice married.

52. Until the erection of the Market Hall in High Street in 1841, and for some time after, the Vegetable Market was held in Hope Street, which on Market days was crowded with stalls, and often a great part of High Street also. At many of these stalls poultry, eggs and butter were also sold.

53. Having thus dealt with the inhabited portion of old Hope Street, we will now describe that portion of it (now called "Regent Street"), which was flanked by fields, and which extended from Bryn y ffynnon House to the township bounds, where the Great Western Railway bridge now is. Walking in this direction away from the town we will first describe the lands on our left, and then returning, deal with those on the other side.

15a. It is thus described in 1777 :—A dwelling house in Hope Street, near the Market Hall, now in the holding of Mr. Peter Hurst, containing a large shop, with a parlour, kitchen, and scullery, a large dining room, and seven lodging rooms, with a workshop and two large wine cellars."

15b. It is thus described in 1777 (December 22nd), when it appears to have been sold by auction :-- " A dwelling house, . . . standing at the corner of the High Street, near the Market Hall, containing a commodious shop fronting two streets, a large dining room, a parlour, kitchen, pantry, scullery, and cellar, five lodging rooms, with garrets over.

54. The Orchard field (No. 36 in the map), which for more than 200 years has belonged to Bryn y ffynnon House, appears to have been formerly a part of one of the Common Fields of Wrexham. It was purchased before 1620 by Thomas Trafford, Esq. The name of this common field appears in Norden's Survey in various forms, of which "Maes Estome" is the most frequent. This probably stands for "Maes Ystum," which would mean "Field of the river bend," and this explanation is the more likely as the field is explicitly stated to have extended to the river, as well as to have stretched along Hope Street.

55. The English Wesleyan Chapel, commonly called "Bryn y ffynnon Chapel" stands on a part of the Orchard Field. The first chapel on this site was erected in 1855, the foundation stone being laid on July 24th of that year, by Adam Bealy, Esq., M.D., grandson of Mr. Richard Williams of The Acrau farm, near Gresford, of whom an account has been given under Salop Street(sec. 17). It took the place of the old Green Chapel, (see Salop Street). This and its appurtenances were now sold, realizing £758 13 4½, but there being a mortgage upon it of £618 3 4, only £140 10 0½ were obtained from it for the building fund of the new chapel. There had, however, been raised about £198 by a bazaar held in August of the previous year. The collection at the laying of the foundation stone amounted to £16 18 5, and other special collections at the opening of the Chapel, at a tea meeting in celebration of it, etc., amounted to £123 16 11. The total cost of the new chapel and of its site was £1,645 18 0½. The Rev. Francis A. West preached the first sermon in it on June 27th, 1856. Mr. James Simpson was the architect, and Mr. James Reynolds Gummow, of Wrexham, (son of Mr. Michael Gummow, and father of the present Messrs. W. H. and M. J. Gummow) the builder. It was a seemly stone structure, standing back from the street and presenting to it a high pitched gable. Within there were two aisles, an organ and singing loft, and behind, schoolrooms and vestries. It included no minister's house, as the Green Chapel property had done, so No. 36 Pen y bryn, was rented of Mr. Meredith Jones (the yearly rent being in 1858, £18), but in 1865, Epworth Lodge in Grove Road was built as a "manse," and is still occupied as such. The last service was held in the first Bryn y ffynnon Chapel on May 25th, 1889, the preacher being the Rev. Joseph Bush, of Newcastle on Tyne, President of the Conference, and it was forthwith pulled down to make way for the new, larger, and more imposing structure which has taken its place.[15a] The contractor for the new chapel was Mr. John Gethin, of Shrewsbury, the builder Mr. James Davies, of Wrexham, and the architects were Messrs. William

15a. The chapel was opened on Friday, September 5th 1890, sermons being preached in the afternoon and evening by the Rev. C. H. Kelly, London, Ex-president of the Conference.

Waddington and Sons, of Manchester and Burnley. The memorial stones were laid on Friday afternoon, July 5th, 1889, one by Sir Robert A. Cunliffe, Bart.; another by Miss Morris, daughter of the mayor, then Evan Morris, Esq. ; a third by G. W. Taylor, Esq.; a fourth by T. C. Jones, Esq.; and the last by Mrs. John Hopley Pierce, on behalf of the children of the Sunday School. The amount raised on the occasion was £402 10 0. The Rev. J. S. Haworth, superintendent of the circuit, gave also £800, a golden egg, as was happily said, laid by a bird of passage. Besides these sums, the trustees possessed for the rebuilding of the chapel, the money left by Mr. James Ollerhead of King Street, formerly a confectioner at one of the two shops at the corner of High Street and Chester Street, which have recently been pulled down. Mr. Ollerhead died November 5th, 1876, aged 74, and left a great deal of property valued at several thousand pounds to the trustees of the Wesleyan Chapel, but as some of the provisions of his will violated the statute of mortmain, the trustees only received a sum considerably under £1,000, but which, by the operation of compound interest, had accumulated, at the time of the pulling down of the old chapel to £1,151. In all, the trustees had, in hand or promised, towards the erection of the new chapel, £3,282 19 0, leaving £2,318 to be raised, of which the bazaar, subsequently held, yielded £620, the remaining sum being soon after raised. The following description of the chapel, taken with few alterations from the report of the Wesleyan Chapel committee for the year 1889, may here fitly be given :—It has a central narthex 30 feet long, approached through side porches. The nave is 63 feet long by 44 feet wide, and there are transepts having a depth of 13 feet extra. At the end of the nave is a chancel (containing the choir seats), having a length of 20 feet with an apsidal end. To the left is the organ chamber, and to the right the minister's and choir vestries. To the rear is a ladies' room, a ladies' store room, a lift from the cellar kitchen, and other conveniences. On the upper floor are two spacious class rooms. Immediately behind the chapel is the school room, with four class rooms to accommodate 330 scholars. The chapel has seats for 650 persons, all on the ground floor, except those in the end gallery over the entrances. The special feature in the plan is the arrangement of the nave, which is reduced to a width of 33 feet by the introduction of a double arcade, used as passages only. The whole of the seats are within the pillars, and have an uninterrupted view of the pulpit, and by means of a central aisle are divided into two blocks. The chapel and schools are designed in the style of 13th Century English Gothic, the walls being of stone throughout. The front includes a spire. The internal wood-work, including the roof timbers (which are exposed to view), are of pitch pine, while the choir stalls and pulpit are of oak. The chancel, narthex, and porches

are tiled.   The windows contain lights in lead, wrought in geomet-
rical patterns, relieved with colour.   The internal arcades (including pillars and arches), the chancel arch, and the jambs and arches
of all doors and windows in the chapel are of chiselled stone.
Complete arrangements for ventilation exist, exhaust shafts being
carried up the tower.   The contracts for the whole building were
let to Mr. John Gethin, of Shrewsbury, for £4,693, exclusive of
the arrangements for lighting and heating, which cost about
£300.[16]

56. The site of St. Mark's Church, which is a chapel of ease,
without any district of its own, is also a part of the old Orchard
Field, and was presented[17] by the late Sir W. Williams Wynn on
two conditions : firstly, that no burials should take place in the
churchyard, and secondly, that the tree which still stands beside
the approach from Regent Street to the church, should be spared.
The church was erected from the plans of the late Mr. Richard
Kyrke Penson, at a cost of over £7,000, a sum which was raised by
public subscription.   It was consecrated May 21st, 1858, the spire,
however, not being completed until June 5th, 1862.   All the seats
are free and unappropriated.   The endowment, as I have already
said (see under Beechley, Wrexham Fechan), was provided by Miss
Mary Anne Bennion, who gave four-fifths of the tithes of Minera,
of the yearly value £115 4 7½.[18]   She gave also the east window, and
£100 towards the erection of the church.   The principal other
subscribers were the Rev. Canon Cunliffe, the vicar, £525 ; Chas.
Kynaston Mainwaring, Esq., of Oteley, and Thomas Irvine, Esq.,
each £200 ; Sir Robert Henry Cunliffe, Bart., of Acton Park, and
John Burton, Esq., of Minera, each £125; Bishop Short, the Marquis
of Westminster, Thomas Fitzhugh, Esq., of Plas Power, Thomas
Taylor Griffith, Esq., of Chester Street, and John Lewis, Esq.,
solicitor, each £100 ; Miss Cunliffe, £80 ; Sir Roger Palmer, Bart.,
of Cefn, Henry Warter Meredith, Esq., of Pentrebychan, Thomas
Lloyd Fitzhugh, Esq., of Plas Power, John Foulkes, Esq., of Rhosddu, and Mrs. Oakley, of Tan y bwlch, each £50 ;   Dr. Edward
Williams, of Holt Street, and Thomas Hughes, Esq., solicitor, each
£30.   The Incorporated Church Building Society and the Dio-
cesan Church Building Society gave also each £400, and the

16. Spite of these efforts the Wesleyans of Wrexham on February 7th, of the
following year (1890) opened a new mission room in Hightown in place of their
old one there.

17. The formal conveyance of the site to the Ecclesiastical Commissioners is
dated April 13th, 1858.

18. The tithes were vested, April 27th, 1858, by Miss Bennion for the benefit
of the clergyman regularly officiating at St. Mark's, in four trustees (Sir W. Williams Wynn, bart. ; Henry Warter Meredith Esq., of Pentrebychan ; Paul Griffith
Panton, Esq., of The Fron, Bangor Isycoed; and Thomas Parry Jones- Parry, Esq.,
of Llwyn Onn); the survivors of whom were empowered to replace by co-optation
those who had died.

Commissioners for Building Churches, £300. Yew trees were planted April 23rd, 1864, by the vicar, Canon Cunliffe, in the churchyard, but they have not grown up. The area of the church-yard, including that of the church, was originally 5,270 square yards, but a great part of this was in 1888 sold for £280 to the Wrexham, Mold, and Connah's Quay Railway Company, the pro-ceeds being applied to the erection of the Welsh Church in Rhosddu Road. The church contains an organ, erected by Whitely of Ches-ter in 1874, at a cost of £540, which took the place of an earlier one by Holditch, for which £120 were allowed ; a pulpit of Caen stone ; a brass lectern, presented by John Lewis, Esq., mayor in 1862-3 ; a font, given by the late Thomas Rowland, Esq., mayor in 1869 ; and other furniture. The communion plate consists of a silver cup " A thank offering presented by Sophia J. Jermyn, Reenadoona, Ireland," and another silver cup, flagon, paten, and platter, " Presented to St. Mark's Church in memory of a mother and brother, by Mrs. Overton, Easter 1872."

57. The following is a list of the curates in charge of St. Mark's Church :—

    1858-68—James Clark Roberts, M.A.[19]
    1868-71—John Williams.[20]
    1871-74—Jas. Harries Gibbon, B.A.[21]

57a. Until Mr. Gibbon left, the curate in charge of St. Mark's was almost regarded as the incumbent of the church, and assumed great power, but since then the vicar of the parish has himself worked it with his staff of curates, and it is for this reason that I give the names of no curates after the name of the Rev. J. Harries Gibbon.

58 The present County Hall and Police Station, next beyond the entrance to St. Mark's Church, were originally the Militia Barracks (built soon after 1857), and were converted to their pres-ent use in 1879, when the new barracks were built in Ellesmere Road. The cannon in the open space in front was captured during the Crimean war.

59. The beautiful Roman Catholic Church, Regent Street, dedicated to Saint Mary, and the rectory attached to it, were built in 1857, by Richard Thompson, Esq., of Stansty Hall, from the designs of the younger Pugin, the cost being something like £9,000. Mr. Thompson also endowed it with £100 a year payable from his estates. The church took the place of the old chapel in King Street, under which, later in this chapter, will be found a history of Roman Catholicism in this town. Ellen, wife of Mr. Thompson,

19. Rev. J. C. Roberts, of Magdalen Hall, Oxford, vicar of Eastbury, 1868 vicar of West Wycombe, 1869 ; rector of Ryton (diocese of Lichfield), 1872.

20. Rev. John Williams, of St. Bees, curate of Holy Trinity, Ripon, 1862, of St. Mary's Bootle, and rector of Newtown, Montgomeryshire, 1871.

21. James Harries Gibbon, now vicar of Halliwell, near Bolton-le-moors.

died at Stansty Hall, November 21st, 1854, aged 52, after the ground had been acquired, but before the church itself had been built upon it,[22] and Mr. Thompson soon after left Stansty, and went to live at Chorley, Lancashire, and never saw the building which his munificence had founded. He caused a costly tomb to be erected to his wife's memory, which stands on the left hand side of the church as one enters it by the Regent Street entrance. It is worth noting that the altar stands at the west, and not at the east, end of the church. The organ, built by Messrs. Gray & Davidson at a cost of £400, was opened July 15th, 1860, and the large bell, cast by Murphy, of Dublin, and which cost £200 (raised by public subscription), was placed in the belfry in 1864.

60. Bradley Road was constructed by the Corporation in 1881, and named after the late George Bradley, Esq., the mayor of that year.

61. The Infirmary was erected on the present site in the year 1838, and has since been several times enlarged, "the Jubilee Wards" being added in 1888. It was founded in 1832, and at first carried on in a house in York Street, since pulled down, just below the Wynnstay Arms. The board room contains a portrait of Thomas Taylor Griffith Esq., one of the founders of the Infirmary.

62. Beyond the Orchard Field was another field (No. 347), belonging in later times to Bryn y ffynnon, and it must have been on this field that the Infirmary was built.

63. Between this field and what is now called "Catherall's Lane" were some lands, which from the beginning of last century belonged to a Mr. Charles Roberts, who had a great deal of other property in the town. In 1780 they belonged to Mr. Williamson of Liverpool, and in 1824 are returned for the first time as the property of Mr. William Harrison, of Lloyd's Bank, at which he was cashier. From about 1811 until his death (March, 1860), he lived at No. 25 Chester Street, a house which he purchased of Richard Lloyd, Esq., and "Harrison's Court" there takes its name from him. By 1844 a house had been built, apparently the present Hope Cottage, and the whole still belonged to Mr. Harrison, and measured 5 A, 0 R, 18 P (Nos. 340, 344, and 345 in the map), No. 339 (measuring 1 R, 15 P, having just been sold to the Shrewsbury and Chester Railway). About this time the late Mr. Thomas Catherall, plasterer, father of the present Mr. Gwilt Catherall, came to live at Hope Cottage, which he ultimately purchased. It is from Mr. Thomas Catherall, that Catherall's Lane takes its name. He was a skilful ornamental plasterer and rather noted for his models of animals. He died October 4th, 1881, aged 84.

22. She was buried in a vault on the left hand side of the walk leading from Regent Street to the church door, and here her husband, who died May 1870, was also afterwards buried.

64. The fields numbered 341, 342 and 343 in the map were aforetime reckoned a part of the area called "Pwll y wrach" of which I shall have something to say presently. But they were generally called for distinction "Burrowes' Land," they having belonged during the early part of last century to Alderman Edward Burrowes, of Chester, whose representatives sold them October 4th, 1750, to Griffith Speed, Esq. (see under No. 58 Hope Street). After his death they passed into the possession of Sir Foster Cunliffe, who conveyed them in 1813, to the Rev. Robert Twiss, of Trefalyn House. In 1844 they belonged to Thomas Taylor Griffith, Esq., who had then recently sold Nos. 341 and 343 to the Shrewsbury and Chester Railway Company.

65. Here I may call attention to an interesting feature in the map, which shows that in 1844 the Shrewsbury and Chester Railway Company had already purchased lands for the construction of of their line, but that the line itself had not yet been made. The lands which they had purchased are represented in the map by the following numbers :—356, 341, 343, 339, 339a, 347, 337, and 335. The line, as originally projected, was called "The North Wales Mineral Railway," and was intended to run ‚from Chester to Wrexham, with a branch from Wrexham to Brymbo. It was then decided to extend the line to Shrewsbury, so that the company owning it came to be called "The Shrewsbury and Chester Railway Company," and the whole now forms a part of the Great Western Railway system. The Act of Parliament authorising the extension to Shrewsbury received the royal assent June 30th. 1845: the North Wales Mineral Railway Company was amalgamated with it in the following year, and the amalgamated line was taken over by the Great Western Railway Company in 1854.

66. A great part of the western boundary of the two townships of Wrexham Regis and Wrexham Abbot is formed by Wat's Dyke, one of the two great boundary dykes, made between the English and the Welsh Whether it is older or later than Offa's Dyke, it is impossible to say. But it is clear from the fact that the ditch is on the western side of the embankment, that it was made by the English and not by the Welsh. I have seen in old deeds very early examples of the Welsh form of the name which generally appears as "Clawdd Wad,"[23] and which may mean "Wad's Dyke." I am inclined to think that, as in the case of Offa's Dyke, so in that of Wat's Dyke, we have a personal name involved, probably some such name as Wada,[23] or at any rate the same name which is preserved in such place-names as Wadsworth, Wadsley, Waddington. and the like. During the making

23. Other forms are "Clauth Wode," and "Clauth Wade."

23a. The actual existence of this name can be proved.

and extension of the Great Western, and Wrexham, Mold, and Connah's Quay Railways, large portions of Wat's Dyke have been removed.

67. Having followed the western side of Regent Street, and reached the township bounds, we now cross the road, and describe the other side. All the fields marked in the map by the numbers 355, 356, 857, 359, 360, 348, 351 and 350 formed, with Nos. 341-3 on the opposite side of the road, an area, once a common field, or two common fields, called "Pwll y wrach," or *The Hag's Pool*, the latter being the name of the pool which still exists, and is situate in the middle of the area. Of this area, the closes numbered 359 and 360 belonged in 1844 to the Acton estate, and at an earlier date apparently 350 also, which, in 1844, was owned by Miss Emma Foulkes. In 1620, John Jeffreys, Esq., of Acton, is described as holding various parcels in Pwll y wrach. In 1844, Nos. 355 and 357 belonged to the vicar of the parish who had recently sold 356 to the Railway Company. According to the rate books, this glebe-land in Pwll y wrach was obtained by exchange from Mrs. Puleston of Hafod y wern towards the end of last century, but what lands were surrendered instead of it I do not know. The Hafod y wern estate, however, still held Nos. 350 aud 348 in Pwll y wrach, but these were ultimately, sold as well as No. 361, to Miss Potts, of Chester. It was through Nos. 348 and 361, that Grosvenor Road was laid out somewhere about 1869. I believe Brynhyfryd was the first house built in it, and Dr. Drinkwater's house opposite was the second.

68. All the land between Pwll y wrach and the inhabited portion of old Hope Street, was bought, a little before 1824, by Thomas Griffith, Esq., surgeon (see under Nos. 7 and 9 Hope Street), of Bryan Cooke, Esq., of Gwasaney, and a great part of it still belongs to his grandson, the Rev Llewelyn Griffith, of Deal.

69. King Street (or rather the western end of it), must, I think, have been laid out on the outer fringe of Mr. Griffith's property, next to Oak Tree Field, a part of the Pwll y wrach area. It was the first residential street formally laid out in this town, the first sign of the expansion of Wrexham. It is mentioned in the rate books for the first time in the year 1828, and as nearly half the houses were then vacant, it is probable that it had only recently been built. The seven houses nearest to Rhosddu Lane formed Gwersyllt Place, were duly numbered, and belonged to Richard Kirk, Esq., of Gwersyllt Hill, having been built on land bought from the Rev. John Pearce, land numbered 4 on the map. Then came three houses, separately numbered, forming Wellington Place, and belonging to Mr. Edward Jones. Wellington Place was followed by the Roman Catholic Chapel (now "The Christian Meeting House,") and by Wynnstay Place, composed of two houses belonging to Captain Watson, of which the first was tenanted by Captain

Morris, and the second (at the corner of King Street and Regent Street) by Miss Kendall. By 1841 the number of houses in King Street had increased to 23.

70. Having mentioned the Roman Catholic Chapel in King Street, it will be well to say something of the later history of Roman Catholicism in the town.[24] When King Street was laid out, Richard Thompson, Esq., (son of John Thompson, Esq., of the Ffrwd Colliery, who in 1828 rented the Brymbo Iron Works) bought one of the plots for building the chapel, but the vendor, when he learned what Mr. Thompson proposed to do, refused to complete the sale, on the plea that he had agreed to sell the ground as a site for a house. Mr. Thompson, therefore, built a house for the priest, all the rooms of which were on the ground floor, while the chapel occupied the whole of the upper story. This is the explanation of the curious arrangement of this building. The King Street Chapel was occupied by the Roman Catholics of Wrexham until Richard Thompson, Esq., above named, then of Stansty Hall, built for them, in the year 1857, the beautiful new church in Regent Street, which has already been described. Before the building of the King Street Chapel, however, a mission had been established in Wrexham under the direction of the Rev. John Briggs, of Chester, afterwards Vicar Apostolic of the Northern District, and ultimately Bishop of Beverley, who celebrated mass in a hired room in Seven Bridge Lane, and afterwards in Cutler's Entry, Charles Street. Wrexham Roman Catholics also sometimes attended at the house of Mr. Thompson, and at Nerquis Hall, the residence of Miss Gifford, where mass was occasionally said. The Rev. D. L. Morton was the first priest resident in Wrexham, and the first baptism registered in the King Street Chapel was performed by the Rev. John Briggs, of Chester, July 18th, 1828. I owe most of this information, as well as the list of priests in charge which follows to a memorandum drawn up by the Rev. Canon Lennon, kindly lent me by the Rev. Canon Hopkins, and to information supplied me by the late John Beirne, Esq. The latter was organist and choirmaster for 32 years. As to the following list of resident prests, all the earlier ones are described as " missioners," the Rev. Dr. Browne being the first " missionary rector."—

24. I have already given in the third volume of this series (*The History of the Older Nonconformity of Wrexham*), a brief account of some Roman Catholics of Wrexham and its neighbourhood during the 17th and 18th centuries. To this account may now be added that on April 17th, 1694, at the Quarter Sessions held at Ruthin, the afternamed were presented by the two high constables ·" ffor popish recusancy."—Robert Trevor, of Esclustra, gent ; Henry Roberts, of Stansty, gent ; James Gooden, of Wrex., practitioner in physic ; Andrew Hill, of the same, cooper ; Eustace Crew, of the same, apothecary ; John Mercer, of the same, body [bodice] maker ; Thomas Bostock, of the same ; Thomas Crue, of Holt. gent ; and Edward Roberts, of Erlas. A " Thomas Crew, of Holt, gent," was buried there June 28th, 1741.

1831—D. L. MORTON.

1833—JOHN TOBIN.

1837—JOHN J. COLLINS.[25]

1839—JOSEPH HELY.

1840—JOHN TOBIN, (the same who had been previously settled
at Wrexham.

1847—JOSEPH JONES.[26]

1850—LEWIS HAVARD.

1851—JOHN COULSTONE, (afterwards of Wilmslow, died June
4th, 1889, aged 67).

1854—JOHN REAH, (canon of Shrewsbury).[27]

1856—JAMES WARD.

1857—WILLIAM HILTON, (returned to Wrexham as priest in
1876.[30]

1857-72—EDWARD F. BROWNE, canon, D.D.[28]

1872-6—AMBROSE LENNON, canon.[29]

1876-83—WILLIAM HILTON, canon.[30]

1883—HENRY HOPKINS, canon.

71. The spacious " Capel Seion," or Chapel of the Welsh
Calvinistic Methodists, was opened on the last Sunday in September 1867, taking the place of the old chapel in Abbot Street, in the
chapter devoted to which will be found an account of the earlier
history of Calvinistic Methodism in this town.   The Rev. Dr. Lewis
Edwards, of Bala, preached the first sermon on the Sunday morning
referred to, the sermon being in Welsh.   The Rev. D. Charles, B.A.
of Abercorn, preached in English in the afternoon, and Dr.
Edwards and Mr. Charles preached in the evening in Welsh.   The
opening services were continued on the Monday, Tuesday, and
Wednesday following, the collections amounting to £121.   There
were then three ministers connected with the church, the Rev. J.
H. Symond, the pastor ; the Rev. Wm. Lewis, late missionary in the
Cassia Hills, India, (who died May 6th, 1890, aged 77); and the Rev.
Richard Jones, who died, October 21st, 1867, aged 49, soon after the
chapel was opened, and was buried in the Dissenters' Graveyard,

25. The Rev. J. J. Collins was a hard-working priest, and accustomed to walk
long distances to administer the sacraments, often as far as Oswestry.

26. The Rev. Joseph Jones had been formerly a Methodist preacher, and was
trained for the priesthood in Brittany.

27. The Rev. John Reah was born near Ushaw College, and died of consump
tion at Poole, Dorset.   The building of the new church was begun in his time.

28. The Rev. Dr. Browne died July 17th, 1872, aged 56, and was buried on
the right hand side of the walk leading from Regent Street to the east door of the
church.   In his time the Brook Street schools were built (see under Brook Street).

29. The Rev. Canon Lennon died March 29th, 1876, aged 66, and was buried
at Liscard Roman Catholic Church.

30. The Rev. Canon Hilton left Wrexham to become president of a college at
Lisbon.

having been in the ministry 22 years. The deacons were Mr. Richard Hughes, Mr. Evan Powell, of No. 6 Town Hill, ironmonger (afterwards of Irvon Villa, Grosvenor Road, a native of Llangammarch, who died December 29th, 1874, aged 60, was buried in the Dissenters' Graveyard, and was father of the present Messrs. John E. Powell and Robert J. Powell); Mr. Richard Brunt, grocer, of No. 16 Town Hill, and Bellevue (who died March 6th, 1883, aged 67), and Edward Francis, the author of *Hanes Dechreuad a Chynydd Methodistiaith yn Ngwrescam*[31] The towers at each corner of the front of the chapel enclose staircases which give access to the side galleries. Within, the chapel is 27 yards long by 14 broad, and provides accomodation for 800 people. Behind, is the schoolroom, built in 1884, which is entered from Egerton Street. In 1869 the number of communicants was 210, of attendants at the services about 570, of scholars on the books of the Sunday School 300, and of Sunday School teachers, 36.

72. The Rev. J. H. Symond left for Towyn, in Merionethshire, about 1873, and was followed in 1875, by the Rev. H. Barrow Williams, who removed in 1889 to Llandudno, and was succeeded, in 1891, by the Rev. E. Morris, M.A., a native of Machynlleth, successively pastor at Aberdovey, and at the Welsh Chapels at Charing Cross and Nassau Street, London.

73. The fields numbered 3 and 5 on the map belonged, in 1884, to Thomas Taylor Griffith, Esq. On this block the Post Office (which had hitherto been held at No. 8 Hope Street) was built in 1885, and soon after, adjoining it, St. James's Hall, while at the same time Duke and Lord Streets were laid out.

74. The present Savings Bank, with its front towards Regent Street, and bounded by Egerton Street on its northern side, was erected in the year 1837, Mr. Edward Welch being the architect. The institution was founded in the year 1832, and previous to its settlement in Regent Street, had been carried on at No. 5 Temple Row, where Mr. Samuel Thomas Baugh's offices now are. Its first actuary was Mr. John Sadler, wine merchant, who on his death, March 16th, 1833, was succeeded by Mr. John Farrar, who remained in office until 1837, when Mr. Bartholomew Dillon (see under No. 34 High Street) was appointed. After his prosecution in December 1842, Mr. Thomas Tyndall, a native of West Bromwich, and a clerk in one of the Wrexham banks, became actuary, and so continued until his death by accidental drowning, August 27th, 1849, when he was succeeded by Mr. Anthony Dillon, the manager of the National Provincial Bank, who resigned in April 1854, giving place to Mr. John Bury, who still holds the office, and to whom I owe the foregoing information.

31. Mr. Edward Francis lived in 1828 and in 1837 at Minera Mill, and subsequently at The Wern farm (otherwise called Ty'n y ddol), Esclusham, and in Abbot Street, Wrexham. He died May 16th, 1876, in the 74th year of his age.

Chapter V.

Henblas Street.

1. The Henblas is mentioned as a street as early as 1620, but it was very short, and then proceeded in a straight line from what is now called "Queen Street" to the open space in front of the Grammar School. When the Manchester Hall, now the Pedler's or General Market, was erected, access was probably made to it both from Chester Street and Henblas Street, and so the latter came to assume its circuitous course. But that part of it which entered Chester Street between the Reform Club and the Old Vaults or "Long Pull" was formerly reckoned part of Kenrick Street (now Bank Street), and not of Henblas Street. When the space in front of the Grammar School was enclosed, a very narrow passage was left between the enclosed ground and the Congregational chapel, so that it was only of use to foot passengers, and it was only widened when in 1883 the Grammar School was bought by the Corporation to form the new Municipal Buildings.

2. The following reference to Henblas Street occurs in Norden's survey (A.D. 1620) :—

"Rent 6d (lease) expired 10 y since. The same (Catherine Jones, widow) holds all that garden and parcel of land called place y kill (Pias y Kiln), and a kiln, with other buildings thereupon remaining, between the streets called y place hen and the lampint. . . . ."

In a deed quoted in the note on p. 78 of my *Hist. of the Older Non-conformity of Wrexham* we find this same "garden or p'cell of land called Place y Kyll in Lampynt" mentioned as adjacent to "the wasteland" on which the schools and property belonging to the poor of Chester Street Congregational Chapel now stand. I have often found in old deeds this word "place" (plas) applied to strips of land on which no building of any kind stood, although in Welsh the word "plas" stands commonly for a "hall."

3. There was, however, in later times, in Henblas Street a large house which was called "The Henblas"—The Old *Hall*, but which cannot be traced earlier than 1742. Inasmuch as it is mentioned in the rate books next to The Rainbow, it may have *faced* Queen

Street, but the premises belonging to it certainly extended along the whole south side of the old Henblas Street, taking in the site of the present Public Hall. This house, together with the Rainbow, belonged in 1780, and for nearly twenty years after, to a certain Rev. John Jones. Who he was I do not know for certain, but he was evidently connected with the Joneses of Coed y glyn, Wrexham (who afterwards owned the property), and I believe he was the Rev. John Jones who was rector of Knockin from 1761 to 1798, and vicar of Llansantffraid yn Mechain from 1783 to 1798. The first occupant that I need name was Mr. John Myddelton, apothecary, who lived here from about 1748 until his death in 1761. He had before lived at what is now 32 High Street, and in the description of that street a full notice of him will be found. He was succeeded in 1764 by the Miss Powell who had hitherto lived at Plas Gwern (see under Tuttle Street), and who was almost certainly Anna Maria Powell, the last of the Powells of Broughton Hall, in the parish of Wrexham. Miss Powell, who was still living at The Henblas in 1771, was followed by Mr. John Jones, stationer, and before 1808 this single house was replaced by three separate houses, and the garden or yard at the back was laid out as " The Birmingham Square," or square for the use of the hardware dealers during the time of the March Fair, Access was obtained to it through the Rainbow passage. A little before 1824, the Yorkshiremen migrated from their own square in Tuttle Street (which was out of the way), and joined with the hardware dealers, and about forty of them bought the Birmingham Square, which henceforth came to be called " The New Yorkshire Square" or "The New Union Hall." It had a gallery around it containing shops, and in this gallery was held a leather market during the first days of the March Fair, which latter used jocularly to be called " The Ides of March." The middle space was open. Ultimately the square was roofed in, and provided with new appointments, and forms now " The Public Hall," which was opened in the year 1873.

4. When the Birmingham Square relinquished its old name, a new square, which was soon after formed on the opposite side of Henblas Street, forthwith adopted it. There were, on the site of the present Vegetable Market, a house, barn, and joiner's yard, the property of Mr. Williamson, and formerly of the Pulfords. The yard just mentioned was formed into a dealers' square and came to be called " The New Birmingham Square." It has since been formed into the Vegetable Market.

5. The present offices of the *Wrexham Advertiser* were erected about the year 1852 or 1853, the building being then called " The Music Hall." It was, however intended to be not so much a concert room, as a hall for lectures and other meetings. It came to be built through the refusal of the owners of the Town Hall to let the room for a lecture by Henry Vincent, and the Liberals of the district

were also anxious to have a building wholly under their own con-
trol.   They saw also in its erection a means of manufacturing
Liberal votes for the boroughs.   The sum therefore required to
build it was divided into shares of £38 each, and among the share-
holders were W. H. Darby, Esq., of Brymbo;   Charles Rawlins,
Esq., senior ,   Charles Rawlins, Esq., junr. ;   Richard C. Rawlins,
Esq., Wm. Rathbone, Esq., of Liverpool, and Thomas Crosfield,
Esq., of Liverpool.   At the last meeting held in the Music Hall a
lecture was delivered by Thomas Cooper, author of *The Purgatory
of Suicides*, the last of a course of lectures on "The Evidences of
Christianity."

6. In 1868, the owners of the Music Hall let it to the proprietors
of *The Wrexham Advertiser* (see ch. IV, sec. 11), one of the proprietors
of which, the late George Bradley, Esq., began to buy up the owners'
shares of the building, and ultimately bought up all, or nearly all
of them.   The first number of the *Wrexham Advertiser* printed at
The Music Hall was dated October 3rd, 1868.

CHAPTER VI

Queen Street.

1. I have repeatedly shown elsewhere how many of the old streets of Wrexham have changed their names, and how often a street bore at the same time more names than one. These two statements are strikingly exemplified in the case of what is now always known as "Queen Street." This street I have found called in 1563, and again in 1620 "Receiver's Street," probably from the fact that one of the receivers of the lordship of Bromfield and Yale had at one time a house therein. This name was subsequently Welshified into "Stryt y Syfwr," which was the equivalent of the English name, and afterwards, as the meaning of it became forgotten, corrupted into "Stryt y Syffern" and "Stryt yr Sovarn,"[1] a name which I find used in the year 1699. Meanwhile the street came to be called "Lower Hope Street" (a name applied to it in 1620 and again in 1701), and "Yspytty Lane," or, by corruption "The Sputty," a name which continued in use until the end of the first quarter of the present century. In the midst of this multiplicity and confusion of apellations, another name—"Queen Street"—was during the last half of last century,[1a] given to it, and although for many years it made but little approach towards general recognition, it had by the beginning of the second quarter of the present century completely established itself, to the exclusion of all the earlier names.

2. In dealing with this street we shall walk along it from Hope Street towards Rhosddu. With that portion of it between the Rainbow and Henblas Street, enough has already been said under Hope Street and Henblas Street. At the Henblas Street corner we shall therefore begin, describing first of all the right hand side.

3. The first house on this side that requires notice is that numbered 19, and occupied by Mr. Ashton Bradley, solicitor. The house representing it can be traced back as far as 1715, and was

1. Mr. W. M. Myddelton has furnished me with an extract from the records of the Denbighshire Quarter Sessions recording that Stephen Burges, high constable of the hundred of Bromfield, on April 21st, 1696, presented at the Quarter Sessions "Mr. Ellis Hughes (see sec 8), for suffering a noysome water cours to come thorow a vacant piece of ground (in the corner of a street bordering to *Sovarn Street*), to the great damage of his neighbours which water cours formerly went and now ought to go another way.

1a. ¶I first find the name "Queen Street" used in the year 1780.

then occupied by Mr. Thomas Robinson, joiner (see *Hist. of Older Nonconformity of Wrexham*, p. 143, note 56), who was succeeded by his son, Mr. John Robinson (see the same, p. 146, note 67). About 1766, Mr. Isaac Smith came to live here and bought the house, but ultimately went to live at Croes Newydd, where he died December 1777. He was largely concerned in opening up the mineral wealth of the Minera district, in connection with which I shall have in the next volume to speak further of him. He was followed by Mrs. Mary Puleston (see under Llwyn Isaf further on in this chapter), who left about the year 1785, and whose successor was Mr. Lloyd, I believe Mr. William Lloyd, surgeon (see under No. 34 High Street), who in his turn, was succeeded towards the end of the century, on his inheriting Plas Power, by his brother-in-law, Mr. Charles Massie, surgeon (see under York Street), who remained there until his death in 1810. Then about 1812, Mr. Thomas Griffith, surgeon, removed hither from Hope Street (see under Nos. 7 to 9 Hope Street). The house then belonged to a Mrs. Edwards, but Mr. Griffith afterwards bought it, and there lived until his death in 1846. His daughters continued to occupy it afterwards, and it still belongs to his grandson the Rev. Thomas Llewelyn Griffith, M.A , vicar of Deal. There are a yard, stables, etc., at the back, with a carriage way into Henblas Street.

4. Queen's Square, a little further down on the same side, is worthy of being studied as the sole survival, very little modified, of the market squares which used to be occupied by tradesmen from various parts of England during the great March Fair. It is approached from Queen Street through a pair of iron gates and under a covered entrance. We then reach an open square, surrounded on two sides (probably on three sides originally), with a covered gallery supported by pillars. In this gallery were shops, and beneath them, on the ground floor, were also shops. The property on which this square was built belonged for the most part to the Hugheses of Chester and Rhosddu (see later in this chapter), and partly to Mr. Thomas Dale, of Oswestry. It was purchased from the former owners by Richard Kirk, Esq., of Gwersyllt Hill, about the end of last century. Mr. Kirk appears to have built the square, which was certainly erected by the year 1804, and I find it specifically called " Queen Square " in 1808. Calico and table linen were the principal articles sold in it. It still belonged to Mr. Kirk in the year 1828.

5. We now cross to the other or west side of the street and must devote a paragraph to Ebenezer Chapel, the Chapel of the Welsh Congregationalists. It was opened March 26th, 1863, the Welsh Congregational Chapel having hitherto been in Pentre'r felin, under which a short account of it will be found. The Rev. Rowland Williams (Hwfa Môn), now of Llangollen, was the minister when the project of building this chapel was first started, but in

1862, while the chapel was still being built, left for Bethesda, Carnarvonshire. Mr. Charles Griffiths, of The King's Mills (see *Hist. of Older Nonconformity of Wrexham*, p. 92, note 46), gave £1,000 to the cost of the chapel, which amounted in all to £2,800, and afterwards £900 towards paying off the debt, and land free for building a vestry at the back of the chapel. Most of this information is obtained from Rees and Thomas' *Hanes Eglwysi Annibynol Cymru*. I give now a list of the ministers who succeeded Mr. Rowland Williams :—

> 1863-1867, OWEN EVANS (came hither from London, went hence to Llanbrynmair).
>
> 1868, JOHN MORLAIS JONES (came hither from Bethesda, Brynmawr, went hence to Brynaman).
>
> 1871, DAVID ROBERTS (Dewi Ogwen, from Carnarvon).

The last named is still minister of the chapel, and the cause has prospered under his direction. He is a well known bard, and master of a sweet and liquid Welsh, and the author of two volumes of "*Pregethau*" or *Sermons*, published by Hughes & Sons, Wrexham, the first volume, printed in 1857 (arriving at a second edition in 1880), and the second volume in 1879. Taking up an American Welsh Magazine a little while ago, I saw in it an article entitled "Gemau Dewi Ogwen," that is *Gems of Dewi Ogwen*, Dewi Ogwen being Mr. Roberts' bardic name. In June 1887 the Oxford University, Miami, Ohio, conferred upon Mr. Roberts the degree of D.D.

6. Between the chapel and the houses next to be described, appears to have been a passage or court called "The Welsh Entry." I find it mentioned in the years 1826 and 1850.

7. The whole group of houses numbered 8 to 10 were I believe built by Mr. John Jones, carpenter, on land belonging to him there towards the end of last century. This Mr. Jones was the father of Mr. John Jones. draper, of Nos. 36 and 37 High Street (see *History of Older Nonconformity of Wrexham*, p. 140, note 46), and of Mr. Edward Jones, architect (see the same, p. 90, note 39). Mr. Jones himself died January 6th, 1796, aged 42. Behind the houses just named he built also a hall for the March Fair, which was approached from Queen Street by the arched passage which still exists between Nos. 9 and 10. It was open in the middle, with a covered gallery around three of its sides, having shops in the gallery and on the ground floor below them. On Mr. Jones' tombstone in the Dissenters' Graveyard, this square is called " The New Linen Hall." In 1818 it is called in the rate books "The Irish Hall" and in 1827 "The Manchester Square," although this name was already appropriated to another hall (see under Chester Street). But it was more commonly called " Jones's Hall." It was still in existence in 1841 and doubtless much later. Linen and fancy goods were the chief commodities sold in it.

8. We now cross the street to the house called "The Yspytty." This, or rather its predecessor, belonged from 1661 (and doubtless earlier) until nearly the end of last century to a family called Hughes, who not merely owned a large freehold farm in Stansty (now represented by The Grange), and a farm in Brymbo called "Tyddyn Broughton," but also a great deal of property in Wrexham. They owned, for example, besides The Yspytty, four other houses in Queen Street, various cottages on the north side of Lampint Street, and in Farndon Street, as well as a good house in High Street which occupied part of the site of the Alliance Assurance Company, and in which Mr. Rowland Samuel long lived (see ch. 1, sec. 22). The first of this family that I can trace is John Hughes, gent, of Stansty, who is mentioned in the year 1647, and again in 1655, and who appears to have died about the time of the Restoration. He married Eleanor (born Puleston), the widow of Hugh Davies, gent, of Cefn y Cwn (see the Davies pedigree under Town Hill). Then at the beginning of the 18th century a Mr. Ellis Hughes is mentioned as owner of The Yspytty, while a Mr. John Hughes, brazier, occupied the High Street house. On February 10th, 1719-20 " John Hughes, brazier, of W., and Eliz. Matthews of Mold parish " were married at Wrexham, and on July 29th, 1730, " Mr. John Hughes, brazier," was buried, having previously, it would appear, removed to Chester. Then another John Hughes, brazier, of Chester, is mentioned, who if not the son of the first John Hughes, brazier, came into possession of all the Hughes' property above mentioned. I have seen his marriage settlement, which is dated May 24th, 1734. He married Elizabeth, daughter of Joseph Spann, gent, of Bromborough, in the county of Chester, with whom he received £500 as a marriage portion. His will was dated October 23rd, 1749, and he was buried at Wrexham on the second of February following, being described in the register as " Mr. John Hughes, of Stansty, brazier." His widow Mrs. Elizabeth Hughes, of Chester, was buried at Wrexham, August 22nd, 1783, and in a deed which I have seen, dated March 22nd, 1786, Elizabeth Hughes, spinster, of Chester, is described as his " only surviving daughter" and in possession of all the family property. I have lost the note of her death, but she appears to have lived until the very end of last century, the High Street and Rhosddu passing into the possession of one Mr. Davenport, while The Yspytty and the cottages adjoining, and in The Lampint, were purchased by Mr. John Evans (see *Hist. of Older Nonconformity of Wrexham*, p. 68, note 13), aforetime a linen draper in High Street.

9. This will suffice, at present, for the *owners* of The Yspytty, and something must now be said of the several *tenants* of it. The first of these that need be named was Mr. Thomas Hayman, attorney at law, who was here in 1742 and 1747, but who removed about 1748, to Ty Meredith, in Chester Street, and ultimately

settled in Holt Street, under which a full account of him will be found. He was followed by Mr. Vincent Price, surgeon, a very important man in his time, who remained at The Yspytty until his death (buried at Wrexham, April 4th, 1782). He married, firstly (September 13th, 1740, at Wrexham) "Mrs. Catherine Broadfoot of this parish," doubtless one of the Broadfoots of Nos. 31 and 40 High Street (probably Catherine, daughter of Mr. John Broadfoot, born March 20th, 1702-3), who was buried September 8th, 1746, and secondly, also at Wrexham (February 18th, 1747-8), Miss Mary Edwards, of Croesnewydd, sister of the wife of the Rev. Thomas Myddelton, vicar of Melton Mowbray, and also perhaps of the wife of Mr. John Myddelton, apothecary, of Wrexham (see the Myddelton pedigree under No. 34 High Street). These ladies were, Mr. W. M. Myddelton tells me, of Puiford, but lived as friends with Miss Mary Myddelton, of Croes Newydd. Mrs. Mary Price was buried at Wrexham, May 16th, 1761. Immediately after, or a little before, Mr. Price's death, The Yspytty seems to to have been rebuilt, for on March 22nd, 1786, it is described as "all that newly erected messuage and dwelling house, with yard, stable, garden, or orchard, etc. . . . heretofore occupied by Vincent Price, surgeon, deceased." Then, about 1789, Mr. John Evans, hitherto a mercer and clothier, at Nos. 36 and 37 High Street (see *Hist. of Older Nonconformity of Wrexham*, p. 136, note 17), came to live at The Yspytty, and then, or soon after, acquired, the house and all the rest of the property adjoining it, and in The Lampint, all of which passed, on his death in 1796, to Mr. John Burton, his nephew, son of his sister Esther (see the same, p. 83, note 30, and p. 86, note 31). In 1799 Mr. Hayman, probably Mr. Watkin Hayman, who was buried at Worthenbury before the end of that same year (see under Holt Street), was tenant at The Yspytty, and Mrs. Hayman was still living there in 1805. Shortly after, Mr. Burton, having relinquished business, retired to the Yspytty, and here he died in 1813, the property passing, on the marriage of his third daughter with the Rev. John Pearce in 1821, to the latter (see *Hist. of Older Nonconformity of Wrexham*, p.p. 89-94), who lived at The Yspytty until his insolvency in 1853. In 1824 the property is described in the rate books as "house and bank," and I have heard from other sources that a bank was once established or intended to be established on these premises. Perhaps banking was one of the many commercial speculations in which Mr. Pearce was at one time or another engaged. After his failure The Yspytty was bought by Mr. John Lewis, solicitor, and it still forms the offices of Messrs. Lewis & Son. The name "Yspytty" means "Hospice."

10. The present Vicarage did not until 1875 belong to the parish at all, although the late vicar, the Rev. Canon Cunliffe, lived there. The Canon gave to the house the name of "Llwyn Isaf"

(Lower Grove), but it had formerly, equally with the house last
described, been known as " The Yspytty." For the house represen-
ted by the present Vicarage, in 1699 and 1700 a certain Mr. Robert
Lloyd was charged ; and in 1701 " Mr. *Godfrey* Lloyd or tenant,"
in 1704 Mr. Robert Lloyd again, in 1704 " Godfrey Lloyd or Mr.
Robert Lloyd," while in 1707, " Mr. Robert Lloyd, yeoman, of
Spotty " having been buried at Wrexham (May 10th, 1706), the
Upper Yspytty had passed, like the lands of Mr. Robert Lloyd in
Wrexham Fechan, into the possession of " Mr. Edward Hanmer or
tenant." This looks, firstly, as though the Mr. Robert Lloyd of
The Yspytty was connected with Mr. Godfrey Lloyd (see under
No. 43 High Street), and was of the family of Lloyd of Rhydwrial,
and secondly, as though the John Lloyd, of Eglwysegl, mentioned
under Wrexham Fechan, was the same as John Lloyd, of Rhydwrial. The latter we know was the father of Mr. Robert Lloyd,
who was the father of the above named Mr. Godfrey Lloyd.

11. The tenant at "The Upper Yspytty " (as for distinction I
may call it), for many years after Mr. Lloyd's death, was one Robert
Samuel, yeoman, who rented and farmed a great deal of the land
adjoining. He remained here until 1727, when he appears to have
removed to Plas Coch, Stansty. While at " The Spotty," as it is
called in the parish registers, he had a son born to him, called
Watkin, baptized March 20th, 1726-7, afterwards probably the
first Watkin Samuel of Plas Coch. From 1728 until after 1732 a certain Mrs Wynne occupied The Upper Yspytty, which is described in
her time as consisting of " house and croft," and she was succeeded
by " Madam Lloyd," who lived there for many years. Then in
1758 Sir Thomas Longueville, Bart., came to live in the house, and
here in the following year he died, being buried in Wrexham
Church, August 30th, 1759, and described in the register as being
" from the Sputty." From 1760 to 1764 the Rev. John Salusbury
occupied the Upper Yspytty, and then removed to Farndon. Who
he was, I do not know, but I find the entries given at foot
relating to him in the Holt register.[1] The next occupier of The
Upper Yspytty was George Ravenscroft, Esq., of whom I have
given a full account under Mount Street, In 1780 the property is
described as belonging to him, and he had also a croft near, which
had formerly belonged to the Acton Hall estate. After Mr.
Ravenscroft's death (between 1780 and 1782), Mrs. Mary Puleston
widow of Philip Puleston, Esq., of Hafod y wern, bought the place

---

1. Kendrick, son of Rev. John Salisbury, of Wrixam, was interrd 10 Mch.
    1762,
John,   „   „   „   „   „   „ 23 Apl., 1762
    Mrs. Elizabeth, wife of Rev. Mr. John Salisbury, dept. this life Feb. 16, and
        was interred the 24 of same month, 1770.
    Mary, dau. of Rev. John Salisbury, of Holt, interred May 11, 1770.
There was also a " Mr. John Salisbury " who was buried at Holt, July 21st, 1757.

of his executors, and here lived until her death September 22nd, 1802. It then passed to her son-in-law, Bryan Cooke, Esq., of Owston, who let it to the Rev. George Warrington, vicar of Hope, (1778-1796), rector of Pleasley (1793-   ), and canon of St. Asaph (1776-1830), who came to live here about 1804. He had previously lived at Plas Grono, Little Acton, and Cefn, all in this parish. I fancy he was son of George Warrington, Esq., (mentioned under sec. 28, ch. iv). His wife, Mrs Mary Warrington, was the only daughter of Henry Stradwick, of Pentre Pant, Shropshire, and she died May 7th, 1802, while Mr. Warrington was living at Cefn, and was buried at Gresford. Mr. Warrington continued to occupy The Upper Yspytty until his death (May   , 1830) being also buried at Gresford. I copy the following entries from the Wrexham parish registers relating to the children of the Rev. George Warrington :—

July 12th, 1769, Geo. Henry, son of the Revd. Geo Warrington, of Place Gronow, Born 14th of May, Bapt.

Nov. 19, 1770, Stradwick, son of the Rev. Mr. Geo. Warrington, of Place Gronow, was born the 21 of October, bapt. (buried at Gresford while an infant).

Nov 15, 1771, Mary Elizabeth, dau. of Mr. Geo. Warrington, of Place Gronnow, born ye 22 of Octo^r. bapt.

Nov. 13, 1772, William, son of the Reverend George Warrington, of Acton was born the 18 of October, bapt.

May 9, 1774, Anne, Dau^r. of the Rev. Mr. Geo. Warrington, of Acton, was born the 5 of May, and baptized the 9 of June (so!).[2]

Aug. 25, 1775, Philips Warrington, son of the Rev. Mr. George Warrington of Acton, was born the 16 of July, Bapt.

Oct. 1, 1776, Hanmer, son of the Reverend Mr. George Warrington of Acton, was born 5 of September, Bapt. (afterwards Consul at Tripoli).

June 4, 1778, Thornhill, son of the Reverend Mr. Geo. Warrington of Acton, was born the 11 of March, Bapt. (afterwards Captain in the 5th Dragoons, and then in the 8th Hussars).

Eliz'th. Dau^r. of Revend Geo. Warrington of Little Acton, was born the 3rd of June, Baptized the 29th of June, baptiz. againe the 3rd of October, 1780.

May 31, 1782, Harriet, Dau^r. of Rev. G. Warrington of Little Acton, by Mary his wife, (born) March 31st, bapt.[3]

12. Until about the beginning of the present century, the land belonging to The Upper Yspytty was rather limited. In front of it, between the house and Rhosddu Lane, was a long narrow strip extending in one direction past the front of The Lower Yspytty, and in the other a long way up Rhosddu Lane. There was also a croft on the other side of the house extending to the backs of the houses in Lampint Street, and also to the backs of those in Chester Street as far as Chester Street House. But on the north side of the

2. Married at Wrexham (October 8th, 1805), to Jacob Ogden Van Cortlandt, bachelor, then captain in 23rd regiment of foot.

3. Married at Wrexham (Nov 18th, 1805), to Pepard Knight, Esq., of this parish.

house, and coming close up to it, was a field of two acres belonging to the glebe, called " Cae'r Ficer " (The Vicar's field), which stretched on the Rhosddu Lane side from the strip before mentioned belonging to the Upper Yspytty towards Chester Street, extending at this end between the back of Chester Street House and the Baptist Chapel. Philip Davies Cooke, Esq., representative of the Hafod y wern Pulestons, afterwards (April 15th, 1825) obtained possesion of Cae'r Ficer by giving the vicar in exchange for it a portion of Pwll y wrach and a field along Rhosddu Lane, numbered 367 on the map, which was then called "Little Dol y Gierf," that is " Little Dol y Geifr," or *Little Goats' meadow*, but since known as *Garden Field*.[4]

13. In 1827 and 1828 The Upper Yspytty is returned in the rate books as belonging to the Rev. John Pearce of the other Yspytty, who must therefore have bought it of Mr. Davies Cooke. After Mr. Warrington's death, the vicar, the Rev. George Cunliffe (see *Hist. of Par. Church of Wrexham*, p. 70), came to live here, the Vicarage itself being unsuitably situated. He subsequently bought the house, and when in 1875 he resigned the incumbency, presented it to the parish of Wrexham, so that it is now, the old Vicarage being sold, the Vicarage of the parish of Wrexham.

14. The building in the grounds of Llwyn Isaf, close to what is now exclusively called " The Yspytty," formed from the beginning of the present century until his death, the offices of Mr. John Hutchinson, attorney (see under Nos. 11 and 12 Hope Street).

15. There were two or three fields along the east side of Rhosddu Lane that were bought by Mrs. Fryer, of the Groves, and incorporated with the Groves estate. Among these was one called " Cae'r Syfwr," that is " The Receiver's Field," but which gradually became corrupted, first, into " Cae Syfern " and then into " Cae Saffron " *(The Saffron Field)*.

16. The Welsh Church, dedicated to Saint David, was built in the Vicarage grounds, in 1889, and the first service was held in it on Saturday, St. David's Day, 1890, although it was not completed until some months afterwards. A great part of the money with which it was built was obtained by the sale to the Wrexham, Mold, and Connah's Quay Railway of a portion of St. Mark's churchyard. It is built of stone, and consists of nave, chancel, organ chamber and vestry, 248 sittings being provided. The architect was Mr. Howell Davies, of Wrexham, and the contractor Mr. J Gethin, of Shrewsbury.

17. Several fields on both sides of Rhosddu Lane were formerly cut up into quillets, and one quillet containing 1R 26P, was still in existence in the year 1830, lying in the field numbered 348 in the map, at that time called " Cae'r dderwen gron," *The field of the round oak,*

4. This and a small close in Stansty were afterwards exchanged for a garden in front of Saint Mark's church.

CHAPTER VII.

Chester Street.

1. Chester Street, often formerly called "Chester Lane," was, as I have elsewhere explained (see *Hist. of Nonconformity of Wrexham,* p. 57, and p. 78 note 21, and p. 127), sometimes, along with Lamb-pit and Holt Streets, regarded as a distinct district, and called "The Lampint," or "The Lampit."

2. As one entered Chester Street from High Street, there would be found at the right hand corner the very ancient inn, since rebuilt, now called "The Feathers," but formerly "The Plume of Feathers," which belonged for at least two hundred years to the Merediths of Pentrebychan. It was a good inn of the second class. The following abstract of a lease I have seen relating to it, may be of interest. The lease is dated January 17th, 1742-3, and is between Thomas Meredith, of Wrexham, Esquire, on the one part, and James Howarth, John Parkes, Thomas Hulme, and John Winterbottom, of Manchester; James Hulton, of Blackley, and Benjamin Blinkhorn, of Pendleton, all of the county palatine of Lancaster, and Ebenezer Gellibrand of Stockport, chapmen, on the other part. The lease grants the Feathers, with a yard adjoining between Chester Street and a certain street leading to the Beast Market, with brew house, large stable, hay chamber and large yard opposite to the sign of the Three Eagles *with privilege to erect booths or shops on any part of the said premises.* We shall meet with the name of one of the Lancashire chapmen again, but it is worth noticing that it was in the yard and rooms of the Old Feathers Inn these chapmen set up their mart for cotton goods at the March fair, which ultimately developed, on another site, into what was called "The Manchester Square."

3. All the houses and land on the east side of Chester Street, up to and including the large house opposite the Municipal Buildings, belonged also to the Merediths of Pentrebychan. This house, which for distinction I am accustomed to call "Ty Meredith," was of considerable importance, and, before its front was modernized more than fifty years ago, must have been very picturesque. Some of the rooms are still very quaint, and over one of the fire-places is a curious bit of old carved oak panelling, which is worth looking at. One or other of the Merediths themselves often lived there, but after they had acquired The Court, this was never the case, and the house was let at rent. It was sometimes divided into

three and sometimes let as one house.   Among those who occupied
it at different times were (1748-1759) Thomas Hayman, Esq.,
(see ch. viii. sec. 4, and Index), (1760-1764) Richard Surridge, (or
Surwich),[1] Esq., and (1764-1770) Rev. John Yale (see Index   ).
But the first tenant concerning whom it is necessary for me to say
anything is Owen Wynne, Esq., of Llwyn, who occupied Ty
Meredith from about 1771 to his death in 1780.   He had already
lived so much in this town and neighbourhood, that three of his
four children were born within the parish of Wrexham.   These
were Watkin Edward (eldest son, afterwards owner of Llwyn),
Owen (who succeeded his brother), and Eleanor (afterwards wife of
Philip Lloyd Fletcher, of Gwernhaulod).   The following are the
entries recording their baptism in the Wrexham registers :—

> Apl. 19, 1754, Watkin Edwards, son of Owen Wynne of Llwyn, Esq.,
> born at Escless 13(th inst).
>
> August 16, 1757, Owen, son of Owen Wynn of Llwyn, Esqr., born at
> Croes Newydd
>
> Oct. 29, 1758, Eleanor, Daur. of Owen Wynn, Esqr., of Llwyn, B(orn)
> 17.

Mr. Owen Wynne married secondly at Wrexham (August 7th,
1772), Mrs. Susannah Lloyd, daughter of Broughton Whitehall,
Esq., and widow of John Lloyd, Esq., of Hafod un nos, his first
wife having died November 16th, 1761, aged 30.

4. The next tenant of Ty Meredith was Mr. Richard Myddelton
Massie Lloyd, who commonly wrote his name "Richard Lloyd" only.
He was one of the sons of Mr. Thomas Lloyd, mercer, High Street,
who was the younger brother of William Lloyd, Esq., the elder,
of Plas Power.   Mr. Richard Lloyd carried on at first the business
of a flannel merchant and had on his premises in Chester Street
a large warehouse for the storing of his stock in trade, but, at least
as early as 1785, started a banking business, which was afterwards
carried on by his son.   The room used as a bank was the
large panelled one which is on your right as you enter the front
door of No. 46.   He married, January 19th, 1782, at Wrexham,
Mary, one of the daughters and co-heiresses of William Bowey, of
by Chester, whom he had two sons and two daughters, namely :—
William, afterwards Sir William Lloyd, knight, of Bryn Estyn, born
October 30th, 1782 ; Mary Ann, born August 27th, 1787, died unmarried January 17th, 1814, and was buried at Wrexham ; Eliza,
born March 6th 1789, died unmarried January 25th, 1814, and was
buried at Wrexham ; and Richard Myddelton Massie, born January
4th, 1794   Mr. Richard Lloyd acquired, about the year 1786, the
kt. estate of Bryn Estyn, formerly belonging to Sir Thomas Kyffyn,

---

1. Richard Surridge, Esq., had formerly lived in Hope Street, and died at
Ty Meredith, being buried at Wrexham, October 24th, 1764.   Compare the names
" Surwich " and " Norwich."

He died at Bath, January 31st, 1814, and was buried there in the church of St. Peter and Paul, and was succeeded in his house and the management of the bank, by his second son, the elder son taking Bryn Estyn, though he seems to have had also, *at first*, some share in the management of the bank, for in 1816 he is described as captain and *banker*. Mr. R. M. M Lloyd, the younger, like his father, seems to have discarded part of his name for he was always called "R. M. Lloyd," and so wrote his signature. He married, first, Charlotte Smith, spinster, of Northampton (settlement before marriage dated May 17th, 1818), by whom he had no issue, and who was buried at Wrexham, September 24th, 1830 ; and secondly Sarah Price, spinster, of Brondyffryn, near Denbigh, daughter I believe of John Price, Esq , of Denbigh, with whom he had £10,720 (settlement before marriage dated October 29th, 1832), who was 17 years younger than himself, and by whom he had issue. Mr. R. M. Lloyd took a prominent position in society and public affairs, and in 1824 was high sheriff of Denbighshire, but in 1849 became hopelessly bankrupt, and as his assets, compared with his liabilities, were absurdly small, many of his depositors were involved in financial ruin, or seriously embarassed. He went to live at Birkenhead, and died May 22nd, 1860, being buried at Wallasey churchyard, where his tombstone may still be seen.

5. We will now cross the street and say something as to the large house which stood formerly where " The Long Pull " now is, and which in 1668 was owned and occupied by Thomas Rosindale, gent, and was until nearly the middle of the next century occupied by his family. It will be simplest, I think, to throw all that I know about this family into the form of a pedigree, (see p. 96).

6. It was Dr. Michael Rosindale who built on leased land adjoining his garden the old Cockpit, " or conveniency for the flighting of cocks," which ultimately passed into the possession of the trustees of the Presbyterian Chapel, and was pulled down in 1884.

7. These Rosindales owned a great deal of other property in Wrexham and the neighbourhood, for example :—The Cock in Farndon Street; the fields numbered 380, 381 and 382 in the map, and some lands adjoining these last in Acton, called "Erw'r groes " and " Erw Sant Silin," (*Saint Silin's Acre*).

8. After the death of Miss Frances Rosindale in 1750, the house seems to have been purchased by Messrs. Blinkhorn & Co., otherwise The Manchester Company, apparently composed of those, or some of those, who had in 1743 leased the Plume of Feathers, and, if the rate books are to be trusted, in their possession it remained until nearly the end of the century. On a part of the garden or orchard was ultimately erected what was called " The Manchester Square," used at the March fair for the sale of cotton goods, while

the house was turned into an inn, and was called in 1771 " The Angel." During the tenancy of Mrs. Worrall, certainly as early as 1786, and as late as 1814, the Post Office was kept here, but was about the latter date transferred to No. 36 Chester Street, the house of Mr. John Roberts, afterwards of Rhyd Broughton. On the site of The Manchester Hall, the Pedlers' or General Market has recently been erected.

9. A full account of the Presbyterian (now Congregational) Chapel has been given in *The History of the Older Nonconformity of Wrexham*, and a detailed history of the old Grammar School, now the Municipal Buildings, will be found at the end of this chapter.

10. Strange as it may seem, many persons, important by reason of their social standing, lived at the house which at the beginning of this century was made into an inn—The Rose and Crown. But we will not speak of these, but pass on[2] to deal with that which is now called

2. Perhaps I should have said something of The Seven Stars at the corner of Lampit and Chester Streets. This house belonged to the Merediths of Pentrebychan. I first find it mentioned as an inn, under the name of "The Star," in the year 1769, being then kept by Mr. John Edisbury.

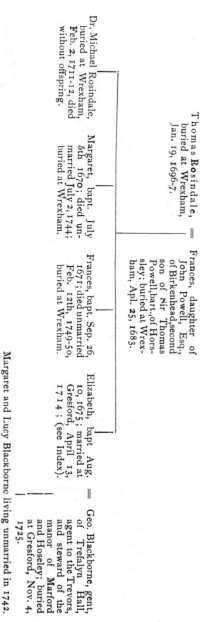

Thomas **Rosindale**, buried at Wrexham, Jan. 19, 1696-7. = Frances, daughter of John Powell, Esq., of Birkenhead, second son of Sir Thomas Powell, bart., of Horsley; buried at Wrexham, Apl. 25, 1683.

Dr. Michael Rosindale, buried at Wrexham, Feb. 2, 1711-12, died without offspring.

Margaret, bapt. July 5th 1670; died unmarried July 2, 1744; buried at Wrexham.

Frances, bapt. Sep. 26, 1671; died unmarried Feb. 12th, 1749-50, buried at Wrexham.

Elizabeth, bapt. Aug. 10, 1675; married at Gresford, April 13, 1714; (see Index). = Geo. Blackborne, gent., of Trefalyn Hall, agent to the Trevors, and steward of the manor of Marford and Hoseley; buried at Gresford, Nov. 4, 1725.

Margaret and Lucy Blackborne living unmarried in 1742.

" Chester Street House." There appears to have been no large house here before 1727 when it is described in the rate books as " Mr. Rd. Jones' new house." The first person of importance whom I can find occupying it was Dr. Apperley. The Apperleys were for two generations so closely connected with the parish that some account must here be given of them, but as this account must be rather a long one, I shall insert it under a distinct heading at the end of this chapter. After Dr. Apperley's death in 1772, John Matthews, Esq., attorney-at-law, came to live in the house, and there continued to live for the rest of his life, with the exception of a few years spent in Wrexham Fechan. During the whole of this time Chester Street House belonged to him. Mr. Matthews was descended through John Matthews, Esq., of Harnage (who died in 1635), from Elystan Glodrudd, and was the head, actually or prospectively, of the family of Matthews of Eyarth and Bostock Hall, Denbighshire.[3] He married at Wrexham, May 18th, 1780, Mary, daughter of William Jones, Esq., of Wrexham Fechan (see ch. xvii, sec. 4), by whom he had the after-named children, all of whom were baptized at Wrexham :—Sarah, born May 28th, bapt. September 28th, 1781, afterwards the wife of John Grey, Esq.;[4] Mary, born June, bapt. September 30th, 1782, died unmarried at Kenure Park, near Dublin (the residence of Sir Wm. Hen. Roger Palmer), May 5th, 1862, and was buried at Wrexham ; Frances, bapt. January 7th, 1785, who married November 23rd, 1820, at Wrexham, the Rev. Nathaniel Roberts, of the parish of Oswestry, afterwards of Cefn Park, near Wrexham ; John, bapt. July 1787 ; and Thomas, born January 26th, 1793, buried at Wrexham, November 20th, 1826. There was a fourth daughter, the date of whose birth or baptism I cannot give—Eleanora, who married March 4th, 1828, Sir Roger William Henry Palmer, Bart., of Kenure Park, county Dublin. I believe both the sons died without issue. Mr. John Matthews was buried at Wrexham, January 13th, 1807, where also was buried his widow, November 24th, 1828.

11. Mrs. Matthews continued to live at Chester Street House until the death of her son Thomas, and then Thomas Taylor Griffith, Esq., F.R.C.S., the skilful and well remembered surgeon

3. Mr. Robert Matthews, the son of the Rev. Maurice Matthews, the second son of John Matthews, Esq., of *Harnage*, was buried at Erbistock, March 10th. 1714-15. He had, by his wife, Prudence, the following sons all baptized at Erbistock :—Robert, born November 28th, 1696 ; Maurice, bapt. November 4th, 1699 ; and John, bapt. July 25th, 1709. From which one of these Mr. John Matthews, of *Wrexham*, was derived, and what was the line of descent, I have been unable to learn

4. Mr. Grey was a Northumberland man, had practised as a surgeon in London, was afterwards for some time resident director of " The Welsh Iron and Coal Mining Company, Coed Talwrn," and lived at Hartsheath. This was in 1825. Charles Matthews in his *Autobiography* gives an amusing account of him.

went to live in it, and there remained for the rest of his life. He
was the son and heir of Thomas Griffith, Esq., of whom a full
account is given under Queen Street. He received his education
at Dr. Daniel Williams' school connected with the old Presbyterian
Chapel, Chester Street (see *Hist. of Nonconformity of Wrexham*, p.
82), and at the Grammar School, Wrexham. After serving his
apprenticeship with his father, he perfected his preparations for his
profession in London, at Leeds, and in Paris. Then he returned
to Wrexham, and for a time was partner with his father, but
ultimately started at Chester Street House a practice of his own.
In the same year, 1826, he married Mary Ann, eldest daughter of
Captain Robertson, of Keavel, Fifeshire, son of Robertson the
historian, and had three children, all baptized at Wrexham Church,
namely :—Thomas Llewelyn, born February, bapt. April
29th, 1828, now the head of the family and rector of Deal ; James
Drummond, born July 22nd, 1829, afterwards of Balliol College,
Oxford, and barrister-at-law ; and Elizabeth, born July 24th, 1832,
who died young, September 1839. Mr. T. T. Griffith had an
extraordinary and well merited reputation as a medical practitioner,
and was much beloved as a man. He was for many years president
of the North Wales branch of the British Medical Association, and
largely concerned in the founding of the Wrexham Infirmary, at
first in York Street, and then in 1838, on its present site. He
founded also the Wrexham Ragged Schools, afterwards called The
Free Schools, now extinct. For many years treasurer of the
Wrexham branch of the Bible Society, he was always an eloquent
speaker at its annual meetings. Not long before his death a sum
of money was raised by public subscription so that his portrait
might be painted and hung in the committee room of the Infirmary.
When the borough was incorporated in 1857, Mr. Griffith was
earnestly pressed to became its first mayor. These solicitations he
resisted, but he gave £200 to the new corporation, which has been
found very useful, and which is known as " Griffith's Fund."
Mr. Griffith was at work almost to the last, dying after a short
illness, July 6th, 1876, aged 81. He was buried in the Old Cemetery.
His wife died the next year, June 4th, 1877, aged 82, and was also
there buried.

12. On the other side of Chester Street, from Holt Street to
Bodhyfryd almost every dwelling represents an ancient house and
has its own history, but I will pass over them all, and only pause
to say something of the house which in recent years has been
called " Bodhyfryd." This house belonged formerly to the
Dymocks of Little Acton, one of whom, Mr. William Dymock,
occupied it till his death in 1764, he being then high sheriff of the
county. To avoid confusion, my account of these Dymocks is
given under a separate heading at the end of this chapter. By
the marriage to Mr. Robert Wynne, of Elizabeth, only daughter

and heir of the above-named Mr. Dymock, Bodhyfryd passed, with the rest of the Dymock property, into the possession of the Wynnes of Garthewin, to whom it still belongs. Mr. Robert Wynne himself occupied Bodhyfryd for a few years (1755.9), and some years later (1801-4) a Captain Thomas Lee, who was engaged in the African trade. Subsequently it was leased for certain lives to Mr. Joseph Cooper (see ch. viii, note 3), and this lease is still in existence. The fields marked on the annexed map, 19, 21, 24, 394, 395, 412, 388 and 389 pertained to this house, and the whole holding contained 19 acres.

13. None of the houses on the other side of Chester Street, north of Chester Street House, seem to require notice, and I have given in my *History of the Nonconformity of Wrexham*, a full account both of the Baptist Chapel, and of the erection of the Groves House. But it is desirable to say something of the history of the house last-named after Mr. James Buttall's death in 1793. Not long after (about 1797), Mrs. Fryer (see *Hist. of Par. Church of Wrexham*, p. 209), widow of John Fryer, Esq., of Aldermanbury, London, took the house and ultimately bought it, and there lived until her death in 1817. Then Mr. Ephraim Parkins bought it, and a Mr. James Jackson started in it a private school which, by one or another, has been carried on ever since. Mr. Jackson was followed, about 1842, by Mr. Matthew Sibson, who in turn was succeeded by Mr. James Parkins, a kinsman of the owner. Then somewhere about 1861 the school was taken in hand by the late honoured Mr. J. Pryce Jones, who died November 24th, 1877, and was followed by Mr. W. J. Russell, B.A. Mrs. Fryer considerably enlarged the lands belonging to The Groves, purchasing several fields near it, so that in 1844, the grounds comprised nearly 22 acres and extended northwards along Chester Road and Rhosddu Lane a little beyond Grove Road, which latter was opened on Mr. Parkins' land about 1855, Bodlondeb and High Grove being the first houses built in it.

14. Bodhyfryd on one side and the Baptist Chapel House on the other were, until about the middle of the present century, the last houses that could be seen along the Chester Road as one passed out of the town towards Chester. Beyond this point, Chester Road was very irregular not merely as to its width, but also as to its direction. The course of the old road can easily be discerned, on the east side of the present Chester Road on both sides of Rhosnessney Lane, by the trees which lined its banks and by other signs. And within Acton Park, it still exists, as a noble double avenue. I have marked by dotted lines on the map of Wrexham, herewith given, a part of its course. It ultimately became identical with the present road which runs between Acton Hall and Acton House and past Pant Iocyn. This road, which we now call " The backway to Gresford," was until towards the end of last century

the highway from Wrexham to Chester. It was continued past Gresford Church, along Pant Lane, past the old Pant Wesleyan Chapel, beyond which it is still quite recognizable, above the present Marford Hill, coming out into the existing high road at Marford between the Marford Arms and the cottage near it, in the back garden of which traces may still be discerned.

15. The fields on both sides of Chester Street were in the sixteenth and seventeenth centuries called "The Common Fields," or "The Town Fields," or in Welsh "Meusydd y Dre." And it will be noticed, on referring to the map, that so late as 1844, the fields numbered 384, 385, 396, 393 and 386, on the east side of Chester Road, were each still called "Townfield," though all of them belonged exclusively to the Acton estate. Indeed all the land west of Chester Street, on each side of Rhosddu Lane and Regent Street, as far as the brook, included "common fields," but as, by the beginning of the seventeenth century, the lands along Chester Road exhibited more strikingly than the lands in any other part of the town the marks characteristic of common fields, the name "Maes y dre" had by this time become restricted to the lands in question. "Meusydd y dre," or more commonly the singular form "Maes y dre" *(Townfield)*, was then formerly the generic name of the area on each side of Chester Road, as far north as Rhosnessney Lane. As I do not possess details of the condition of this area, earlier than the beginning of the seventeenth century, I shall give an account of it as it was at that time, and at times somewhat later. This area was not an open tract, but consisted of many enclosed pieces of land, with the names of which we shall make ourselves acquainted as we proceed. But each close contained various strips of land, each strip belonging to a different owner. Often the same owner had several strips in the same close, separated from one another by strips belonging to other owners. These strips were called in English "pieces," "parcels" and "quillets," and in Welsh "drylliau" *(pieces)*, "ysgythrau" *(cuttings)*, but much more commonly "Erwau" *(acres)*. In local deeds, in fact, the strips are often described as "those pieces or *errowes* of land under known metes and bounds" situate in such and such closes. At the time I am speaking of, the quillets, as I shall henceforth call them, varied a great deal in area, but this was in great measure because, even before the end of the 16th century, the process of adding quillet to quillet, by purchase or exchange, had already begun. Many of the quillets had specific names, as "Erw Gam" *(Crooked Acre)*, "Erw glai" *(The Clay Acre)*, "Erw'r Stryt" *(The Street Acre)*, "Erw'r Pwll" *(The Pool Acre)*, "Erwau'r Ysgubor" *(The Barn Acres)*, "Erw Fechan" *(The Little Acre)*, "Erw Fawr" *(The Big Acre)*, "Erw Dda" *(The Good Acre)*, "Erw Goch" *(The Red Acre)*, "Erw'r Delyn *(Acre of the Harp)*, and the like. Not all the names of the quillets were compounded of the

word " erw " but most of them were, and from this fact, and from the fact already mentioned that the general name for these strips was " errowes," I am inclined to believe that an " erw " or acre, was taken to be their normal area. Now it can be proved up to the hilt, that "the customary acre" of Wrexham and all the regions adjacent, was in the 16th, 17th and 18th centuries regarded as containing 10,240 square yards, and that this customary acre was divided into four roods, each containing 2,560 square yards. It is also clear from a study of the Welsh laws that the word " erw," which so often occurs therein, would be much more accurately translated " rood " than " acre," and, although abov., following modern usage, I have translated " erw " as " acre," I have little doubt that the erw was really the customary rood or " cyfar " of 2,560 square yards. The Venedotian Code mentions a measuring rod containing 16 of Dyfnwal's feet—" gwialen gyhyd a'r hir iau," *a rod equal in length to the long yoke.* As Dyfnwal's foot contained 9 inches, the rod in question was equal to one of 12 statute feet in length. If with this rod we set out a strip 8 rods broad, and 20 rods long, as they actually do in Brecknockshire to this day, we get the rood of 2,560 square yards, called in Brecknockshire and also in the lordships of Hope and Mold, "a cyfar." But neither in field names nor in the immediate neighbourhood of Wrexham, have I met with the word "cyfar," though four or five miles to the north west it was in common use. In fact, it would seem that the area called in and near Hope and Mold a " cyfar," was in and near Wrexham called an "erw," and that both the cyfar and the erw contained 2,560 square yards. The strips were not separated from each other, in later times at any rate, by balks or strips of unploughed land, but their extent was marked by four " merestones" set at their four corners on which the initials of the owners were cut.

16. And here, before I go further, it may be well to explain in what sense the Common Fields were common. They were not, as far back at least as the end of the 16th century, common in the sense of belonging to the community. The strips in the common fields belonged either to freeholders or to leaseholders who had a right, on a certain fine being paid, to the renewal of their leases from the lord, and so had a definite property in them. The fields were only common in this sense, that the closes were not held by a single person, but by many persons who held various portions or quillets in them. I cannot even find that there were rights of pasture or any other rights exercised over them by the community at any time of the year. One of the closes containing quillets belonging to three several persons was called "Cae Marthin Fychan " (*The field of Martin the Little*), showing that it had originally belonged to a single person—Martin the Little. I have already in the first volume of this series—*The History of Ancient*

Tenures of Land in the Marches of North Wales—explained how the quillets in the Common Fields were in part the result of the operation of the common plough (which produced the *normal* quillets containing one erw or cyfar each), and in part the result of the operation of the custom of gavelkind, or equal distribution of the property of a deceased owner among his children (which produced those quillets, which, though of equal area in the same field contained more or less than an acre).

17. There are two other interesting points as to the quillets in the Town Fields, of which something may be said. First, as already has been pointed out, some of them belonged to freeholders, and others (the largest number of them), to leaseholders; but the freeholders' quillets were intermixed in the strangest way with those of the leaseholders. Secondly, although a group of quillets (generally from three to six), scattered over the Town Fields is stated in old surveys and deeds to *pertain* to some ancient messuage in the town itself, it did not pertain *indissolubly* thereto, and I find that even at the end of the 16th century owners of ancient messuages in the town, had begun to sell their quillets in the Town Fields to other quillet holders, who wished to enlarge their holdings. And this process has gone on continuously to the present day until not a single quillet is now left.

18. Having said so much of the general characteristics of the old Town Fields, we will now descend to particulars. And we will describe as far as possible the character of the fields in detail on the west side of Chester Road, walking northwards from the Baptist Chapel to the township bounds, and returning on the other side of the road.

19. The quilleted close nearest the town, within which the Groves House was built, was called "Pant y crydd" (*The shoemaker's hollow*), and immediately adjoining it was another quilleted close called "Pant y glofer" (*The glover's hollow*). Pant y crydd, and I suppose Pant y glofèr also, was situated in an area known as "Maes y dre ucha" (*The Upper Town Field*). About the year 1765, Mr. Jas. Buttall bought certain quillets in these fields, and in June of the year following made an exchange of some of these with others belonging to Thomas Meredith, Esq., of Pentrebychan, so as to get as much land lying together as possible to serve as grounds for the house which he had already built in Pant y crydd. I have been permitted to take a tracing of the plan of these two fields attached to the deed of exchange, and a copy of this I herewith give as an illustration of the manner in which, so late as the middle of last century, after all the attempts made to abolish quillets, many of the fields of Wrexham were still cut up. In a map of 1825 three quillets in the Groves ground belonging to the Pentrebychan estate are still shown, but in the map of 1844 they are not marked, but when the National Eisteddfod pavilion was being

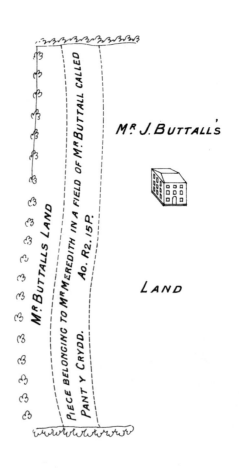

MR J.BUTTALL'S

LAND

PLOT OF TWO FIELDS IN WREXHAM REGIS A.D. 176●

The Quick hedges are marked thus :- ᴄ₃₅₅₃₅₃

Meres are marked thus :- --------------

Mr. MEREDITH'S LAND

A PIECE BELONGING TO Mr. BUTTALL ON THE
S.W. SIDE OF PANT Y GLOFER.
A R P
0 . 3 . 7

Mr. BUTTALL'S LAND.

PIECE
BELONGING
TO Mr. MEREDITH
IN A FIELD OF Mr.
BUTTALL CALLED PANT
Y GLOFER. A. R. P.
0 . 1 . 2

ROAD FROM WREXHAM TO CHESTER

N

WOODALL, MINSHALL & THOMAS, LITHOS. WREXHAM.

erected in a field belonging to Roseneath, immediately north of Grove Park, when the workmen were digging a trench for the gas pipes, they disinterred an old mere-stone with the letters T.M. upon it, letters which were doubtless the initials of the name of Thomas Meredith, Esq.

20. North of Pant y glofer were other quilleted closes, one of which is called in Norden's Survey of A.D. 1620 " Kae yr Synor," which should probably be written, according to modern spelling " Cae'r swynwr " (*The wizard's field*), and of which another of considerable size is variously named in the aforesaid survey. It is ten times called " Tale y gyfer," and once " Tal y geifr." I fancy the proper form of the name should be "Talar y geifr " (*The goats' headland*), and it is certain that two fields were until recent times (see the map) called " The Goat's Meadow" and " The Goat's Field " which must have occupied the site, or part of the site, of the close whose name is now under discussion.

21. Crossing the lane leading to Rhosddu we come now to the three fields marked in the map 380, 381, and 382. These fields belonged in 1620, except one parcel of two customary acres called "Y Wern" (*The alder marsh*), to Michael Jones and Catherine Jones, his mother (then recently dead), and were known in English as "Acton Moor " and in Welsh as " Gwaun y terfyn " (*The boundary moor*) which latter was a very suitable name, as their outer edge formed the boundary between the townships of Wrexham Regis and Acton. About the time of the Restoration, they belonged to Thomas Rosindale of Chester Street (see sec. 5), whose descendants, Margaret and Frances Rosindale, and Elizabeth Blackborne, mortgaged them to Mr. Edward Brown of Liverpool, from whose executors they were bought about the year 1752 by Mr. Thomas Hayman (see under Holt Street), whose heirs sold them (September 29th, 1789) to Sir Foster Cunliffe, Bart., then of Saighton, Cheshire, afterwards of Acton Hall. By this time the fields had lost their old name, and No. 382 had come to be called " Cae aderyn y bwn " (*The field of the bittern*). The area of the last named field was much diminished soon after by the formation of the new Chester Road, so that a large portion of it became enclosed in Acton Park.

22. We now cross the Chester Road, and deal with that portion of the township of Wrexham Regis which lies within Acton Park. Next the old Chester Road and on the east side of it were two closes belonging in 1620 to John Jeffreys, Esq., of which one was called " Cae Erddylad " (*Erddylad's field*), and the other " Cae tan y wern Acton " (*Field below Acton Alder Marsh*). The former of these names appears to have been corrupted to " Erw'r tyfod," and in 1790 a memorandum appears in the rate books that a part of "Cae aderyn y bwn " (on the other side of Chester Road) had been added to " Erw'r tyfod," a memorandum which gives the

approximate date of the construction of the new Chester Road.
John Jeffreys, Esq. also possessed at the same time another close
at the eastern end of that portion of Wrexham Regis which now
lies within Acton Park, which was called "Cae Wad," a name
which continued in use until the park was enclosed towards the
end of last century. But until a little before that operation was
completed a great part of Wrexham Regis now within the park
did not belong to the Acton estate at all, but belonged to the
Traverses of Trefalyn House, and of this portion (which was called
"The Two Werns"), Sir Foster Cunliffe is for the first time
returned in the rate books as the owner in the year 1789. "Cae
Wad" is a very curious name, and means, I believe "Wad's Field,"
a name which ore cannot but compare with "Clawdd Wad," the
Welsh name for Wat's Dyke.

23. The whole of the triangular area between Chester Road on
the west, Rhosnessney Lane on the north, and the footpath which
connects these two highways, an area which comprises over $56\frac{1}{2}$
acres, belonged in 1844 with the exception of Nos. 388 and 389[5] to
the Acton estate. But this was not always so. This area was
formerly full of intermixed quillets belonging to different persons.
The first John Jeffreys, Esq., of Acton, bought a good many of
these quillets. Ellis Yonge, Esq., who came into possession
of Acton in 1747 gradually bought other quillets in the same area,
and this process was continued by Sir Foster Cunliffe, Bart. (who
bought Acton in 1787), and by his son Sir Robert Henry Cunliffe,
Bart., until the area was brought to the condition in which it is
shown in the map of 1844.

24. Many of the closes within this area bore names that are
worthy of record. There were "Maes y dre isaf" (*The lower
town field*), "Maes y dre fawr" (*The great town field*),
"Tiroedd ceimion" (*Crooked lands*), "Perth y benglog" (*Bush of
the skull*), "Plas Iorwerth ap Einion" (*Place of Iorwerth ap
Einion*), and Erw glai. Of none of these do I know the exact
position, except the last named, and this was originally part of
Talar y geifr on the opposite side of the way, from which it was
cut off when the new Chester Road was made. It was on Erw
glai that Beech's barn stood.

25. In the fields numbered 397 and 398 on the map is an avenue
of trees parallel with and just above the present Rhosnessney
Lane. I believe this avenue represents the *old* Rhosnessney Lane,
that it was abandoned, on account of the difference of level, when
the Chester Road was made, and that the present lane, or rather
the western end of it, was at that time made.

---

5. The two fields numbered 388 and 389, which look like enclosed quillets,
belong to Bodhyfryd, 388 containing 3R 30P, and 389, 3R 35P.

26. I owe to Sir Robert A. Cunliffe, Bart., who has kindly permitted me to examine his deeds, the opportunity of making myself acquainted with many of the foregoing particulars relating to the Common Fields of Wrexham, particulars which show how much those fields differed from the Common Fields of England.

WREXHAM GRAMMAR SCHOOL.

27. Valentine Broughton, an alderman of Chester, and a member of the family of Broughton of Marchwiel, Bersham, and Broughton, who died June 18th, 1603, left the sum of £6 13 4 a year for ever "towards the maintenance of the schoolmaster for the time being in the town of Wrexham, for the education of youth in good condition and learning there."[6] Valentine Broughton is generally reckoned the founder of the Grammar School of Wrexham, but in his bequest the schoolmaster is assumed to be already existing, and in the will of Edward Jones, Esq., of Plas Cadwgan (dated January 7th, 1580-1, proved May 20th, 1581), occurs the following passage:—" In case a benefice or living, of £30 yearly at the least, be obtained from the Bp. of St. Asaph, it is to be for finding a free school at Wrexham, and my Exors. to give £18 to the use thereof, over and above the £18 heretofore bequeathed by Sr. David ap Edwarde late vicar of Ruabon." I find from the Ruabon registers that the full name of the vicar just mentioned was David ap Edward ap David ap Robert. If this Sir David ap Edward was not of the testator's family (as Mr. Jones' will suggests) it was probably David ap Edward ap David ap Robert of Plas Issa, Stansty, who was certainly a contemporary of the vicar, and like him was sometimes called " David Edwards."

28. In Norden's Survey of 1620 a " barn in the Lampint" is described as being " adjacent to the schoolhouse," from which it appears that the schoolhouse stood then where it has stood down to our own time. This also is probably the schoolhouse which elsewhere in the same survey is described as held freely by the [church] wardens, with a garden of one customary rood (2560 square yards), at an annual quit rent of 2d. The large open space between the school and Chester Street, where was then a great pool called " Y Pwll Mawr," did not at that time, or did not belong wholly, to the school.

29. I can find no further mention of Wrexham School, or of any of its masters, until 1657, when, under date October 19th Philip Henry writes in his diary " my good friend MR. MADDOCKS usher of Wrexham School dyed." A little later we find a MR. JEFFREY WILLIAMS mentioned as usher of the school, and in the Chirk

6. Alderman Broughton left besides, £3 6 8 to the singing men and "quiristers" in the parish church of Wrexham, but *ultimately* both bequests were paid to the schoolmaster.

Castle Account Books (as Mr. W. M. Myddelton tells me), there is recorded under date July 30th, 1664, the gift of 40s to " Mr. Jeffrey Williams, usher of the Schoole of Wrexham, towards the enlarginge of the scholehoase of Wrexham." Mr. Jeffrey Williams was buried in the churchyard, August 19th, 1683, when he is described as "schoolmaster of Wrex." Now during the whole time of Mr. Williams' connection with Wrexham School MR. AMBROSE LEWIS (see *Hist. of Par. Church of Wrexham*, p. 75, sec. 10) is also described as connected with the school. It is pretty certain he was *head* master and that Mr. Williams was subordinate to him. Licensed in 1662, Mr. Lewis was still "schoolmr." in 1678, and was buried in Wrexham churchyard, January 2nd, 1698-9, but had, it seems evident, ceased to be connected with the school for a long time before his death. He was a man of considerable local importance, but as I have said a great deal about him in my *Hist. of the Older Nonconformity of Wrexham*, I will say nothing further of him here.

30. As no records belonging to the school were found when in 1880 it was finally closed, in attempting to compile a fuller list of the masters than has yet been published, I am thrown back on such references to the earlier masters as can be found in the parish registers and elsewhere, in doing which, however, I am exposed to the danger of naming some as masters who were merely ushers.

31. In May 1686, the burial of " MR. STEPHEN JONES, schoolmaster of Wrex." is recorded in the registers.

32. Towards the end of the 17th century the name of a MR. JOHN STODDART begins to be mentioned. On October 23rd, 1624, he was married at Wrexham Church, to "Mrs. Christian Andrews" (grand-daughter of Captain Roger Myddelton of Plas Cadwgan), and on March 2nd, 1696-7, the baptism of his son Hugh is recorded. As he is called " John Stoddart, gent," the probability is that he was not in orders. I do not find him mentioned after 1699. He lived in Bridge Street.

33. A few years later the name of MR. THOMAS UPTON, who although he lived in The Green, was I believe, a master of The Grammar School, occurs :—The following entries relating to him in the parish register may be quoted :—

> May 18, 1707, Elizabeth, Da. of Thomas Upton, Schoolmaster, of the green, born 12, Bapt. 18th.
> Sept. 12, 1707, Tho., son of Tho. Upton, Schoolmaster of Wrexham, Buryed.
> Mch. 26, 1708, Mr. Thomas Upton, Schoolmaster of green Buryed.

34. Then in 1715 comes this entry :—" Sept. MR. WM. LLOYD, Head Schoolmaster, Buryed."

35. In 1717 about £80 were raised by subscription to repair the schoolhouse, which had become very ruinous (Archdeacon Thomas).

36. In September 1723, the REV. JOHN APPLETON is specifically described as "headmaster of Wrexham Grammar School" and this is the first time that I have found the school called "The Grammar School." On April 30th, 1725, Mr. Appleton was married at Erbistock to Eleanor Pulford, who appears to have been a daughter of Alexander Pulford, gent, of Wrexham (see ch. xvii, sec. 31). The two following entries relating to Mr. Appleton occur in the parish registers :—

Nov. 23, 1729, Alexander, child of Mr. John Appleton, Schoolmaster, of W'em, Buryed.

Dec. 8, 1729, Elinor, wife of Mr. John Appelton, Schoolmaster, Buryed.

In Mr. Appleton's time, Mr. John Roberts (buried March 16th, 1724-5), was usher.

37. After 1729 I do not find Mr. Appleton mentioned, and it is this very year that Archdeacon Thomas gives for the appointment of a certain Mr. Pulford, M.A., as head master, but I never find him mentioned as such, and he certainly was not master during the years immediately preceding the appointment of the Rev. Thomas Williams, the next master on the Archdeacon's list. There was actually, however, a REV. THOMAS PULFORD, M.A. belonging to an important local family (that into which Mr. Appleton married), who I think in 1730 became curate of Harthill, in Cheshire, and who ultimately retired to Wrexham, where he was buried December 30th, 1768. The probability therefore is that this was the Mr. Pulford who was appointed in 1729, and that he was master of the school for one year only.

38. I do not know who succeeded Mr. Pulford but the REV. WM. LEWIS was the next head master whom I find mentioned. Thomas Pennant was a pupil in the school during his time. Mr. Lewis was buried February 28th, 1743-4. There is a tablet to his memory in the parish church (see *Hist of Par. Church of Wrexham*, p. 214, (52).

39. Who was the immediate successor of Mr. Lewis I have been unable to discover.

40. With the appointment of the REV. THOMAS WILLIAMS, B.A., we come at last to firm ground. Archdeacon Thomas gives (and I do not doubt, correctly) 1748 as the year of his appointment, but his name does not occur in the rate books until 1752, when he was living in the house now called "The Rose and Crown," where he continued to reside until the year before his death. He was vicar of Pennant Melangell, but did not reside there. The following entries relating to him occur in the parish registers :—

Dec. 5, 1752, John son of the Revd. Mr. Thomas Williams, Schoolmaster, Baptized.

Mch. 12, 1756, Vaughan Richard, son of the Rev. Thomas Williams, Schoolmr., born Feb. 11.

May 13, 1757, The Revd. Mr. Thomas Williams, Schoolmaster of Wrexham School, Buryed.

41. Mr. Williams was succeeded as headmaster by the REV. ROBERT PRICE, B.A. He came from Hope, where he married (November 12th, 1754), Elizabeth, daughter of Griffith Jones, gent, of Colomendy, in that parish. It appears from the rate books that he lived during the years 1756-1767 in the same house in Chester Street which his predecessor had occupied before him. In 1765 he became rector of Bodfari, but did not reside there, though he held that benefice until his death, but when appointed, in 1768, to the curacy of Berse, near Wrexham, he resigned the head mastership of the school, and spent the rest of his days at Berse Drelincourt. He had many children, of whom four died young, but the afternamed appear to have grown up:—Robert (bapt. November 2nd, 1759); Thomas (born June 5th, 1764); Jane (born April 1st, 1768); Elizabeth (born January 8th, 1771); Ann (born July 16th, 1775), and Catherine. His daughter Ann became afterwards the wife of the Rev. Edward Whitley (see *Hist. of Par. Church of Wrexham*, p. 79, note 19), his successor in the curacy of Berse. Another daughter, Catherine, married at Wrexham (February 23rd, 1800), Lieut. Johnson Butler Carruthers, of the King's Own, or 4th regiment of infantry, who appears to have lived at one time with his father in law. Mr. Price died August 31st, 1811, aged 81, and was buried at Hope, where also was buried his wife, who died October 1780, aged 49.

42. In 1769 and 1770, and probably before, a Mr. Jones was an under-master. He is described as "usher of the latin school."

43. In 1770 the REV. CHARLES ANSON TISDAILE, an Irishman by birth, was appointed head master, but in 1772, resigned to become head master of Oswestry Grammar School. He officiated as clergyman for many years, but was afterwards found to have never been ordained. While in Wrexham he had, for assistant, David Richards, then about 19 years of age, afterwards well known, under the name "Dafydd Ionawr," as a Welsh poet. One of his poems, "Cywydd y Drindod," was printed at Wrexham in 1793.

44. Mr. Tisdaile was succeeded by the REV. EDWARD DAVIES, B.A. He married Elizabeth, daughter of Mr. Thomas Smith, of Hafod Wen, Esclusham Above. In 1796 he became rector of Llanarmon Dyffryn Ceiriog, but still for many years lived at Wrexham, occupying a large house where are now the offices of Mr. J. Allington Hughes, and the surgery of Drs. Williams and Evans In 1804 he resigned the mastership, being I suspect required by Bishop Horsley to personally discharge the duties of his benefice, and went to live at Llanarmon. He died February 1811, aged 63, and was buried at Wrexham, where his widow was also buried March 9th, 1812.

45. Up to this date none of the headmasters had lived at the school, which was in fact no more than a schoolroom, and had no dwelling house attached. But about the year 1800 this school-

room was pulled down, the whole space between its site and Chester Street enclosed, and the present building erected. After this time the masters always lived at the school house. Under Mr. Davies the number of scholars very much declined.

46. The next master was the REV. JAMES SMEDLEY who came from Westminster School. In the parish register the burials of Mrs. Catherine Smedley (October 1805) his wife, and Thomas Hill Smedley (April 5th, 1808) his son, are recorded. In 1809 he resigned and became curate of Hope, where he also kept a school.

47. The REV. SAMUEL NORMAN succeeded Mr. Smedley, and made the school very flourishing, although its efficiency was seriously threatened in 1812 by the master being deprived of £60 of the £101 out of Lady Jeffreys' Charity (see *Hist. of Par. Church of Wrexham*, pp. 204 and 205), which had for a long time been paid to him. These sixty pounds were now applied to the maintenence of the Lancasterian Boys' School in the Beast Market, an appropriation made by the bishop, in consequence of the resolutions passed at several vestry meetings as to the misapplication of this charity (*Ibid*, pp. 172 and 173). The following entry relating to Mr. Norman may be quoted :—"June 26, 1812, Samuel Shaw, S(on) of the Revd. Samuel Norman, schoolmaster, by his wife Elizabeth, born, Janr. 31, 1812 [Baptized]." Mr. Norman died April 1813, of typhus fever, and was buried in Wrexham Church, where there is a tablet to his memory (see *Hist of Par. Church of Wrexham*, p. 207).

48. The next master was the Rev. John Kendal. He was married when he came to Wrexham, and had then one son at least, John, who appears to have assisted him at the Grammar School. His wife Sarah (born Walton), died December 1814, and is buried at the old cemetery. On June 18th, 1816, " John Kendall, clerk, and Elizabeth Hughes of Croesnewydd," were married at Wrexham, but I think the bridegroom on this occasion was John Kendal, *junior*, and that the Rev. Wm. Kendal, for twenty five years vicar of Birch in Hopwood (who died April 1881, aged 57), was the son and not the brother of John Kendal, junior. The Rev. John Kendal, senior, had in fact when the future vicar of Birch was born, already a son named William. However this may be, Mr. John Kendal, senior, married (January 4th, 1825), Miss Sarah Hill, of the parish of Wrexham, by whom he had at least five children, of whom three died young, and William (born July 8th, 1829), died February 1860, at the age of 28. Soon after Mr. Kendal came hither, the bishop deprived (in 1817) the master of the residue (£41 a year) of Lady Jeffreys' charity, which had become applied to the Grammar School. Mr. Kendal died January 21st, 1838, aged 64, having been master for 25 years, and having carried on the school with great success under great

difficulties. There is a tomb to his memory, and to the memory of many of his family in the old cemetery.

49. At the death of Mr. Kendal, the REV. DAVID ROBERTS became schoolmaster, but was succeeded in 1843, or soon after, by MR. JOSEPH FLOATER. Mr. Floater was neither a clergyman nor a graduate, but he was a learned man, and deserved to succeed. Nevertheless, the school began from this time to decline. Mr. Floater died August 14th, 1868, and was buried in the Old Cemetery, where Mary, his wife, who died July 1861, also lies.

50. Mr. Floater's successor was the REV. THOMAS KIRK, M.A., under whom the school became extinct, and who in 1880 was required to resign.

51. Among the distinguished persons who were educated, as boys, at the Grammar School of Wrexham, the following may be named :—Thomas Pennant, author of "Tours in North Wales," "British Zoology," and other works ; Robert Price, of Gilar, called "the patriot of his native country;" the Rev. Peter Roberts, the author of many theological books, and works on Welsh antiquities[7]; Thomas Taylor Griffith, Esq., F.R.C.S., of Wrexham ; and, it is probable, the famous Morgan Lloyd of Wrexham, better known as " Morgan Llwyd o Wynedd."

52. I do not intend to give here a full account of the endowments belonging to the school, having already done this in Appendix V. of my *History of the Parish Church*, but I should like to avail myself of this opportunity of making a few additions to that account. The Rev. Ralph Weld who bequeathed £100 to the school, was probably the nephew and not the son of the Ralph Weld mentioned in note 16, p. 87, of my *Hist. of Par. Church of Wrexham.* He was rector of Great Saxham, near Bury St. Edmunds, but was a native of this town. His will was made in 1715, and the executors of it were the Rev. Joseph Weld of Hayder, county of Lincoln, and Mary Wragg, of Wrexham, widow [of Thomas Wragg, exciseman, of Wrexham]. Therein he speaks of his sister, Mary Powell, of Wrexham, widow, as still living. The Gwen Eyton who also gave a bequest to the Grammar School, was, I have since discovered, the widow of Bartholomew Davies, butcher, of Wrexham, who was the son of David ap John Robert, glover, (see p. 47), and a member of the important local family of Davies of Wrexham. She was buried 1st of July 1684.

53. The endowments of the old Grammar School are now applied to providing seven exhibitions of the yearly value of £15, tenable for three years at any school higher than elementary, or at any technical school approved by the governors. Candidates must belong to the ancient parish of Wrexham, and the exhibitions are

7. Peter Roberts was a native of Ruabon, but his father, John Roberts, who was a watchmaker, removed soon after Peter's birth to Wrexham, where he lived on Town Hill, in the shop now known as No. 3.

divided into two classes. Five are for candidates from public elementary schools within the old parish, three for boys and two for girls. The other two exhibitions, one for boys and one for girls, are open to pupils in schools other than elementary, or under private tuition. The exhibitions are obtained by examination, the syllabus for which is that of the North Wales Scholarship Association.

54. The old Grammar School, altered and enlarged, forms now the Municipal Buildings of Wrexham.

55. At the northern end of the Grammar School yard, opening into Chester Street, was the old fire engine house which belonged to the parish. After the Corporation acquired the school, they built a new engine house at the back of the old one, purchasing the latter and its site of the churchwardens in the year 1883, for the sum of £20.

THE FAMILY OF APPERLEY.

56. "Nimrod" (Mr. Chas. Jas. Apperley) makes great fun over the three facts that he never asked, that his father never told him, and that indeed he never knew, who his grandfather was. Now there was living in Chester Street House, Wrexham, from about 1742 to the end of his life, a Dr. James Apperley who certainly belonged to Nimrod's family. I cannot speak out of the confidence born of positive knowledge, but I think he must either have been the father or the uncle of Mr. Thomas Apperley (Nimrod's father). Anyhow, he was a very well known man in his day. He was settled in Wrexham before 1742, but for how long and where he then lived, I cannot learn. He married Alethea, the elder daughter of Richard Clayton, Esq., of Brymbo Hall. His wife was buried at Wrexham, May 12th, 1740, and he was himself buried there thirty two years after, January 1772. He was a doctor of medicine, but whether he actually practised or not, I do not know. He often appears to have lived at Brymbo Hall. Mr. Thomas Apperley was educated at Oriel College, Oxford, and accompanied the second Sir Watkin Williams-Wynn in his grand tour of Europe. He married March 3rd, 1773, being then 43 years old, Anne, daughter of the Rev. William Wynne, A.M., late rector of Llangynhafal, of the family of Wynne of Maes y neuadd, Merionethshire. Soon after his marriage he removed from Wrexham to Plas Grono, in the township of Esclusham Below. All his children were baptized at Wrexham Church, namely :—Thomas (born February 21st, bapt. March 28th, 1774); Anne (born November 12th, bapt. December 29th, 1775) ; Frances (bapt, September 5th, 1777); Charles James (bapt. October 7th, 1778) ; Harriet, (born January 10th, bapt. April 1st, 1780); Maria

(born August 5th [1781], bapt. March 2nd, 1782); Catherine, (born April 15th, bapt. May 27th, 1783) ; and Elizabeth, (born January 23rd, bapt. November 11th, 1785). Of these, Charles James afterwards developed into the famous sporting writer known as "Nimrod," the author ot *My life and Times, The Life and Death of the Celebrated John Mytton*, etc., and married Elizabeth, daughter of William Wynne, Esq., of The Wern, Carnarvonshire, and sister of William Wynne, Esq., of Peniarth. Mr. Thomas Apperley was an excellent classical scholar, and afforded by his studious habits and polished manners, a singular contrast to the hard drinking, hard hunting squires with which the neighbourhood then abounded. He published, in 1793, a little volume, printed at Wrexham by Richard Marsh, entitled *Essays and Reflections, Religous and Moral*. He was an acquaintance and correspondent of Dr. Johnson, and according to "Nimrod," a letter was found among his papers after his death which showed that Bishop Percy had sent him a copy of his *Collection of Ancient Ballads* that he might revise it before it should go to the press. Moreover his son tells us that what was said of Dr. Johnson might with truth be said of him, that "he was a lay preacher of morality and a strict observer of it himself." On the other hand he was somewhat of "a church glutton," and " in his zeal for the Church could not be in charity with a Dissenter," so that " if he heard of one of his tradesmen turning Methodist, as the vulgar term is, he would instantly send for his bill and have done with him, saying: If he has become a Methodist it is preparatory to his becoming a rogue."

57. When to all this has been added that Mr. Apperley was "of diminutive stature, not exceeding 5 feet 5 inches in height but well proportioned " ; that he was a justice of the peace and deputy lieutenant of the county ; and that he died in the 86th year of his life—all has been said about him that there is need to say.

THE DYMOCKS OF LITTLE ACTON AND BODHYFRYD, WREXHAM.

———

58. The Dymocks of Little Acton were probably connected with the Dymocks of Penley, and were certainly connected with the Dymocks of Sontley in the parish of Marchwiel, though I cannot state the exact nature of that connection.[8] The year 1694 is the earliest date at which I have found them mentioned as seated at

———

8 As to the Dymocks of Marchwiel, no information concerning them. having ever been published, I have thought the following extracts from the Marchwiel registers may be of interest :

"John, the son of Edward Dymock and Elizabeth his wife baptized January the 7th, 1652 (1652-3)."

Little Acton, though they were doubtless there before. They afterwards obtained Bodhyfryd, Wrexham, and ultimately, by marriage, the estates of James Morgan, gent, namely: Stansty Lodge and the land pertaining to it, and certain lands in Brymbo, all of which property ultimately passed into the possession of the Wynnes of Garthewin.

59. I have compiled from various sources the accompanying pedigree of the family which I believe to be correct, though there are two or three conjectural points in it.

60. The following extracts from the parish registers relate to various Dymocks of Wrexham parish, whom I cannot assign to their right place in the family history :—

Extracts from Wrexham Parish Registers :

Oct. 1634, Jane, the daughter of Griffith Dymock was bapt. the same daie (4th). Nov. 1634, Jane, the daughter of Griffith Dymock, was bapt. the thirde of November.

Nov. 1636, Magdalen, filia Gruffini Dymock 1⁰ Aprilis (bapt. fuit). Sep. 27, 1676, William Dymock, buryed. Margaret Dymock was b(uried) in w(oollen) the tenth day of February 1679-80.

Jan. 1, 1693-4, Elizabeth Dimmock, widdow of Bersham, Buried.

Oct. 1697. Thomas Bulkeley, of Esclusham, and Mary Dymock, of Marchwiel, were Maryed.

November 11th, 1765, William Simpson, of Hatfield, coy. York, Esqr., and Miss Elizabeth Dymock of this parish, Spinster, Married.

Extract from Marchwiel Register :

Jany. 1712-3, Elizabeth Dymock, of Acton, was buried Jan. ye 10th.

Extracts from Bangor-is-y-coed Register :

June 6th, 1724, Mrs. Dymock of Actin, in the parish of Wrexham, buried.

Aug. 14, 1729, Mrs. Dymock, of Actin, in the parish of Wrexham, widow, buried.

———————

William, the son of Edward Dymock and Elizabeth his wife, baptized March the 23rd, 1656 (1656-7).

William ye son of Thomas Dymock and Rose his wife, was bapt. the **March,** (1668

William Dymock the son of Thomas Dymock and Rose his wife was buried Aug. 11th, (1671).

William, the son of Thomas Dymock and Rose his wife, was bap. Aug. 7, (1672).

William Dymock [the elder], was buried Sept. ye 27, (1676).

Elizabeth ye wife of Edward Dymock, was buried Nov. ye 23rd, 76, (1676).

Thomas Dymock was buried Oct. 26, 1677.

Thomas Dymock was buried July the 29, (1683).

William Dymock, the son of Rose Dymock, was buried Nov. 9, (1684).

Edward Dymock of Sontley, was buried July 7, 1686.

Joseph Dymock of Sontley, was buried Dec. ye 4, (1706).

The name of Thomas Dymock, gent, of Sontley, is mentioned in the year 1620.

DYMOCKS OF ACTON AND WREXHAM.

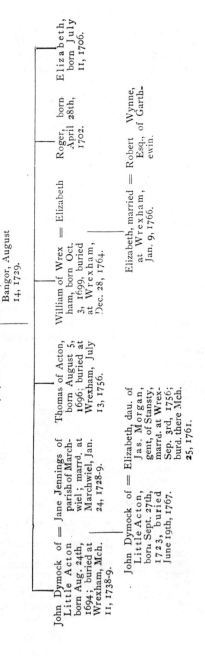

John Dymock of = Ellen, daughter of
Acton; buried at   Thos. Puleston,
Marchwiel, Apl.   gent, of Pick-
6, 1706.   hill, buried at
  Bangor, August
  14, 1729.

John Dymock of = Jane Jennings of
Little Acton,   parish of March-
born Aug. 24th,   wiel; marrd. at
1694; buried at   Marchwiel, Jan.
Wrexham, Mch.   24, 1728-9.
11, 1738-9.

Thomas of Acton,
born August 5,
1696; buried at
Wrexham, July
13, 1756.

William of Wrex = Elizabeth
ham, born Oct.
3, 1699, buried
at Wrexham,
Dec. 28, 1764.

Roger, born
April 28th,
1702.

Elizabeth,
born July
11, 1706.

John Dymock of = Elizabeth, dau. of
Little Acton,   Jas. Morgan,
born Sept. 27th,   gent, of Stansty,
1723, buried   marrd. at Wrex-
June 19th, 1767.   ham. Sep. 3rd, 1756;
  burd. there Mch.
  25, 1761.

Elizabeth, married = Robert Wynne,
at Wrexham,   Esq., of Garth-
Jan. 9, 1766.   ewin.

CHAPTER VIII.

฿olt Street.

1. I have already said that Holt Street was formerly, and far on into the last century, regarded as a part of The Lampint   The name " Holt Street " does not occur till towards the close of the century, and I am inclined to believe, when it was felt necessary to find a more distinctive name for it, that it was called " Five Barn Street " before it was called " Holt Street." The former of these two names occurs in a deed dated 1749, and I believe that what we now know as Holt Street was intended to be designated by that title.

2. Holt Street must have presented, a hundred years ago and more, quite a rural appearance.   There were few houses in it, and many barns and orchards.   As one entered it from Chester Street there was on the right hand side, after passing the corner house, a barn, connected with which were a stable, coach house, gardens and orchards leading to the house in Charles Street, lately occupied by Wrexham Water Works Company, and known as No. 5.   Then, where Regis Place and Holt Street House now are, were two other large houses, the first having a barn, and beyond was an orchard.   On the other side of the street, opposite the barn first-named, were two other barns which still stand : then came the Friends' Meeting House and Burial Ground, and the plot of meadow, still open, across which one could see to Acton Park, and on the other side of this was what is now called " Holt Street Cottage."

3. We will deal first of all, with the house and barn which stood where Regis Place now is, and which can be traced back in the rate books as far as the year 1700.   They were then, and until 1722, occupied by Mr. John Hopson, who was buried at Gresford, September 18th, 1722, and afterwards by Mrs. Hopson, who was buried in the same place, May 14th, 1734.   These then passed into the occupation and ownership of Mr. Edward Whetnall, who was a carpenter, joiner, and timber merchant in a large way of business, and who acquired much property in the town, in particular a large house in Charles Street (now numbered 10 and 11), the premises of which gave him a back way from his Holt Street property, which must have been very desirable.   Then, after a short occu-

pation by a Mr. Edward Budd, who was buried at Gresford,[1] May
20th, 1782, Mr. Samuel Cooper entered upon the tenancy of the
premises which he ultimately purchased.   He was a timber
merchant and coach builder, and prospered in business.   He
bought the large house in Charles Street, formerly Mr. Whetnall's,
where Cutler's Entry now is, and appears to have rebuilt it, so that
to him the coming of that Entry into existence is probably due.
Towards the end of his life,. he built, instead of the single house in
which he had hitherto lived, the various houses and cottages as
they now stand in Regis Place.   He died January 1st, 1810, aged
62. Mr. Joseph Cooper, his eldest son, succeeded him in business, or
rather took his place before he died.   He was, like his father, of a
thrifty and acquisitive disposition, and gradually bought a great
deal of property—the Dunks Farm, Abenbury ; the farm now
called "Bron Haul," near King's Mills; Holt Street House; and Holt
Street Cottage ; The Rose and Crown, Chester Street, and the
group of houses reaching round into Lambpit Street to which it
belongs; and a lease for lives of the Bodhyfryd property in Chester
Street [see sec. 12].   He died February 22nd, 1856, aged 75.
Of his children three daughters survived.   His youngest daughter,
Sarah, married July 17th, 1838, Edward Williams, Esq., M.D., who
for so many years has lived at Holt Street House; another
daughter, Mary, married July 1st, 1840, Mr. Owen Owen Williams,
brother of Dr.Edward Williams, and son of Mr John Williams,
tanner, of Denbigh; and a third daughter, Ellen, married the late
George Harvey Williams, Esq., M.D., of Oswestry, a cousin of Dr.
Edward Williams.   After Mr. Joseph Cooper's death, his son-in-
law, Mr. Owen Owen Williams (who lived at Holt Street Cottage,
and died April 3rd, 1872), ultimately carried on the timber business
which is now represented by that of Mr. Edward Meredith Jones.
As to his carriage building business, this was now taken up by
the brothers Messrs. James and Joseph Jackson (sons of William
Jackson, dyer,) and Robert Jones, who adopted the name of
Jackson and Jones.   These three had been in Mr. Cooper's employ-
ment, and were very well known men   The brothers Jackson were
active members of the Chester Street Congregational Church, and
Mr. Joseph Jackson was a deacon there: Mr. James Jackson was
the father of Mr. Thomas Evans Jackson of Chevet Hey, and Mr.
Robert Jones was the father of John Jones, Esq., of St. Johns,
an ex-mayor of Wrexham.   After a time Mr. Joseph Jackson
and Mr. Robert Jones retired from the business, which was then
carried on under the name of Jackson and Sons, and has recently
been sold by Mr. Thomas Evans Jackson to Messrs. Morgan and
Co., of London.

1. There seems to have been a curious tendency in the occupants of these
premises to be buried at Gresford ; three already named were buried there, and the
Coopers, presently to be named, were there also buried.

4. The house which stood on the site of the present Holt Street House was originally divided into two dwellings, and no one of importance lived there until Mr. Thomas Hayman, who had hitherto occupied Ty Meredith (see under sec. 3, ch. vii), and who had before occupied The Yspytty (see page 88), came to dwell in it. He owned as well as occupied it, but whether it was he or his successor, Mr. Griffith, who rebuilt it, I do not know. Here Mr. Hayman, who was an attorney, lived from about the year 1759 till his death. He married Eleanor, one of the daughters of John Puleston, Esq., of Pickhill Hall, by whom he had four children, of whom one died an infant:—Anne (bapt February 19th, 1753); John (bapt. October 2nd, 1754); Thomas Puleston (born February 26th, 1756) ; and Watkin (bapt. April 4th, 1761). Of the above named children, John, the eldest son, was afterwards well known as Major Hayman of the 9th Regiment : there is a tablet to his memory in Gresford Church :[2] he married Frances, daughter of Thomas Boycott, Esq. (see ch. iv, sec. 28); one of his daughters, Frances Louise, married Captain Somerville, R.N., afterwards 17th Baron Somerville. Mr. Thomas Hayman's only daughter, Anne, became " Privy Purse " to Queen Caroline, while she was Princess of Wales, and afterwards retired to Gresford, where (as Mr. Trevor Parkins tells me), she built Glasfryn, and there lived until her death, December 15th, 1847. Watkin, Mr. Hayman's youngest son was a cripple, but had a great reputation as a wit and punster. I quote the following passages concerning him from Nimrod's *Life and Times.*

Watkin Hayman, for he knew no other appellation, was one of those who seemed to think, with Fielding's Allworthy, that life is but an entertainment, and that the best way to treat it is to enjoy it to the last ...... He had the wit of Voltaire, and in readiness of retort was unequalled by any man that I have since met with in life. Then how exactly did he verify the assertion of Bacon, that deformed persons are commonly even with nature. Nature had "done ill" by him in making him a cripple from his birth; but the superiority of his intellect, his talent for amusing conversation and his singing, in which he was unequalled among professionals, rendered him more than quits with her on that score. But nature still stood his friend. So far from being aware of his deformity---he could not move without a crutch---Polyphemus-like he would have looked for the reflection of his own person in the stream, if no mirror had been at hand ; and his dress was generally that of the most conspicuously attractive character.

5. Mr. Thomas Hayman died in 1783, and was buried at Gresford, June 19th: his widow ultimately went to live at Gresford, and was there buried, November 21st 1809, aged 80.

6. After Mr. Hayman's death, his house in Holt Street was bought by Mr. Robert Griffith of Hafod y bwch. To this Mr. Griffith and his descendants I have thought it best to dedicate a

2 Major Hayman died August 14th, 1839.

special article at the end of this chapter. After 1820, the year of Mr. Thomas Murhall Griffith's death, Holt Street House was occupied for short periods by various tenants, and was afterwards bought by Mr. Joseph Cooper, whose son-in-law, Dr. Edward Williams, has occupied it for something like fifty years.

7. I have now dealt fully with the south side of Holt Street, and will pass to the north side. Of the Friends' Meeting House that stood here, so much has already been said in my *Hist. of Older Nonconformity of Wrexham*, that I need say nothing more concerning it in this place. But something should be said of the meadow or croft that lay between the meeting house and Holt Street Cottage, and which now takes in the whole site of the former. This croft which, in its original condition, was a little over two acres in area, is a detached portion of Wrexham Abbot. At the further end of it, parallel with Holt Street, was, until 1881, a quillet of 15 perches belonging to the vicar of Wrexham. The rest of the croft pertained to Holt Street Cottage which adjoins it, and is also situated in Wrexham Abbot. Holt Street Cottage is really a good old house which I find described as new in the year 1726, and which then belonged to Mr. William Jones, the parish clerk. It was ultimately purchased by Mr. Thomas Hayman, attorney, and has since shared the same fortunes as Holt Street House, belonging successively to the Griffiths, to Mr. Joseph Cooper, and to the heirs of the latter. From 1806 to 1814, Mr. Thomas Edgworth, solicitor (see ch. xvii, sec. 9), lived in Holt Street Cottage, and from 1826 for many years Mr. Edwin Wyatt, solicitor, afterwards of Bryn Tirion, Bersham, also occupied it, and was followed by Mr. Owen Owen Williams.

The FAMILY of MURHALL GRIFFITH.

8. The family which, for distinction, I call that of " *Murhall* Griffith," though originally it was called "Griffith " simply, were, according to the statement on their tombstone in Marchwiel Churchyard, "lineally descended from the ancient family of Griffith of Old Marton and Dinthill Hall, Salop." The first of them connected with this parish was Mr. Joseph Griffith, at first of Sontley in the parish of Marchwiel, who towards the close of his life, came to occupy as a tenant Hafod y bwch *Fawr*, Llyn Tro, and Ty'n y Celyn, all in the township of Esclusham Below Dyke, and who lived at Hafod y bwch. He was buried at Marchwiel, August 10th, 1744. His son, Mr. Robert Griffith, followed him at Hafod y bwch, and there remained for at least 40 years. He married (in 1762) Margaret, eldest daughter of John Jones, Esq., of Pen y bryn, in the parish of Ruabon, by Barbara, his wife (eldest daughter of Edward Hughes, Esq., of Ceidiog, near Ruthin), and

PEDIGREE OF FAMILY OF MURHALL GRIFFITH.

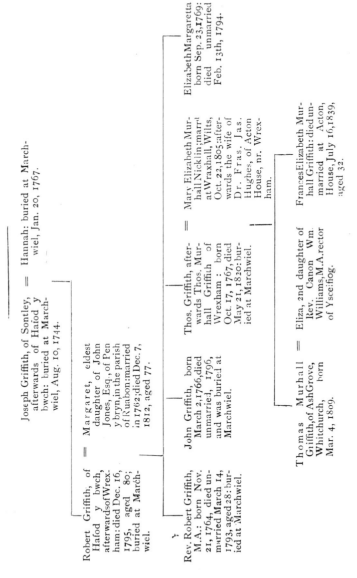

Joseph Griffith, of Sontley, afterwards of Hafod y bwch: buried at Marchwiel, Aug. 10, 1744. = Hannah: buried at Marchwiel, Jan. 20, 1767.

Robert Griffith, of Hafod y bwch, afterwards of Wrexham: died Dec. 16, 1795, aged 80; buried at Marchwiel. = Margaret, eldest daughter of John Jones, Esq, of Pen y bryn, in the parish of Ruabon: married in 1762; died Dec. 7, 1812, aged 77.

Rev. Robert Griffith, M.A.: born Nov. 21, 1764, died unmarried March 14, 1793, aged 28: buried at Marchwiel.

John Griffith, born March 2, 1766, died unmarried, 1796, and was buried at Marchwiel.

Thos. Griffith, afterwards Thos. Murhall Griffith of Wrexham: born Oct. 17, 1767, died May 21, 1820: buried at Marchwiel. = Mary Elizabeth Murhall Nicklin; marr'l at Wraxhall, Wilts, Oct. 22, 1805: afterwards the wife of Dr. Fras. Jas. Hughes, of Acton House, nr. Wrexham.

Elizabeth Margaretta born Sep. 23, 1769; died unmarried Feb. 13th, 1794.

Thomas Murhall Griffith, of Ash Grove, Whitchurch, born Mar. 4, 1809. = Eliza, 2nd daughter of Rev. Canon Wm. Williams, M.A. rector of Ysceifiog.

Frances Elizabeth Murhall Griffith: died unmarried at Acton, House, July 16, 1839, aged 32.

had four children, three sons and one daughter, all particulars relating to whom are given in the annexed pedigree. Somewhere about the year 1788, Mr. Griffith purchased Holt Street House, Wrexham, and came to live there. He had previously acquired a great deal of valuable property in the town and parish of Wrexham, namely :—" The Three Pigeons " in Hope Street, where are now the Lion Stores ; The Machine (now The Red Cow) in Pen y bryn; the Walnut Tree Farm, Rhosddu ; four houses in Town Hill (see ch. iii, sec. 16) ; Rockwood and Daisy Bank Farms, Broughton ; and Penrhos Issa and College Farms, Brymbo. His eldest son pre-deceased him, and his second son, Mr. John Griffith, who succeeded him in 1795, died in less than a year afterwards, and was followed by his brother, Mr. Thomas Griffith of Holt Street House. This Mr. Griffith married, October 22nd, 1805, Mary Elizabeth Murhall Nicklin, only daughter of the Rev. Joseph Nicklin, of Bradford, Wilts, by his wife Mary, sister to Thomas Murhall, Esq., of Great Ash, Whitchurch, Salop. By this marriage Mr. Griffith ultimately acquired the estate of Great Ash, and, in consequence, assumed in 1813 the name of Murhall-Griffith, instead of Griffith. He had one son, Thomas Murhall-Griffith, who inherited his estates, and one daughter, who died unmarried. He was high-sheriff of Denbighshire in 1813. He died in 1820, and was buried at Marchwiel. His son, the second Mr. Thomas Murhall Griffith, lived for some time at Acton House with his mother, who had married Dr. Hughes of that place, and afterwards sold Holt Street House, and went to live at Great Ash.

Chapter IX

Lambpit Street.

1. I have elsewhere explained (see *History of Older Nonconformity of Wrexham*, p. 57), that "The Lampint" was formerly the name, not of a single street merely, but of a distinct district, which comprised the whole of the present Lambpit and Holt Streets, and the lower part of Chester Street. In later times it became restricted to what is now called "Lambpit Street," with which alone in this chapter we have to do.

2. As to the name, "The Lampint" or "Y Lampint" is undoubtedly more ancient and correct than "Lambpit" though I have not the slightest idea what "Lampint" means. The district in question is mentioned twenty three times in Norden's *Survey*, and is once called therein "Lampyat" but in every other instance either "Lampint" or "Y Lampint."[1] In other ancient deeds and records the form "Lampint" almost invariably occurs. But the form "Lambpit" or rather "Lampit" (*Loam pit*) though less ancient, is itself fairly old. The unintelligibility of the other name led people at an early date to adopt one which conveyed to the mind some real meaning. The existence of the great pool in the Lampint (in front of the Grammar School), contributed also no doubt to the adoption of the name "Lambpit Street." Nevertheless, it is only during the present century that the latter has finally established itself, and some old fashioned people still talk of "The Lampint," and are historically right in doing so.

3. The only houses in Lambpit Street that need to be described are those on the south side, between the corner of Chester Street and Pearce's Court. All these belonged formerly to the Traverses (see *Hist. of the Older Nonconformity of Wrexham*, p. 66, note 8), who derived them from Mr. Edward Mainwaring, and they appear previously to have been occupied by Mrs. Barbour, widow of Captain Gerald Barbour (see *Hist. of Par. Church of Wrexham*, p. 131). The group of houses, now four or five in number, between Chester Street and the kiln, formed during the last century two only,

---

1. The transcriber has once, by mistaking "c" for "t," a mistake often made written "Lampinc."

which were sometimes combined into one. In one of these Mr. Edward Mainwaring himself lived and died. In another lived from 1728 for several years Mr. William Henry, who was the father of Dr. Thomas Henry, F.R.S. (see ch. iv, sec. 35, and Index). Mr. Henry afterwards went to live in Hope Street (see p. 65), and was succeeded in the Lampint by Mr. Edward Lloyd, who had the whole house. Mr. Lloyd was an attorney (see Index and pedigree of family of Davies in ch. iii), who died May 1808, at the age of 98), and was buried at Wrexham. He left the Lampint about the year 1751. Then in 1801 another attorney, Mr. John Jones, came to occupy the easternmost of the two houses now referred to, and there continued until his death, July 5th, 1815, at the age of 64. He was called "Mr. Jones of Bryn Deino" to distinguish him from another Mr. John Jones, also an attorney, who was living at Wrexham at the same time. After this date, no one lived in these houses that need be named. A little before the year 1824, they passed from the possession of the representatives of the Traverses to that of the late Mr. Joseph Cooper (see ch. viii, sec. 3). The kiln adjoining them is mentioned in 1699, and there has been one on that spot ever since. On the other side of the kiln, in one of the houses belonging to the Traverses, lived, from about 1718 to his death, Mr. John Santhy, and his widow after him. Mr. Santhy was I believe, the last representative of an important Welsh family seated for centuries within the township of Burton, in the parish of Gresford. He was buried at Gresford, May 27th, 1721. About the year 1824 or a little earlier, these houses and the kiln were purchased by Mr. John Williams, maltster, late of the Talbot, who appears to have rebuilt the former, making one large seemly house of red brick, containing three distinct tenements in one of which he himself lived until his death (February 20th, 1839).

4. The Traverses possessed a great deal of property in Wrexham. Besides the houses in the Lampint just described, and the house, now the Rose and Crown in Chester Street, they had the Office in Mount Street (see ch. xiv, sec. 11-13), three houses in Hope Street, on each side of what is now Bank Street (see ch. iv, sec. 42), and several cottages on the north side of the Beast Market. They had also some land along or near Rhosddu Road, and several fields along Chester Road, including two called "The Werns," within what is now Actcn Park. This quite apart from their large property in Allington.

Chapter X.

Charles Street.

1. The Street now called "Charles Street" was formerly, and until late in the last century, called "Beast Market Street," and was even regarded sometimes as a part of the Beastmarket itself: 1788 is the first year in which I have met with the name "Charles Street," though it was doubtless given before that date, just as the name of "Beast Market Street" continued to be used for a long time after it.

2. In our account of this street we will begin with its north side, that side which is on our left hand as we go from High Street to the Beast Market.

3. The first house that calls for notice is that which stood on the site of the office of the Wrexham Water Works Company. Here was living in 1715, and until his death in 1730, Edward Hanmer, gent, postmaster of Wrexham. He had previously had a shop in High Street. I do not know to what family he belonged. He owned not merely the house in which he lived, but the two houses between it and the Feathers Yard, as well as a small house in Holt Street at the back af his premises. He owned also a farm of 51½ acres in Abenbury, one of 29½ acres in Erlas, a quillet in Pant y crydd ; Erw'r on, adjoining Pant y crydd; and all the afternamed fields in Wrexham Fechan :—Erw ddu (near Coed y glyn) ; Erw eurych (near Bowling Green); Cae bryn ; Cae yscawen; Clark's croft ; Cae llidiart ; Cai clai ; and Cae Lewis. Mr. Hanmer died in 1730-1. and was buried on February 12th of that year, at Wrexham, where his wife, Mrs. Alice Hanmer, who followed him in the occupation of his house, was also buried, May 12th, 1744.[1] He had at least four children, all of whom died young, and after his widow's death there was long litigation as to the disposition of his property, which in 1799 was ordered to be sold by auction, and was then dispersed. The house is at that time thus described :—" The materials and ground place of a very large house and walled garden in Charles Street aforesaid, formerly

---

1. Eleanora and Mary Hartnall of Isleworth, spinsters, are in August, 1764, described as the devisees of Mrs. Alice Hanmer, widow, of Wrexham, and as such sold some lands formerly the property of Mr. Edward Hanmer.

occupied by the late Mrs. [Hannah] Smith,[2] the collector's widow, and now untenanted; with a stable, barn, coach-house, gardens and orchards which lead from the house into Holt Street, in the occupation of Mrs. Treen." Mr. Thomas Penson bought the house at the auction in 1799, together with the cottage in Holt Street, giving £345 for the "lot," and went to live in the former of the two, where he remained until some date between 1814 and 1818, when it was sold, having previously been rebuilt, to Mr. John Foulkes, attorney at law, about whom as the founder of a Wrexham family something must now be said.

4. Mr. John Foulkes was a native of Cefn, near St. Asaph, and a nephew of Mr. John Hutchinson, attorney at law, who came from Abergele. When he first started in practice he occupied a house in Hope Street, in the court adjoining Mr. Weaver's house, where he remained until he removed to Charles Street. I have some reason to believe that he married, for his first wife, Miss Martha Price, daughter of Mr. Daniel Price (*see Hist. of Par. Church of Wrexham*, p. 105), by whom he had, among other children, a son, John (his eldest child, bapt. January 8th, 1802), who succeeded him. Mrs. Foulkes died July 9th, 1816, aged 44, and Mr. Foulkes married subsequently (September 19th, 1817), at Wrexham, Miss Sarah Langford, a daughter of Mr. Joseph Langford, sadler, of Wrexham (see p. 24, sec. 16), by whom he had one son, William Langford Foulkes, born December 5th, 1818, afterwards a well known barrister on the North Wales Circuit, who died at Apothecary's Hall, Llai, near Gresford, October 26th, 1887, and was buried at Hope.[3] I have heard the following story of Mr. John Foulkes, senior, that if in his walks a magpie crossed his path, he would make with his stick the sign of a cross upon the ground, and say:—" Devil, I defy thee." He died at Elwy House, King Street, October 6th, 1833, aged 59. Mr. John Foulkes, junior, succeeded his father at Charles Street, and was clerk to the Bromfield bench of magistrates, who met for a long while in his offices. He built Rhosddu Lodge and Ashfield, and was the first to live in the former house. He married (February 3rd, 1829), Miss Elizabeth Bennion, only daughter of William Bennion, Esq., of Plas Grono. He had a son, since deceased, Wm. Bennion Foulkes, who was an officer in the 5th Dragoons. Martha, his

---

2. Mr. Edward Smith, who was collector of excise (see *Hist. of Par. Church of Wrexham*, p. 206), occupied this house after the death of Mrs. Hanmer.

3. Mr. Langford Foulkes was rather notable as being one of the four barristers who succeeded in preventing attorneys from pleading (as they had hitherto been accustomed to do), at the Ruthin and Mold Quarter Sessions. In 1852 he contested, as a Liberal, the Denbigh Boroughs against the Hon. Frederick Richard West, of Ruthin Castle, but was defeated by 74 votes (362 to 288). In later years he acted as a revising barrister.

eldest daughter (bapt. November 29th, 1831), married Mr. H. J. Byron, the well known dramatic writer ; Henriette, the second daughter (bapt. April 13th, 1834), married at Wrexham (October 10th, 1860), Mr. Wm. Carew Hazlitt, an equally well known literary man, son of William Hazlitt, barrister, and grandson of the famous William Hazlitt, the essayist ; Mary Elizabeth, another daughter, married at Wrexham (July 9th, 1861), Robert George Wynne Wrench, son of the Rev. Henry Ovenden Wrench, and died March 3rd, 1865, aged 27, being buried at Wrexham ; another daughter married Peter Ormrod, Esq., of Pen y lan, in the parish of Ruabon, son of Thomas Ormrod, Esq., of Bolton; and Benedicta, the youngest daughter, married at Wrexham, John Kenrick, Esq., of Wynne Hall.   Mr. John Foulkes died December 21st, 1861, aged 60.

5. The Wrexham Water Works Company whose offices until lately occupied the house which has just been described, was formed in 1864 to supply the parliamentary borough of Wrexham, and authorised to abstract water by means of a dam across the brook near Pentrebychan, the water being stored in the reservoir (constructed in 1867) by Packsaddle Bridge, along the Ruabon Road.   Further powers were obtained in 1874, by virtue of which the Cae Llwyd reservoir, on the hills, was constructed in 1876 and 1877, and the area of supply was extended so as to include Gresford, Marford, Rossett, Llai, Burton etc.   By another Act obtained, powers were obtained to construct the Marford Hill reservoir (made in 1882), and the Gronwen reservoir (made in 1884), and the Company now supplies a large part of Cheshire, including nearly all the Eaton estate from Farndon to Saighton, where a water tower is now being built.

6. Moving up the street, we come to No. 6, which is only here mentioned because I find that in 1784 and 1785, the house that occupied its site was called "The Lamb."   Something may be said also as to Nos. 7 and 8 : the house that stood here was occupied, from about the year 1758 to nearly the end of the century, first by Mr. Thomas Williamson, *cutler*, and afterwards by his widow, and was commonly called "The Cutler's," so when the present two houses were built instead of it, with an entry between, this entry came to be called "Cutler's Entry."   The large house which stood where Nos. 10 and 11 now are, belonged originally to the Griffiths of the Cefn in Abenbury, and in 1757 is described as "a certain messuage in the Beast Market:" it was then sold to Mr. Edward Whetnall (see p. 115, sec. 2 and 3), who owned also Nos. 7 and 8.   Many notable people have lived in this house, but too much space would be taken up if I were to enumerate them.   The Elephant and Castle, now No. 13, is first named as such in the rate books of 1788, and belonged two years after, as it belongs still, to some one of the name of Birch.   But about the middle of last

century it belonged to the Mr. Edward Whetnall already named, and the tenant was one Simon Randles, who paid £8 a year rent, but in 1761 Mr. Whetnall provided some additional accomodation, and a curious arrangement between landlord and tenant was then made, namely, that Randles should pay £2 a year additional rent, allowing Mr. Whetnall to make his own brewings in the new brewing kitchen, and charging other people 9d a brewing. The house next to the Elephant and Castle, now The Hat, is a very old one, though perhaps not so old as the following inscription, which is carved on a slab built into the wall of one of its rooms :

1. 6. I. N. 2. 7.

If the initials in this inscription stand for I.H., it is curious that the house and its appurtenant kiln were occupied in 1699, by one James Hanchett, who had the same initials. From about 1750 until his death in 1777, Edward Pennant, gent, lived in this house. In 1788 it was an Inn, and called "The Green Man," nor can I find the name of "The Hat" applied to it before the year 1808.

7. Crossing the street, we pause at Nos. 14 and 15, which are subdivisions of a house whose antiquity is in great measure concealed by a plastered front. I have seen a deed, dated October 20th, 1650, by which William Linley, of Norwich, leased this house, or the predecessor of it, to Edward Thomas, corvisor, who then dwelled in it, for the lives of Margaret, his wife, Jonathan, his elder, and Samuel, his younger son. This Edward Thomas was, as I have shown in my *Hist. of the Older Nonconformity of Wrexham*, (see note, p. 31), a rather important person in this town during the Commonwealth epoch, while his son Jonathan, became Dr. Jonathan Edwards, Vice Chancellor of the University of Oxford. Mary Presland, a daughter of his wife by her first husband, married Thomas Davies, gent, of Wrexham (see p. 48, sec. 21), whose grand-daughter, Mary Davies, married David Thelwall, Esq., of Blaen Iâl. This house thus came into the Thelwall family, and here Mrs. Thelwall, widow of the abovenamed Mr. David Thelwall, lived for many years.

8. The next house westward, No. 16, represents that in which in 1661, Mr. David Phillips, chandler, lived As he possessed the estate now called "Bron Haul," near King's Mills, he is often called David Phillips, *gent*. He was buried September 24th, 1670, and was followed by Mr. Wm. Phillips his son. Then there came another Mr. David Phillips, and finally, this house and the land near King's Mills, passed into the possession of Roger Kenyon, Esq., by whom the two were sold to separate purchasers.

9. "The Blossoms Inn" (No. 23), I do not find mentioned under that name earlier than 1780, although it was plainly an inn long before, for the tenant of it in 1732—Thomas Stringer—is described as "innkeeper and carpenter."

10. The tannery behind No. 22 was founded about 1825, by the
late venerable Mr. Meredith Jones (who died November 21st, 1888,
aged 91), son of Edward Jones, smith and maltster, of Pen y bryn,
and father of many well known sons, among whom may be mentioned Mr. Edward Meredith Jones, J.P., timber merchant; Mr.
Richard Meredith Jones, general manager of the North and South
Wales Bank, Liverpool ; and Mr. John Meredith Jones, J.P.,
leather manufacturer.

CHAPTER XI.

The Beast Market.

1. The Beast Market is mentioned in a Latin deed of the 3rd year of Edward IV. under the name " Mercatus averriorum," and in Norden's Survey of 1620 under that of " Forum Bestiale."

2. Many persons still living remember Lady Jeffreys' School and the Pinfold in the Beast Market. The former of these stood opposite the ends of Charles Street and Seven Bridge Lane. It seems to have been erected about the year 1812, and to have been conducted at first according to the principles of Mr. John Lancaster. It was still standing in 1833, but was closed about the year 1851, and was subsequently replaced by a school in another part of the Beast Market, which ceased to be used when, in 1884, the new National Schools were built, and has since been sold to the Salvation Army.

3. Adjoining Lady Jeffreys' School, and nearer Farndon Street was the Pinfold.[1] This served for the township of Wrexham Regis, as the Pinfold on Pen y bryn served for Wrexham Abbot. The Pinfold in the Beast Market was still standing in 1833, but was removed before 1844.

4. At the lower end of the Beast Market was a great pool—the " magnum stagnum " of Norden's Survey, which has since been filled up, and close at hand, in recent years, stood the stocks. The Corporation pays £10 a year rent to the Crown for the Beast Market.

5. Having thus dealt with the inner portion of the Beast Market, we will now treat of its outer edge. And we will begin with the portion next Charles Street, working round by the Smithfield and Farndon Street to Seven Bridge Lane.

6. Where the large house now is which Mr. H. Venables Palin, surgeon, occupies, and which is called " Crescent House," there were, in 1742, three houses, in one of which[1a] lived John Pulford,

1. Mr. W. M. Myddelton has communicated to me the substance of an agreement, dated January 9th,1694-5, between Jonathan Moore, gent, of Erddig, and the inhabitants of Wrexham Regis, whereby Mr. Moore undertakes to make a new Pinfold in Wrexham Regis, in the place where the old one then stood, before the 1st of March following, and also " a sufficient doucking stoole," in consideration of £8, he to find materials.

1a. In this or in one of the other two houses, afterwards lived Mr. Thomas Powell, attorney at law, who was buried at Wrexham, February 6th, 1788.

gent, a member of a family elsewhere dealt with (see pp. 20 and 34-36). In the year 1760 these houses are described as belonging to Mr. Taylor, probably Mr. Robert Taylor, of Llwyn y cnottie, as to whom and as to whose family, an account will be given in the next and final volume of this series.[2] Then about the beginning of the present century, they came into the possession of Mr. John Eddowes about whom I shall have much to say further on in this chapter, and who had married (at Gresford, June 6th, 1766), Mr. Robert Taylor's daughter, Elizabeth. It is probable that it was through his wife, that Mr. John Eddowes acquired the property, and he it was in all likelihood who built the present house. He certainly lived in that house, and it still belonged to the family in 1857. Then from about 1824 to 1826 Mr. Vernon Poole Royle, surgeon, occupied the Crescent House, and was followed by Mr. John Dickenson, surgeon, who bought the house of Mr. Eddowes, of Birkenhead,[3] and lived there until his death (March 19th, 1887, aged 77), when he was succeeded by his nephew, Mr. H. Venables Palin, M.B., Major of Wrexham, 1889-1891.

7. There was formerly a delightful, winding, hedge-lined country lane, leading from the Beast Market to The Dunks, part of which has since been straightened and vulgarized into Smithfield Road. At the corner of this lane and of the Beast Market, a little before the year 1818, Mr. Thomas Penson erected a theatre, and close to it, in the aforesaid lane, which now came to be called "Theatre Lane," a house for himself. Mr. Penson was an auctioneer, architect, and mason, who had hitherto lived at what is now No. 28 Bridge Street, and who afterwards (see ch. x, sec. 3), built the house in Charles Street (No. 5), in which the Wrexham Water Works Company's offices lately were. He married (February 7th, 1787), at Wrexham, Miss Charlotte Brown, died March 30th, 1824, and was buried in the old Cemetery. One of his sons, Mr. John William Todd Penson (bapt. August 19th, 1796), was an artist, who married at Wrexham (April 23rd, 1823), Miss Catherine Roberts, Post-mistress, a very beautiful woman, of 36 Chester Street, where he himself lived until his death (April, 1826). Another son, Mr. Thomas Penson, also an architect, was surveyor for many years for the counties of Denbigh and Montgomery : he lived at first at Gwersyllt Hill, a house which he obtained through his wife, Frances, daughter of Richard Kirk, Esq., and which he refronted. He was the father of the late Mr. Thomas Mainwaring Penson, architect, of Chester, of the late Mr. Richard Kyrke Penson, F.R.I.B.A., of Ludlow, and of other children.

8. I believe I am right in saying that the Theatre was built only a little before 1818, for although I have seen a play bill for

2. This Mr. Robert Taylor married (February 23rd, 1762), at Wrexham, Sarah Pulford, and it was perhaps through this marriage that the property came into his possession.

the year 1802, in which "The Theatre, Wrexham " is mentioned, I think this was only a large room used for the representation of plays, perhaps the upper room of the Town Hall, and not a theatre properly so called. The play bill just mentioned announces a representation of Macbeth, under the management of Mr. Nunns, and among the names of the performers are those of Mr. Fairbairn, Mr. Stanton, Mrs. Stanton and Miss Stanton. Now when Mr. Penson built the Theatre, or, as it was more commonly called, the Play-house, he leased it to the Mr. Stanton who was one of the players of 1802. The latter had a Company which performed also regularly at Oswestry, Ellesmere, Drayton, and perhaps elsewhere. At different times, Sheridan Knowles, Miss Foote, and Charles Matthews have acted upon the boards of this theatre.

9. After Mr. Penson's death, the theatre and house were sold to Mr. John Jones, a son of Mr. Edward Jones, of Pwll y go, Bersham, who lived there until his death, February, 1837, in his 78th year.

10. In 1875, the theatre was converted into a Temperance Hall, being purchased by a company of gentlemen interested in the welfare of their fellow townsmen. After being used for two or three years by the Salvation Army, it was in 1889 sold to Messrs. Powell and Whittaker, agricultural implement makers, who have rebuilt the front, having first sold a portion to the Corporation for rounding off the corner next the Smithfield.

11. Between the two lanes leading from the Beast Market to the Dunks, lanes now represented by Smithfield and Crescent Roads, was a farm of $15\frac{1}{4}$ acres (numbered on the map 440, 441, 443, and 444), belonging to the Merediths of Pentrebychan. It was nicknamed "The Barrens," but I do not think it ever had any real and generally recognized name. There was a farm-house belonging to it which disappeared in later years, the lands being then always let to the tenant of the Feathers Inn, a house which also belonged to the Merediths. In 1699, one Robert ab Arthur was tenant of The Barrens, whose widow and children adopted the surname of Barthur. A part of this farm, of about two acres extent, was sold in the year 1875, to the Corporation to form the present Smithfield. The field taken for the latter appears to have been that called "Cae'r cigyddion "—*Butcher's Field*, a rather curious fact.

12. Passing from the Smithfield along the east side of the Beast Market, we come, just past the old National Schools (now the Salvation Army Barracks), upon the remains of an old tannery, which was in actual operation three or four years ago. The first tanner seated in this spot was the Mr. William Poynton, aforetime of The Walks, to whose memory there is a tablet in the parish church (see *Hist. of Par. Church of Wrexham*, p. 213). He died in 1746, and was followed by another William Poynton, doubtless his

3 Thomas Stanton Eddowes, Alderman of Birkenhead, son of the last Mr. John Eddowes of Wrexham, born May 16th, 1803, died March 6th, 1883

son, who died March 16th, 1766   Mr. Poynton was succeeded in his tannery in the Beast Market (described in the rate books as " a house and two crofts,") by Mr. John Eddowes.   This Mr. Eddowes had married (November 1750) Mary Poynton, a fact which explains his settlement at Mr. Poynton's tannery, after the death of the latter.   Mr. Eddowes had himself occupied and owned a tannery at what was then still called " Pentre'r felin newydd," just below the bridge at King's Mills, which his father, John Eddowes, the first (descended from an old family of Abenbury freeholders), had started before :742.   John Eddowes the second, was succeeded at the Beast Market tannery by his son, John Eddowes the third, who was buried at Marchwiel, November 19th, 1799, aged 46, and he again by his son, John Eddowes the fourth, who died May 21st, 1812, aged 35, and was buried in Wrexham churchyard.   The last named John Eddowes married Miss Mary Brown, daughter of Mr. Jonathan Brown, grocer, of High Street, Wrexham.   He had two brothers, William Owen Eddowes (see *Hist. of Par. Church of Wrexham*, p. 114, note 324), and Charles Eddowes. blind from manhood, to whose memory there is a pathetic tribute on his tombstone in the churchyard.   After her husband's death, Mrs. Eddowes continued to carry on, by help of her brother in law, William Owen Eddowes, the Beast Market tannery, but it was ultimately sold, about the year 1825, to Mr. William Pierce (who died March 3rd, 1880, aged 91), and was worked until a few years ago by Mr. Walter Jones, tanner and currier, of 22 Charles Street. The lands annexed to the house and tannery are numbered 72, 73, 74, 76, and 418 on the annexed map and comprised nearly 2½ acres.

13. Mr. Alderman Thomas Stanton Eddowes (of Birkenhead, who died March 6th, 1883), son of Mr. John Eddowes the fourth, was in partnership with Mr. Thomas Murray Gladstone, who had married his sister Frances, forming thus the well known firm of Gladstone, Eddowes and Company, ship-anchor makers, &c., of Liverpool.   Elizabeth, daughter of John Eddowes the third, had also married Mr. James Gladstone, of Liverpool, father of Mr. Thomas Murray Gladstone.   The annexed pedigree will make the connection of the two families of Eddowes and Gladstone clear, and will also show how the honourable family of Gladstone is connected with Wrexham by other links than those supplied by the Eddowes family.   The Mr. James Williamson, mentioned in the pedigree, whose daughter married Mr. John Murray Gladstone, came to Wrexham from London.

14. Farndon Street was always formerly reckoned a part of the Beast Market, and the name is itself quite recent. I shall, therefore, following the ancient arrangement, include Farndon Street in my survey of the Beast Market, going up along the south, and returning along the north side.

EDDOWES AND GLADSTONE.

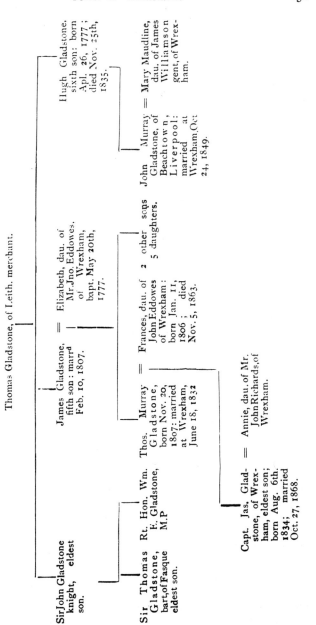

Thomas Gladstone, of Leith, merchant.

Hugh Gladstone, sixth son: born Apl. 26, 1777; died Nov. 25th, 1835.

James Gladstone, fifth son: marrd Feb. 10, 1807. = Elizabeth, dau. of Mr. Jno. Eddowes, of Wrexham, bapt. May 20th, 1777.

John Murray Gladstone, of Beachtown, Liverpool: married at Wrexham, Oct 24, 1849. = Mary Maudline, dau. of James Williamson gent, of Wrexham.

Sir John Gladstone, knight, eldest son.

Frances, dau. of John Eddowes of Wrexham: born Jan. 11, 1806 ; died Nov. 5, 1863. = Thos. Murray Gladstone, born Nov. 20, 1807: married at Wrexham, June 18, 1832

2 other sons 5 daughters.

Sir Thomas Gladstone, bart, of Fasque eldest son.

Rt. Hon. Wm. E. Gladstone, M.P

Capt. Jas. Gladstone, of Wrexham, eldest son; born Aug. 6th. 1834; married Oct. 27, 1868. = Annie, dau. of Mr. John Richards, of Wrexham.

15. On the south side of the street, were a house and barn owned by the Thelwalls of Blaen Iàl, mentioned as belonging to them as early as 1702, and as late as 1828. The barn, which was still standing in 1843, and was subsequently burnt down, was really a tithe barn. The Thelwalls were the owners of the tithes of the townships of Abenbury Fawr, Abenbury Fechan, Gourton and Bieston, and subsequently of those of Wrexham Regis and Wrexham Abbot also; and it was in this barn that the tithes taken by the Thelwalls were actually stored.

16. Between Mr. Thelwall's property and the Bull's Head was a house standing a little into the street, and which I only mention here on account of its curious name—"The Old Maid's House."

17. Further on was the Cock Inn, called by that name as early as the year 1699, a name recently changed to that of the Victoria Tavern. It belonged formerly to the Rosindales of Chester Street, (see pp. 95 and 96).

18. On the north side of the street there is nothing calling for notice except it be the tablet in front of some cottages nearly opposite the Cock, which I cannot interpret, I ought however, perhaps to say that Harrison's Court takes its name from Mr. John Harrison, glazier, of Abbot Street, (see *Hist. of Par. Church of Wrexham*, p. 109, note 280 f)

	M.
J.	M.
	1774.

19. We are now back again in the Beast Market proper, and passing along its northern side. Here, close to the beginning of Farndon Street, was a public house, which in 1728, was called "The Bear," in 1742 "The Green Dragon," and in 1774, "The Griffin," but which seems to have passed out of existence before the end of the last century. And at the corner, or nearly at the corner, of this side of the Beast Market and of Seven Bridge Lane, was "The Red Cow," mentioned under that name in 1742, and again in 1828. This north side of the Beast Market was, according to the report to the Board of Health in 1849, in a most disgusting sanitary condition. " Here are cellar dwellings, no drainage, and in parts much sickness." The details, which are given in the report, are better imagined than quoted.

20. Seven Bridge Lane is so important that I shall treat it, as I have done Farndon Street, under the head of the Beast Market. But I must protest against the attempt which has been made to substitute, for the ancient, pleasing, and significant name of Seven Bridge Lane, the new, absurd, and meaningless name of Market Street. There appears to have been once an open drain along the length of this lane, carrying off the storm-water from Holt Street down to the Beast Market and the great pool there. Over this open drain were probably placed a few plats for crossing it, which were dignified by the title of bridges, and so the name

Seven Bridge Lane may have arisen, a name certainly as old as 1720, and doubtless much older. The open drain just mentioned must have been subsequently covered over, for the Sanitary report of 1849 declares that " Seven Bridge Lane is the only street in the town with a tolerable sewer," but that none of the houses communicated with it, and that the mortality in the lane was 35.4 in the thousand. There were, and still are, several old timbered cottages in Seven Bridge Lane, but there never was more than one house of any importance. This latter is described as new in 1742, and there pertained to it, a kiln and croft.[4] Here lived Mr. John Perrott, formerly a mercer at Nos. 4 and 5 High Street, who was buried May 9th, 1773.

21. Having thus dealt with the Beast Market and the smaller streets opening into it, we must treat of some of the fields and lands that lay near it.

22. Going out of Farndon Street along Holt Road, on our left between the road just named and Cooper's Lane, were four fields (numbered on the annexed map 390-2, and 414), belonging to the Merediths of Pentrebychan, three of which were called " Acrau hirion," " Borthgray,"[5] and " Cae'r fron," which last was an abbreviation of " Cae'r fron pwll yr uwd." In 1620 Acrau hirion was divided into two quillets. These fields had an area of about 21 acres, and on part of them the house called " Beaconsfield " was built in 1881, by Mr. Edmund Mason.

23. The field numbered on the map 411 and another, now belonging to the Acton estate, were purchased May 20th, 1765, of the Rev. Edward Hughes, of Radway (see p. 17, note 1), by Ellis Yonge, Esq., of Acton. They were then called " Frenchman's Field " and " Hill field," and a barn seems to have stood on one of them.

24. We now come, on both sides of the road, to that great detached portion of Wrexham Abbot, comprising 123.3 acres, in which Spring Lodge and the Town Depôt stand, and which will be best dealt with when we come to treat of the township to which it belongs.

25. We therefore cross the road to the Town Depôt and Slaughter House (built about 1864) Now in old surveys and deeds frequent mention is made of a pool, or rather of a field, called " Pwll yr vwd," a name which we must read " Pwll yr uwd,"

---

4. This croft included a great part of the land lying between Seven Bridge Lane, Beast Market, Farndon and Holt Streets, and contained nearly an acre.

5. I once thought that " Borthgrey " should probably be altered to " Berthgrey," e and o being often indistinguishable in ancient deeds, but I have since seen an old deed in which this field is called " Borth Gre," a name which would prob· ably mean The Stud Pasture.

which means *Porridge Pool*,[6] and which was transferred at an early
date to the farm house just named, known in later times as "Spring
Lodge." Now all the indications contained in the aforesaid surveys
and deeds go to prove that Pwll yr uwd was situated in the low-
lying part of Wrexham Regis, adjoining Holt Road and the Town
Depot. Well, there are two very interesting statements made as
to Pwll yr uwd in Norden's Survey (A.D. 1620). Norden says it
had formerly been the place of public execution ("locus executionis
malef'c'r") and common pertaining to the town of Wrexham,
but enclosed and granted by lease dated 23rd year of Queen Elizabeth.

26. And here it may be well to say that just as, roughly speaking, all the lands, *included in Wrexham Regis*, on the north side of
Holt Road, belonged to the Common *Fields* of Wrexham, so, with
the exception of the quilletted crofts at the back of Farndon Street,
and of the east side of the Beast Market, all the lands lying south
of Holt Road pertained at one time, it is quite clear, to the Common *Pasture* of Wrexham. As we come to describe these lands
we shall find, in their names and characteristics, full evidence of
this statement. This Common Pasture would then stretch from
Holt Road to the old lands of the Hafod y wern estate, taking in
Bryn Gwiail lands, The Dunks, The Caeau, The Green, The
Barrens, etc. Nay, it is probable that the Hafod y wern estate was
itself taken out of this common pasture, which would then be an
unbroken tract of land stretching as far as Glyn Park, which we
know to have been the lord's demesne. But, except perhaps The
Green, all this pasture appears to have been enclosed before the 17th
century, for Norden's jurors declared in 1623 that there was "no
common or waste within this mannor."

27. So much by way of introduction. Now, keeping to the
south side of the road, let us pass along it from the Town Depot
towards Holt Street. The long ridge on our left is almost certainly that which is called in Norden's Survey "Bron pwll yr uwd.'
Pwll yr uwd Brow. And now we find ourselves in a strip of
Wrexham Abbot, taking in a part of the road, running parallel
with it, and stretching to the corner of Farndon Street: it contains
only half an acre of land, and belonged wholly to the vicar of
Wrexham. Roughly parallel with this strip, though starting from
the back of Farndon Street at a point nearer the Beastmarket proper,
was another detached strip of Wrexham Abbot, but somewhat
larger than the first, containing exactly two acres of land. It was

---

6. How this pool came to have such a name, it would be useless to guess, but
that this was actually its name there can be no doubt In the earlier parish registers it is called "Pwll yr ywd," and old people so pronounce it. In later times
persons who could not explain the name, have spelled it "Pwll yr wydd" *Goosepoo*
or "Pwll yr hwyad" *Duckpool*, but there is absolutely no authority for either of
these forms.

called formerly " Cae'r pant," *Field of the hollow*, and now " The Hollow Croft." It includes three quillets, whereof one belonged to the poor of Wrexham, and another until 1881 to the vicar, the vicar's quillet (whose area was one acre), being called " Dryll y ficer," *The vicar's piece*. I have elsewhere (see *Hist. Ancient Tenures of Land, etc.*, p. 21), sufficiently discussed the question of these detached portions, and so am exempt from saying anything more about them here.

28. Norden mentions a field "on the east side of " or " near " the Beast Market, which he calls at different times " Bryn Gwain," " Bryn Gwean," and " Bryn Gwyan." The first of these names is evidently the more correct, and stands for " Bryn gwaun," *The layland hill*, a name which affords further evidence of the existence of waste land adjacent to it. Valentine Tilston had eight parcels in it, John Nicholas one parcel, and John Jeffreys, Esq., another parcel of three butts. In later times I do not find Bryn gwaun mentioned at all. But at the beginning of the last century a close a little east of the Beast Market is mentioned in the rate books, which is variously spelled " Bryn gwyel," " Bryn gwiel," and " Bryn gwell," all names apparently meant for " Bryn gwiail " *the twigs hill*, or *Hill of the twigs or rods*. The tithe-map compiler in 1844, without any authority, altered this name to " Bryn y fwyell" *The hill of the axe*, a name which I unfortunately adopted in my *Town Fields and Folk of Wrexham in the Reign of James I.* Bryn gwiail, with other lands adjoining, belonged, when they are first mentioned in the rate books, to the Pulford family, but about the year 1785 passed into the possession of John Ellis, Esq., of Eyton Cottage, in the parish of Bangor is y coed, and in 1844 still belonged to Captain Henry Ellis, a representative of the same family. They consisted then of five closes (numbered in the annexed map 419-422, and 425), and comprised over 21 acres,

29. Adjoining the lands last named are what are now called " The Dunks." The Dunks form a large tract of land occupying portions of the townships of Wrexham Regis, Wrexham Abbot, and Abenbury Fawr. Norden, in 1620, distinctly describes them as " mores," supplying thus a further proof that the lands between Holt Road and the township boundary at this point were formerly waste. The true and ancient name of The Dunks is " Gwern Dwnc," and this name is met with as late as the year 1746. The process by which " Gwern Dwnc " became degraded into the form " The Dunks " is very well illustrated in the parish rate books in which the lands in question are called in 1746 " Gwern Dunk," in 1750 " Wern Dunks " and in 1764 " The Dunks." Within Gwern Dwnc, along the township border was a hill called " Bryn Twnc." It is evident that " Gwern Dwnc " and " Bryn Twnc " contain the same word. " Gwern Dwnc " means *The twnc alder marsh*, and " Bryn twnc " *The twnc hill*. " Twnc (connected with " tyngu,"

to swear) was the name of a particular rent or tribute formerly paid by all Welsh land holders to the lord of the commote.   The suggestion made in the note on page 111 of my *History of Ancient Tenures* as to the reason why Bryn Twnc and Gwern Dwnc got their name must be taken as a suggestion only, and not as representing my settled opinion.   The lands called " The Dunks " which belonged to Wrexham Regis were comprised in 1844 in two closes, and had an area of a little over seven acres.   From the beginning of the last century to rather late in it, they belonged to Mr. Charles Roberts : in 1780 they belonged to a Mr. Williamson, of Liverpool, and were still in his possession in 1819 ; in 1827, Col. Salusbury (John Lloyd Salusbury, Esq., of Penaner), had them, and he still had them in 1844.

30. We now come to the estate of the Pulestons of Hafod y wern, which on account of its own importance, and of the importance of its possessors, deserves a separate chapter.

Madoc Puleston : =
Living in 1413, second son of
Robert Puleston, of Emral,
by his wife, Lowry

John Puleston, of Bers. = Alswn Fechan, daur of Howel   Edward Puleston
divided with his   ap Ieuan ap Gruffydd, of   second son :
brother Edward the   Bersham, by Alswn, daur of   ancestor of the
moiety of his father's   Howel ap Goronwy, of   Pulestons of
lands : died in 1461   Hafod y wern   Cristionydd,
   and the Davieses
   of Erlas

(1) Alice, daur of Thos. = JOHN PULESTON, = (2) Alice, daur of Hugh
   Salusbury, of   *the old*, Chamberlain   Lewis, of Presadd-
   Lleweni, no issue   of North Wales   fed, Anglesea,
(3) Elen, daur of Sir   died in 1480
   Robt. Whitney, Kt.

The Pulestons of Bers,   JOHN PULESTON, = Ellen (or Elizabeth)
and the Pulestons of   sirnamed "Tir Môn,". because   daur of Piers
Pwll yr uwd, see   he was there brought up :   Stanley, Esq., of
chap. xxvi   high Sheriff in 1544   Ewloe

PIERS PULESTON, = Catherine, da : of   Richard Puleston,   Roger Puleston, of É▪
mentioned in 1547   Sir Thos. Hanmer,   second son : mard Jane   Eltham, third son :
and 1554   of Hanmer, Bart.   daur of Gruffydd ap   mard Dorothy, daur
   Edward ap Morgan,   of Thos. Powell, Esq
   of Brymbo Hall

JOHN PULESTON, = Jane, daur and co-heir   (2) Henry Puleston   —Jane, O.S.P.
living in 1597   of John Almer, of   (3) John Puleston, junr.   —Dorothy
   Almer   (4) Wm. Puleston, O.S.P.   —Ellen
   (5) Roger Puleston, of Highgate   —Margaret
   (6) Edward Puleston   —Emma (or Eva)
   (7) Richard Puleston   —Ales
   (8) Nicholas Puleston   —Katherine
   (see note 3)   —Ellen

Edward Puleston = Margaret, daur of   —Hugh Puleston, O.S.P.   (1) Mary, daur of John =
living in 1597   Humphrey Ellis,   —Roger Puleston, O.S.P.   Lloyd, of Wigginton,
   Esq., of Althrey,   —Richard Puleston, O.S.P.   near Llanfarthin (St.
   O.S.P., afterwards   —Ermine, O.S.P.   Martin's)
   wife of Rice Lloyd,   —Emlyn, O.S.P.
   gent.   Ele

f Hafod y wern are given in capitals.

ngharad, daur of
David ap Grono,
ap Iorwerth, of
Llai

Margaret = Morgan ap Ednyfed,   Angharad = Ellis Eyton, Esq.,
         of Broughton   of Ruabon
     The Broughtons   John ap Ellis Eyton
      of Broughton
     and Marchwiel

a = (1) John Lewis, Esq.,   Elinor = Wm. Coctmor   —(3) Jane = John Wynne ap David ap
      of Gwersyllt Ucha   2nd dau. of Llanlleched   Howel ap Ieuan of Bersham
  (2) John Brereton   —(4) Jonet = John Wynne Roberts, of
  (3) Wm. Hookes   Hafod y bwch, Sergeant at Arms
                                      —(5) Elizth = Robert Sontley, of Sontley
                                      —(6) Lily = Roger Decka, of Ryton, ap
                                        David Decka Fychan
                                   —(7) Emlyn = John Wynne Sutton, ap
                                        David Sutton, of Gwersyllt
                                 —(8) Katherine = Owen Roe, of Malpas

ohn Wynne Lloyd, of Plas y Bada, Ruabon
Wm. Almer, of Almer and Pant Iocyn
Rhydderch ap Richard
Edward Wynn, of Cop
Warburton, of Arley
ohn Parry, of Marchwiel
Valentine Tilston, of Wrexham, son of John Tilston, gent., of
      Wrexham (see App. iv)

OBERT PULESTON = (2) Susanna daur of Hugh Meredith, gent., of Pentrebychan, living in 1652

— = (1) Hugh Davies, gent of Wrexham —Jane   Ellen, wife of   Mary, wife of
  = (2) John Hughes, Attorney at Law —Ermine, o.s.p. Fras. Freeman   Wm. King, of
       Stansty   near Leeds   London
                                                   Abbey, Kent

ROBERT PULESTON = Jane, daur of John   George Puleston,   Susanna = (1) Stephen Warma
                 Wynne, gent., of   bapt. at Wrexham,   of London
                 "Copperleny,"   Aug. 12, 1622   (2) George May, 2
                 Flintshire   son of Sir Th
                                                             May, of Mayfi

JOHN PULESTON = Eleanor, daur of Sr
born 1603, buried at   Kenrick Eyton, of
Wrexham, Nov. 13,   Eyton Isaf : buried
1674   at Wrexham, Mch.
                 30, 1709

Robert Puleston,   JOHN PULESTON = Dorothy, daur and   Kenrick, born   Edward, born   Gerard
born at Eyton,   born 1658 : married   co-heir of John   Mar. 25,   Mch. 12,   Apl.I
Aug. 30, 1656,   at Gresford, Oct.22,   Lloyd, gent., of   1663 : liv-   1664, : liv-   bapt.
living May 4,   1692 : burd at Wrex-   y Fferm, Flint-   ing May 4,   ing in 1676   28, 1
1676   ham, Apl· 24, 1713   shire, burd at   1676   Wre
                      (see Sec. 5)   Wrexham, Sept.
                                   11, 1741

JOHN PULESTON, born = Dorothy, 3rd daur of   RICHARD PULESTON, = Mary, daur c
July 23, bapt. Aug 1,   Eubule Thelwall, Esq.,   12 Aug., bapt. 21 Aug.,   Egerton, D
1693, at Wrexham : mar-   of Nant clwyd, died   1694, at Wrexham : marrd   Astbury, Ci
riage settlement dated 21   Apl. 23, and buried Apl.   at Lit. Budworth Church·   ied 17 Jan.,
Aug., 1722 : buried at   30, 1745 at Wrexham   Cheshire: buried at Wrex-   Budworth,
Wrexham, Dec. 27, 1737   ham, Dec. 14, 1744   buried ther
(see sec. 5)

Dorothy, buried at Wrexham, Mch. 17, 172¾   PHILIP PULESTON, = Mary, youngst daur of
Susan,   "   "   Dec. 6, 1730   born at Chester, Apl.16,   Robt. Davies, Esq.,
John,   "   ,,   Aug. 26, 1734   1741 : bapt. at St. John's   of Gwys aney : died
                                             Church there: died Apl.   at the Yspytty, Sept.
                                             10, 1776 : burd at   22, 1802, aged 63 :
                                             Wrexham   buried at Wrexham,
                                                                    Sept. 27

FRANCES PULESTON, = Bryan Cooke
sole heir, born 30 Oct.:   Owston, Y
bapt. at Wrexham, Nov.   of Anthou
29, 1765 : married at   Esq., of t
Wrexham, Dec. 18, 1786 :   died Nov.
died Jan. 1, 1818 : buried
at Owston Church

PHILIP DAVIES COOKE,
of Gwysaney, Owston, etc.,
born Aug. 11, 1793 : died
Nov. 20, 1853 : buried at
Owston

PHILIP BRYAN DAVIES COOK
born Mch. 2, 1832

LESTON, Esq., by his *second* Wife.

—Thomas Puleston, o.s.p. - Rose Puleston, o.s.p.	—Prudence = Thos. Noy, of Pendre, St. Barrians, Cornwall —Margaret = John Hagley, of Colchester —Catherine = Richard Eyton, of Erbistock, son of Sir Gerald Eyton, of Eyton Isaf

born
1669
Apl.
9, at
am

Peter, born
Dec.7,1761,
bapt. Dec.
28, at 1671,
Dec.9,1675
Wrexham

Eleanor born 1655 = Edward Partington of Chester, mercer
at Gwysaney, married at Wrexham,

Mary died 1659

Anne, born 26 Jan. buried 1 Mch in N. Chancel of Wrexham Church | 1661

Susanna, born Feb. 3, 166$\frac{6}{7}$

Jane, born Mar. 12, 1672 (see note 8)

Rev. Philip, rector of hire : marr-3$\frac{8}{8}$, at Little Cheshire :

Kenrick, born Feb. 7: bapt. Feb 18, 169$\frac{3}{4}$, at Wrexham : buried there Dec. 20, 1698

Edward Puleston, born Oct. 23, bapt. Nov. 4, 1697, at Wrexham, afterwards of Jesus College, Oxford : admitted to holy orders, Mch. 10, 172$\frac{2}{3}$: buried at Wrexham, Jan. 2, 173$\frac{1}{2}$

Dorothy, bapt. at Wrexham, July 30, 1700 (see note 9)

Frances, bapt. at Wrexham, Dec. 2, 1744 : died unmarried at Chester, Nov. 14. 1804 : buried at Wrexham, Nov. 18

sq., of
s, son
Cooke,
same :
1821

Lady Helena Caroline, eldest daur of George 3rd Earl of Kingston

Chapter XII

Ibafod y wern and the Pulestons of Wrexham.

1. The Hafod y wern estate, lying between what I take to be the old Common Pasture of Wrexham and the lord's demesne of Glyn Park, suggests the probability of its having been carved out of the one or the other, and granted by the lord of the commote to the first holder of it for services rendered. Indeed the very name of the house shows that it must have been built on land more or less waste, " Hafod y wern" meaning " Summer Shieling of the alder marsh," and "hafodau" or "summer shielings" being merely temporary dwellings, erected for the convenience of those who tended the sheep and cattle at their summer pastures. However this may have been, Hafod y wern was in 1620, and long before, the principal free estate in the manor. The first holder of it *who actually lived there*, appears to have been Hwfa ap Iorwerth, youngest son of Iorwerth ap Ieuaf of Llwynonn. The pedigree of his descendents, holders of Hafod y wern, is given on page 119 of the 3rd volume of *Powys Fadog* (taken from the Harleian M.S.S.), and is copied in an abbreviated form as below :—

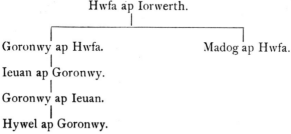

Hwfa ap Iorwerth.

Goronwy ap Hwfa.   Madog ap Hwfa.

Ieuan ap Goronwy.

Goronwy ap Ieuan.

Hywel ap Goronwy.

No dates are appended in the pedigree to any of these names, but it is possible to supply approximate dates to some of them. Thus, it is almost certain that the Madog ap Hwfa, or Madog Athro, who became vicar of Wrexham in 1294,[1] was son of the Hwfa ap

---

1. In most Roman Catholic countries, the parish priest is generally a peasant, a man of the people, but in mediæval Wales large numbers of the priests were sons of gentlemen or uchelwyr.

Iorwerth, who heads the pedigree, and as to the Hywel ap Goronwy, whose name ends it, there is in existence a "marwnad" or "elegy" on his death, composed by Lewis Glyn Cothi, whose period of political activity belongs, roughly speaking, to the middle of the 15th century.   In this elegy occurs the line " Mae Gwrec- sam am wr o'm iaith," that is "Wrexham is [the town] for a man of my language," showing how thoroughly Welsh at that time Wrexham was.   The Hywel ap Goronwy just named was the last inheritor of Hafod y wern in the direct male line of the old Welsh family of that place.   He left two daughters, of whom Alswn (the Welsh form of Alice) had Hafod y wern for her portion, and married Hywel ap Ieuan ap Gruffydd, of Bersham (living in 1467), by whom she had one daughter, Alswn, sole heiress of Hafod y wern, who married John Puleston, Esq., of Bers (Plas ym Mhers, now called " Upper Berse "), eldest son of Madoc Puleston, Esq.[1a]   It was in this way that the Pulestons came into possession of Hafod y wern, but they still continued for a time to live at Bers.   It is true that in the Puleston pedigree at Gwysaney, compiled in 1665, John Puleston, the grandson of Madoc Puleston, is described as of Hafod y wern, but I have almost invariably found this John Puleston's son (also called John Puleston), described as of Tir Môn, and his grandson, Piers Puleston, as of Burras.   There is no doubt, however, that Piers Puleston's son and successor, John Puleston, not merely owned Hafod y wern, but lived there.   And as to John Puleston Tir Môn himself, he is described in the marriage settlement, dated October 31st, 154½, of his daughter Jane, as " John Puleston, the elder, esquire, of *Wrexham*."   As the provisions of the marriage settlement, (still in the possession of his descendant, Philip Bryan Davies Cooke, Esq., of Gwysaney) are very peculiar, it may be well to summarize, and in part, quote them.   The agreement is between John ap David ap Howel (son and heir of David ap Howel, of Bersham), gent, and the above named John Puleston, Esq., in anticipation of the marriage of the said John ap David with Jane Puleston, daughter of the said John Puleston.   "The said John Puleston covenaunteth and graunteth to brynge the said Jane his dochter to the churche dure in ye same state as she is nowe, and ther wed and take to her husband the said John ap David and also to arey hir to hir wedyng accordyng to hir degree, and also to pay the said John ap David the somme of six and thirtty poundes xiiis iiiid . . . . . . and also to fynd the said John ap David and Jane his wiffe meates and drinkes and logyng the space of oon yere immedyatly following the marriage, and at the yeres yende to delyver and geve to the said John and Jane reasonable

---

1a. A full account of the Pulestons of Bers will appear in the next volume.

Beddyng " (*Arch Camb.* 1878 vol., p. 70). Mr. John Puleston (the son of Mr. Piers Puleston), indubitably lived at Hafod y wern, and was followed by his son Robert Puleston, who was succeeded by his son of the same name, as the annexed pedigree shows.[2] The first of these two I guess to be the Robert Puleston who was buried at Wrexham, November 21st, 1621. If so, he is also the Robert Puleston, Esq., specifically described as of Hafod y wern, referred to in two documents belonging respectively to the years 1612 and 1620. In the first of these documents he stipulates for the maintenance of his sister Ellen, who had married Valentine Tilston (see *Hist. of Older Nonconformity of Wrexham*, p. 10), but who had quarrelled with her husband, and was then living apart from him. The second document is *Norden's Survey of the Manor of Wrexham Regis* (A.D. 1620), and herein a minute description is given of the Hafod y wern estate, and this description I will translate out of Norden's Latin, giving also in brackets translations of the Welsh field names:—"[Chief] Rent, 15ˢ; Robert Puleston Esq., holds, as free, one capital messuage called Hauod y werne, barn, stables, orchards, gardens, and closes or parcels of land to the same pertaining, being arable, meadow and pasture land, called by these names:—1. Kae Stacie (*Stacy's field*); 2. Kae Cor (*The stall field*); 3. Lloyn y Cocksuite (probably *The Cockshoot Grove*); 4. Y Cae Mawr (*The big field*); 5. Kaer vallen (Cae'r afallen, *The apple tree field*); 6. Dole dda (*The good meaaow*), which should probably be "Dol ddu," *Black meadow;* 7. Grost y kerddorion (evidently "Groft y cerddorion," *The singers' croft*); 8. Kaer g oise (*Field of the cross*); 9. The field beyond the mill; 10. Errow vechan (*Little acre*); 11. Y wern vechan (*The little aldermarsh*); 12. The Coppie; 13. One close of land beyond the river . . . . two cottages, a garden and . . . . by the New Mill, and . . . . and garden in Pentre velyn yr Abbat, and one parcel of land adjacent to the same, containing in all, by estimation, one hundred [customary] acres." These 100 customary acres would be equal to about 211½ statute acres, so that

2. The first half of this pedigree is copied, with but few additions, by the permission of Ph. B. Davies-Cooke, Esq., from the Puleston pedigree at Gwysaney: the second half I have compiled, for the most part, from entries in the parish registers, and is not I fear, owing to the gaps in the latter, quite complete. Among various local wills, which I have had copied at Somerset House, is one of John Puleston, of Wrexham, gent, "about to pass into parts beyond seas in her Maties Service of the Wars." As the will was dated September 18th, 1589, and proved June 2nd, 1590, it is probable that Mr. John Puleston died abroad, and that he took part in the expedition of Sir Francis Drake and Sir John Norris, which took the suburbs of Lisbon and burned Vigo. He speaks of his "late father Nicholas Puleston" (probably eighth son of John Puleston, of Hafod y wern, son of Piers Puleston), and of his mother in law Dorothy Puleston, wife of Nicholas Puleston. He left his messuage and lands in Wrexham to his friend William Meredith, of London, gent. In Norden's Survey it is stated that in the 1569 Nicholas Puleston surrendered a tenement, garden, orchard and barn in the Beast Market, Wrexham, to the use of his son, John Puleston.

the estate in 1620 was much larger than the present estate, which only contains about 84½ acres,[3] and comprises the fields, etc., marked on the map 458, 458a, 459-468, 475 and 476. As to the "smithie and a little parcell of ffreehold land of Robert Puleston in Pentre yr velin Abad" (so elsewhere described), this was a detached portion of Wrexham Regis lying in Wrexham Abbot, which is not now reckoned as belonging to the former manor. The Robert Puleston, Esq., now under consideration, married Susanna, daughter of Hugh Meredith, Esq. (of Pentrebychan), whose will is dated 1652, who therein describes herself as "widow," and mentions her grandson John Puleston. He was succeeded by his son and successor of the same name, probably the Robert Puleston who died June 23rd, 1634, and was buried at Wrexham three days after. There is a beautiful portrait of him at Gwysaney, painted in the year 1632, when he was 19 years of age. He married Jane, daughter of John Wynne, Esq., of Cop, Flintshire, and was followed at Hafod y wern by his son, John Puleston, Esq., who was nominated at The Restoration one of the knights of the proposed order of the Royal Oak.

2. I have the pleasure of giving on the opposite page a drawing of the old house of Hafod y wern drawn by Lady Helena Cooke, which her son the present Ph. Bryan Davies-Cooke, Esq., has been good enough to allow my wife to copy. The portion to the left of the picture was removed about 1829 by the late Ph. Davies-Cooke, Esq. It contained the great hall, which was provided with a dais, wainscot, and "painted hangings." The rest of the building was pulled down and the new house built by the present Mr. Davies-Cooke. The top of the old chimney of Hafod y wern House is still preserved at Gwysaney, and Mr. Davies-Cooke tells me that, from its ornamentation, he judges it to be of the reign of Henry VII, but a beam in the house contained the date 1611.

3. Although the Pulestons were still described as "of Hafod y wern," they themselves after about the year 1757 lived elsewhere, either at the house described on pp. 143 & 144, at the Upper Yspytty, at Esclus Hall, or at Chester, the old house of Hafod y wern being let as a farmstead, and as such it has continued down to our own days. About 1869, Philip Bryan Davies Cooke, Esq. let Hafod y wern as a sewage farm to the Corporation of Wrexham, which in 1872 sublet it to Lieut-Col. Alfred S. Jones, V.C., who afterwards relinquished it, and the lease being now run out, the Corporation are making arrangements for dealing with the sewage on the Five Fords Farm, further from the town.

---

3. The total area of the Puleston estates in Wrexham, in the third quarter of last century, as estimated for crown rent, was about 255 acres. Nearly the whole of the township of Burras Hwfa, an estate of about 50 acres in Gresford, and lands elsewhere also belonged to them, and at The Restoration the annual income of John Puleston, Esq., of Hafod y wern, was estimated at £2,500.

OLD HAFOD Y WERN HOUSE.

From a drawing by LADY HELENA CAROLINE COOKE.

4. In this paragraph I give such details, from the parish registers relating to the Pulestons as (for sufficient reasons), are not incorporated in the pedigree given in this chapter :—

Margaret,[4] the daughter of Robert Puleston, was baptized the xiii daie Feb., 1620-1.

Robert, the supposed son of Jn. Puleston, was baptized the xi daie Apl, 1621.

Hughe,[5] the sonne of Hughe Puleston, was baptized the x daie Aug., 1621.

Thomas,[5] the sonne of Hughe Puleston, was baptized the xxth daie Apl, 1623.

Mrs. Elizabeth Puleston[6], the wief of Robert Puleston Ar., buried the xviith daie Apl., 1623.

Catherine, the daughter[4] of Robert Puleston was baptized the xth daie Apl., 1624.

Ffrances,[5] the daughter of Hughe Puleston, was baptized the ix daie Mch., 1624-5.

Ermina Puleston[7],	sepult fuit 13o die	Novembris,		1636.
Elena Puleston,	,, ,, 3° ,,	Maij,		1637.
Thomas Puleston,[5]	,, ,, 16° ,,	Decembris,		,,
Rogerus Puleston,	., ,, 18° ,,	Aprilis,		1639
Rosa Puleston,[4]	,, ,, 13° ,,	Junij,		,,

Feb. 5, 1679-80, Mrs. Jane Lloyd, of Havod y wern, widdow, was Buryed.

Jan. 3, 1699-1700, Mr. Morgan Jones, of Mould, and Mrs. Jane Puleston,[8] of Havod y wern, married.

May 8, 1702, Mrs. Mary Puleston, widdow, of the Beast Market, buryed.

Apl. 24, 1713, John Puleston, Esq., of Havod y werne, was Buryed.

Dec. 27, 1737, John Puleston, of Havod y wern, Esq., Buried.

Jan. 29, 1745-6, Miss Dorothy Puleston,[9] of Havod y wern, spinster, Buryed.

Nov. 12, 1750, Madam Frances Puleston, Widw. of Richard Puleston, of Havod y wern, Esq., died the 8th, Buryed.

4. I suppose children of the first Robert Puleston, Esq., of Hafod y wern, by his second wife: see pedigree.

5. I suppose children of Hugh Puleston, gent, of Pwll yr uwd.

6. Probably the wife of Robert Puleston, Esq., son of William Puleston, gent, of Pwll yr uwd.

7. I suppose a daughter of the first Robert Puleston, Esq., of Hafod y wern, by his first wife.

8. Probably a daughter of John Puleston, Esq., by his wife Eleanor, daughter of Sir Kenrick Eyton: see pedigree.

9. Probably daughter of John Puleston, Esq., by his wife Dorothy, daughter of John Lloyd, Esq : see pedigree.

Sept. 2, 1791, Harriet Emma,[11] Dr. of Bryan and Frances Cooke, Esq., W.R., born July 20, Bapt.

5. In nearly all the Puleston pedigrees which I have seen, the John Puleston, Esq., who married Miss Dorothy Lloyd, of Fferm, is said to have died in 1722, but the parish registers and rate books unite in showing that he died in 1713, according to the above given extract. The registers and rate books also show that this John Puleston, Esq., was followed immediately by his son of the same name, who however, dying without surviving issue, was succeeded by his brother Richard. The ordinary pedigree represents the latter as succeeding to the estate immediately on the death of his father.

6. Ermine Puleston, spinster, of Richmond, Surrey, by her will, dated 1699, directs her body to be buried at Leamington, Warwickshire. To what branch of the Puleston family she belonged, I do not know.

11. Harriet Emma Cooke, died December 9th, 1798, and was buried at Owston Church. Her brother, afterwards the late Philip Davies-Cooke, Esq., and her elder sister Mary Frances (according to *The Seize Quarters of the family of Bryan Cooke, Esq.*, by William Bryan Cooke, Esq., 1857), were also born in Wrexham, but I cannot find any record of their baptism in the parish register. Miss Mary Frances Cooke married the Rev. William Margesson, vicar of Mountfield.

CHAPTER XIII.

York Street.

1. I have never found the street, now known as "York Street," called by that name before the year 1780. Its earlier name was "Street Below Churchyard," a name which though distinctive, was awkward, and non-conformable to English usages in the matter of street names. It has been supposed that York Street was named after Yorkshire Square, towards which it led, but the latter is mentioned for the first time in the rate books in 1786, while the name of the former occurs, as we have seen, in 1780. An old name—"Love Lane"—which was popularly given to Mount Street appears to have been also sometimes applied to York Street, though, as I have said, it was usually designated during the 18th century "Street Below Churchyard," and more rarely "Street Below The Eagles." A still earlier and more interesting name was "Swine Market Street" or "Marchnad y Moch," and it is specifically so called in a will dated March 22nd, 1750-1. It is a pity that this name was ever abandoned.

2. The only house on the *east* side of this street of which I need say anything is that which is now "The Black Horse Inn," and was aforetime "The Old Hop Pole." Originally it was a private house of some pretensions,[1] and belonged to the Pulestons of Hafod y wern, many important people at one time or another occupying it. Of most of those I shall have other opportunities of speaking, and shall therefore now deal only with Mr. Charles Massie, surgeon, who lived here from 1781 until the end of the century, succeeding, in the tenancy of the house, his brother in law, Mr. Wm. Lloyd, surgeon, son of Wm. Lloyd, Esq., the elder, of Plas Power.[2] The following *abbreviated* pedigree will show how much intermixed were the Massies of Coddington, Cheshire, and the Lloyds of Plaspower, and will also show whence the Lloyds of

---

1. In 1799, I find it described as "a large house and yard, coach-house, brewhouse and . . . . in the holding of Mr. Massie," at the yearly rent of £40. It was sold in the year named, by Bryan Cooke, Esq., the representative of the Pulestons.

2. Mr. Massie went afterwards to live at No. 19 Queen Street (now occupied by Mr. Ashton Bradley), where he remained until his death (June 24th, 1810).

Chester Street (see pp. 94 and 95), got their name of Massie. Mr.
Charles Massie, of York Street, married at Bangor is y coed
(January 29th, 1787), Benedicta, daughter of Robert Lloyd, gent,
of the family of Lloyd of Maesmynan, and brother of the Rev
Frederick Lloyd, M.A. rector of Bangor. I have attached the names
of his seven children to the annexed pedigree. His daughter, Maria
Benedicta, married, September 8th, 1813, at Wrexham, Maurice
Evans, gent, of the parish of Marylebone, the baptism of whose
daughter, Mary Isabella, is recorded (June 7th, 1817), in the
Wrexham register, Mr. Evans being then described as of Bryn y
ffynnon, doubtless of Bryn y ffynnon *Lodge*, where Mr. Charles
Massie's widow then lived.

3. There is no other house in York Street concerning which it
seems necessary to say anything.

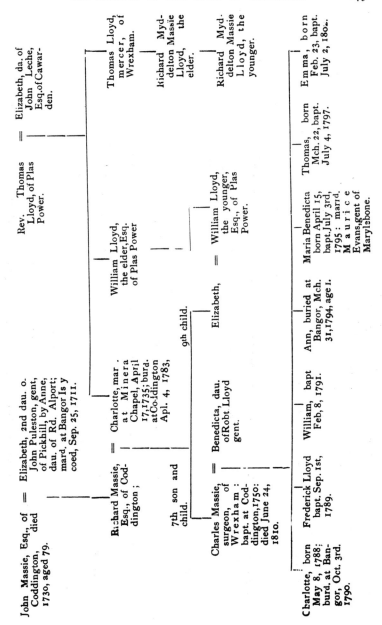

John Massie, Esq., of Coddington, died 1730, aged 79. = Elizabeth, 2nd dau. o. John Puleston, gent, of Pickhill, by Anne, dau. of Rd. Alport; mard. at Bangor Is y coed, Sep. 25, 1711.

Rev. Thomas Lloyd, of Plas Power. = Elizabeth, da. of John Leche, Esq. of Cawarden.

Thomas Lloyd, mercer, of Wrexham.

Richard Myddelton Massie Lloyd, the elder.

Richard Myddelton Massie Lloyd, the younger.

Richard Massie, Esq., of Coddington; = Charlotte, mar. at Minera Chapel, April 17, 1735; burd. at Co-ldington Apl. 4, 1783,

William Lloyd, the elder, Esq. of Plas Power

7th son and child.

Charles Massie, surgeon, of Wrexham: bapt. at Coddington, 1750: died June 24, 1810. = Benedicta, dau. of Robt Lloyd gent.

9th child.

Elizabeth, = William Lloyd, the younger, Esq., of Plas Power.

Charlotte, born May 8, 1788; burd. at Bangor, Oct. 3rd. 1790.

Frederick Lloyd bapt. Sep. 1st, 1789.

William, bapt Feb. 8, 1791.

Ann, buried at Bangor, Mch. 31, 1794, age 1.

Maria Benedicta born April 15, bapt. July 3rd, 1795 : marrd. Maurice Evans, gent of Marylsbone.

Thomas, born Mch. 22, bapt. July 4, 1797.

Emma, born Feb. 23, bapt. July 2, 1802.

Chapter XIV

Mount Street.

1. Mount Street was, until the middle of last century, commonly called "Love Lane," and afterwards "The Green," and it was not until the end of the century that the name "Mount Street" became really established.

2. Strange as it may seem, looking at its present condition, "The Green" was formerly one of the best esteemed streets in the town. There were four really good houses in it, which I shall describe in their proper place. At the bottom of the street were the open fields, while at the other end, visible at the top of the Green steps between and above houses with high and picturesque roofs and gables, was the east end of the parish church.

3. Tuttle Street formerly entered Mount Street almost at the foot of The Green steps, while next The Nag's Head, where the end of Tuttle Street now is, were some cottages belonging to the Merediths of Pentrebychan.

4. I cannot with any confidence trace the house now called "The Nag's Head" earlier than 1742, at which date it was occupied by one Samuel Davies. He was succeeded by Mr. Jonathan Davies, who was buried in Wrexham churchyard, October 8th, 1766, and who owned Plas Gwern and much other property in Tuttle Street and elsewhere. These Davieses were indeed of some consideration in their time. Mrs. Elizabeth Davies, one of this family, married (at Gresford, September 8th, 1731), Thomas Blackborne, gent, of Allington.[1]

5. The house next to The Nag's Head, now the offices of Messrs. F. W. Soames and Co., which about the end of last century came to be called "Mount Street House," was always of some importance. It has recently been stuccoed and altered in various ways, but it was originally a good looking red brick house, and had, I remember, in its eastern end, three or four windows with well moulded oaken mullions. In 1699, the year in which I first find

---

1. She survived her husband and died in her house at Pont Tuttle, and was buried in the Dissenters' Graveyard, May 2nd, 1755.

this house (or its predecessor), mentioned on the rate books, it was occupied by, or belonged to, Ellis Lloyd, Esq., of Pen y lan, and in 1715, and again in 1724, it is described as the house of Mr. Eubule Lloyd, who was Mr. Ellis Lloyd's nephew and successor. Then in 1724 and in 1726, one James Mytton, Esq., was living in it, and after his death, his widow, " Madam Mytton," as she was called, occupied it for many years, until in fact the date (about 1749) when George Ravenscroft, Esq., came to live in it. Mr. Ravenscroft was one of the dozen most considerable men in the Wrexham of his time, and at the close of this chapter, I have, in a separate section, told all about him that I know. After Mr. Ravenscroft's removal in 1765 to Llwyn Isaf, the Rev. John Lloyd, curate (see *Hist. of Par Church of Wrexham*, p. 78, note 16), occupied Mount Street House for many years, and was followed in 1781 by the Rev. John Yale, of Yale, who was still living there in 1793. In 1797 I find Mr. George Kenyon, second son of Roger Kenyon, Esq., of Cefn, described as the tenant of the house, and here he remained until on the death of his father he removed to Cefn itself. All the gentlemen just named were tenants merely. The owner in 1783 was a Mr. John Jones, who died soon after ; then in 1783 Mr. William Jones is returned as owner, and in 1797 and again in 1808 Mr. Samuel Jones. Whether the Mr. John Jones, surgeon, who in 1811 came to live in Mount Street House, and who also owned it, was a member of the same family, I do not know. He practised as a surgeon there until his death (February 11th, 1824, aged 42), and his widow continued to occupy the house for something like twenty years after. The late Mr. Wm. Denson Jones, solicitor, of Wrexham (born March 23rd, 1809, baptized September 21st, 1809), was the surgeon's son. Afterwards Mr. William Rowe, civil engineer, and at one time surveyor to the Bersham and Brymbo ironworks, acquired the house and lived in it. He was an absent minded man, and his putting up his umbrella as he was passing down the aisle of the church at morning service, was long remembered as a joke against him. But I shall show in the last volume of this work that he posssessed qualities and capacities which are much more worthy of remembrance, and that he had his part in much which abides still

6. The house which has just been described took its name from the street in which it stood : the house of which we have now to speak—The Mount—gave its name to the same street.

7. It is generally believed that The Mount was originally called " Plas Steward." If this was the fact, of which I am not convinced, the following translated entry from Norden's Survey (A.D. 1620), relates to it :—

" Rent 13s 4d . . . Hugh ap Robert (Richard Hughes), currier (or skinner CORIARIUS), holds a fair tenement with curtilage and garden upon the mount there, called Place Steward, by the way leading from the graveyard towards The Green; one cottage and garden pertaining to the same on the

west side of the aforesaid Green ; and one other tenement, curtilage, and
garden . . . . directly opposite Place Steward ; and five closes of land,
whereof the first is called Bryn y Vagh, containing by estimation four acres,
the second is a parcel of meadow lying at the foot of the same, the third
one other meadow adjacent to the same . . . . . . the fourth, which is also
another parcel adjacent, is called Kae Denter, the fifth is one other close
there called Bryn y vellin, [held] by lease granted among other things to
Thomas Wynn, and dated 17th March in the 45th [year of Queen] Elizabeth. 9 [customary] acres."

8. The first time that I find The Mount mentioned under that
name is in the year 1699, when Lady Eyton of Lower Eyton, was
living there.   In 1704 Miss Anne Davies, here nearly always
called "Madam Davies," a daughter of Mytton Davies, Esq., of
Gwysanau and Llanerch, came to The Mount where she remained
for forty years.[2]   With her lived her sister Catherine, Lady
Williams, widow of Sir William Williams, bart., of Plas Ward,
who continued to occupy The Mount, after Miss Davies' death.
These ladies were noted for their liberalily, and few appealed to
them in vain that had some charitable object for their plea.   I
find that each of them gave £50 towards building the Wrexham
Workhouse, and indeed almost every scheme of public usefulness
started in this district during their lives was furthered by the
pecuniary aid which they rendered.   Elizabeth, one of their sisters
married Thomas Eyton, Esq., of Leeswood, to whose eldest son,
also named Thomas Eyton, The Mount passed on Lady Williams'
death,[3] and who regularly lived there until the end of his life.
Of this Mr. Eyton, "Nimrod" thus writes in his usual familiar
style :—"This gentleman was in appearance a true specimen of the
old English squire of those days, a stamp then fast wearing away.
But what a bundle of prejudices was he ! Fancy his refusing to
dine at any man's house, where he was not certain of finding a
batter pudding so hard that it might have been tossed over the
roof without spoiling the form; and a certain description of wine
glass—a very small one, perhaps twenty to the dozen—which
would enable him to drink a bumper to every toast.   Although I
was young when he died, I have a perfect recollection of "Old Tom
Eyton," as he was always called, on his cropped brown gelding,
which he considered a hunter, but which would not now be thought
fast enough for one of our fast mails."

9. I have seen an inventory, made in 1776, of the household
furniture of The Mount, and it is plain from this that the house
was, during Mr. Eyton's time, unusually well furnished, and that
his establishment was maintained in good style.   The kitchen was
especially well supplied.   There was also a capital stock of china,
and in 1787 a fair quantity of plate.   Some of the supposed

2. Died October 20th, 1744. buried at Mold.
3. Lady Williams died February 20th, 1749-50, and was buried at Mold.

ornaments were doubtless very inartistic, as " the shell work in the chimney piece with curtains and rod," "the castle of shell work in the dining room with painted and guilt stand," and the like, but some of the rooms must have looked rather handsome. There were two bedrooms, for example, called " The Yellow Damask Room," and " The Crimson Damask Room," because not merely were they hung respectively with yellow and crimson damask, but the bed drapery and counterpane, the chair covers and cushions were all of the same material : they were furnished also each with a gilt and burnished table, and a pair of gilt sconces. In one of the rooms was a beautiful mantelpiece of black oak carven with flowers on the jambs and below the mantel shelf, and continued upwards so as to form a frame for a mirror. This has since been removed, and the house is now unroofed and gutted.

10. Mrs. Eyton of The Mount died in December 1767, and was buried on the 17th of that month at Mold. Mr. Thomas Eyton himself died June 6th, 1787, leaving no children behind him, a son, Edward (baptized at Wrexham, October 2nd, 1748), having predeceased him.[3a] His heir was his next brother, the Rev John Eyton, A.M., rector of Erbistock (1744-1755), curate of Berse Drelincourt (1755-1768), rector also of Westbury, Salop, and vicar of Pulverbatch, Salop, who married in 1753, Miss Penelope Grey Hope, only daughter of George Hope, Esq., of Dodleston and Broughton, in the parish of Hawarden, and of Hope Hall, Flintshire, the last of her race. The Rev. John Eyton had many children, of whom six were baptized at Wrexham, and I give at foot,[4] copies of entries relating to them in the Wrexham registers. He died July 1781, and was buried on the 15th of that month at Hope, in the register of which parish he is described as the "Rev. John Eyton of *Wrexham*." From about 1788 to 1800 The Mount was tenanted by Robert Dod, Esq.,[4a] at a rent of £40 a year. It

3a. Mr. Eyton appears to one time to have lived at Plas Jenkins, Abenbury Fawr, and he is described as of Abenbury when his son Edward was baptized.

4. Dec. 30, 1754, Hope, son of the Rev. Mr. John Eyton, Rec[r.] of Erbistock, born 19 Nov. Bapt.
Mch. 8, 1756, Robert, son of the Rev. Mr. John Eyton, of W.R. born Feb. 1, Bapt.
Jany. 22, 1761, Letitia, Dau[r]. of the Rev. John and Penelope Eyton of Bersham, born Dec. 22, 1760, Bapt.
Nov. 28, 1763, Eliz. Dau[r]. of the Rev. John Eyton of Ber'h'm [born] Oct. 29, Bapt.
Mch. 28, 1765, Ann, Dau[r]. of Rev. Mr. John Eyton of bersham Chap. born 16 of feb. Bapt.
May 20, 1766, Catherine, Dau[r]. of the Rev. Mr. John Eyton of Bersham, born ye first Bapt.

4a. I believe this gentleman was Robert Dod, Esq., of Cloverley (descended from the Dods of Edge, Cheshire), who married Mary, second daughter of Broughton Whitehall, Esq., and who was thus connected by marriage with the Davieses, his wife's elder sister, Elizabeth, having married Peter Davies, Esq., of Broughton, Flintshire, and her younger sister Robert Davies, Esq., of Gwysaney.

is evident from the extract given at foot[5] that the Rev. John Eyton's son and successor, the Rev. Hope Eyton,[6] also lived for a time at The Mount, where he was succeeded by his sister, Miss Letitia Eyton (a daughter of the Rev. John Eyton), who shortly after (before 1808) till her death, January 4th, 1836, took up her residence at The Priory. In June 1806, The Mount was sold for £900, by the Rev. Hope W. Eyton to Messrs. John, Samuel, and Thomas Barker, merchants, of Manchester, sons of Mr. John Barker, so that with the proceeds realized thereby, the land tax might be redeemed on the rest of the Leeswood estate.[7] At this time the property is described as consisting of a mansion house, stables, coach house, other out-buildings, and a cottage (The Lodge) abutting on Mount Street, together with gardens and nearly two acres of meadow. All of this came ultimately into the sole possession of Samuel Barker, Esq., of Manchester, who died in November 1834. Ultimately a suit at law took place among Mr. Barker's devisees, and by a decree of Chancery, dated July 26th, 1852, the property was ordered to be sold, and underwent various changes of ownership. Various gentlemen bought it in February 1871, for £475, and formed it into a Working Mens' Institute. This did not succeed, so about ten years ago the surviving trustees sold it for £1,050, and invested the money, the interest of which is at present applied to the purchase of books for the Wrexham Free Library. The building will shortly be pulled down to make way for the Wrexham and Ellesmere Railway.

11. The next house of importance on the same side of Mount Street as The Mount, and between it and the end of the street, was called "The Office." It stood a little back from the street, and there were iron railings in front of it. I first find it mentioned in 1663, when it is thus described in the rate books—"the house where the office is kept." In 1665, Major Manley of Erbistock, afterwards Sir Francis Manley, was living at The Office, where he remained for several years. Then we lose sight of it for a long time, but in 1702 we find Kenrick Eyton, Esq., of Lower Eyton, charged for it, and afterwards his son, Mr. Gerard Eyton, attorney, who died there in the year 1715. His widow married soon after Mr. John Travers, of whom and of whose family, I have given a long account in my "History of the Older Nonconformity of Wrexham," (see p. 66, note). To the Traverses and their assigns it henceforth belonged until the beginning of the present century, and

5. Sept. 24, 1793, Wm. Wynne, son of the Rev. Hope and Mary Eyton of Mount, born Aug. 6 Bapt.
6. The Rev. Hope Eyton, M.A., of Leeswood, vicar of Pennant and rector of Llangynog 1744-7 ; rector of Nannerch 1746-7 ; vicar of Corwen 1747-9 ; vicar of Mold 1792-1825 ; died November 22nd, 1828, aged 70.
7. Two farms in Abenbury, namely Cae mynach and Plas Jenkins, which had belonged to Mr. Eyton, appear to have sold about the same time as The Mount.

MOUNT HOUSE. 1890.

MOUNT HOUSE. 1890

here Mr. Travers himself appears to have lived until he removed to Trefalyn. In 1731, Dr. Lloyd is charged for the Office. This must be the Dr. Rossendale Lloyd, a son of Foulk Lloyd, Esq., of Foxhall, Denbighshire, and Aston, Shropshire, who lived in Wrexham, and here died, and was buried (September, 1734). In the *Gentleman's Magazine* for February, 1735, there is a " Poetical Essay on his death." All his children were baptized here, namely:— Thomas (born February 7th, 1726-7); Mary (bapt. November 13th, 1728); Rossendale (bapt. December 18th, 1730); William (bapt. November 17th, 1731), afterwards the Rev. William Lloyd, the owner of Aston ; and Philip (bapt. September 2nd, 1734). Mrs. Jane Lloyd, widow of Dr. Rossendale Lloyd (daughter of Robert Davies, Esq., of Gwysaney), was buried with her husband at Wrexham, September 29th, 1775.

12. Dr. Lloyd was followed at The Office by Thomas Kyffyn, Esq., of Maenan, who was an attorney in the town, but did not remain here after 1744. Bryn Estyn and Perth y Bi, near Wrexham, belonged to him, and he was the father of Sir Thomas Kyffyn, knight.

13. The next tenant of The Office of whom I have any record, was the Rev. John Yale, of Yale (1769-1780), who was followed by a certain Mrs. Newton (1781-1800). Subsequently, The Office passed into the possession of Mr. Samuel Kenrick, of The Bank, was divided into two tenements, and was at last pulled down. Mr. William Overton remembers the Office, which his mother's first husband, Mr. John Parry, maltster, occupied for a short time.

14. Passing to the other side of the street, nearly opposite The Mount, where Brown's Court and the house west of it now are, was a house which from 1699 to 1826 at least, was called " Carnarvon Hall," for what reason I cannot understand. During the years 1742-4 it is also strangely called in the rate books " Steward's Hall," a name still more difficult to explain, for " Plas Steward " (which is the Welsh counterpart of the name " Steward's Hall ") was almost certainly on the other side of the street, and, as has already been said, is probably to be identified with The Mount. As far back as I can trace, and down to the end of last century, it belonged to the Marchwiel Hall estate. None of its tenants were of sufficient importance to be here named.

15. In a tablet on the front of of the White Lion Inn (the license of which was relinquished in 1889), on the same side of Mount Street and at the west end of it, is the inscription

S.

R.   A.

1725.

These letters stand for Robert and A——Shefton.[8] Behind the

8. This Robert Shefton died February 24th, 1755, aged 62.

White Lion was an old bowling green.

16. Before leaving Mount Street, it may be well to say that The Cross Keys, the third house east of Brown's Court, is one of the oldest public houses in Wrexham, and perhaps the oldest that retains its ancient name. I can trace it with certainty as far back as 1721, and as in 1661 the Cross Keys is mentioned as in the Green district, it is probable that we can trace it back as far as this latter date. Of course, the house has been rebuilt since 1661.

17. In order to show the relative importance in the middle of last century of the several houses in Mount Street which I have mentioned, I give the amounts at which they were severally assessed in the year 1742:—The Mount 5s 6d; Mount Street House 4s; Nag's Head 3s 3d ; Plas Gwern 3s ; The Office :s; White Lion 2s 4d ; Carnarvon Hall 2s ; Cross Keys 10d.

18. As The Caeau (*The Fields*) is very near Mount Street, it may be well to say here what is necessary to report concerning it. It is a very ancient farm, and is distinctly mentioned in the rate books in the year 1668. In the third quarter of last century it was charged for chief rent as containing 38 acres, but in 1844 it contained only 19A, 3R, 0P, of land. It was occupied between 1704 and 1738 by Mr. John Jones, a noted *almanaciwr*, or almanac maker (see *Hist. of Older Nonconformity of Wrexham*, p. 62, note 5). I do not know that it is needful to say anything concerning any of the later tenants. The Caeau belonged in the 18th century and early part of the 19th century, to the Hafod y wern estate, but was ultimately, I believe, sold by Mr. Bryan Cooke, the representative of the Pulestons, to Mr. Potts of Chester, who sold it to Mr. Ebenezer Pike of Bessborough, County Cork.

19. The Dog Kennel, now almost swallowed up in the works of Messrs. J. Meredith Jones & Sons, was a small house and farm, or rather set of market gardens, which also belonged to the Hafod y wern estate, but which, with other portions of that estate, including The Caeau, passed, about the year 1825, into the possession of Miss Potts of Chester. Mr. Thomas Bury tells me that Miss Potts of Chester sold what remained of The Caeau and Dog Kennel farms in November 1876, to Mr. Pike of Bessborough, County Cork, who died March 29th, 1883, and whose widow sold it in June 1884 to the late Mr. Benjamin Piercy of Marchwiel Hall, for the extension of the Wrexham, Mold and Connahs Quay Railway. Mr. Pike contracted, in July 1877, with Mr. Charles Huxley for the making of the various roads that now cross the old estate, including the extension of Rivulet Road, which had hitherto reached no further than the entrance to the Gas Works, and which was first laid out to the extent just named about the year 1873. The Caeau Road and Mount Pleasant are ancient trackways, the first leading to the Caeau, and the other to the Dog Kennel.

20. It may be also appropriate here to say something as to what

is called " The Eagles Meadow," a large flat area of ancient grass-
land, comprising originally nearly nine acres, which lies between
Mount Street, York Street, Charles Street, the Beastmarket and
Smithfield Road, the houses in Charles Street and on the west side
of the Beast Market being perched on the ridge which lifts itself on
these sides above the meadow. This piece of land belonged as far
back as I can trace to the Wynnstay estate, and has been almost
invariably let to the occupier of the Wynnstay Arms, formerly
called " The Eagles," whence the name of the meadow. At one
time the sewage of a large part of the town was allowed to run into
a channel in this meadow, where it was backed up, so that the
more solid part might accumulate and be sold as manure, while the
liquid part found its way into the brook. The meadow became in
this way a regular plague spot, and the mortality in 1847-9 among
the inhabitants of York Street, which bounded the Eagles' meadow
on one side, was 51.6, and in Mount Street, which bounded it on
another side, 46.6 in the thousand. A sufficient explanation of
this high rate of mortality of York Street might, however, have
been found in the condition at that time of the street itself, for
" all the wells between it and the churchyard were tainted," while
" on the opposite side, its courts, which were numerous and crowded,
descended to the margin of the Eagles' Meadow, and in some of
them were large open manure tanks excavated in the marshy soil."
Enough of this unpleasant subject.

21. Eagle Street which leads from Mount Street to the Eagles
Meadow, was made to assume its present form by the erection of a
row of cottages on its eastern side in 1848 by Mr. Michael Gummow, and it then received its present name.

THE RAVENSCROFTS OF WREXHAM.

22. George Ravenscroft, Esq., belonged, it is supposed, to the
family of Ravenscroft of Bretton, but I can neither prove the connection nor give the name of his father. I first find him mentioned
in the rate book for 1745, when he lived in Wrexham Fechan,
whence, as has been said, he removed in 1749 to Mount Street
House, and thence in 1765 to the house now called Llwyn Isaf
(The Vicarage), where he remained for the rest of his life. This
last named house is described as belonging to him. He owned also
the White Lion in Mount Street, and a large farm in Brymbo, which
appears to have been that called " Pentre Saeson." He married
Elizabeth, daughter of John Puleston, Esq., of Pickhill Hall. and
sister of the Rev. Dr. Puleston of Worthenbury, and had by her
many children, all of whom, the afternamed, were baptized at
Wrexham Church :—Charles (born April 1st, 1746); Jane (bapt.
March 1747-8); Edward (born December 23rd, 1748); Eleanor

(bapt. January 13th, 1749, buried November 5th, 1760); John (born November 22nd, 1750); Frances (bapt. July 16th, 1753); Elizabeth (born July 5th, 1754); Peter (bapt. September 20th, 1755); Harriet Constantia (born August 1st, 1758); Thomas (born October 10th, 1760, buried January 17th, 1761); and Philip (born March 21st, 1762, buried August 15th, 1765). There were, besides a daughter, Elizabeth, who must have died young, baptized at Bangor-is-y-coed, and a son Robert, who was buried at Wrexham, September 18th, 1756. I cannot give the date of Mr. Ravenscroft's death nor the place of his burial, but his death must have taken place between the years 1781 and 1783. Something must now be said as to his children. Mr. Edward Ravenscroft, one of his sons, married in 1796, Emma, daughter of Thomas Boycott, Esq., late of Bryn y ffynnon, Wrexham, and presented in 1809 to the parish, the sun dial that is still in Wrexham churchyard. Peter Ravenscroft, another of the sons, was in holy orders, and his name appears as officiating at baptisms, marriages, and burials in the Wrexham registers at various dates between 1803 and 1809 and again between 1826 and 1834, but whether he was beneficed or not I do not know. Harriet Constantia, one of Mr. George Ravenscroft's daughters, married (October 2nd, 1781), at Wrexham, Richard Jenkins, Esq., of Eaton Constantine ; and another daughter (Miss Elizabeth Ravenscroft, I believe), married a Mr. Vanburgh.

Chapter XV

Tuttle Street.

1. I have already said something as to Tuttle Street, under the head of Mount Street, and to this the reader is referred.

2. The name "Tuttle" was aforetime written here "Tothill" and "Toothill." It is of course an English name. There are Toothills innumerable scattered over England, and though the name occurs elsewhere in Wales than at Wrexham and Burras (both, be it remembered, east of Offa's Dyke), it never, I believe, occurs except as the name of a hill close to one of the great *English-built* castles. There are Toothills, still so called, at Rhuddlan, Conway, Carnarvon, Harlech, and I think at Criccieth. I am disposed to agree with the late Canon Williams that a *toothill* means a "look-out hill," like the Welsh "gwylfa." The Canon says that the word "tut" is still in common use in mining countries, and that "tutwork" means "exploring work."

3. Where then was the Wrexham Toothill? If Tuttle Street had always been as short as it now is, we might have supposed it to be that on which Plas Gwern formerly stood, or even that on which the Parish Church now stands, but it is certain that Tuttle Street was formerly taken as extending beyond the brook to the top of what is now called 'Madeira Hill" (a name not older than this century), which I have actually found called "Tuttle Hill." It is thus impossible to speak certainly as to the situation of the Wrexham Toothill, and it is equally impossible to say anything confidently as to the circumstances under which it acquired its name.

4 The bridge over the brook at the foot of Tuttle Street is called now, as formerly, "Pont Tuttle" or "Tuttle Bridge." But Pont Tuttle was so late as 1748, and doubtless a good deal later, a wooden foot bridge merely.

5. The most important house in Tuttle Street was that which before the end of the seventeenth century was called "Plas Gwern"[1]

---

1. "Plas Gwern" means "Alder marsh Hall" or "Carr Hall." The word "carr" although it has not established itself in literary English, has been current in the folk speech of nearly every part of England, and is the exact equivalent of the Welsh "gwern." It is a pity so good a word should go out of use. There was probably a "gwern" or "carr" between Plas Gwern and the brook.

and which has recently (1888) been pulled down. It stood at the back of the Nag's Head in the premises of Messrs. F. W. Soames and Company. I believe the very hill on which it was placed is now levelled. I present herewith reproductions of two sketches of it.

6. I have some reason for believing that Plas Gwern is the same house is that which was, in the time of Queen Elizabeth and King James I, called " Y Bryn " or " *The Hill.*" A description in Norden's Survey of a property well known to me, which adjoined The Bryn forms the main ground of this belief. Still I cannot be absolutely certain. The following is the description of The Bryn itself in Norden's Survey A.D. 1620 :—

"[Chief] Rent 3d, [Lease] 23 yea' in being. Richard Trevor, knight, (Sir Richard Trevor of Trefalyn) holds one fair tenement lately built next the mount ("juxta monticulum) there called Y Bryn, with garden adjacent to the same demised, with other property (" inter alia ") to Francis Lloyd (by a lease) dated 11 Dec. 45th year of Elizabeth. . . . Also three cottages, garden and stable together adjacent in the street leading towards " Y Bont bren," or " The Wooden Bridge " was doubtless Pont Tuttle, and the street Tuttle Street.

7. At the Restoration, Mrs. Elizabeth Jones, a benefactress to the parish (see *Hist. Par. Church of Wrexham*, p. 136), lived apparently at Plas Gwern, but the first time that I find the house specifically called by this name is in the year 1685, when Mr. John Maddocks, described in the parish register as " John Maddocks of Place Gwern, gent," was buried (February 26th). Just after this date a certain Charles Bradshaw, Esq., to whose only daughter, Alice, there is a brass in the parish church (see *Hist. of Par. Church of Wrexham*, p. 211), lived there for some time. I have notes of various persons of consequence who subsequently occupied Plas Gwern, but as they were there only a short time it is scarcely worth while to mention them. Something must be said, however, of Mr. George Blackborne, who lived at Plas Gwern from 1703 to 1706. His first wife was, I believe, Margaret, daughter of Thomas Powell, Esq., of Horsley and Pant Iocyn. His daughter, Anna Maria (born March 5th, 1703-4, buried at Wrexham, August 9th, 1704), and his son, Thomas, (born May 7th, 1706) were both baptized at Wrexham. He afterwards went to live, first at Groft y Castell (The Roft), and then at Trefalyn Hall, both in the parish of Gresford, and became steward of the manor of Marford and Hoseley in succession to a Mr. Thomas Blackborne. Mr. George Blackborne became also, it would appear, agent of the Trevalyn Hall estate, and married, for his second wife, Miss Elizabeth Rosindale of Wrexham (see page 96). Of his son Thomas we shall have to speak presently. At this time Plas Gwern is described as consisting of "house, barn and kiln."

WEST FRONT, 1887

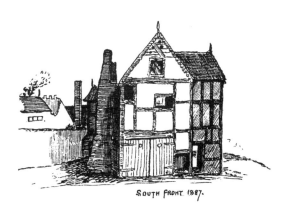

SOUTH FRONT, 1887.

PLAS GWERN.

PHOTO-LITHO? BY

WOODALL. MINSHALL & THOMAS, WREXHAM.

8. Not long after this Plas Gwern was in the possession of a family named Davies, the same Davieses to whom the Nag's Head belonged (see page 146), and henceforth the Nag's Head and Plas Gwern formed part of the same property. On September 8th, 1731, Mrs. Elizabeth Davies, a member of this same family, married at Gresford, a Mr. Thomas Blackborne, son apparently of the Mr George Blackborne already mentioned. Mr. Blackborne appears to have lived at Pont Tuttle, a house which belonged to the Davieses (see sec. 11), and Plas Gwern was thenceforth also rated in his name. Mr. Thomas Blackborne was buried at Gresford, February 20th, 1760, and his wife at the Dissenters' Graveyard, Wrexham, May 2nd, 1755. There appears to have been no issue of this marriage, and both Plas Gwern and Pont Tuttle reverted to the Davieses From 1752 to 1762 a Miss Powell lived at Plas Gwern, and afterwards Mr. John Kenrick, junior, of Wynne Hall (see *Hist. of Older Nonconformity of Wrexham*, p. 75). From this time no person of any importance occupied the place, and I have now little more to say about it. I have seen a placard announcing that there were to be sold by auction at the Old Nag's Head, Wrexham, on Monday, June 7th, 1773, " a messuage called Plas Gwern, in the occupation of Mr. Kenrick, a field called " Cae Denter," a field called " Pen Crach," and eight small houses in Tuttle Street. Plas Gwern does not appear, however, at that time to have been sold, as it was long afterwards returned as belonging to Miss Davies. Its subsequent history need not detain us.

9. Here it is necessary to say that the east side of Tuttle Street is in Wrexham Regis, and the west side in Wrexham Abbot, but though I wish, as far as possible, to treat each township separately, I intend to deal with each street as a whole, even though it may be situated in different townships.

10. We now accordingly cross from the east side of Tuttle Street to the west side, and here, in 1715, at the foot of the churchyard steps, were a house and kiln with much land appertaining thereto, which belonged to Philip Jones, the parish clerk, and afterwards to his son, William Jones, also parish clerk. A part of this property was afterwards purchased by Mr. William Edwards, tanner, of the Palis (see ch. xx, sec. 17 and 18), and therein was built about the year 1788, what was called " Yorkshire Square." This consisted of a large open space surrounded by small one storied shops for the use of the dealers in Yorkshire cloth, who resorted to the great March Fair, and who had hitherto been accommodated at the Town Hall. When a little before 1824 the Yorkshiremen left this square (see under Henblas Street), these shops were converted into cottages. The following is a description given in 1849 of this square in a *Report to the General Board of Health on the Town of*

Wrexham :—

" Here are altogether 35 tenements with one privy, and that in a state quite unapproachable. The court is occupied by dung pits and collections of filth, and in parts sodden with ordure. The privy of these cottages drains into a succession of open pools of soil, which extend at the back of other cottages, and into a public way opening from Tuttle Street. The sickness here is severe, and the mortality 38.2 in 1000."

11. Lower down the same side of Tuttle Street, and close to the brook and bridge was a good house, which from its nearness to the latter was called after it " Pont Tuttle." A large meadow pertain- ed to it. From 1715 to 1730, Mrs. Davies (one of the Davieses mentioned in connection with the Nag's Head and Plas Gwern), was rated for it, but when Mrs. Elizabeth Davies married Mr. Thomas Blackborne, the latter came to live at Pont Tuttle, and there continued until his death in 1760. Then the property pass- ed to Mr. Jonathan Davies of the Nag's Head, who let it to William Hughes, tanner, and in 1763 mortgaged it to John Hanmer, gent, of Overton, Flintshire. The property is thus described in the in- dentures of mortgage :—" All that messuage, tenement, and dwell- ing house in Tothill Street in Wrexham Abbot, and the toft or court railed in before the same, and the garden and skin house and yard, and the garden and old orchard leased to William Hughes, tanner, to erect bark bays, and make skin pits therein, and the two pieces of land in Wrexham Regis called Cae Denter and Cae Bryn Crach."[2] Soon after, the property came into the possession of Mr. James Jones, tanner, one of whose family (I believe his daughter, Elizabeth Jones), married Mr. John Burton of High Street, after- wards of The Yspytty (see *Hist. of Older Nonconformity of Wrex- ham*, p. 83, note 31), who ultimately came to own a part of it, the other part – the meadow, comprising about 2½ roods, passing into the possession of another tanner, Mr. Beardsworth of Pen y bryn. Mr. Burton's portion descended to his daughters, Miss Burton and Mrs. Pierce, and it was, I think, on this portion that the iron found- ary was erected, which was carried on by Mr. Edward Jones (see *Hist. of Older Nonconformity of Wrexham*, p. 90, note 40), and which still exists.

12. I will now deal with the house of Edward Ellis gent, of whom I have said something in note 4, p. 208 of *The History of the Parish Church of Wrexham*. Since that note was compiled, how- ever, I have learned a great deal more about him. If he was, as I conjectured, the son of Mr. John Ellis, apothecary, of Wrexham, he was of the stock of the Ellises of Eyton, in the parish of Bangor is y coed. In a deed dated February 1788 he is described as son of John Ellis, gent. In 1795, John Ellis, gent, of Liverpool, is des- cribed as his eldest surviving son, and in 1803, Edward Ellis, the younger, gent, of Wrexham, as his eldest surviving son. Edward

2. Cae Denter was on the opposite side of the brook, and is noticed elsewhere. Cae Bryn Crach was, I believe where Mr. Thomas Bury's house now is.

Ellis, the younger, had by his wife, Mary (afterwards the wife of Robert Wright of Widnes), two daughters, of whom Maria Clementina died young, and the other, Mary Ellis, spinster, of Everton, near Liverpool, was living in 1821. Edward Ellis, the younger, as well as his brother Robert, died in the lifetime of their father, and in 1821, Jane, Esther, Eleanor and Theophila were the only surviving children of Edward Ellis, the elder. Jane was then the wife of Edward Jones of The Eagles Inn, Wrexham, but had been before, I believe, the wife of Samuel Hughes of Wrexham (I suppose Samuel Hughes, grocer, of 58 Hope Street); Esther was the wife of Charles Edward Studley, gent, of Overton, Flintshire ; Eleanor was the wife of a Mr. Thomas Jones ; and Theophila was the wife of Francis Williamson (probably Francis Williamson, tinman, of 10 Hope Street, Wrexham). Mr. Ellis's property was rather extensive. Besides Mount Pleasant and the land belonging to it in Pen y bryn and Ty Gwyn farm in Acton, he owned three houses at Pont Tuttle (in one of which he lived), four houses and a warehouse on the north side of College Street, four houses in Stryt Draw, several houses on west side of York Street, including the Black Horse (now the Royal Ship), and five cottages in the Beast Market.

[Since the above was in type I have found mention made of "George Ravenscroft, of Wrexham, gent." on Oct. 9, 1738.]

Chapter XVI.

Salop Street.

1. Salop Road, like Mount Street, and even more frequently than Mount Street, was before our own days, commonly called " The Green," and the bridge which carried it across the brook to Wrexham Fechan was known always as " The Green Bridge "[1] In the third quarter of the last century all of what still remained of The Green, except the workhouse, belonged to the Pulestons of Hafod y wern. As Salop Street at that time differed strangely from its present condition, I have given a copy of a plan of it, in the possession of Ph. B. Davies Cooke, Esq., of Gwysaney, who has permitted me to copy it. One of the houses on The Green, owned by Philip Puleston, Esq., was that of Mr. John Peers, skinner, with skin-house and garden appurtenant to it. It would seem as though Mr. Peers' skin house stood where Messrs. J. Meredith Jones & Sons' works now are, and also as though after Mr. Pears' time there was no skin house on this spot until the time of Mr. Evan Morris, to be mentioned in the next paragraph. At any rate there is no charge for any skinyard here in the parish rate books during that interval.

2. Mr. Evan Morris, skinner, grandfather (not uncle, as I said in note 28, p. 112 of my *History of the Older Nonconformity of Wrexham*), of the late Sir Evan Morris, kt., established himself in business, between 1819 and 1824, as aforesaid, on part of the site now occupied by Messrs J. M. Jones & Sons' extensive works, and there continued for something like thirty years. He was ultimately succeeded by Messrs. John Meredith Jones and Charles Rocke, tanners and leather manufacturers, a firm which since the retirement from it at the beginning of 1888 of Mr. Rocke, has adopted the style or name of J. Meredith Jones and Sons.

3. A little further on the same side of the road on the way to the bridge, was the Workhouse. This was erected before the year

---

1. This bridge (called "Pont y Greene" in 1648, and "The Green Bridge" in more recent times), was rebuilt by the late Peter Walker, Esq., in April, 1877, under the name of "The Willow Bridge."

	A – R – P
7. RICHARD JONES, FOR NEW HOUSE	0 – 0 – 4
THOS. DAVIES' LATE FIELD.	2 – 2 – 1
	2 – 2 – 5
8. A·NN JAMES, HOUSE & GARDEN.	0 – 0 – 3
9. EDWARD PHILLIPS HOUSE 5 DWELLINGS.	0 – 0 – 5
10. ELLIS JAMES ONE DWELLING ADJOINING THE HOUSE IN POSSESSION OF JOHN PIERS.	0 – 0 – 1
11. JOHN PIERS FOR HOUSE UPON THE GREEN, HOUSE, SKIN HOUSE AND GARDEN.	0 – 0 –32
12. WREXHAM GREEN EXCLUDING THE WORKHOUSE.	0 – 3 – 11

PLAN OF WREXHAM GREEN
IN THIRD QUARTER OF
EIGHTEENTH CENTURY.

WOODALL, MINSHALL & THOMAS, LITHOS, WREXHAM.

1737, and largely it would appear, by voluntary contributions. The following list of subscribers towards its erection and maintenance has been preserved :—

Lady Williams [of The Mount], (see page 148),

£50 0 0

Mrs. Anne Davies,   ,,   (see page 148) £50 0 0
Mrs. Drelincourt (of Berse Drelincourt) £10 for five years.
Miss Bennett (*See Hist. of Par. Church of Wrexham*, p. 202, note 2g) ... ... £10 for five years.
Miss [Mary] Myddelton (of Croes Newydd) £10 ,,
Mrs. Mytton (see page 147) ... ... £5 for five years.
Robert Williams, Esq.[2] ... £5 a year during pleasure.
Richard Puleston, Esq. (of Hafod y wern) ... £4 0 0
Jas. Apperley, Esq. (see page 111) £5 0 0
Simon Yorke, Esq. £5 5 0
Mrs. Williams £1 16 0
Mrs. Lloyd £1 1 0

4. Afterwards (in 1747), Mrs. Drelincourt collected £63 17 0 "for discharging Workhouse debts," and a list of those who then subscribed is given on p. 202 of my *History of the Parish Church.*

5. The Workhouse was still standing in Salop Street in 1833, and a part of the wall that fenced it was until 1891 in existence, giving access to Havelock Square.

6. Immediately adjoining the workhouse and near the bridge, but standing back from the road, was the old Bridewell of Wrexham. The Bridewell is specifically described in the year 1698 as being in The Green. The following extracts from the parish registers, relating more or less to the old jail of the town may be given —

Jan. 1625-6, William ap William, the und^r gaoler, was buried the xiith daie.

Aug. 18, 1702, Lowry, wife of Richard Williams, of W.A. hangemon, poor, was Buryed.

Dec. 18, 1709, David Owen, whipper, of Bridewell, was Buryed,

7. Here I suppose was kept and used "the cuckstoole belonging to the town of Wrexham Regis," which at the Quarter Sessions held at Wrexham, July 12th, 1698, was presented as being "out of repaire and repaireable by the inhabitants of ye sd Town of Wrexham," (see p. 127, note 1). A cuckstool was a chair in which scolding women were placed in order to duck them. It is very likely that they were ducked in the brook which ran round two sides of the Bridewell, but we cannot be certain of this, for there is a pool near the Great Western Station called "Pwll y wrach" *The Hag's Pool*, and there were many other pools within the town very suitable for such a purpose.

---

2. Robert Williams, Esq., of Bryn y ffynnon, Wrexham, afterwards of Erbistock, brother of the first Sir Watkin Williams-Wynn.

8. The Bridewell was still standing in Salop Street in the year
1833. The site of it is now occupied by Havelock Square, and
the old gate which led into its precincts stood until the year 1891
in Salop Street, and formed the entrance from the latter into
Havelock Square.

9. Immediately opposite the Bridewell, adjoining the brook, on
the western side of Salop Street, were the original gas works of
Wrexham. These were erected in the year 1827 by a firm styled
"Keay, Edwards, and Company." In 1839 the present Gas Company was formed, and in the following year gas works were erected
in Willow Lane, where the malt kilns of the late Mr. Peter Walker
now are, and shortly afterwards the new Company purchased the
works, mains, and rights of the original Company. Until January
1st, 1844, although gas was supplied in some cases by meters, when
it was charged 10s per 1000 cubic feet, it was supplied generally
"by contract" by six different tariffs according to the form of
burner used. In 1840 the following were the terms per annum,
for "a single jet" and for an "Argand No. 3" burner, the burners
not being allowed to be lighted before sunset.

Burner.	Till 8 o'clock.	Till 9 o'clock.	Till 10 o'clock.	Till 11 o'clock.	Till 12 o'clock.
Single Jet ...	19s.	26s.	30s.	35s.	40s.
Argand No. 3 ...	42s.	63s.	72s.	88s.	100s.

Those who took the gas until 8 o'clock only, were not allowed to
light it before the 21st of August, nor after the 21st April, and if
gas was lighted on Sundays the above charges were increased by
one-sixth. If also any person was found burning gas after the hour
contracted for, a charge was made for the whole of the quarter for
the hour at which it was discovered alight. On Saturday nights
however. the lights were allowed to burn for two hours after the
hour agreed upon without additional charge. Payments were to
be made half yearly.[3] A little before 1870, when the Company
obtained Parliamentary powers, a portion of The Dog Kennel farm
was purchased as a site for an additional gas holder, which is still
in use and is capable of containing 65,000 feet of gas. Soon after
1870, a fire occurring at the Willow Lane Works, the directors

3. I find that in 1850 the Gas Company paid for their coals 7s 6d a ton delivered,
and got for their gas 8s a 1000 cubic feet, so that if they knew their work, they
must at that time have been doing an exceedingly profitable business. In 1862,
Mr. John Rowe, son of Mr. William Rowe, of Mount Street House, was appointed
manager.

determined to abandon them altogether and erect new works, including offices and manager's house, at the bottom of Wrexham Fechan, on the site adjoining the additional gas holder already mentioned. This was accomplished in 1871. The works were extended in the year 1886, and the total storage capacity now amounts to 365,000 feet. I owe nearly all these particulars to the courtesy of Mr. Walker, the present manager of the Gas Company.

10. Nearly opposite the end of Rivulet Road was the first Wesleyan Chapel built in Wrexham. It was commonly called "The Green Chapel," and it is commemorated by the lane called "Chapel Lane."

11. Having thus mentioned this chapel, I shall now proceed to give what I have been able to learn of the early history of Wesleyan Methodism in this town.

The HISTORY of EARLY WESLEYAN METHODISM in WREXHAM.

12. The history of *early* Wesleyan Methodism in this town is veiled in mystery. We know, however, that a society was established here as early as 1772, and that Wrexham was then in the Chester circuit. There is reason to believe that the first meetings were held in what was afterwards called "Hughes' Yard" (see under College Street), then the yard of Mr. Benjamin Parry, and apparently in Mr. Parry's house also. Meetings were also subsequently held in a cottage in Chapel Street, next the Independent Chapel-house, where the house called "Bryn Awel" now is. The history of the connection of Samuel Bradburn with early Wesleyanism in this town is very interesting. Under College Street I have recorded the local tradition as to this connection in his own words. Samuel Bradburn's father was also named Samuel Bradburn, a godly and upright man, who married (at Chester in 1740), "the only daughter of Samuel Jones, a noted gardener of Wrexham," probably one of the Joneses who were so long connected with The Dog Kennel. By a shameful device Samuel Bradburn, the elder, was taken to have enlisted, and, his wife accompanying him, he served in the continental wars for many years, and Samuel Bradburn, the younger, was born at Gibraltar, October 5th, 1751, and was twelve years old when his father's regiment returned to England. After his discharge the father settled in Chester, and there young Samuel Bradburn was apprenticed to a shoemaker, and was "converted" and there, after a sad falling away into sinful courses, once more gave his heart to God, and again joined himself with the Methodists. Now comes an account written by himself, of his first three visits to Wrexham. "Having"

he says " been frequently pressed by persons in the society, and also by some of my wife's relations, to spend a few days with them at Wrexham, I took an opportunity of going thither at Easter, 1772. I found every one very loving and free, and I might have been happy had not my mind been so perplexed about preaching, but the distraction of my thoughts induced me to return home the day after I went, in a most disagreeable frame of mind. As the same people continued to importune me, and my time was now at my own disposal, having completed my apprenticeship, January 1st, 1772, I went at Whitsuntide, and spent several days among them, more to my satisfaction than before. I met their class, prayed, and sang hymns with them from house to house : they even prevailed upon me to give two or three public exhortations to the people who assembled with a desire to hear preaching. In these exhortations I found much freedom, both in spirit and speech, but still stifled the thoughts of preaching as much as I could, though my conscience smote me, and many severe threatenings passed through my mind, till feeling no rest, and nothing prospering that I undertook, I determined to leave home, and travel till the end and nature of these things more clearly appeared." Accordingly, he went to Liverpool in July, 1772, working here at his trade, but returned to Chester in November. " At this time " he continues, " I went to see my old friends at Wrexham, designing to remain and work there till the spring, intending then to go to London ; but God appointed it otherwise. During my stay at Wrexham, I wrought with one of the leaders who is now in Paradise. He often spoke closely to me on the subject of preaching, frequently mentioning the sad *woe* if I obeyed not, insomuch that I was overwhelmed with fear lest I should be disobedient to the call of God, or should run when he did not send me. However, I kept my former resolution, prayed much and lived near to God, and he made darkness light. On Sunday, February 7th, 1772, Mr. Gardiner, of Tottenham,[3a] intended to preach at noon, and as I was going to the preaching house, brother H. said :—" something makes me fear that Mr. Gardiner will not come ; if he does not, I hope you will no longer let the devil keep you silent." I felt my mind greatly affected while he was speaking to me, but did not say a great deal, not having much doubt of Mr. Gardiner's coming. As he was an admired preacher, a crowded congregation attended to hear him. We waited in the room until the people began to go away, when I was requested to preach. O my God ! Thou alone knowest what I then felt. My whole frame was so affected that I could scarcely speak or see ; I trembled in such a manner that, but for supporting myself by the pulpit, I should have fallen to the ground. While they were singing the first hymn, I lifted up my heart to God, and prayed that if I was going to act agreeably to

3a. Probably Mr. Gardner, of Tattenhall Wood, Cheshire.

His will He would assist me ; if not, that I might be kept from proceeding. I continued very long in the first prayer, found much encouragement of heart, and a good deal of courage, though I could not look the people in the face during the sermon. Some days before, I had been reading the account of St. Paul's proceedings at Corinth and Ephesus ; on opening the bible, I was led to the same passage, and took for my text part of the second verse of the nineteenth chapter of the Acts of the Apostles, "Have ye received the Holy Ghost since ye believed ?" I endeavoured to shew in what sense every Christian receives the Holy Ghost viz: — as a convincing, assisting, comforting and purifying Spirit, and pointed out, as well as I could, the necessity of thus receiving the Spirit of God, from the state we are in without him, being ignorant, helpless, miserable, and unclean creatures ; I then exhorted them to examine themselves, whether they had thus received the Holy Ghost, etc. Upon the whole the people seemed much affected, and I found such satisfaction in my mind that I gave notice we should meet again in the evening ; but I durst not say I would preach, being afraid to call myself a preacher." Here we evidently have, in Mr. Bradburn's own words, an account of the same incident, which, as reported by local tradition, is somewhat differently given in the chapter relating to College Street. It is plain that the sermon was preached not in the open air in a yard, but in a room furnished with a pulpit, but the room was probably in Mr. Parry's house and approached from what was afterwards called "Hughes' Yard." Mr. Bradburn continues :—
"In the evening many of the congregation were obliged to go away for want of room ; and I felt myself so raised above everything I had ever experienced before, that I spoke between two and three hours on that sweet passage which had often been blessed to my soul, John i, 43 and following verses. I preached at Wrexham the Thursday and Monday following, and on Monday returned home" to Chester. At Chester he was put upon the plan as a local preacher, and Wrexham being then in the Chester circuit, preached at Wrexham several times afterwards by due appointment. At the Conference of 1774 his name appeared on the minutes as one of the three travelling preachers of the Liverpool circuit, and in 1799 he, as I have already said, became President of the Conference. being then one of the most eloquent and popular preachers in the Connexion. It should also be said that the famous Thomas Olivers visited Wrexham after he had begun to preach. He was the author of the two well known hymns beginning "The God of Abraham praise," and "Lo! He comes with clouds descending." Mr. Olivers in his *Autobiography*, mentions this visit. but does not give the date, which, however, must have been before 1753. Nor does he mention a curious incident at Wrexham, an account of which I have read somewhere but cannot

now trace.   Thomas Boycott, Esq., of Brynyffynnon (see page 62), being a magistrate, when Mr. Olivers preached at Wrexham, signed a warrant for his arrest, and threatened to have him whipped out of the town unless he promised to preach no more in it, tried in short to "boycott" him, a curious fact, seeing that the verb "boycott" with the meaning now attached to it, is a creation of our own days.

13. I have already said that it seems probable that Mr. Bradburn's Wrexham relatives were the Joneses of The Dog Kennel. And I may here add that The Dog Kennel produced another Wesleyan minister, the Rev. Edward Jones, son of Mr. Thomas Jones,[4] market gardener, of The Dog Kennel, who on August 10th, 1841, being then stationed at Chester, married at Wrexham, Harriet, daughter of Thomas Roberts, maltster.

14. There is a local tradition that Mr. Wesley once paid a brief visit to Wrexham (see under College Street), preaching from an upper window of a house on Town Hill, now numbered 2, and occupied by Mr. E. R. Palmer, shoemaker. But although no mention appears to be made of this visit in Mr Wesley's journal, it seems certain that this tradition is trustworthy.

15. At the Conference of 1803 Wrexham was separated from Chester, and made the head of a circuit which included Oswestry. It had two ministers, of whom one lived at Wrexham, and the other at Oswestry. This arrangement continued until 1811, when Oswestry was made into a separate Circuit, but in 1822 was again amalgamated with Wrexham, and so continued until 1869. In September, 1813, the circuit plan included the afternamed stations, the number of members, and the quarterly contributions from each place being also given :—Wrexham, 60 (£3 10 0) ; Whitchurch 76 (£6 11 6) ;[5] Aston 30 (£2 4 0) ; Dodsgreen, 14 (10s.) ; Broughall, 20 (14s. 6d.) ; Bronington, 13, (25s.) ; Noman's Heath, 22 (£1 8 6) ; Duckington, 17 (10s.) ; Holling Lane, 11 (19s.) ; Overton, 19 (12s. 6d.); Bedwell, 12 (2s. 6d.); Cefn Mawr, 15 (27s.) ; Moss. 11, (7s); Holt, 5, (11s. 6d.) ; and Rackery, 0 (10s.) ; the total number of members being 325, and the total quarterly income £21 10 6. In June 1823, after the Oswestry circuit was again annexed to that of Wrexham, the places on the plan, with the quarterly contributions, were as follows : Wrexham, £11 16 0 ; Cross Lanes and Bangor, 21s. ; Overton, £2 ; Rhosmadoc, £1 7 7 ; Ruabon, 16s. ; Cefn, 21s. ; Bersham, 17s. 6d. ; Moss, £1 15 5 ; Gresford, £1 15 10 ; Lightwood Green, 6s. 5d. ; Penley, 14s. 7½d. ;

---

4. Old Mr. Thomas Jones, of The Dog Kennel, died November 30th, 1868, aged 87, his family having been connected with The Dog Kennel for more than a hundred years. Prochorus Roberts, son of the Rev. Edward Jones, died June 11th, 1832, in the 23rd year of his age, and was buried in Wrexham churchyard.

5. In 1815, Whitchurch was made the head of a new circuit.

Caergwrle, £2 18 8 ; Farndon, 6s. ; Greenwalls, 10s. ; Ponkey, £1 10 11 ; Bangor, ; Oswestry,£2 2 0 ; Wern, 21s. ; St, Martin's, :7s. o½d. ; Chirk, £1 10 10 ; Dudleston Heath, 20s.; Ellesmere, 25s. ; Porthywaen, 7s. ; Treflach Wood, 6s. 6d. ; Rhosygadfan, 20s. ; Tregynon, 4s. Spite of the amalgamation of the circuits, the two were always regarded in a measure as distinct, there being a Wrexham and an Oswestry side. I shall therefore only deal with those places which were worked from Wrexham. Overton was for a long time a flourishing cause, there being in September, 1830, 40 members there, a number which in March, 1839, had fallen to 3, and the place was the next quarter left off the plan. Rhosmadoc appears for the first time in June, 1816, having taken the place of Yellow Oak (which is first mentioned in March, 1815), and had 20 members in September 1832, but appeared in the plan f or the last time in December, 1835. Ruabon is mentioned for the first time in September. 1815, but was left off in April, 1818, reappearing in June, 1822, left off again in December, 1835, but once more showing itself with 16 members in March, 1838, and has continued to the present time. Since September, 1815, Cefr and Moss have kept their place on the plan. In September, 1815, the Cross Lanes cause takes the place of Bedwell, and in June, 1823 is amalgamated with that of Bangor, but in December, 1828 the name " Cross Lanes " disappears altogether, only Bangor being mentioned, a state of things which continues until September, 1833, and in the following March the Cross Lanes Society is returned as composed of seven members. The present chapel at Cross Lanes was built in the year 1834. Bangor itself first appears on the plan in September, 1819, and the quarterly meeting was held at the Dungrey, Bangor, June 24th, 1814 ; in June. 1823, as I have already said, Cross Lanes and Bangor were united, but were afterwards severed, Bangor having in June, 1836 only two members, and ceasing to be mentioned in the plan of March, 1838. Lightwood Green, in the parish of Overton, is first mentioned in January. 1816, and its name continued on the plan until March, 1835. The name of the Rackery disappears from the plan in September, 1815, but was replaced in April, 1820 by Gresford, a chapel being built in the Pant in 1822, which was replaced in 1879 by the present elegant building on the Chester Road, Gresford ; in March, 1832, the society there c omprised only 8 members, and in March, 1850, only 12. Bersham first appears on the plan in September 1815, and in September, 1829, was amalgamated with Rhostyllen, but was separated from the latter in April, 1826, and has continued a distinct society to the present time. The present chapel at Bersham was built in the year 1840. Penley was put on the plan in October, 1818, but was given up in 1826. Preaching began to be held at Greenwalls, the house of Mr. Samuel Williams, in the beginning of 1819, but ceased towards the end of 1823. The Society at Caergwrle was established at the end of 1819, and

speedily became very flourishing.   Ponkey first appears in the plan
in April, 1821, and appears for the last time in December, 1835.
Adwy'r Clawdd first appears on the plan of June, 1838, but is
dropped from that of September, 1840, to reappear in June, 1841.
The other places whose names occur for a short time on the early
plans are : Knolton Bryn, (1816) ; Rhosnessney (1819) ; Y Fedw
Coed in Eyton (1819 and 1820) ; Gwastad (1820 and 1821) ;
Farndon (1822-4) ; Crabtree Green (1824-1830) ; Holt (1813 and
1814, and 1832) ; Rhosllanerchrugog (1837 and 1838) ; King's
Mills (1847-1853) ; Ffrwd (1848-1853) ; The Forge, Abenbury
(1853) ;   and   Minera (1854-5).

16. From   this   long   digression   we   return to the town of
Wrexham.   In 1805 the Chapel in Salop Road, or in " The Green "
as it was always then called, was opened, and a sermon preached
at the opening service, January 1, 1805, or at one of the opening
services, by the Rev. Samuel Bradburn, and was published at
Bolton.   It was entitled "God shining forth from between the
Cherubim."   A minister's house, very small and poor, stood behind
the chapel.   In 1807, Wrexham was in the North Wales District
with the Rev. Owen Davies, himself a native of Wrexham, for the
chairman, who writing from Denbigh March 5th, 1807, to
Dr. Coke, says of the new chapel at Amlwch, that it was the best
in North Wales, " except that at Wrexham." In 1809, and again
in 1819, Wrexham was in the Shrewsbury District, but was afterwards allotted to the Liverpool District, in which it still continues.

17. A little before the time the Green Chapel was opened, a Mr.
John Williams came to settle as a draper, at the corner of Church
Street and Town Hill, and there remained until his death Nov.
15th, 1832, aged 63. (see under Church Street).   He married
Elizabeth, daughter of Mr. Benjamin Gilpin, of Bersham Furnace,
and sister of the well known Gilbert Gilpin, by whom he had one
daughter, Mary, who was the first wife of Mr. T. C. Jones.   Mr.
John Williams was a Wesleyan, and the eldest son of Mr. Richard
Williams, of Yr Acré farm, in the parish of Gresford, (that is *The
Acres*, corruptly called " The Rackery ")   This Mr. Richard
Williams was so devoted a Wesleyan, and so closely associated
with the rise of Wesleyanism in this district, that it is necessary
to say something about him.   He came to Yr Acré from Cheshire
somewhere about the year 1763, and immediately opened his house
for Methodist preaching, which was held there for about fifty years,
he being the leader of the class that met in it.   He married in
London, Elizabeth, second daughter of Mr. Richard Gardner, of
Tattenhall Wood, Cheshire, and had nine children who reached
maturity, six daughters and three sons.   Of the three sons, besides
Mr. John Williams, of Wrexham, there were Mr. Richard
Williams, of Green Walls farm, near Chester, father of the present
Mrs. T. C. Jones, and Mr. Samuel Williams, of Chester, whose

grandsons (sons of Mr. John Guest Williams, of Chester), have recently bought Yr Acré farm, in which their great grandfather so long lived. Of the daughters, Ann married the Rev. Samuel Warren, A.M., LL.D., then a Wesleyan minister (see note 11), and died in London December 2nd 1823, aged 43, being buried in the City Road Chapel graveyard.[6] Elizabeth became the wife of the Rev. George Morley, Wesleyan minister, twice President of the Conference ;[7] Martha married the Rev. Joseph Roberts, Wesleyan minister ; Phyllis married Mr. John Downes, a hat manufacturer, of Manchester ; Mary married Mr. Adam Bealey, a bleacher, of Radcliffe, Lancashire, and became the mother of Dr. Adam Bealey, of Harrogate (see page 72) ; while the eldest daughter, Margaret, married in 1796 John Copner Williams, Esq., solicitor, of Mold, afterwards of Denbigh, whose daughter married the Rev. Thomas Wynne-Edwards, M.A., vicar of Rhuddlan. Old Mr. Richard Williams, of Yr Acré, died July 12th, 1816, in the 79th year of his age, and was buried in Gresford churchyard. Mr. T. C. Jones has a portrait of him in oil, as well as one of his son Mr. John Williams, draper, of Wrexham.

18. The leading early Wesleyans in Wrexham, besides Mr. John Williams and Mr John Hughes (already mentioned) were Mr. William Matthews, shoemaker, of Charles Street, where Mr. Southern's shop now is (No. 21) ; Mr. John Farrer (see pages 18 and 19), and Mr. William Carman,[8] clothier, of Town Hill, who was circuit steward for many years. In the circuit, perhaps the chief man was Mr. James Platt, of Fens Hall, who was living there in 1814. At a later date the chief Wrexham Wesleyans were the present Mr. T. C. Jones, Mr. Samuel Thomas Baugh, the late Messrs. John Gittins[9] and Meredith Jones (see under No. 22 Charles Street), and, in the circuit, Mr. George Powell, of Ruabon.

19. In the early days of Methodism in this town, a horse was kept to enable the minister to travel through the circuit, and the cost of this was very considerable, the charge for its maintenance being almost as great as the charge for the maintenance of the minister himself. In those days, in fact, the salaries of the minis-

6. Her husband Dr. Warren, published (1827) a very interesting Memoir of her.

7. Mrs. Morley was the grandmother of Mrs John Gittins, of Plas yn Llwyn, who possesses a very beautiful portrait of her.

8. Mr. William Carman was a brother of the late Mr. John Carman, Clothier, who had a shop a little lower down on the same (north) side of Town Hill, and was father of Mary Ann, the first wife of the late Mr. John Gittins. He died April 2nd, 1844, aged 50, and was buried in the Old Cemetery.

9. Mr. John Gittins, J.P., was for many years an Ironmonger at No. 7 Hope Street, and the father of the present Mr. John Colemere Gittins, of the same place. He retired from business in 1882, and died suddenly at Plas yn Lllwyn, November 5th, 1887, aged 65. He was a Class Leader, Local Preacher, and several times Circuit Steward.

ters, or "the preachers" (as they were always then called), were exceedingly small, and nothing but an overpowering sense of duty could have inspired them to undergo such hardships as their small incomes must have involved. Of course a furnished house, such as it was, was provided for them, their travelling expenses were paid, allowances were often made to them when they were sick,[10] and other allowances were sometimes made under special circumstances. Still, spite of all this, the smallness of the salaries on which the preachers had to subsist is very striking. Thus, during the quarter ending October 2nd, 1815, only £5 5 0 were paid to the Rev. James Fussell, an educated man, formerly an under graduate at Oxford, as his "quarterage," £2 2 0 more as his wife's "quarterage," and £1 19 0 as "board," but in the quarter immediately succeeding Mrs. Fussell's "quarterage" was not paid. Inasmuch as it seems probable, from other entries in the account book, that the "board" was only the repayment of sums Mr. Fussell had expended in his travels through the circuit, £28 a year was the most that Mr. Fussell ever received. But the tendency was, as time went on, to increase the minister's salary, and in 1823 £8 a year began to be allowed for a servant. Nevertheless, even as late as 1858, the salary of the elder (or Wrexham) minister was only £96 a year, while that of the younger (or Oswestry) minister was only £52 4 a year.

20. Indeed it is surprising how small the total income of the circuit was. In October, 1813, the total quarterly receipts from the classes throughout the whole circuit (which, be it remembered, included Oswestry and the stations connected with it), amounted to only £20 10 6, and in March, 1856 to only £47 9 1. In 1831 the first grant to the circuit from the Contingent Fund was made, but was discontinued in 1856. These, and special contributions were the sole sources of income, nor were quarterly collections made until after 1850, and in March, 1859 these only realized £14 7 5.

21. In 1827 there were in the Wrexham circuit, 8 chapels, 20 local preachers, and 392 members. The latter amounted at Christmas, 1832, to 499, but had fallen by March, 1840, to 279, and had only risen by December, 1854 to 375. The present numbers (March 1890) are: 15 chapels. 32 local preachers, and 572 members.

22. The early Circuit Stewards' book includes no other items of special interest than those incorporated in the foregoing narative, except the following in December 1845 : "Expenses connected with opposing Maynooth Endowment Bill 10s."

10   In the old Circuit Stewards' book which Mr. William Thomas has kindly allowed me to see, there are notes of frequent payments for "medicine," evidently for the preachers. The following entries may be quoted : June 29, 1819. Doctor's Bill, £2 ; March, 1834, presented to Mr. Griffiths (Rev. Joseph Griffiths) on account of afflictions, £5 ; 1814, Mrs. Jordan's confinement £3 3.

23. The Green Chapel continued to be used until 1855, when it was sold to the Wesleyan Reformers, and the first Brynyffnnon Chapel was built, and under Hope Street, pages 72-74, some account of that chapel will be found. When the Wesleyan Reformers died out in Wrexham, the chapel was sold to the late Mr. Thomas Rowland (Mayor in 1869-70) who pulled it down, and built the houses composing Chapel Place on its site. From the time of the building of the Brynyffnnon Chapel commenced the period of the increasing and abiding prosperity of the Wesleyans of Wrexham.

24. In 1855, the year when the new chapel was opened, the circuit plan included the following stations : Wrexham, Cross Lanes, Moss, Ruabon, Cefn, Caergwrle, Gresford, Bersham, Adwy, Oswestry, Ellesmere, Dudleston, Overton, Lodge, Llangollen Road or Jubilee Chapel, Selattyn and Hengoed.

25. I give the following annotated list of the ministers that have been stationed in the Wrexham Circuit from the beginning :—

1803-4	George Lowe, Edward Linnell.
1804-5	do. do.
1805-6	John Sydserff, Samuel Warren.[11]
1806-7	do. do.
1807-8	William Harrison, sen. ; John James.
1808-9	Anthony B. Seckerson,[12] (from Chester); John James
1809-10	do. William Baker, jun.
1810-11	do. William Worth.
1811-12	William Timperley, do.
1812-13	do Luke Barlow.
1813-14	John Jordan, Joseph Pretty.
1814-15	do. do.
1815-16	James Fussell (came hither from Oswestry ; see under Wrexham Fechan)
1816-17	do.
1817-18	do.
1818-19	Hugh Beech.
1819-20	do.
1820-21	do.
1821-22	James Mortimer.
1822-23	do. Hugh Carter. James Fussell, Supernumerary,

11. Samuel Warren, M.A., L.L.D., married Anne, eldest daughter of Mr. Richard Williams, of Yr Acré, in Gresford parish (see before) : about 1832 he joined the Church of England and became ultimately Rector of All Souls, Every Street, Manchester. One of his sons was Samuel Warren, Q.C., Author of " The Diary of a Late Physician," and of other works ; he was born at Yr Acré when his mother was on a visit there. Dr. Warren died May 23rd, 1862, aged 81.

12. Anthony B. Seckerson was a rather noted preacher. A portrait of him is given in the Methodist Magazine for December, 1809, when he was at Wrexham.

1823-24	John A. Lomas, Thomas Pearson, James Fussell, [Supernumerary.
1824-25	John Hughes (from Brecon), William Davies (3rd)do.
1825-26	do. do. do. do.
1825-26	Jonathan Turner (from Caermarthen), John Oliver (from Kington), James Fussell, Supernumerary.
1827-28	Jonathan Turner, John Wheelhouse (from Newtown), James Fussell, Supernumerary.
1828-29	Charles Janion, John Wheelhouse, do. [James Fussell, Supernumerary.
1829-30	Thomas Gee, Thomas Jones do.
1830-31	Henry Tuck, do. do.
1831-32	Edward Jones, (1st) (from Durham), Samuel Dawson,
1832-33	do. Samuel Dawson [James Fussell, Supernumerary.
1833-34	Joseph Griffith, jun., James Corbett do.
1834-35	do. John Hornby do.
1835-36	do- Thomas Pearson, jun, do.
1836-37	Hugh Carter, George Hughes do.
1837-38	do, Richard Petch do.
1838-39	Thomas Hall, (from Brigg), Joseph Sykes, do.
1839-40	do. John Ward, jun.
1840-41	Luke Heywood, Thomas Denham.
1841-42	John Hornby, Samuel Lucas (sec.)
1842-43	Francis Barker, Joseph Whitehead.
1843-44	do. do.
1844-45	William Ricketts, Frederick Payne
1845-46	do. Elisha Balley.
1846-47	do. do.
1847-48	William Coullas, George Buckley.
1848-49	Robert Mainwaring, John Eaton.
1849-50	do. do.
1850-51	Thomas Haswell, Thomas H. Brocklehurst.
1851-52	Robert Totherick, James M. Cranswick.
1852-53	do. Joseph Hirst.
1853-54	Benjamin Slack, Samuel Atkinson (2nd)
1854-55	do. do.
1855-56	do. do.
1856-57	Samuel Hooley, Ishmael Jones, Griffith Hughes, [Supernumerary.
1857-58	do· John M Pilter do.
1858-59	do. do do.
1859-60	Seth Dixon (1st) ; Alfred Freeman do.
1860-61	do. George G. S. Thomas do.
1861-62	Jacob Turvey, David Stewart do.
1862-63	do. do. do.
1863-64	do. James Daniel do.
1864-65	John S. Jones, James Daniel

1865-66	John S. Jones, James Daniel
1866-67	do. Joseph Agar Beet,[17] Henry Needle.
1867-68	Frederick Payne, do do.
1868-69	do. Edward R. Edwards, William Wilson, Supernumerary.[13]
1869-70	Frederick Payne, Edward R. Edwards,
1870-71	Joshua Priestley,[14] John S. Simon.
1871-72	do· Thomas H. Mawson
1872-73	do. do.
1873-74	William Shaw (B) Charles Onions.[15]
1874-75	do. do.
1875-76	do. Sidney Mees.[16]
1876-77	John G. Cox, Henry A. Young, Joseph Agar Beet, Supernumerary.[17]
1877-78	John M. Bamford, George H. Barker.
1878-79	do. do.
1879-80	do. Alfred Johnson.
1880-81	Ebenezer Evans, do.
1881-82	do. do.
1882-83	do. Percy Watson.
1883-84	Joseph Agar Beet,[17] Percy Watson.
1884-85	do. do.
1885-86	James W. Eacott, George Gibson (B) ;[18] Ebenezer [Evans, Supernumerary.
1886-87	do. George Gibson do.
1887-88	do. do. do.
1888-90	James Sewell Haworth,[19] Samuel Mort[20] do.
1890-91	do. do.
1891-92	J. M. Mangles,[21] J. Bateman.

13 Married Elizabeth, third daughter of Mr. Richard Williams, of Greenwalls: died May 14th, 1869, aged 67, and was buried in Gresford Churchyard.

14 Joshua Priestley, a member of the same family as Dr. Priestley, of Birmingham : died April 3rd, 1863 at Accrington, aged 73. He was a native of Birstall.

15 Charles Onions, afterwards changed his name to Wenyon, married Eliza Morley, second daughter of the late Mr. John Gittins, of Wrexham, obtained the degree of M.D. from the University of Edinburgh, and went out as a medical missionary to China, and is now stationed at Fat Sham.

16 Mr. Sidney Mees married shortly after his stay in Wrexham, a daughter of the late Mr. Nuttall, of Llangollen.

17 Rev. Joseph Agar Beet married Sarah, only daughter of Mr. Samuel Thomas Baugh, of Plaspenyddol, Bersham, near Wrexham, is author of various homiletical works, and was transferred in 1885 to become Theological Tutor at Richmond College.

18 Rev. George Gibson removed to Leith.

19 Son of Richard Haworth, Esq., cotton manufacturer, of Manchester, educated under the late Mr. Pryce Jones at the Grove School, Wrexham, and went from Wrexham to Hastings.

20 Went from Wrexham to Margate.

21 Came from Newark to Wrexham.

PART II

CHAPTER XVII

WREXHAM FECHAN.

1. The name "Wrexham Fechan," which means "Little Wrex-ham," is now applied exclusively to the little stretch of street, part of the Ellesmere Road, which struggles up from The Willow Bridge to the mouth of Bryn y cabanau Lane (so called). But formerly it was a name of much wider application, Erddig Lane for example, being described as in Wrexham Fechan. Wrexham Fechan, in fact, so late as the beginning of the 17th century was the name of a distinct township, although ever since 1660, at any rate, it has been treated as a part of Wrexham Regis. What were the exact boundaries of the old township of Wrexham Fechan I cannot discover, but from various indications I do not think I shall be far wrong in saying that it included all that part of the present township of Wrexham Regis which lies on the right bank of the Gwenfro. What is now called Wrexham Fechan is the old street of the township. the only part of it in which a group of houses stood. In the present chapter we shall deal first of all with Wrexham Fechan in this narrower sense, and then treat of it in the larger sense, describing the fields and estates belonging to Wrexham Fechan which lay beyond the street. or group of houses, now exclusively so called.

2. Beginning with what is now known as Wrexham Fechan, we will stand at The Green Bridge, and speak first of The Bridge House on the right hand side of the road. The first time I have met with this house (or the predecessor of this house), called by this name is in the year 1768, but the house itself can be traced back as far as 1742. In 1780 it is described as belonging to William Jones, Esq , of Wrexham Fechan, and in 1793 to John Jones, Esq., of the same (see page 176), but in 1794 it belonged to John Meller Esq. (see page 42 note 1a), who still owned it in 1808, but before 1818 it had been bought by the Rev. Wm.

Browne, minister of the Presbyterian Chapel, who let The Bridge
.Bridge House as an inn, but converted part of the premises by the
brook side, where Willow Lane now is, into a skin yard for his son
Mr. William Browne.   I believe the present house was built by
Mr. Michael Gummow, who in 1857 was the owner of it.

3. Keeping along the same side of the street (for there were at
this point no houses on the opposite side), we come, at the
corner of the street and of Bennion's Lane, to The Green
Dragon, which is mentioned under that name in 1742. It belonged in 1808 to Mr. Thomas Stephenton, of Willow House, but was
sold after his death to Mrs. Bennion, of Beechley.

4 At the opposite corner of Bennion's Lane is the important house
now called "Beechley," a name which, though quite modern, I
shall adopt for distinction sake, the house having formerly no
specific name, except that for a time it was called "Dursley's"
or Darsley's, from a person of that name who occupied the place in
the early part of last century.   Mr. Dursley (or Darsley) was there
in 1715 and also in 1717, but not afterwards ; nevertheless the
estate was called by his name long after 1742.   After this gentleman's time the house and lands passed into the possession of one
Thomas Jones, and in 1726 "the new house" here is mentioned
in the rate books, an interesting entry, since it gives us the approximate date of the erection of the later house.   In 1742 the
latter was vacant, but in 1747 and 1748 both house and lands were
occupied by George Ravenscroft, Esq.[1] (see pages 147 and 153),
and were charged for church rate at 3/5, Hafod y wern being
charged during the same years at 20/9. Then in 1749 Mr. William
Jones, the first of the important family of Jones of Wrexham
Fechan, came to occupy the estate, and then or at a later date
acquired it.   In 1747 he was living at Plas Gwern, and about
1753, started in business as a wine merchant at the Vaults in
Abbot Street (see under Abbot Street).   This business about the
year 1765 he relinquished and lived afterwards as a private
gentleman at his house in Wrexham Fechan, becoming High Sheriff
of the county in 1774.   He was, as we shall directly see, a son of the
Rev. William Jones, curate, of Erbistock, and was baptized there
October 10th, 1724.   Not naming those who died young, the following are the names of those children of his who were baptized at
Wrexham :—1 Jane bapt. November 8th, 1749 ; 2 William, bapt.
January 18th, 1750-51 whom I suppose to have succeeded him,
and who married at Wrexham (June 15th, 1771), Mary King, of
the parish of Marylebone, Middlesex ; 3 Mary, born May 2nd, 1752,
afterwards the wife of John Matthews, Esq., of Wrexham (see
page 97); 4 John, bapt. August 1756 ; 5 Thomas, bapt. December
16th, 1757 ; 6 Richard, bapt. September 20th, 1759 ; 7 Bridget, bapt.

1. He had for two years before lived in another house in Wrexham Fechan
which I cannot identify.

August 9th, 1763; and 8 Edward Lloyd, born November 16th, 1765.
In the Wrexham registers the two following entries occur :—
" Mch. 23, 1776, William Jones, of Wrexham Vechan, Esq.,
Buried ;" and " Feb. 26, 1782, William Jones, of Wrexham Vechan, Esq,, Buried." From these and other entries in the registers
and rate books, the impression is borne in upon the mind that
William Jones. Esq., the son of the Rev. William Jones, died in
1776, and was succeeded by his son of the same name, who dying
without issue in 1782, was succeeded by his brother next in age,
John Jones, Esq. In the Marford Court Rolls, on the other hand,
under date December 11th, 1792, John Jones, Esq., of Wrexham, is
described as the *eldest* son of the first William Jones, Esq., of
Wrexham Fechan, a statement which, however, may perhaps be
taken to mean that he was the eldest son *then surviving*, and
therefore the heir at law.   The elucidation of the history
of this family is beset with special difficulties owing to the
similarity of the names involved.   In any case, it is certain
that after the decease of the Mr. William Jones who died
in 1782, his property passed by inheritance into the possession of Mr. John Jones. This Mr. John Jones, the record of
whose baptism I cannot find in the parish registers, appears after
his brother's (or father's) death, not to have occupied Beechley at
all, and beyond the names of his children (William Price Jones,
who died unmarried and intestate, and Henry Stephens Jones,
ribbon weaver, of Coventry), I know nothing of his history.
    5. Having said this much by way of introduction, it becomes
necessary to give further particulars as to the history of the Joneses
of Wrexham Fechan.   The Rev. William Jones, curate of
Erbistock, married at Ruabon (August 30th, 1719) Ann Lloyd,
spinster, sister, and afterwards one of the two heirs of Edward
Lloyd, Esq., of Llwyn y maen, near Oswestry. This Mr. Edward
Lloyd had married, for his first wife Maria, only daughter of
Edward Lloyd, Esq., of Horsley, in the parish of Gresford. By
this wife he had no children, and his children (Edward Richard
and Frances Phebe) by his second wife (Bridget), died without issue.
His two sisters, Ann and Catherine, became thus entitled after
his death, to equal moieties of what remained of the Horsley Hall
(as well as I suppose of the Llwyn y maen) estate. One of the two
sisters, as we have seen, married the Rev. William Jones. His
son, the first William Jones, Esq., of Wrexham Fechan, was thus
the heir of a moiety of Horsley and probably of Llwyn y maen, or
of part of it.   He had also the house and lands in Wrexham
Fechan aforetime called " Dursley's," with which were incorporated
another small house and croft. We have seen moreover, that he
owned The Bridge House, Wrexham Fechan, and The Vaults at
the corner of Abbot Street and Black Chamber Street, in which he
had for a time carried on business. The whole group of houses
between The Sun and The Bull in Abbot Street also belonged to
him.

6. The rate books for the years 1772-1779 are lost, but from those of 1780 we find that although Beechley then still belonged to the Joneses, it was occupied by Major Bell (see Index). In 1781 it was occupied by Mr. Hughes, in 1783 and 1784 by Mr. George Warrington (see page 61), and in 1786 by Mr. Hodgkins. Then about 1793 or 1794 it was acquired by Thomas Bennion, Esq., attorney at law, and in his occupation, and in that of his daughters, it remained until past the middle of the present century. Bennion's Lane, which adjoined much of his property in Wrexham Fechan, took its name from him. The whole of the property of the Joneses did not pass into his possession, The Bridge House and the house and shop in Abbot Street, for example, passed into other hands. So also did a field along Bennion'sLane which had been a part of the old Dursley lands. On the other hand his widow added The Green Dragon to the Wrexham Fechan estate, and he himself bought a house adjoining Beechley, which he converted into an office, and which still stands in the Beechley grounds. This became the office of Messrs Kenyon and Bennion, his partner being George Kenyon, Esq., son of Roger Kenyon, Esq., of Cefn, and this firm did the greater part of the legal business then transacted in Wrexham. After Mr. Bennion's death, Mr. Kenyon took into partnership Mr. Philip Parry, who lived at The Court, and the firm became known as Messrs Kenyon and Parry. Then from 1817 until his death in 1829, Mr. Kenyon practised as a solicitor in the office aforesaid in his own name alone. In 1844, the fields numbered 207, 209, 210, 216, 217, 492, 498, 499, 500, and 515 in the annexed map, belonged to Beechley. Mr. Thomas Bennion was the eldest son of Mr. Bennion, of Parcau (Parkey), Pickhill, and Mr. John Bennion of Old Sontley, and William Bennion, Esq., of Plas Grono, in Esclusham Below, afterwards of Ashfield, in Stansty, were his brothers.[2] He married Miss Jane Edge, the heiress of an estate in Overton parish (Flintshire), which included Sodyllt, Queen's Bridge, and other farms, and had by her five daughters, all baptized at Wrexham, and all I believe, buried at Overton. Their names were—Dorothea (born February 7th, bapt. April 24th, 1793, died   1852); Caroline (born October 28th, 1795, bapt. February 12th, 1796, died February 6th, 1847); Mary Anne, (born September 1st, bapt. September 4th, 1797, died   );

2. The above-named Mr. John Bennion, of Sontley, had, amongst others, two sons, one of whom, Thomas, was of Burras Lodge, and the other, John, a solicitor, of Wrexham, first of 29 Chester Street, afterwards of Island Green, in our notice of which a further account will be given of him ; and a daughter, Maria, who became the wife of Mr. Thomas Acton, of Rhyd Broughton, and the mother of the present Mr. T. Bennion Acton, solicitor. There was also a Mr. Joseph Bennion, who was related to the same family, who in 1808 was living at Croes Newydd, and in connection with whom the following entries occur in the parish registers :

Dec. 20, 1808, Joseph, S. of Mr. Joseph and Camilla Bennion, Croesnewydd, Buried.

June 20, 1812, Camilla Caroline. wife of Mr. Joseph Bennion, Æt 35. Buried.

Feb. 27, 1819, Joseph Bennion Esq., London, Æt 39 Buried.

Ellen Eliza (bapt. September 12th, 1801); and Jane (bapt. October 24th, 1801). Mr. Thomas Bennion died November 14th, 1803, aged 43, and was buried at Overton, where also was buried his wife, who died March 10th, 1840, aged 76.   His widow, Mrs. Jane Bennion, continued to occupy Beechley to the end of her life. There also remained until the time of their death her three eldest daughters.   These three ladies, who never married, were extraordinarily munificent.   Miss Dorothea Bennion rebuilt in 1850 the south aisle of Overton Church.   She also, in conjunction with her sister, Miss Mary Anne Bennion, erected, to the memory of her sister Caroline, the Bennion Almshouses at Overton.   Miss Mary Anne Bennion gave in 1858, £100 towards the erection of St. Mark's Church, Wrexham. and purchased four-fifths of the great tithes of Minera from Richard Thompson, Esq., for the perpetual endowment of it.   The east window of stained glass in the same church, to the memory of Albert, Prince Consort, was also set up by her at a cost of £440.   Mr. John Lewis, solicitor, ultimately succeeded Miss Bennion at Beechley, gave it its present name, and still lives there.

7.   The next house in Wrexham Fechan on the same side of the way which we must notice is that next but one to Beechley. In 1785 and 1791, Mr. John Matthews attorney (see page 97) from Chester Street lived here, and afterwards (1791-3) Mr. Harris, attorney, who was succeeded by the Rev. Humphrey Maysmore, curate.   Then about 1805 George Griffiths, Esq. (see *History of Parish Church*, p 115, note 354), afterwards of The Mount, bought the house, and here lived until after 1814, when Mr. Benjamin Octave Corlett set up a school in it, which continued until about 1826.   In all the entries relating to Mr. Corlett in the parish register, the word "Schoolmaster," following his name, has been erased, and the word "Gentleman" substituted for it—a piece of snobbery, for a schoolmaster he was, and no one need be ashamed of so honourable a calling. The Rev. James Fussell, who had from 1815 to 1818 been the regular Wesleyan Minister stationed in Wrexham, followed, about 1822, Mr. Corlett as a schoolmaster at this house, and there lived for many years, dying at Poplar Cottage January 18th, 1839, aged 56, and was buried in the grave of the Tomkinsons of Mount Street, and the Owenses of Felin Puleston.   He was a native of Road, Somerset.

8.   Beyond the house just described came that called "The Travellers' Rest," now an Inn, but formerly a small farmstead, or market gardener's house, having the fields attached to it which are numbered in the map 220-225, and containing about 3a. 3r. 34p. of land. This holding belonged during the last and the first quarter of the present century to the Pulestons, of Hafodywern, and their successors, but about the year 1825 was sold to Mr. Potts, of Chester.

9. At the western corner of Ellesmere Road and "Bryn y Cabanau Lane" is the house called "Gatefield," named probably, as we shall presently see, from a field adjoining known as "Cae Llidiart," which means "Gate field" in English. This house is first mentioned in the rate books for 1824, but as those for 1819-1823 are lost, it may have been built three or four years before 1824. In the year last-named it is described as the property of Mr. Edward Crewe (see under College Street), and as occupied by Mrs. Abraham. Two fields called "Cae Llidiart" and "Barn Field" (the latter so-named from the old barn which still stands in Bryn y cabanau Lane, and which was built by Mr. Crewe), were also owned by Mr. Crewe, but were let apart from the house : they were probably those marked 495 and 497 in the map. Then about 1827 Mr. Crewe sold the two fields to Miss Potts, and the house to Mr. Thos. Edgworth, solicitor, afterwards the first mayor of Wrexham, and in the following year Mr. Edgworth himself went to live in the house, and there continued until nearly the end of his life. As the Edgworths were a family of some importance, and long connected with the parishes of Wrexham, Holt, and Marchwiel, I have given an account of them in a separate notice at the end of this chapter.

10. We have, hitherto, kept on the same (or right-hand) side of the street, called Wrexham Fechan from the Green Bridge upwards. On the other side back to the Gwenfro were nothing but fields, all (or nearly) belonging in 1844 to Miss Potts, of Chester, whose father had bought them of Philip Davies Cooke, Esq., the representative of the Pulestons, of Hafod y wern, the former owners of them. Among these lands were two fields, marked 453 and 454 on the map, which were called "The Heltrees," a name on which I can throw no light. The lower Heltree or "Hiltre" (as it is called in one deed), is now intersected by Rivulet Road, and the Gasworks occupy a portion of it. Adjoining the Heltrees (but I do not know on which side of them), were two fields called "Cae brenhin mawr" and "Cae brenhin bychan," that is "*The Great King's Field*" and "*The Little King's Field*,"—interesting names because they show that the land about here belonged formerly to the lord's demesre, and so seem to confirm what I have said in ch. xii, sec. 1. Like the Heltrees, these two fields pertained in later times to the Pulestons, of Hafod y wern.

11. As to "Bryn y cabanau lane," it is by no means certain that this is the true form of the name. "Bryn y cabanau" means "Hill of the cabins," but old people call it "Brynyky Banyky," of course a corrupt name, but not, necessarily, a corruption of "Bryn y cabanau," which represents, probably, only an attempt to rationalize a name of which the original form is doubtful.[2a] In fact, I have seen

2a. "Bryn y cabanau" is not only a late, but one may freely say, a manufactured name. Nevertheless, on the assumption that it is ancient and correct, the

a group of deeds of last century, wherein, instead of "Bryn y cabanau," the forms "Bryn y gwiban" and "Bryn y gwibane" occur. This, of course, disposes of "Bryn y cabanau," but still leaves the true form of the name uncertain. "Bryn y gwiban" would mean "Hill of the fly," while "Bryn y chwiban" (an alternative form which suggests itself), would mean "Hill of the whistle," neither of them names that can be regarded as satisfactory. I shall speak of this lane again on page 181.

12. Continuing our course past Gatefield along the Ellesmere Road, there were in the year 1844 no houses on the left hand until one came to Bron Haul, and on the right to the King's Mill *House*.

13. In 1844, Thomas Edgworth, Esq., owned the fields numbered 469-471 (containing 29 acres), on the one side of Whitegates Lane leading to Hafod y wern, and Thomas Taylor Griffith, owned the fields numbered on the map 452, 455 to 457 (containing nearly 16 acres), on the other side of the lane. This lane had, hitherto, been very crooked, and these gentlemen straightened it, making it take its present course. Mr. Edgworth's fields were ultimately bought by Peter Walker, Esq., of Coed y glyn, who built the farm buildings and labourers' cottages on the east side of the lane which now stand there.

14. The fields just named had been bought by Mr. Griffith and Mr. Edgworth, of the Potts, of Chester. The latter possessed, during the early part of this century, a very large quantity of land in Wrexham. In 1844 Miss Ann Potts and Mrs. Ann Potts, widow, owned, between them, the Dog Kennel estate, containing the areas numbered 149, 153-7, and 214, and comprising 9a. 0r. 32p., the Travellers' Rest estate, the field opposite the Travellers' Rest (numbered 215, and containing 3a. 2r. 30p.), the Heltrees adjoining (Nos. 453 and 454, containing 7a. 0. 3p.), the Caeau estate, a group of fields along " Bryn y cabanau" lane (numbered in the map 494-7, 501, 502, 506, 508, and 509, containing 36a. 0r. 28p., see sec. 17), and a group of lands in the Pwll y wrach area, near the Great Western Railway Station (see page 78), the whole amounting to 79a. 3r. 7p., all close to a rapidly growing town, and capable of being let at good rents. If to these we add the lands sold to Messrs. Griffith and Edgworth, we shall get a total area of 124a. 2r. 27p.

15. The abandoned railway that crosses the Ellesmere Road was intended to go to Whitchurch, and to work with the Wrexham, Mold, and Connah's Quay Line. It was started about the year 1863, and abandoned about 1866.

16. The Barracks in Ellesmere Road were erected in 1877, the old Barracks of the 23rd Royal Welsh Fusiliers being the present County Hall in Regent Street.

---

statement has been made that on the hill so called, during the plague (date not given), cabins were erected for the accommodation of the sufferers. And so history is made.

17. There were formerly in Wrexham Fechan seven fields belonging to the Acton Hàll Estate, From various indications I guess that one of those fields (which came to be called " Egerton's Croft,"and was on the right-hand side of Ellesmere Road, above King's Mill House), was bought by Miss Bennion, of Beechley, and is, probably that marked 492 on the map. The other six fields lay, I am sure, along what is now called " Bryn y cabanau lane," The following is the description of the seven fields in Norden's Survey of A D., 1620 :—[Chief Rent], 6s. 8d. The same [John Jeffreys, Esq., of Acton], holds in Wrexham Fechan seven closes of land, purchased of Richard Williams, being formerly the land of Richard Smith, called by these names following : 1. Kæ truin uaine ["Cae trwyn faen,"—*Field of the stone snout*]. 2. Pant y feiriad ["Pant yr offeiriad,"—*The priest's hollow*]. 3. Y crachdire [Scabland, *i.e.*, Poor land]. 4. Kae gwalchmaie [*"Gwalchmai's field"*]. 5. Errow y dwr [*The Water acre*]. 6. Kae y groise ["Cae'r groes,"—*"Field of the cross*]. 7. Kae lloydin [probably " Cae llydan,"—*Broadfield*], containing. by estimation, 15 [customary] acres," equal to nearly 32 statute acres. Some of the names above-quoted are very interesting. All are now forgotten, but most of them were still remembered during the latter part of last century. In fact, there is at Gwysaney a map of these fields with the names given. As one goes along " Bryn y cabanau lane," the field numbered 494 was " Pant yr offeiriad," that numbered 502 was " Crachdir," while " Cae trwyn faen" adjoined " Pant yr offeiriad" to the west. On the other side of the lane, where 501 now is, were " Erw Ddwr," " Pitfield," and " Erw Crachdir." The field called " Bryn y gwyban," after which the lane was named, appears to be that numbered 508 in the map. These seven fields were leased in 1668 by John Jeffreys, Esq., to Arthur Harper, and afterwards were purchased by the Pulestors, of Hafod y wern, whose representatives, Bryan Cooke, Esq. (or his son) sold them to Mr. Potts, of Chester.

18. The King's Mill House appears to have been erected on lands which, in 1690 and again in 1715, are described as belonging to John Weston, of Marchwiel. In 1724 John Meller, Esq., of Erddig, is rated for "Weston's late lands," and in 1742, though Weston's late *lands* there are mentioned, no mention is made of any house The house, however, had come into existence by 1780, and was then, as now, a part of the Erddig estate.

19. As to the farm now called " Bron Haul " on the opposite side of the road to King's Mill *House*, this was erected on lands belonging to the heirs of Mr. David Phillips, who was buried at Wrexham, September 24th, 1670 (see page 125). In 1771 they were still called " Mr. Phillips' lands," but before 1780 they had been purchased by Roger Kenyon, Esq., of Cefn. In 1828 they still belonged to the Cefn estate, and are described as " lands" only, no house being mentioned. They were subsequently sold to Mr. Joseph Cooper (see page 116), who I believe, built

the present farmhouse, and are still possessed by his representatives. In 1844 the house was certainly in existence, and had attached to it 24 acres of land, comprising the fields numbered 472-4, 477-9, 483-5.

20. The group of cottages and smithy in the hollow down by the bridge and opposite the King's Mills, formed together with another group of cottages adjoining in Abenbury, a hamlet which until a hundred years ago was called ' Pentre'r Felin Newydd " (*Hamlet of the New Mill*), but is now known simply as " The Pentre."

21. I have already said that the King's Mill was aforetime the lord's mill of Wrexham Regis, and that here, and here only, were the inhabitants of the township allowed to grind. The following statement of the sixteen jurymen empanelled by John Norden to assist him in his survey in the year 1620 may usefully be quoted : " They [the jurymen] say that the Prince his highness hath a custome water mill in this mannour, called Y Vellyn Newydd, or New Mill, whereat the tenauntes and inhabitantes of this manno' of Wrexham and of other townships[3] are bounde to grinde ; and that Roger Bellot, gent, hath a lease of the same mill (amongst other things) under the great seale of England for three lives in being, at the rent of ten poundes, six shillings, eight pence, p'ann, and now in the tenure of Robert Puleston, Esquire, who had the same at the hands of the said Roger Bellot, and is kept in very good reparac'on."

22. The King's Mills subsequently passed into the possession of the Edisburys of Erddig, and have ever since belonged to the Erddig estate. The provision as to all the inhabitants of Wrexham Regis grinding their corn at these mills, and nowhere else, became subsequently modified into a commutation fee for all who did not grind their *malt* there, and this fee was collected within the memory of some now or recently living.

23. Having thus completed our survey of the street known as Wrexham Fechan and of Ellesmere Road, let us now, starting from Wrexham Fechan, walk along what is now called " Bennion's Lane," in the direction of Sontley Lane. Here we come to what were, aforetime, the Common Fields of Wrexham Fechan. On our right was, until recently a field, numbered 206 in the map, which, in later times, was called the " Upper Hirdir" or "Lesser Hirdir" ("Hirdir"—*Longland*), but which was originally called "Grofft Tuddir," or " Grofft Tudor," that is *"Tuddir's Croft,"* or *"Tudor's Croft"* Across this, the street called " Salusbury Park," or " Salusbury Road," now runs. In 1620 David ap John Robert (see under College Street) owned half of Grofft Tuddir, John Lloyd, of

---

3. Probably of all the bond townships of the commote or rhaglotry of Wrexham.

Eglwysegl, having at the same time two parcels of land in the same by right of Elizabeth ferch Hugh, his wife. The half of GrofftTuddir which David ap John Robert possessed had, a few years before, consisted of at least three parcels or quillets, one having been purchased by him in 1616, of Hugh Jones, gent, of Bedwell, and Owen Jones, gent, of Gourton, another of Maud ferch Hugh, sister of the above-named Elizabeth ferch Hugh (and formerly the land of her father Hugh ap David ap Hugh), while the third was a parcel called " Erw Jamys" (*James' acre*), also purchased of the same Maud ferch Hugh, which adjoined Grofft Tuddir on the south. David ap John Robert appears to have subsequently bought of John Lloyd the other half, or two parcels of Grofft Tuddir, and thus got the whole field (which then contained a little over five statute acres) into his hands. I give these particulars so as to show how the severally-owned quillets or strips of land in a single field *sometimes* arose. Hugh ap David ap Hugh had several fields in Wrexham Fechan which, after his death, were partitioned among his two daughters, but not so that one daughter had one group of fields and the other another, but so that, in the case of this field at any rate, the two daughters had certain parts of the same field. Grofft Tuddir descended from David ap John Robert to his representatives, the Davieses of Wrexham, from them by marriage to the Thelwalls, of Blaen Iàl, and so to John Lloyd Salusbury, Esq. (see page 32, sec. 36), nephew of the last Simon Thelwall, Esq., of Blaen Ial. This Mr. Salusbury, in the year 1844, still owned Grofft Tuddir, then called " The Lesser Hirdir," and it was from him that Salusbury Road or Salisbury Park got its name, while Hirdir Lodge in Salisbury Park was called after the latter name of Grofft Tuddir.

24. Nearly all the fields along Bennion's Lane belonged in 1620 to the above named John Lloyd, of Eglwysegl (at an earlier date called John Lloyd, gent, of Wrexham), and came to him through Elizabeth ferch Hugh, his wife. These lands extended back on the left hand side of the lane to Sontley Lane and Glyn Park, and amounted in all to 42 customary acres (equal to nearly 89 statute acres), of which 40 acres were freehold. Much of this land, as we shall presently see, was sold to David ap John Robert, but what remained was afterwards possessed by Mr. Robert Lloyd, yeoman, of Yspytty (see page 90), Wrexham (probably John Lloyd's heir), who was buried at Wrexham, May 10th, 1706, and then became the property of Mr. Edward Hanmer (see page 122).

25. Returning now to Bennion's Lane, and proceeding towards Sontley Lane, there was in 1620, on the right hand side after passing Grofft Tuddir, a field belonging to John Lloyd, called "Cae'r ysgawen," *the elder tree field*. This is probably represented by the two fields numbered 537 and 538 in the map.

26. A little further along the same side was a piece of leasehold land of 4¼ statute acres, also held in 1620 by John Lloyd, called "Cae'r garnedd," that is " Field of the burial heap." I do not doubt that the *carnedd* commemorated in the name of this field was the tumulus marked on the map in No. 534, from which Hillbury, Mr. John Bury's house, built in 1862-3, was named [4]

27. Going now to the other side of the lane, and still keeping our face towards Sontley Lane, we may notice the two fields numbered 514 and 516, and called in the tithe map of 1844 " Pen y gilio." It is pretty certain that these represent the close which in 1620 belonged to John Lloyd, and was then called " Pen y geilyed" which perhaps stands for " Pen y geilwad " *The Ploughman's head*, a ploughman being often called " geilwad," which really means a " caller." During the last century they belonged to Willow House.

28. Then at the corner of Bennion's and Sontley Lanes was a close called " Cae'r deon," *The dean's field*. David ap John Robert bought it in 1615 of Hugh Berse, of Wrexham, weaver, Richard Berse having bought it, in 1587, of George Salusbury, gent, of Chester. David ap John Robert bought also of John Lloyd, or of his sister in law Maud ferch Hugh, other lands adjoining, so that his property here is now represented by the fields marked 510, 511, 517, 520 in the map. All these fields have now lost their ancient names, but it is possible to give the older names of most of them, though not possible to say which field bore which name. Besides Cae'r deon, there was Cae'r porth (*The gate field*), immediately south of Cae'r deon ; Cae'r ysgubor (*The barn field*); Cae'r llwyn (*The grove field*) ; Cae cockshoot (*The cockshoot field*) ; Yr acre (*The acres*); Maes Gwrecsam Fechan (*Wrexham Fechan field*); and, if I remember rightly, " Yr ysgythrau " (*The cuttings*), which is described as adjoining Glyn Park. In three of these names— Yr acre, Yr ysgythrau, and Maes Gwrecsam Fechan — we seem to have evidence of the distribution of separately owned quilletts over this area. As to Maes Gwrecsam Fechan we know this to be the case. It belonged partly to Hugh [ap] David, and partly to Humphrey Ellis, Esq., of Althrey, in the parish of Bangor is y coed—but Hugh David's portion did not lie all together in one part of the field, and Mr. Ellis's portion all together in the remaining portion of the field, but the portion of the one consisted of separate strips or quilletts mixed together, so that first came a strip belonging to Hugh David, then another belonging to Mr. Ellis, then a third belonging to Hugh David, and so on, Mr. Ellis having in all five separate parcels. These, of course, were relics of what, in this district at any rate, was a defunct system of tenure,

4. When this tumulus was cleared away it was found to contain " a circular heap of stones enclosing made ground, and near the summit of the mound a cist of red sandstone, etc , protecting an old funeral urn and bones. The fragments of the pottery were marked with a rude ornamental design. *Wrexham Advertiser.*

and Hugh David secured a lease for three lives from Mr. Ellis of his quilletts in Maes Gwrecsam Fechan, so that he might cultivate the field according to rational and more modern methods. In 1626 accordingly, David ap John Robert, having already bought, or being about to buy John Lloyd's portion of the field, bought of Roger Ellis, Esq., son of Mr. Humphrey Ellis, his portion also, so as to get the whole of the close into his own hands. In doing this he followed a custom which was already being widely adopted, and which has been followed ever since, so that now the number of separately owned quilletts in this neighbourhood is very small. The description of Mr. Ellis' five quilletts in Maes Gwrecsam Fechan in the deed of purchase executed between Roger Ellis, Esq., and David ap John Robert is so interesting that I have thought it worth while to reproduce it :—"All those fiue peeces or p'cells of land w'th thapp'tennes Lyeingeseuallie w'hin a clausure or field called Maes Gwrecsam Vechan, whereof the first is all that peece or p'cell of lands lying in the west side and towards the south ende of the said field, containeinge Tenne pikes or butts of Landes, be yt more or lesse wth a headland in the south end thereof. The seconde is all that peece or p'cell of land lyeing about the midst of the said field, and allsoe towards the south end thereof contayneing sixteene butts of Lande, be yt more or less. The third is all that peece or parcell lyeing in the east side of the said field, and likewise in the south ende of the same, contayneing eight butts of Land . . . . . at either end thereof. The fourth is all that peece or parcell allsoe in the East side of the said clausure or field, and towards the north pte thereof contayneing five butts of land, whereof Two butts are about six Kodes in Leangth. And the fifte is all that little peece, being in the north ende of the same field and containinge Three Butts of land be yt more or less." It is to be noted that the quilletts sold were not of equal size. If we look at No. 510 in the map we shall see a quillett still left in it, represented by the long narrow portion thereof which intervenes between Nos. 512 and 501. It is very probable that "Maes Gwrecsam Fechan" was once the name for the whole tract of land which lay between Ellesmere Road, Bennion's Lane, Sontley Lane and Glyn Park, and that it was full of quilletts separately owned and intermingled, but that by 1620, by the process which we have seen in operation, most of them had been abolished, and the name had become restricted to the small tract in which separately owned quilletts still lay. The group of fields of which we have been speaking as having been acquired by David ap John Robert was still in 1844 in the possession of John Lloyd Salusbury, Esq., his heir.

29. We have now turned into Sontley Lane, and are walking towards the river. Beyond the fields we have just described all the lands on the both sides of the road belong to the Erddig Estate, and as we pause on the top of the brow and look down into the pleasant "glyn" or valley, with the river flowing through it, we

look down into what was aforetime Glyn Park, of which we shall have more to say presently.

30. Now let us make another excursion into the old *township* of Wrexham Fechan, starting from Tuttle Bridge, going up Madeira Hill, turning to the right along Poplar Road, and so into Erddig Lane.

31. Just as we begin to mount Madeira Hill, we come on the left-hand side, between the brook and Willow Road, where the late Mr. Walker's Brewery now is, to the site of an important old house, which, in later times, came to be called " Willow House." It is shown in the view of Wrexham, published in 1748. I believe it to be the property represented in Norden's Survey of Wrexham, in the following words : " George Goldsmith, and Maria his wife, hold, by right of the said Maria . . . . two cottages and gardens in Wrexham Vechan, one barn, dovehouse and orchard there, and five closes or parcels of land called—1. Y Kae Mayn ["Y Cae maen"—*The stone field*]. 2. Errow gand [" Erw gam"—*Crooked acre*]. 3. Errow vechan [" Erw fechan"—*Little acre*]. 4. Kaer kutt ["Cae'r cut"—*Field of the hut*], and 5. Yr hirdire [" Yr hirdir"—*The longland*]. This last-named field survived until quite recent times, being numbered 539 on the map, and has given its name to a district—The Hirdir—now covered with houses and streets. The other lands lay between The Hirdir and Grofft Tuddir on the one side, and Willow House on the other, stretching along Madeira Hill, and even backwards to Bennion's Lane, and the street which is now solely called Wrexham Fechan. When and by whom Willow House was built I do not know. I believe the Mr. George Goldsmith, above-named, to have been a brother of the Mr. Thomas Goldsmith, who is mentioned in the account of the Shirehall, under Town Hill. Before 1699, another Mr. George Goldsmith was seated here (see *Hist. of Par Church of Wrexham*, pp. 143-145). He was somehow connected with the Pulford family, the name Ursula being common to the two families, and his son who was buried at Wrexham, March 18th, 168$\frac{6}{7}$, being named Richard *Pulford* Goldsmith. His wife, Ursula, was buried September 30th, 1704, and he himself on December 11th, following. He was succeeded at Willow House, then and long afterwards called " Pont Tuttle," by Mr. Alexander Pulford. This Mr. Pulford had, besides three sons who died young, at least three daughters, namely :—Ursula (born May 13th, 1695), Elinor (born July 11th, 1705, who married at Erbistock, April 30th, 1725, Rev. John Appleton, master of the Wrexham Grammar School, and was buried December 8th, 1729, her infant son, Alexander, having died the month before), and Catherine (born August 7th, 1708), who married at Wrexham May 15th, 1728, Ralph Wragg, gent, son of Mr. Thomas Wragg, surveyor of excise, and had several children, of whom one was Thomas Wragg, gent, of Wrexham (buried at Wrexham, May 22nd, 1771), whom we will call Thos.

Wragg, *the elder*, to distinguish him from his son, Thomas Wragg, gent, of Liverpool, whom we will call Thos. Wragg, *the younger*. Mr. Alexander Pulford had also, I believe, another daughter, who married Mr. John Stephenton (see page 26). Mr. Alexander Pulford's wife was buried February 5th, 1710, and Mr. Pulford himself June 12th, 1726. Then, after an interval, the Rev. Thomas Pulford lived here until his death in 1768. I believe this Mr. Thomas Pulford was a son of Mr. Alexander Pulford, for I find him described in a deed which I have examined as a brother to the above-named Mrs. Elizabeth Stephenton, and uncle to Mr. Thomas Wragg (probably Thomas Wragg *the elder*). At any rate he inherited Mr. Alexander Pulford's property. He appears to have been for a short time (in 1729) head master of Wrexham Grammar School, and from 1730 to 1768, curate of Harthill, Cheshire. After his death Mrs. Elizabeth Stephenton, his sister, and Thos. Wragg, gent, of Liverpool, being his heirs-at-law, agreed to submit the division of his estate, which was very considerable, to the arbitration of Thomas Boydell, of Trefalyn, and Thomas Jones, gent, of Wrexham (see hereafter). The arbitrators awarded the Willow House estate as part of Mrs. Stephenton's share of Mr. Pulford's property, which estate is described in the award as that dwelling house wherein the late Mr. Thos. Pulford had formerly lived, then occupied by the said Mrs. Stephenton, the cut-buildings, garden and orchard belonging to it, as well as those fields in Wrexham Regis [held therewith], namely, Barn field, with the barn and cottage standing upon it, the Hirdir, Cae'r cut, "Penny giliad" (Pen y geilwad, see sec. 27), and the crofts adjoining to it, and the Bronydd, and all that messuage, stables, garden and croft in Wrexham Fechan, in the occupation of John Woods (the Bridge House). Before 1780 Willow House was let to Captain Thos. Jones, theretofore of The Court, and here he remained until his death, October 26th, 1799, aged 61, being shot in a duel at Elles- mere (see *Hist. of Par. Church of Wrexham*, p. 215, note 24). Captain Jones was the son of Mr. Thomas Jones, by his wife Margaretta Maria, eldest daughter of Sir Thomas Longueville, of Esclus Hall and Prestatyn.[5] He married, firstly, at Wrexham May 4th, 1767), "Miss Jane Jones," and by her had one son, Thomas Longueville Jones, born September 18th, bapt. October 14th, 1768, who afterwards assumed the surname of Longueville, came into possession of the Longueville estate at Prestatyn, and became the father of the late Thomas Longueville, Esq., of Pen y lan, Oswestry. Captain Jones' first wife died October 1st, 1768, and was buried at Wrexham. He married, secondly, Ann Lloyd, by whom he had nine children, all baptized at Wrexham, namely, 1. Edward, born 17th April, 1774, afterwards father of late Rev.

---

5. I suppose the following entry in Wrexham Parish Registers refers to a younger brother of Capt. Jones :--Oct. 24th, 1747. Edward, son of Mr. Thos. Jones, of Postatin [Prestatin] Baptized.

Harry Longueville Jones, editor of *Archæologia Cambrensis*.
2. Richard, born June 13th, 1775, who died unmarried in the Isle
of Jamaica, August 23rd, 1799.   3. Hugh, born September 20th,
1776, the ancestors of the Joneses of Lark Hill, Lancashire, and
Badsworth Hall, Yorks.   4. Charles, a twin, born August 28th,
1777.   5. Ann, a twin, born August 29th, 1777, who married
(October 29th, 1798), James Boydell, Esq., of Llai, in the parish of
Gresford, died August 23rd, 1799, without issue, and was buried at
Wrexham.   6. Harry, a daughter, born November 11th, 1778, and
died an infant.   7. Elizabeth, born November 20th, 1779.
8. Harriet, born December 4th, 1780, who became the wife of
Francis Edge Barker, Esq., of Llyndir, in the parish of Gresford,
and died February 17th, 1846, and 9. Maria, born April 17th, 1782,
who became the wife of Thos. Lowndes, Esq.   Mrs. Ann Jones,
Captain Jones' second wife, died June 27th, 1796, aged 52.

32. After Captain Jones' death, Thomas Stephenton, Esq. (see
pages 26 and 27), the owner of the house, and the representative of the ancient family of Pulford, to whom it had belonged,
came to live in it, and here remained until his death in December,
1825.   He was one of the sons of Mr. Stephen Stephenton (see
page 38), attorney-at-law, born November 5th, 1757, and was
buried in the Old Cemetery.   In the rate books for 1827 and 1828
Willow House is returned as belonging to Miss Thompson, and as
occupied by Mr. Gronow.   In a map of 1833 it is described as the
house of Thomas Broster, Esq.   In 1843 and 1850 the late
Mr. Robert Humphreys Jones, solicitor, was living in it, and in
1857 it still belonged to him.   It was called "Willow House" from
a willow which overhung the brook.   Soon after, Mr. Richard
Evans, of the New Hop Pole, York Street, afterwards the late
Alderman Evans, father of Alderman R. W. Evans, of Chester
Street, bought the Willow House, starting a brewery there.   This
brewery was purchased in 1860 by the late Mr. Peter Walker
(see sec. 43), who had already been connected, as pupil to Mr. Joseph
Clark, with the brewing business in Wrexham, when he was about
17 years old, but had, subsequently, started several wine and spirit
businesses in Liverpool.   How he prospered at the Willow Brewery
is very well known.   The extensive buildings there, now tenant-
less, were erected by him.   Before his death he had made
arrangements for transferring his business to Burton, and the
foundation stone of his new building was laid February 17th, 1882,
the Willow Brewery in Wrexham being closed in September, 1883.

33. I do not know whether Willow Lane had any existence
before the early part of the present century, and certainly "Madeira
Hill" was a still later name.   The street so named was formerly regarded as a part of Tuttle Street, and was called "Tuttle Hill"
at least as late as 1826.   The year 1831 is the first in which I have
found the name Madeira Hill mentioned.

34. In taking the course marked off for ourselves, going up Madeira Hill and turning at the top along Poplar Road into Erddig Lane, we have Wrexham Regis (formerly Wrexham Fechan) on our left, and Wrexham Abbot on our right, but, until we come into Erddig Lane, we shall describe both sides of the street in the same chapter, this being the course least calculated to cause confusion.

35. Let us now then describe the Wrexham Abbot side of Madeira Hill. The houses at the foot of the hill on this side appear to have been built by Mr. William Edwards, tanner, of The Palis, or his widow (see under Penybryn), on a field called "Cae deintyr" (*The tenter field*). In the largest of these houses, whereto is attached a kiln, which overlooks the brook, several of the Edwards family lived, and here in 1825 died his widow, Mrs. Jane Edwards, and his son Charles Edwards, Esq., the latter, of cholera morbus.

36. The greater part of the land on the other side of Madeira Hill belonged originally, as I have already said, to Willow House, and this was certainly the case with the Barnfield, on which has in recent years been built a blind alley called by the same name.

37. Having reached the top of Madeira Hill, we turn to the right into Poplar Road. Indeed this is the only way we could, until about the middle of the present century, have taken, for although there were two footpaths from the top of Madeira Hill into Bennion's Lane (one across Grofft Tudor or the Lesser Hirdir, and one across the Hirdir, properly so called), there was no other public road from Madeira Hill than Poplar Road.

38. On the left or Wrexham Regis side of Poplar Road (itself a modern name), was a large close called "Fairfield," and on the right or Wrexham Abbot side other fields which belonged at the beginning of this century to Mr. Edward Davies, joiner, of the Kiln House, Stryd Draw. At the two ends of this group of fields, between 1817 and 1824, Mr. Davies built two houses, one called "Poplar Cottage" (which included two separate dwellings) at the corner of Madeira Hill and Poplar Road, and one called "Holton Cottage," in which Mr. Alexander Fyfe, master of the British Schools, lived at the time of his death, and now occupied by the Rev. Dr. Roberts.

39. Coming to the end of Poplar Road we turn to the left into Erddig Lane, along another side of Fairfield, still having for a while, Wrexham Regis on our left hand, anh Wrexham Abbot on our right. On this latter side was built in 1811, or a little before, by Mrs. Edwards, widow of Mr. William Edwards, tanner (see above), a good house called "Fairfield House." Here from July, 1819, the Rev. John Hughes, brother of Mr. Richard Hughes, of No. 56 Hope Street (see page 70,) carried on for many years an academy for training young men for the Calvinistic Methodist ministry, but broke up his Academy at the end of 1834, and

ultimately went to Liverpool, where he died (August 8th. 1860, aged 63), and was buried at Smithdown Lane Cemetery.[6] Continuing our course along Erddig Lane, we plunge, for a space, at the point where Sontley Lane begins, into a portion of Wrexham Abbot, but presently, as we near Coed y glyn, have once more Wrexham Regis on our left hand, and Wrexham Abbot on our right.   Nearly all this portion of Wrexham Abbot pertains to The Court estate which we shall describe under the township to which it belongs, but Coed y glyn is in Wrexham Regis (formerly Wrexham Fechan) and must be described here.

41. "Coed y glyn" means "The Glyn Wood" and takes its name from The Glyn Park, of which we shall say something hereafter.   The first mention that I have met with of Coed y glyn as a farm holding, occurs on July 5th, 1688-9, when Philip Griffith, of Coed y glyn, was buried in Wrexham Churchyard.   But this Philip Griffith is charged in the rate books as far back as 1661, for

6. The Rev. John Hughes was the third son of Mr. Hugh Hughes, of Adwy'r Clawdd, carpenter, and Mr. John Hughes followed the same trade until he was 18 years of age. Mr. Hugh Hughes, of the Adwy, was the third son of Mr. Richard Hughes, of Sarphlle, near Llanarmon Dyffryn Ceiriog, and came to the Adwy about 1780. where he died August 10th, 1850, aged 87. He married Mary, only daughter of Edward Davies, of the Adwy, by whom he had several children, whereof in this series we shall only have occasion to mention three—the subject of this note, born February 11th, 1796 (the third son), Mr. Richard Hughes (see page 70), of High Street, and Mr. Edward Hughes, of the New Mills.   Mr. John Hughes, although he was not recognised as a preacher until the time of the Cymdeithasfa held at Mold in February, 1821, and was not ordained until 1892, began to preach in 1813, when only 17 years of age, his first sermon being given at Bersham, and preached often afterwards before his formal recognition.   He set up in September, 1815, a school at Cross Street, in the parish of Hope, which, after six months, he removed to Caergwrle, and in the middle of August, 1817, went to Chester "for the sake of learning the elements of Greek and Latin."   In 1819 he opened Fairfield House as an Academy.   Among the names of the ministers who were trained there the following may be mentioned :--Foulk Evans, Machynlleth ; Dafydd Rolant, o'r Bala ; Daniel Evans, Harlech ; Robert Jones, Sir Fôn ; Robert Thomas, Llidiardau ;   Richard Williams, Liverpool ; John Jones, Pontycysylltau ; John Jones, Carmel ;   John Davies, Nerquis ; David Jones, Treborth ; Robert Hughes, Gaerwen ; Richard Edwards, Llangollen ; Griffith Williams, Llanfachreth, Sir Fôn ; Lewis Jones, Bala ; Roger Edwards, Mold ; Edward Evans, afterwards of America ;   Robert Williams, Aberdyfi ; Thomas Francis, Wrexham ; Humphrey Evans, Maethlon, Meirionydd ; John Evans, Llansantffraid ; James Donne, Llangefni, and John Rogers, afterwards an English minister at Bridport.   The great book on which he was engaged, and which he afterwards published when living in Liverpool, was *Methodistiaeth Cymru*, in three volumes, the last of which was published in 1856, by Messrs. Hughes and Son, Wrexham. Both while at Wrexham and after he removed to Lsverpool he took great pains in working up the English causes of this district, and was called "Esgob yr Goror," or "Bishop of the Marches."   While at Wrexham he was accustomed to preach on Sundays at the Rossett, Cross Street, Llai, Burton, Townditch, Glan y pwll, Yellow Oak, Puleston Mills, and other places.   He was twice married, his first wife, whom he married in 1820, being Miss Mary Anne Jones, Tir Llanerch, Corwen.   He married his second wife in June, 1833. All these particulars I have obtained from "*Bnchdraeth y diwiddar Barchedig John Hughes, Liverpool*," by the Revs. Roger Edwards, Mold, and John Hughes, Liverpool, published in Wrexham, by Messrs. R. Hughes and Son.

apparently this very holding. In 1790, Richard Jones, gent, is mentioned as the agent of the Erddig Hall estate, and in 1729 went to live at Coed y glyn, which belonged to that estate, and there remained until his death in 1741. He was followed by John Jones, gent, but I do not know whether the latter was Mr. Richard Jones' son, or whether he was also agent for the Erddig estate. Nor do I know exactly when he died, but I judge somewhere about 1759. Of his two daughters, Ann, the elder, was one of the early adherents of Calvinistic Methodism in this neighbourhood, was a member of the society at Adwy'r Clawdd, and became the first wife of Mr. Richard Jones, ironmonger, of High Street (see page 18), being, with her husband, the chief means of starting a Calvinistic Methodist cause in this town. She died November 6th, 1793.[7] Jane, the second daughter of Mr. John Jones, the elder, of Coed y glyn, married the Rev. Jenkin Lewis, of Penybryn Chapel, Wrexham (*see Hist. of Older Nonconformity of Wrexham,* p. 117), and lies buried in the Dissenters' graveyard, Wrexham. The ultimate successor of Mr. John Jones, the elder, at Coed y glyn was his son, Mr. John Jones, the younger. He also appears, in the earlier part of his life, to have been a Calvinistic Methodist, and there seems to be little doubt that it was at Coed y glyn that the first Methodist preachers who visited Wrexham were entertained. He married at Wrexham (November 2nd, 1775), Penelope, daughter of the Rev. Thomas Myddelton, vicar of Melton Mowbray (see pages 27 and 28), and lived at first at Pentre'r felin House, Wrexham, his mother occupying Coed y glyn, but removed to the latter house before 1793. He had one daughter, Mary, who married at Wrexham, Edward Dymock, Esq., of Penley, Flintshire. Mr. John Jones died May 5th, 1817, aged 79, according to his brass in the parish church, which is probably correct, but aged 84 according to the entry in the burial register. Mrs. Jones continued to occupy Coed y glyn until about 1827, and then I believe went to live with her daughter Mrs. Dymock. She died March 12th, 1841. Having said this much it may be well to give all the entries that I have noticed in the parish registers relating to the Joneses of Coed y glyn :—

Dec. 6, 1734, Ann, wife of Mr. Richd. Jones, Stewart to Mr. Yorke, buried.

Dec. 5, 1741, Mr. Richard Jones, of Coed y glyn, Steward at Erthig, buried.

July 17, 1743, Ann, Da. of Mr. John Jones, of Coed y glyn, born June 15th, baptized.

July 10, 1745, Jane, Da. of Mr. John Jones, of Coed y glyn, born 3, baptized.

Apl. 23, 1753, William, son of John Jones, of Coed y glyn, gent, born 5, baptized,

Mch. 22, 1772, Francis, wife of Mr. Richard Jones, of Coydaglynn, buried.

---

7. Mr. Edward Francis, in his *Hanes Dechreuad a Chynydd y Methodistiaid Calfinaidd yn Ngwrecsam,* says that "though, in a sense, but young, she was nevertheless, a mother in Israel," It is evident that she was a kind, devoted, pure, and high minded woman, and her memory was long green.

Nov. 2, 1775, John Jones, Bachelor, and Penelope Myddelton, Spinster, both of this parish, married.

Mch. 3, 1779, Mr. Richd. Jones, from London,   buried.

Mch. 2, 1781, Mary, dau. of John and Penelope Jones, Pentrevelin, born 22 Feb., baptized.

Apl. 24, 1787, Rev. Jenkin Lewis, and Jane Jones, both of this par.   married.

June 16, 1834, Edward Dymock, of Penley, Esq., and Mary Jones, of parish of Wrexham, married.

May 16, 1817, John Jones, Esq., Coed y glyn, 84,   buried.

42. Mrs. Penelope Jones was followed at Coed y glyn, according to the rate books by   Myddelton, Esq.   The latter Mr. W. M. Myddelton tells me, was the Rev. Robert Myddelton, of Gwaunynog, son of the Rev. Dr. Myddelton, rector of Rotherhithe (see the Myddelton pedigree opposite page 28).   He sold the Gwaunynog estate, and died at Rhyl in 1876, aged 81.   He married Louisa, daughter of Sir George Wm. Farmer, of Mount Pleasant, Sussex, and had an only son, Robert, Captain in the Denbighshire Militia, who died in 1858.   In 1843 and 1844, Thomas Wynne Eyton, Esq., second son of the Rev. Hope Eyton, of Leeswood, was living at Coed y glyn, and in 1857 Miss Eyton.

43. There were attached in 1844 to Coed y glyn, the fields and crofts numbered in the map 530, 531, 532, 542, 543, 544, and 546, which included in all nearly 41 acres.   Soon after, Coed y glyn passed into the occupation of the late Peter Walker, Esq., of whom I have already given some account, while speaking cf Willow House and Ellesmere Road.   At Coed y glyn he remained until his death, April 13th, 1882, aged 61, being buried in the Ruthin Road Cemetery, where also lies buried his first wife Agnes, who died August 30th, 1864, aged 46.   He was exceedingly liberal and popular, and after having been made mayor in 1866-7, was re-elected at the close of his year of office.   His portrait hangs in the Council chamber of the Borough.   In politics he was a Conservative, and announced his intention, not long before his death, of coming out as second Conservative candidate for the County of Denbigh, then undivided, in opposition to Mr. Geo. Osborne Morgan, the Liberal member.   He presented to the Parish Church the stone pulpit which still stands there, and which cost 200 guineas, and promised £1000 towards the building of the new schools, Madeira Hill, a sum which was afterwards paid by his executors.   He had several children of whom three daughters survived:—(1) Margaret Agnes, who married at Wrexham (November 10th, 1880), the Rev. Meredith Hamer, at that time curate of Berse Drelincourt; (2) Elizabeth Anne, who was born January 23rd, 1862, married (September 20th, 1882.) at St. George's, Hanover Square, Mr. Richard Henry Venables Kyrke, eldest son of Richard Venables Kyrke, Esq., then of Nant y ffrith, now of Pen y wern, in the parish of Hope, and who died July 18th, 1885, and is buried in the New Cemetery, Wrexham; and (3) Laura Louise who married (September 20th, 1882), at St. George's, Hanover Square, Francis

James Vaughan-Williams, Esq., then of The Court, Wrexham, and registrar of the County Court there, but now of 49 Rutland Gate, Hyde Park. Mr. Peter Walker was a brother of Mr. John Walker, and of Sir Andrew B. Walker, Bart., both of Liverpool. He acquired towards the end of his life a shooting estate in Ayrshire called " Auchenflower."

44. After Mr. Walker's death, his widow left Coed y Glyn, which is now occupied by Sir Robert Eyles Egerton, K.C.S.I., formerly Lieutenant-Governor of the Punjab, third son of William Egerton, Esq., of Gresford Lodge.

45. We now come to a part of Erddig Park, entering through the Lodge gates, which was formerly in the older Glyn Park. Glyn Park, however, contained much land that is not included in Erddig Park, while the latter includes, in its turn, much land that was not included in Glyn Park. Of Glyn Park I hope to give a full description in the next volume of this series. But of two or three points concerning it I may say something here. First, it was very ancient, for I find it mentioned on September 29th, 1397, when the king appointed, during his pleasure, Geoffrey (or Griffri) de Kynaston, " one of our archers," to be keeper of it for life, at 6d. a day. It was then called " Glynthwedock Parc," that is " Glyn Clywedog Park," or " The Park of the Dale of The Clywedog." It appears, in fact, to have included the whole dale of the Clywedog with the hills on each side, from a point below Little Erddig to the King's Mills on Ellesmere Road. As we have seen, it belonged to the lord of the commote, and in 1620 is described as demesne land, although then disparked and cut up into separate holdings. Part of it only was in the township of Wrexham, but within this part were situate what were called " The French Mills." Although two sketches of these mills are in existence, it is impossible to indicate their exact site. But I shall not be far wrong in saying that they stood near the bridge that spans the Clywedog, between Erddig Lodge and Erddig Hall. The first time that I have found them called " The French Mills" is in the year 1699, but they are mentioned without being named in 1620, when they are described as " two mills under one roof," and there was then " a ferme house near the mills." A still older name for them was " Melin Coed y Glyn," which occurs in the reign of Queen Elizabeth (exact year not discoverable), a name which means " Coed y Glyn Mill," or " Mill of the Dale Wood." They are mentioned for the last time in the rate books in the year 1804, and were then still called " The French Mills." It will, doubtless, be asked how these mills came to acquire so strange a name as that just mentioned. The following is the explanation that has occurred to myself I have already said that all tenants of Wrexham Regis (whether free or leasehold)

were bound to grind at the King's Mills, Ellesmere Road. But those who had acquired portions of the Glyn Park, which was demesne land, were not subject to this obligation, and as standing in the lord's place, were free to erect mills at which they themselves and the inhabitants of the free townships adjoining (but not those of Wrexham) could grind their corn. The mills were thus the franc or free mills, or the mills of the franchise or liberty of Glyn Park, a name which might afterwards become corrupted into "The French Mills." This explanation may not be correct, but it is the best I can give.

The EDGWORTHS of HOLT and MARCHWIEL.

46. Thomas Edgworth, the first of this family of whom we have any note, settled at Holt in the County of Denbigh, about the middle of the 16th century. The Edgeworths, of Edgeworthtown, county Longford—to which, Richard Lovel, "the inventor of the telegraph," and Maria Edgeworth, the novelist, belonged—are said to have sprung from the same stock. Thomas Edgworth, of Holt, had a son, Roger Edgworth, who was an attorney, and one of the jurers that assisted, in A.D. 1620, John Norden in his survey of the town of Holt and Manor of Hewlington. Roger Edgworth was buried in the church of Holt, near the spot marked by his initials on the north wall. His son, Thomas, married Martha, daughter of John Sadler (see *Hist. of Older Nonconformity of Wrexham*, p. 4), and probably the last resident in it prior to its demolition. The son of this Thomas Edgworth does not appear, but his grandson—another Thomas—removed to Wrexham, and lived at first in the churchyard there[1]. I find him described in 1707, as a "felt maker," and in 1709 and again in 1712, as a "castor maker," a castor being a beaver hat. He, subsequently (before 1715), removed to the house in High Street, which after-

---

1. Up to this point my information as to the Edgworths is derived from an account in an old copy of the *Wrexham Advertiser*, an account probably supplied by one of the family, but I noticed in the Holt registers, the two following entries :

"Margret Edgworth, wife of Roger Edgworth, gent, was buried Sept. 11, 1666."

"Rog. Edgworth, generosus et Notarius Publicus de Hoult sepult fuit . . . . die Maii, 1668."

I noticed also on the register towards the end of the 17th century, entries relating to the baptism of several children of Thomas and of John Edgworth : one of these last was probably the father of the first Thomas Edgworth of *Wrexham*.

wards became the "The Bear" (see page 19), and occupied part of the site of the present Market Hall. Here he carried on the business of a hatter, and here he died. being buried (March 13th, 1721), near the south door of the church. His widow, Mrs. Ann Edgworth, lived in the same house until her death, December, 1743. His daughter, Elizabeth (born November 13th, 1707), married (February 18th, 1731), Mr. Samuel Crew, of the parish of Holt. His son, John Edgworth, born November 19th, 1712, was twice married. The first wife of this Mr. John Edgworth, by whom he appears to have acquired some property at Ashton, Lancashire, was Elizabeth, daughter of the Rev. Harry Style, rector of Stockport. Upon her death, Mr. Edgworth sold his property at Ashton, where he had resided, and returned to his native country. He lived at first, from about 1751 to 1753, at the College in Wrexham Churchyard, whence he removed to Plas Grono, in Esclusham Below, marrying in 1764, Sarah, sister of Mr. John Matthews, attorney-at-law, of Wrexham, (see page 97). At Plas Grono was born his elder son, John (born October 21st, 1765, baptized at Wrexham, November 24th). Thence he removed to Hoseley, in the parish of Gresford, where were born his daughter Ann (baptized at Gresford, October 8th, 1768), who became the second wife of Mr. Richard Brown, solicitor, of Wrexham (see *Hist. of the Older Nonconformity of Wrexham*, p. 116), and his younger son, Thomas (baptized at Gresford, September 3rd, 1771). Finally, Mr. John Edgworth went to live at Bryn y Grog, in the parish of Marchwiel, where he, for the most part, thenceforth lived, though in the entry relating to his burial in Marchwiel register, he is described as "John Edgworth, of Wrexham, Esq." He died November 25th, 1798, aged 86, his widow dying December 12th, 1817, aged 74. She appears to have lived during her widowhood, at what is now No. 36 Pen y bryn, Wrexham. John and Thomas, the two sons of the Thomas and Sarah Edgworth last-named both held commissions in the Wrexham Volunteers, and, subsequently, in the East Denbighshire Militia, John being major in the latter, and were both barristers at law. John, the elder, lived at Bryn y Grog, where he died, July 7th, 1826, aged 61. He was twice married, his first wife, Mrs. Tyldesley Edgworth, dying January 1st, 1800, aged 30. His second wife, Mrs. Margaret Edgworth, a daughter of John Matthews, of Burras Lodge, Gourton (whom he married at Wrexham, July 7th, 1801), survived him, dying November 14th, 1861, aged 86. This Mr. John Edgworth was in actual possession of Bryn y grog, though I am not fully certain how he acquired it, whether by inheritance from his father, or by purchase. In 1800, however, I find it stated that a part of the old Marchwiel estate, probably Croes y mab, had been sold to him, and in September, 1811, he bought of Sir Thos. Hanmer, Bart., of Bettisfield (representing a mortgage), another portion of that estate in Abenbury and Marchwiel.   He left all his estate to his wife Margaret, for the term of her natural life, and afterwards to his nephew, Thomas Edgworth.   His brother, Thomas, the younger son of Mr. John Edgworth, *the elder*, married in 1804, at St. Anne's Church, Liverpool, Elizabeth, one of the daughters of Mr. Edward Meredith, the well-known baritone.   He appears to have lived at first at Holt Street Cottage, Wrexham.   His only son, Thomas, afterwards first mayor of Wrexham, was born January 30th, 1805, and baptized at Wrexham, January 29th, 1807.   He afterwards removed to Burras Lodge, and finally to Bryn y grog   He died April 16th, 1830. aged 58, and was buried at Marchwiel, where also was buried his widow, who died February 2nd, 1851, aged 81. Mr. Thos. Edgworth, the only child of Thomas and Elizabeth Edgworth, was articled at Stockport, and passed his examination in London at the same time as Mr. John James, late Town Clerk of Wrexham, both of whom soon after established themselves in practice in this town.   In 1836 he became Clerk to the Guardians, an appoint- ment which he ultimately resigned, but his appointment as Registrar of the County Court[2] he continued to hold until the time of his death.   He married, at Guilsfield Church, June 11th, 1844, Miss Eliza Jane Robarts, of Welshpool, an only child of Jas. Robarts, Esq.   He originated the Market Hall Company, buying, before the Company was established, the site on which the Hall was subsequently built, including the house in which his great grandfather had carried on business.   He was also a warm sup- porter of the Wrexham, Mold, and Connah's Quay Railway Company, of which he was a director until the end of his life. His offices in late years were on the east side of the churchyard, immediately north of what was used to be called "The Green Steps."   Of fine presence, genial in manners, liberal, and cultivated, he was wonderfully popular, and his popularity may be said to have reached its height when he was unamimously elected in 1857 the first mayor of Wrexham, but it began to decline when he threw him- self with his customary energy into the execution of the necessary sanitary reforms which the new Corporation undertook.   At the expiration of his year of office his re-election was proposed, but another member of the Council was brought forward in opposition to him.   The voting was equal, and as his opponent had voted for himself, Mr. Edgworth gave his casting vote in his own favour, and so became mayor a second year.   This action increased his unpopu- larity, and he gradually withdrew himself from public life. About 1866 he retired from practice, resigning it to Mr. J. Devereux Pugh, whom he had taken into partnership some twenty or more years before, and went to live at Bryn y grog, where he died

---

2. The County Court Offices were then on the north side of the churchyard, between the end of Church Street and The Nef.

January 7th, 1868, in the 63rd year of his age.   He left two sons and two daughters. Of the sons, the elder, the Rev. Roger Edgworth, rector of Bridport, was born at Gatefield, May 13th, 1849, and between 1880 and 1885 sold the whole of the Bryn y grog and Croes y mab estates.   The second, Thomas John Edgworth, Esq., is a solicitor at Eastbourne, Sussex.

Part III.—WREXHAM ABBOT,

Introduction.

CHAPTER XVIII.

1. The township of Wrexham Abbot, the limits of which are indicated by the dotted lines on the map, came into existence in the year 1200, when Gruffydd ap Madoc Maelor, Prince of Powys Fadog, granted to the monks of Valle Crucis, then newly established in Yale, a portion of the township of Wrexham Fawr.[1] The whole area of Wrexham Abbot, including its detached portions lying in Wrexham Regis, is 351.164 acres, while Wrexham Regis including Wrexham Fechan, contains 952.948 acres. But a large portion of what is now called Wrexham Abbot—" The Parcau " (see Index), the original area of which is uncertain, was reckoned until 1828 at least, as part of Wrexham Regis. This portion formed, it is probable, the site of the " llys " or court of the lord of the commote, and so was reserved. So that in this respect Wrexham Abbot is now larger than it formerly was. In another respect, however, it is much smaller. For it is quite clear that a portion of the summer pasture on the mountains, belonging to the lord of the commote or rhaglotry of Wrexham, was also granted to the monks of Valle Crucis. This summer pasture still pertained to Wrexham in the year 1631, and is then described as containing 100 [customary] acres (equal to 215.7 statute acres) of mountain land, the bounds whereof are described, being parcels of land in the township of Minera, called " Havodir, Estel, y ffynnon Wen," " Nant yr Euryn, and Receiver's Meadow, 5 acre, loyd (Coed) Eva 3 acres." From the description of this tract, its area, and the mention of " Y ffynnon wen" (the situation of which is well known), it seems evident that the portion of the lord's Hafodir which was granted with Wrexham Abbot to Valle Crucis was that tract of land, 205 acres in area, which is now reckoned as a detached portion of Esclusham Above, which is partly surrounded by Minera, and which includes Lester's Lime Works, and the Minera Company's Lime Works, as well as a farm called " Hafod y werger "

The unappropriated part of Wrexham was afterwards called " Wrexham Regis " or *King's Wrexham*. " Wrexham Fawr," which means *Great Wrexham*, seems to have been the early name for what was afterwards known as Wrexham Regis and Wrexham Abad *(Abbot's Wrexham)*, as distinguished from Wrexham Fechan (Little Wrexham). And I find in a deed dated 1616 the name as actually used in this sense. On the other hand, later in the same century the name " Wrexham Fawr " is used as equivalent to " Wrexham Regis."

2. I forgot to say that the "Bailiwick of Wrexham," as that name appears in the Abbey accounts, appears to have included Stansty Issa (or Stansty Abbatis), as well as Wrexham Abbot. The value of the bailiwick of Wrexham, as described in The Valor Ecclesiasticus of Henry VIII 1535, is thus given :—

Balli'at de Wrexham
Val' in

Reddit' assis' ib'm p. annu.	xiiii^{li} ii$_s$ viii$_d$
Firma molend' ib'm p. annu.	c^s
P'quis cur'co'ibs annis	Liii$_s$ iiii$_d$

That is, the rents of assise of the bailiwick of Wrexham were £14 2 8 a year, the farm of the mill £5, and the purquisites of court there in ordinary years £2 13 4, the total yearly income received by the Abbot from the bailiwick being £21 16 0. Out of these were paid the fees of the two bailiffs, that of Edward ap Rhys being £1, and that of Guttyn Madoc 13^s 4^d. Edward ap Rhys was also subseneschall of the Abbot.

3. After the suppression of Valle Crucis in 1535, Henry VIII granted to Sir William Pickering, knight (of Oswaldkirk, Yorks), a lease for 21 years of the monastery and its possessions, including the manor of Wrexham Abbot, and the rectorial tithes of the parish of Wrexham. This lease was dated July 5th, in the 29th year of the king's reign (1537). For the manor of Wrexham Abbot, Sir William covenanted to pay an annual rent of £4 8 10, for the Abbot's mills there £5, and for the tithes £5. Edward ap Rees was then bailiff of Wrexham Abbot, and his salary £2 a year. On the 7th of July 1551, Edward IV renewed the above named lease to Sir William Pickering. Sir William died in January 1574, bequeathing his lease of Valle Crucis to his daughter Hester, who married Edward Wotton, Esq. (son of Sir Thomas Wotton, knight, of Bocton Malherbe), afterwards Sir Edward Wotton, K.B. Then in the 25th year of her reign, Queen Elizabeth granted the lease of the monastery, manor, and tithes, apparently for thirty years, to the above-mentioned Edward Wotton. Hester, his wife, died May 8th, 1592, and Sir Edward (created Lord Wotton, of Marley, May 13th, 1603), afterwards married Margaretta, daughter of Philip, Lord Wharton. James I, on the 30th of May, in the third year of his reign, renewed the lease for one hundred years from the end of the thirty years then in being, and on the 29th of April, in the second year of his reign, granted the monastery to Lord Wotton, and to his heirs, *for ever*. At his death, Lord Wotton left the monastery to his widow, the lady Margaret. In January, 165$\frac{1}{2}$, the monastery of Valle Crucis is returned as in the holding of "Lady Margaret Wotton," as well as various "Tythes and Tenementes in severall Towneshippes" of the lordship of Bromfield and Yale. I do not doubt that the manor of Wrexham Abbot also belonged to her, as in a parish paper of the year 1635, "Lady

Wotton" is returned as the largest non-resident landowner in the parish of Wrexham. Lady Wotton's estate was sequestered by the Parliament, who sold, September 1st, 1651, Valle Crucis and its appurtenances to Michael Lea, gent, and John Lawson, citizen and grocer, both of London, for the sum of £3306 6 7⅞.

4. At what time, and under what circumstances, the manor of Wrexham Abbot, or that portion of it which was not already alienated, passed into the possession of the Wynnstay family, I do not know, but I have seen a declaration by Sir John Wynn, of Watstay, (afterwards Wynnstay), that all the property of Lord Wotton in the late monastery of Valle Crucis became vested by purchase in his father Henry Wynn, Esq.   The year of the purchase appears to have been 1663, but my abstract of the deed was written out so hastily, having little time to spare and many documents to examine, that the date appears in the abstract very badly written, and I cannot be absolutely certain that it is quite correct.   Certain it is, however, that soon after the restoration, the owners of Watstay became owners of Wrexham Abbot, as they still are.   Before this had happened, however, the Abbot's Court House, the head of the manor of Wrexham Abbot, almost certainly the same as the present house called " The Court," had been alienated, and as the Court Estate is of some importance, and the deeds belonging to it (which, through the kindness of Lieut.-Col. Meredith, I have been permitted to see), throw considerable light on the tenures of Wrexham Abbot, I have decided to devote to the history of The Court a distinct chapter.

Edward Lhuyd mentions in his *Itinerary* (written at the end of the 17th century), a cross called " Croes gareg " (*Stone cross*), as standing somewhere in Wrexham Abbot (probably in the main portion of the township), but does not indicate its precise locality.

CHAPTER XIX.

The Court Estate, Wrexham Abbot.

1. At the beginning of the 17th century, Lancelot ap Ellis Tudor, gent, was living at the Court, which he held by lease of Sir Edward Wotton, and on April 1st, 1616, Edward Meredith, "citizen and draper, of London" (brother of Sir William Meredith, of Stansty, and of Hugh Meredith, Esq., the first of the Merediths of Pentrebychan), bought this lease of Lancelot ap Ellis, for £80. Then on October the 16th following, Hugh Meredith, of the parish of Wrexham, gent, Humphrey Berrington, of London, haberdasher, and Edward Lloyd, of London, yeoman, bought the Court estate of the Right Hon. Lord Edward Wotton, for £350[1]. The following is a summary of the description of The Court in the indentures of sale :—All that messuage or tenement commonly called The Courte, situate in Wrexham Abbot, now in the tenure of Lancelot ap Ellis, or his under-tenants, and two parcels of land commonly called y dolydd, late in the possession of John Owen, of Wrexham, deceased, and lately occupied with the said messuage by Lancelot ap Ellis and Ellis Tudor, his father, and all other buildings, lands, and hereditaments to the same messuage belonging, and also free common of pasture, turbary, and liberty to dig, delve, and take turf in and upon the mountains (see ch. xviii, sec. 1), and all other the waste grounds of the said Edward Lord Wotton, lately belonging to the lately-dissolved monastery of Valle Crucis, other than such as are now enclosed." There were reserved to Lord Wotton and his heirs, all timber growing upon the estate, and all "mynes of tynn, lead, and coales," as well open as hidden with liberty to dig and break the ground, paying reasonable compensation for the same. And the vendees were to hold the estate of the said Edward Lord Wotton, as of his manor of Wrexham Abbot, in free and common socage, by fealty, and the rents, heriot, relief, and suit of court and service within the said manor, and suit of mill and custom to the mills, that is to say, yielding to the

---

1. In a deed of 1607 a tenant of Lord Wotton engaged to pay his rent at "The Abbot's Court House," but after the sale of the estate in 1616 this name never occurs.

said Lord Wotton the annual rent of thirty shillings, in two equal
portions, on the feast of the Annunciation of our Lady, and on the
feast of St. Michael the Archangel, at the north porch of the parish
church at Wrexham, and twenty shillings for a rent heriot[2], and
ten shillings for a relief at the death of every tenant of the said
premises, or of any part thereof, and " shall grynde all their and
every of their gryst and mulcture and all kynde of corn and grayne,
at the Mill or Mills now of the said Lord Wootton, aforesaid," and
on every alienation of the premises, or any part thereof, shall
render a fine of 12d. to the said Lord Wotton, into the hands of
the steward of the said manor, and shall make due presentment of
every such alienation before the steward, or his deputy for the
time being, to be entered of record in the court of the said manor."
On September 26th, 1618, the above-named Hugh Meredith,
Humphrey Berrington, and Edward Lloyd, leased The Court for
ten years, to William Stokes, cordwainer, of Wrexham, at £35 a
year, to be paid in one full sum " at the north door or porch" of
the parish church of Wrexham.

   2. In 1701, John Wynne, gent, of whom I have spoken under
Hope Street (see page 65), became tenant of The Court, and there
remained for some years, and was followed, before 1720, by Roger
Lewis, a farmer.

   3. In 1726, The Court was owned by Sir Roger Meredith, Bart.,
of Leeds Abbey, Kent (great grandson of Sir William Meredith,
Knt., of Stansty, above-named), who sold it for £1670, on August
1st, 1726, to his kinsman, Mr. Richard Meredith, of Bristol, fifth
son of Ellis Meredith, Esq., of Pentrebychan (who was great
grandson of the Hugh Meredith, Esq., above named). Along with
the Court estate was sold a piece of land adjoining, called " Bron
Bwdle" (*Boodle's Brow*, from a former owner, John Boodle), and
another piece of land called " Cae'r march du" (*The black horse-
field*, see No. 326 in map), and a seat or pew in the south " isle" of
Wrexham Church.   Mr. Richard Meredith married Elizabeth,
only daughter of Charles Myddelton, Esq., of Broughton, by whom
he only had one daughter, who died an infant.   He lived at The
Court until his death, 1744, being buried December 30th of that
year at Wrexham, leaving The Court to his widow, who lived there
until her death, and was buried May 22nd, 1759, with her husband,
bequeathing The Court to her husband's nephew, the second
Thos. Meredith Esq., of Pentrebychan, and as a part of that estate,
it has ever since continued.   Mrs. Richard Meredith survived her
nephew-in-law, but the widow of the latter, Mrs. Margaret
Meredith, appears to have lived here for some years.   Then, after her
death on April 1st, 1774, The Court was leased for six years to The

   2. In a deed dated 1607, relating to another messuage in Wrexham Abbot, the
heriot to be rendered was 7s 6d., and this was the amount of the heriot in
Wrexham Regis, and in other manors in the lordship of Bromfield.

Bersham Iron Company at £33 a year.   Four pieces of land were also leased therewith, namely, The Fir Tree Field, The Higher Wood, Bron Boodle, and The Barn Croft.   This lease must have been afterwards renewed, for John Wilkinson, Esq, one of the two members of the Bersham Company, lived here from 1774 until 1791, and William Wilkinson, Esq., the other brother, from before 1799 until after 1800.   Then from 1806 until after 1817, Philip Parry, Esq., of the firm of Kenyon and Parry, solicitors (see ch. xvii, sec. 6), was tenant, and afterwards John Eddowes Bowman, Esq., banker (see page 69, note 1).   In 1844, Henry Warter Meredith, Esq., of Pentrebychan, appears himself to have been living at The Court.

4.   What was the original area of The Court estate when Mr. Richard Meredith bought it in 1726, I do not know, but it is certain that the Merediths gradually enlarged it by the purchase of various -fields adjoining.   In 1844, the estate included the fields numbered 301 to 307, 309a, 311 to 313, 316, 540, 541, and contained, 76a. 3r. 25p., or, if we include Cae'r march du, 84a. 3r. 25p.

5.   Until the year 1881, the field numbered 316 was not built upon, and there was a public path along the side of it furthest from The Court, from Erddig Lane to Ruabon Road, coming out in the Oak Tree Tavern yard.   It was called in Welsh " Cae bryn" (*Hill field*), and in English " Oak Tree Field," and "Fairy Field." It contained a rather large round tumulus, called "The Fairy Mount," crowned by an ancient oak, which, until lately, was full of vigour, and put forth, yearly, a fair crop of leaves, but is now dead.   In 1881, Col. Meredith opened out this field, making two roads across it (Fairy Road and Belmont Road), and soon after the several houses that now line those roads were built.   On February, 25th, 1882, Mr. W. E. Samuel, who had purchased the plot which included the Fairy Mount made a cutting into the latter, and found, according to *The Wrexham Advertiser*, on the original level of the ground, about 25 feet from where the opening was commenced, and at a depth of 8 feet (from the top of the tumulus), a heap of human bones.   The bones were very much decomposed, and no urn or cistvaen was found, nor even any considerable quantity of stones near them.   A little distance from the bones and towards the north, were found four fine fragments of rude pottery, not in good preservation, but still sufficiently large to give an idea of what shaped vessel they had composed, and which appears to have been an old drinking cup of small size."   No flint weapons were found,   The opening was cut into the mound from east to west.

6.   The field numbered 540, formerly called " Bryn Crach" (*Scabby Hill*), and perhaps part of 541, form now the site of Stratfield House, the residence of Mr. W. E. Samuel, and of Oaklands the residence of Mr. Thomas Bury.

7. Bron Boodle was exchanged in 1789, with Wm. Lloyd, Esq., of Plas Power, for two fields near Pentrebychan, part of the Ty'n y celyn property, but afterwards passed into the possession of Mr. Yorke, of Erddig, and is now in Erddig Park.

8. The most striking feature to an antiquarian in The Court estate is Wat's Dyke, which traverses it, passing quite close to the house, and is here in a fine state of preservation. Following it until we come to the Ruabon Road, we reach the boundary of the township in this direction, and find ourselves upon a road which, as we walk toward the town, along Pen y bryn and Bridge Street, will afford us plenty of materials for another chapter.

CHAPTER XX.

Ruabon Road, Pen y bryn, Stryd Draw, and Bridge Street.

1. Emerging from The Court Wood at the point where Ruabon Road cuts through Wat's Dyke, we stand at the boundary of the township in this direction. Wat's Dyke, in fact, at this point and and all along its northern course, divides the township of Wrexham Abbot from that of Bersham.

2. Setting our face towards the town, the narrow strips on our right hand marked 310 and 314 on the map, represent the course of the old Ruabon Road, which went through the village of Y Felin Puleston, and so into what is still called the old Ruabon Road. At what date the present road was constructed, I do not know, certainly less than a hundred years ago, for a map dated 1789 shows the Ruabon Road as running through Y Felin Puleston, and no other road leading thither. The present road was made through part of a field called "Cae'r cleifion," to be mentioned in the next paragraph, the site of the old road being given in exchange.

8. On our left is the New Cemetery, which was consecrated July 3rd, 1876. It originally was identical with the field marked 325 in the map, part of Cae'r cleifion, and was extended eastward in 1890, taking in another portion of Cae'r cleifion, a judicious precaution, since the easternmost portion of the latter was then being rapidly built over. "Cae'r cleifion" means "The sick folks' field," but in an old Latin deed, as well as in the *Valor Ecclesiasticus* of Henry VIII, it is called "Terra leprosorum," that is *The lepers' land*, and the probability is strong that there was formerly "a clafdy" or *lazar house* on this spot. But I have said enough of this on page 59 of my *History of the Parish Church of Wrexham*. Having formerly belonged to the bishops of St. Asaph, Cae'r cleifion passed afterwards into the possession of Ambrose Lewis, of Wrexham (see the same, page 81), and so was ultimately inherited by Bamford Hesketh, Esq., of Gwrych Castle, Abergele, who still owned it in 1844, when its area was 13 acres.

4. In Ruabon Road, just opposite the lane which bounds the easternmost end of Cae'r cleifion (now widened and called "Victoria Road"), was a toll gate which remained until about 1878.

5. Cae Siacman (*Jackman's field*), now more commonly called "Cae Siac" (that is *Shack's* or *Jack's field*), numbered 323 in the map, I first find mentioned under that name in the year 1707 when Sir John Conway, of Esclus Hall, and Bodrhryddan, was charged for it in the rate books. In 1780 and for some years thereafter, it belonged to John Humberstone Cawley, Esq., also of Esclus Hall, but afterwards was bought by Mr. John Valentine, of The Caeau, and ultimately passed into the possession of the Foulkeses (see page 123), and in 1844 belonged to Wm. L. Foulkes, Esq., and including the croft numbered 320 which is now built over, contained 13A, 1R, 10P.

6. There is a tradition that the portion of the Ruthin turnpike road which leads from Pen y bryn to the corner of Bellevue Road was not made until the end of last century. This may be true, but it is certain that it was already in existence in 1784, for in the deed dated in that year, by which Sir Watkin Williams Wynn made over the site of the Old Cemetery, that site is described as "abutting upon the southern side of the turnpike road leading from Wrexham to Ruthin,"

7. The field numbered 318 on our right hand side, formed part of the land belonging to what was once an important house, immediately opposite the mouth of the Ruthin Road. Through this field the two streets called Wellington Road and Bath Road were in 1862 laid out.

8. Some account of the important house mentioned in the last paragraph must now be given. On April 24th, 1624, Anne Goldsmith, widow of Thomas Goldsmith, gent (see note 1, page 40), sold to David ap John Robert (see the pedigree of the Davies in the chapter iii), " all that barn and orchard adjoining in Pen y bryn Wrexham, lately purchased of Henry Hughes, gent, by Thomas Goldsmith," the vendor's late husband. This barn appears to have been afterwards used as a tithe barn, for the Davieses owned the tithes of Wrexham (see under College Street), and stowed them in a barn on Pen y bryn. It is probable that this barn and orchard afterwards descended to Hugh Davies, ironmonger, a younger son of Hugh Davies, gent (see under College Street), and grandson of the above named David ap John Robert, and that here, on retiring from business, he erected in 1676, the house which came afterwards to be called " The Red House." His wife's name was Ruth, and the tablet that he set up, bearing his own and his wife's initials, still exists on the front of one of the cottages that occupy the site of the old house (see *Hist. of Older Nonconformity of Wrexham*, p. 58). Other lands were probably afterwards added to it. That No. 318 pertained to the house we know, and that No. 186 belonged to it as well as other fields is almost certain. Thus in 1699 while The Court estate is charged 5s in the rate books, the Red House and lands are charged 4s 6d, nearly as much, and in

1702 they are actually charged more. Afterwards as The Court estate grew, the latter is assessed at a higher rate, being in 1742 charged 19s, while Mr. Davies' house and lands are charged 6s, but that the house was a good one is clear from the fact that in the year just named it is charged exactly half of the whole property. This property after the death of Hugh Davies, gent, *the second*, became the property of his son Hugh Davies, gent, *the third*, and afterwards of his son, Joseph Davies, merchant, of Liverpool (who was living in the year 1749), and finally of Adam Davies, gent, of Liverpool (the eldest son of Mr. Joseph Davies), who appears to have sold it about the year 1764. By 1780 it had passed into the possesssion of Edward Ellis, gent, of Tuttle Street, and was still his at the time of his death in 1822. The property is described in 1820 as consisting of a messuage, barn, timber yard, garden, and three cottages in Pen y bryn, and various parcels of land in or near Pen y bryn containing in all 8A, 1R, 1P. To distinguish it from the other Red House, the messuage was latterly called Prospect House. After the death of Mr. Edward Ellis this property was broken up, most of the land being purchased by Richard Browne, Esq., of Pen y bryn House.. Whether the old house was wholly pulled down, or whether the cottages which occupy its site were constructe1 out of it, I cannot discover.

9. Next to The Red House were, and still are, the Bowling Green, and annexed to it the Bowling Green Inn. The first time that I find the Bowling Green mentioned on this site is in the year 1698, and the first time I find it specifically mentioned, as forming part of the Wynnstay estate, is in the year 1780, though there are plentg of indications that it belonged to that estate long before. It was sold by Sir Watkin Williams Wynn, between 1844 and 1857. The premises are rather extensive, and comprise nearly an acre of land.

10. Continuing along the same side of Pen y bryn, just above the Red Cow, were some cottages, one of which, from at least as early as 1757 down to the end of the last century, was *occupied* by a club called the Senior Society, and all of which are described in 1780 as *owned* by that society. In the church accounts for 1799, I find the "steward of the Senior Society" mentioned. Before 1808, the Society had sold its property in Pen y bryn, which, in that year, consisted of four cottages owned by one Mrs. Edwards, who afterwards built on the ground at the back, facing Erddig Lane, the house called "Fairfield House." The members of the Senior Society afterwards held their meetings at The Black Lion, in Hope Street. Now that I am speaking of the Senior Society, I may as well copy a memorandum I possess, dated 1841, giving a list of the Friendly Societies then existing in Wrexham :— Senior Society, founded in 1744, meeting at Black Lion ; Union Society, founded in 1766, meeting at Pigeons [now Lion Stores, Hope Street], 180

members ; Friendly Union Society, founded in 1807, meeting at
The Fleece ; Ancient Britons, founded in 1824, meeting at The
Highgate Inn, 83 members ; Foresters, founded in 1840, meeting
at the Carnarvon Castle, 42 members ; Ivorites, founded in 1836,
meeting at Three Tuns, 150 members ; Royal Cambrians, meeting
at Nag's Head ; Odd Fellows, founded 1821, meeting at Greyhound,
250 members ; Odd Fellows, meeting at Coach and Horses [High
Street] ; United, founded in 1772, meeting at Blossoms Inn, 135
members ; Amicable, founded in 1769, meeting at Blossoms, 160
members, and Waterloo, founded in 1816, meeting at Red Lion,
194 members." Most of those societies were wrecked by the
failure, in 1849, of Lloyd's Bank, in which they had deposited their
funds ; notwithstanding, later in the year, the following societies
celebrated their anniversaries :— The Cambrian Lodge Order of
Odd Fellows, at the Coach and Horses ; The Prince of Wales
Lodge, at The Bowling Green ; The Ancient Britons' Lodge at
The Feathers, and the Court Prince of Wales Lodge of Foresters,
at The Fleece.

11. The site of the Red Cow (sometimes called the Brown Cow)
and yard was formerly occupied by a barn, which can be traced about
two centuries back in the rate books. In 1780, this barn, no house
being mentioned, is returned as belonging to Robt. Griffith, Gent.,
the ancester of the Murhall-Griffith family (see pages 117 and 118),
and in 1813 the premises still belonged to Thos. Murhall-Griffith, Esq.
In 1804, the first reference to the weighing machine in the road in
front occurs, and in 1808 the house is first mentioned, the whole
premises being described as consisting of a house, machine, barn, yard,
etc.   Shortly after (1813) Mr. Thos. Murhall-Griffith, sold the
property, which was now commonly known as " The Machine," to
Mr. Jas. Phœnix. The first time I find the house spoken of as a
public house, and called the Red Cow, is in the year 1843, and in
the year following it is returned as belonging to Mr. James Stokes.

12. The four houses next below the Red Cow, numbered 7 to
10, are only interesting as occupying the site of three messuages,
formerly belonging to the Buttalls, ancestors of Jonathan Buttall,
Gainsborough's " Blue Boy" (see *Hist. of Older Nonconformity of
of Wrexham*, pp. 79-82). In 1799 they are still returned as belonging to Jonathan Buttall, Esq., and, shortly after, as consisting of
six houses, which, about 1812, passed into the possession of John
Hughes, joiner, who had already acquired all the other houses
between them and the Three Jolly Drovers, next to be mentioned
Soon after, he pulled down the six houses, and erected the four
that still stand there.

13 We come now to the house at the corner of Pen y bryn and
Chapel Street. This part of Pen y bryn has, in comparatively
recent years, been lowered, so that the roadway is much lower than
the footpaths on each side. Thus, high as it now is, it is less high

than it formerly was. This fact earned for this part of the street the name of "Highgate," a circumstance which not only gives a clue to the name of the inn (The Highgate Inn) opposite, but also explains how the house now to be described came to be called, in later times, "The Cask in Highgate." Its original name, however, was "Three Jolly Drovers," a name which I first find applied to it in 1792. In 1833 it was called "The Light Dragoon," but its popular name was "The Cask in Highgate." It has since been re-built, and is now "The Albion Vaults."

14. Having reached the corner of Chapel Street, and the latter being very short, and regarded, at one time, as a part of Pen y bryn, we may as well here describe it. "Pen y bryn" appears to have been, at one time, the name of a district and not exclusively of the street now solely so called. When the name "Pen y bryn" became specialized, it became necessary to find a specific name for the street now known as "Chapel Street," which thus came to be called "Stryt Draw" (*Yonder Street*), a name which I first find mentioned in 1788. After the Pen y bryn Chapel was built in 1789, the street came gradually to be called "Chapel Street," and this name has, in recent years, completely displaced the old name given to it.

15. As we enter the street the large house on our right-hand side, called "Pen y bryn House," attracts our notice. This house was built about 1808, or a little before, by Mr. Richard Browne, a well-to-do attorney, who had previously lived at No. 36 Pen y bryn, and of whom a tolerably full account is given in Note 4, p. 116, of my *Hist. of Older Nonconformity in Wrexham*, where, however, by a printer's error, the date of his death is given as 1826 instead of 1836. The garden, until recently, included the site of the present Clovelly Cottage. Mrs. Brown, widow, was followed by Mr. Joseph Clark, brewer, mayor in 1864-5, who died here.

16. The house which faces the end of Chapel Street represents a very old holding, which consisted of house, barn, and croft, and was called "Oulton's," from one Richard Oulton, who was living there at least as early as 1699. "Old Richard Oulton, of Pen y bryn" was buried at Wrexham, September 5th, 1722. Mrs. Hannah Oulton was still there in 1744. In 1770 it is first mentioned as belonging to Edward Ellis, gent, of Tuttle Street, who probably derived it from his father-in-law, Robert Samuel, who for several years before had been charged for it in the rate books. The croft appears to have stretched from the house all along one side of Poplar Road to Madeira Hill, including the areas numbered 177, 188, and 189 in the map, which certainly belonged to the property in later times. In 1804, Mr. Edward Davies, joiner, was owner of all this property, and he soon after built the house and kiln at the top of Stryt Draw, and subsequently the houses called Holton Cottage (late the residence of Mr. AlexanderFyfe, of the British Schools), and Poplar Cottage.

17. All the land on the north side of Stryt Draw, including the site of the Congregational Chapel, appears to have belonged to the house in Pen y bryn, formerly called " The Palace," but now represented by " Bryn Issa," the property during the latter part of last and the earlier part of the present century, of a family named Edwards.

18. The property represented by the house now called Bryn Issa in Pen y bryn was rather extensive. It included the site of the present Cambrian Brewery, as well as the field on the north side of Chapel Street, numbered 174 on the map, which appears to have been called " Cae Barty" (Cae Barcdy, or *Tan house field*),. where the house then stood, the whole containing more than two acres. To these was afterwards added " Cae Deintyr" (No. 175 in the map), the original area of which was over two acres. As to the house, this was formerly called " The Palace," which should, how-ever, probably be spelled " Palis," the latter being an adopted Welsh name, meaning a place enclosed with *palis*. I am not sure that I have noticed the house called by that name before 1765, when Mr. William Edwards came into occupation of the premises, and converted them into a tannery. Here Mr. Edwards lived until his death September 7th, 1779, aged 7—. He was exceedingly prosperous, and acquired a great deal of property in the town, besides the premises which he himself occupied. He was a member of the family of Edwards, of Stansty, being probably a brother of old Mr. John Edwards, *farmer*, of that township. He was twice married, and had many children, among whom may be mentioned Thomas, his successor, John Edwards, currier, of The Well House (see ch. xxvii, sec. 4), Charles Edwards, Esq., of Madeira Hill, and, perhaps, Mr. Watkin Edwards, maltster, of Island Green. Mr. Thomas Edwards, who succeeded his father at The Palis, was also a tanner, and was very prosperous. He was com-monly called " The King, of Pen y bryn," as his brother John was called " The Duke." He was buried May 6th, 1830, and is called in the register " Thomas Edwards, Esq." I should say that Bryn Issa is now numbered as belonging to Bridge Street, but was always formerly, and until recent years, regarded as situate in Pen y bryn.

19. In 1844 the old Palace property belonged to Parry Jones, Esq., while the tannery formed the site of a brewery which was carried on at that time by Messrs Clarke and Orford, but after Mr. Orford's death, by Mr. Clarke alone for many years. The chief member of the firm was Mr. Joseph Clarke, wine merchant (see page 71). He lived during the latter part of his life at Pen y bryn House, Chapel Street, and there died, December 7th, 1881, aged 77. The premises are now those of The Cambrian Brewery, and belong to Wm. J. Sisson, Esq.

20. No. 7 Bridge Street, to which, keeping along the same side of the road, we next come, represents the house of the Beardsworths,

tanners, who derived it from the Williamses, tanners. Of these
families I have given a full account in my *History of the Older Nonconformity of Wrexham*, especially in note 14, p, 68 of that volume.
But I have there made a mistake in saying that their tannery
occupied part of the site of Mr. Sisson's brewery. In reality it
stretched between what is now Mr Sisson's brewery and Bridge
Street, and was the same tannery as that occupied by the late
Mr. Hugh Price. The premises extended beyond the river and are
approached by a cartway from Tuttle Street and by a footpath
through Victoria Terrace from Bridge Street.

21. The King's Head (No. 5 Bridge Street) belonged originally
to the Stephentons (see page 26 and Index), but in 1780 to
Thomas Jones, gent, and in 1808 to Edward Rowland,
Esq., of Gardden Lodge. In 1786 Hugh Evans, surgeon, came
hither from Abbot Street, and here he died, and was buried
February 22nd, 1779, being described in the register as of " Pen y
bryn," for all Bridge Street was reckoned formerly as a part of
Pen y bryn. This Mr. Evans had among other children a
daughter, Mary Evans (born 1st, bapt. 23rd July, 1763). It is not
unlikely that the latter was the Mary Evans with whom Samuel
Taylor Coleridge was once in love, and who is mentioned in a
letter of the poet presently to be quoted. When I was going
through the parish registers and the registers of the two ancient
meeting houses of Wrexham, I took note of every Mary Evans
recorded. Unfortunately, I forgot that the poet mentions in his
letter " Miss E. Evans," Mary Evans' sister, and though I noticed
that Mr. Hugh Evans, surgeon, had many children, I am not able
to say whether among them was a daughter whose christian name
began with the letter E ; but the above named Mary Evans was
the only one, who in point of age and condition, could be in any
way regarded as the one whom the poet Coleridge mentions in the
following extract from a letter written by him July 22nd, 1794,
during his tour in Wales, to his friend Martin :—" At Wrexham,
the tower is most magnificent ; and in the church is a white marble
monument of Lady Middleton, superior, *mea quidem sententia*, to
anything in Westminster Abbey. It had entirely escaped my
memory that Wrexham was the residence of Miss E. Evans, a
young lady with whom, in happier days, I had been in habits of
fraternal correspondence. She lives with her grandmother.[2] As I
was standing at the window of the inn, she passed by, and with
her, to my utter astonishment, her sister Mary Evans, *quam afflictum et perdite amabam*, yea, even to anguish. They both started
and gave a short cry, almost a faint shriek. I sickened, and well

2. If Mary Evans was the daughter of Mr. Hugh Evans, and was in 1794
residing in Wrexham, unmarried, both her father and mother would be at that
time dead, and she would probably be living with some of her relations, or as
Coleridge supposes, she might have been married.

nigh fainted, but instantly retired. Had I appeared to recognize ner, my fortitude would not have supported me.

> Vivit, sed mihi non vivit—nova forte marita
> Ah ! dolor ! alterius carà a cervice pependit
> Vos, mala fide valete accensæ insomnia mentis,
> Littora amata valete ! vale ah ! formosa Maria."[2a]

Hucks informed me that the two sisters walked by the window four or five times, as if anxiously. Doubtless they think themselves deceived by some face strangely like me. God bless her ! her image is in the sanctuary of my bosom. and never can it be torn from thence but with the strings that grapple my heart to life. This circumstance made me quite ill. I had been wandering among the wild wood scenery and terrible graces of the Welsh mountains to wear away, not to revive, the images of the past. But love is a local anguish : I am fifty miles distant and not half so miserable."[3]

22. Mrs. Evans, who is charged for the last time in the rate books of 1789 for No. 5 Bridge Street, was immediately followed by Joseph Burton, innkeeper, and it is in his time that I first find the house called " The King's Head," a name which it has retained ever since.

23. No. 4 Bridge Street, now The Carnarvon Castle, became an inn late in the present century, at some date between 1833 and 1843.

24. "The Horns," the last house on this side of Bridge Street, and next the bridge itself, I first find called by that name in the year 1702, but until about 1758, it was much less of an inn, if an inn at all, than the place of business for a series of flax dressers, curriers, and tanners. About the beginning of the present century its name was changed, and it came to be called "The King's Arms" and it is mentioned under that name in the books of 1808 and 1817, but in those of 1824 it is again called " The Horns," and so has continued to be called ever since.

25. Having thus reached the bottom of Pen y bryn, or Bridge Street, and described the whole of the south side, we will now return to the mouth of Ruthin Road, and walk townwards, describing the other side of Pen y bryn, and of Bridge Street.

2a. My friend, Mr. J. Arthur Thomas, to whom I showed these lines, offered me the following versified rendering of them :—
> " She lives, yet lives not mine to be,
> Methinks another's bride is she
> And clings to his embrace. Ah me !
> " Farewell my hot soul's cheating dream,
> Farewell the fields that dearest seem,
> Farewell to Mary, beauty's beam."

3. I owe my knowledge of this letter to my friend, Mr. Edward Meredith Jones, who made a copy of the letter, which copy I have followed.

THE PENTICE, PENYBRYN   DETAILS OF GABLE

From a Photo. by J. OSWELL BURY, Esq.

THE PENTICE, PENYBRYN

26. All the houses between Ruthin Road and Tenters' Square appear originally, and until after 1732, to have been small. The most important of them was an old house, which has, within the last few months, been pulled down, and was called "The Pentice," of which I give a drawing, copied by my wife from a photograph. "Penthouse" is a corruption of "Pentice." The upper story of this old building projected over the footpath, and was supported by stone pillars, and on the top of its front gable was a stone bearing the inscription—

$$\text{T} \quad \begin{matrix} \text{W} \\ 1691 \end{matrix} \quad \text{E}$$

that is, W. & E. T. Now in 1699, one Thomas Whitehead is charged in the rate books for a house on or near this very spot, and I suppose this was the T. W. who is commemorated in the inscription. He was a stone carver, and afterwards let the house to tenants, and was buried at Wrexham July 11th, 1708. A croft pertained to the house, and it appears from the rate books as though it extended from Ruthin Road to Tenters' Square, and as though what is now the Swan Inn Pen y bryn, and Bryn Castle, were afterwards built at the two ends of it.

27. The rate books for 1727-1741 are wanting, but in those of 1742, Mr. Vaughan Jones, is charged for house and land in Pen y bryn. It is quite certain that the house is that which is *now* represented by "Bryn Castle." I have suggested in the *Hist. of the Par. Church of Wrexham*, p. 77, note 10, that this Mr. Vaughan Jones was one of the family of Jones, of Llandysilio Hall, but I am not now sure whether in making this suggestion I was not led astray by the regrettable similarity of Welsh surnames. In any case, after 1742, from 1743 to 1753, Mr. *Richard* Jones was charged for the house and land in question, and afterwards, until 1768, Mrs. Jones. Then the property passed into possession of one John Griffiths, who continued to own it until after the end of last century. In 1780, the house had become a tavern, and was called "The Peedin Inn," a name which I cannot explain, but which I sometimes doubtfully fancy to be a corruption of "pioden"—a *magpie*. In 1808, the property is described as consisting of house, kiln, and croft, and it had by that time passed into the possession of Mr. John Jones, maltster. The year just named is the last in which I find the house called "The Peedin Inn," and 1811 the first in which it is called "Bryn Castle." In 1812 it became the property of Mr. Jonathan Moore, maltster, who let the house as a private dwelling, and used the malt kiln for his own business. It ultimately became the property of the late Mr. James Edisbury.

28. On a part of the land belonging to The Peedin Inn, the New Swan Inn, at the corner of Ruthin Road and Pen y bryn, was built. It is first charged in the rate books for 1804 and first called "The Swan" in those of 1824.

29. The predecessor of the house now numbered 35 was formerly a rather important one, and consisted of house and barn, belonging, during the early part of last century and until about 1769, to a family called Bradshaw, of which family a Mr. Thomas Bradshaw, scrivener, of Wrexham, was a member.   Then it passed into the possession of Mr. Joseph Jackson, clothier (see on page 33), and here, from about 1730 to 1790, lived Mr. John Meller, merchant (see page 42 note 1a).   Richard Benjamin, gent, of Rhosnessney, son of Richard Benjamin, gent, of the same, by his wife, Elizabeth Dannald (*see Hist. of Older Nonconformity of Wrexham*, p. 63, note 7), married, April 2nd, 1793, Sophia Bruen, daughter of this Mr. Meller[4], and so acquired the house in Pen y bryn, and after his wife's death, sold it by auction, March 10th, 1800, to Mr. Thos. Edwards, of The Red Lion, High Street, the property being then described as comprising " a good and commodious house consisting of two good parlours, kitchen and back kitchen on ground floor, four good lodging rooms on first floor, and a tea room commanding a beautiful and extensive view of the hills, with suitable garrets in the attic storey ; good cellars, brewhouse, stable, cowhouse and granary, with a walled garden containing stock of choice fruit trees."   In 1808, Joseph Warter, Esq., was living here, and here lived until his death, November 11th, 1811.   He married Margarette Meredith, sister and heiress of Dr. Thomas Meredith, of Pentrebychan, and his son Henry assumed the name of Meredith, and was the father of the present Lieut.-Col. Henry Warter Meredith, of Pentrebychan.   Then about 1815, Mr. Richard Eyton Edwards, woolstapler, son of the Mr. Thos. Edwards, of The Lion, already mentioned, occupied the premises, and still occupied them in 1828.   He married, November 29th, 1814, Harriet, daughter of Mr. Thos. Edwards, tanner, of Pen y bryn (see sec. 18).   He died April 9th, 1838, aged 41, at his house in King Street, and in that year Richard Edwards, of Wrexham, gent, is returned as his heir.

30. The house numbered 36, next to the house last described, belonged in 1780 to John Meredith, of Y Felin Puleston, smith, brother of Mrs. John Jones, of the Miners' Arms (see under College Street).   After Mr. John Meredith's death (September 18th, 1874, aged 46), it passed into the possession of the last named, then into that of her son, Mr. Edward Jones, smith and maltster, and ultimately into that of her grandson, the late Mr. Meredith Jones, of Charles Street.   Here

---

4. I believe the " Mr. John Meller, of Pen y brinn, gent," who was buried at Wrexham, March 12th, 1779, was the father of the above named Mr. John Meller. The latter besides his daughter, Sophia Bruen, who married Mr. Richard Benjamin, of Rhosnessney, had another daughter, Dorothy Langford (born November 19th, 1774), who married at Wrexham, (June 6th, 1798), Mr. Richard Stanley, of Rotherham ; and two sons—Richard (born December 15th, 1777), called in 1807 Captain Meller, of Isle of Man ; and John Langford, described in 1820 as of Rhosnessney.

came to live in 1789, Mr. Richard Browne, attorney, already mentioned in Sec. 15, and here he remained until he built a house for himself in Chapel street. For many years, until the erection of Epworth Lodge in Grove Road (about 1865), it was the residence of the Superintendent Minister of the Wrexham Wesleyan Methodist Circuit.

31. " The Highgate Inn" (No. 41), I first find mentioned under that name in the year 1680.

32. The property where Mr. Chadwick's brewery now is, and the two cottages[5] below it, are returned in 1770 as belonging to Edward Meredith, smith, of Y Felin Puleston, wrongly said to have been the father of the still-remembered singer of the same name, and passed after his death, in April, 1777, to his son John Meredith, above named. The latter appears to have died without issue, and so they came into possession of his sister, Mrs. Mary Jones, wife of Mr. John Jones, of The Miners' Arms (see under College Street), whose son, Mr. Edward Jones, smith and maltster, had his smithy, dwelling house, and malt house, on this spot (the site of Mr. Chadwick's brewery), the whole remaining very little altered until five or six years ago. He married Eleanor, daughter of William Catleugh, of Hawarden, whose wife Elizabeth (baptized at the Presbyterian Chapel, Chester Street, June 22nd, 1779), was a daughter of Peter Trail, a Scotchman, and one of the foremen at the Bersham Iron Works. Mr. Edward Jones died March 3rd, 1812, aged 47. and his son was the late Mr. Meredith Jones (see p. 126).

33. Where Nos. 28 and 29 Bridge Street and the Eagle Brewery now are, were, formerly, two houses belonging to the Wynnstay estate. These, or the representatives of these, can be traced as far back as 1724. But in 1718 a house called " The Porch House" is mentioned in the rate books, in a position which shows that it must be on or near the site of these two houses, and in the rate books for 1708, Sir John Wynn, of Wynnstay. is charged for this Porch House, so that it is nearly certain that the latter stood where Nos. 28 and 29 now stand. Among the tenants of No. 28 the first of any importance was Mr. Thos. Penson, who came hither in 1786, and who remained until about 1799, when he removed, first to Charles Street, and afterwards to the Beast Market (see page 128). In 1816 and 1817 the Rev. William Browne, minister of the Presbyterian Chapel, Chester Street, was living here, and between 1824 and 1828 the Rev. Ebenezer Williams, senior curate of the parish. As to No. 29, in 1780 and 1781 a certain Dr. Worthington was the tenant, who was succeeded by Mr. Thomas

5. One of these two cottages were occupied during a great part of last century by Owen Davies, tailor and stay maker, whose son Owen (baptized at the parish church May 28th, 1752), became afterwards a Wesleyan minister, and one of the pioneers of Wesleyan Methodism in North Wales.

Griffith, surgeon, who remained here until about 1788 (see page 53). In 1805, Mr. Edward Evans, tanner (see *Hist. of Older Nonconformity of Wrexham*, p. 79, note 24), came to live in the house, and he was still living there in 1828. I have heard his son say that he could walk from the back premises of his house to his tannery, which occupied the site of the *Old* Pentrefelin Brewery, without going into Brook Street. In 1826 this house is described as in Pen y bryn, a fact which shows how modern is the practice according to which the street between Pen y bryn and the Horns' Bridge is called "Bridge Street." Between 1844 and 1857, Sir Watkin Williams Wynn sold Nos. 28 and 29 to Mr. Thomas Williams, who had hitherto been tenant of one of them, and who had already started the brewery, which, from its connection with Wynnstay family, he had called "The Eagle Brewery."

34. The premises of Mr. William Pierce, cabinet maker (No. 31 Bridge Street), were composed originally of at least two houses, belonging to the Lloyds, of Plas Power.[6] In that one which was nearer to the bridge, from 1745 until his death in 1775, lived Mr. Thomas Hussey, weaver. His daughter Mary Anne married Richard Bickerton, a naval officer, afterwards Rear-Admiral of the Blue, who was created a baronet in 1778, and whose son, Sir Richard Hussey Bickerton, Bart., was also a distinguished naval officer and Rear-Admiral of the Red. This fact I did not know when I was working through the parish registers, and therefore though I remember Mr. Hussey's name being several times mentioned, cannot give the date of baptism of his daughter Mary Ann, afterwards Lady Bickerton. The surname "Bickerton" was itself rather common in and around Wrexham during last century, but whether Admiral Bickerton sprung from any of the Bickertons of this neighbourhood, I do not know. Both these houses were taken about 1804 by Mr. William Owen, joiner, who died March 19th, 1844, aged 72, and whose daughter, Elizabeth, was the wife of the late Alexander Wilson Edwards, Esq.

35. The house at the corner of Bridge Street and Brook Street, recently rebuilt, belonged formerly to the Wynnstay estate. In 1769 it is described as "Mr. John Jackson's new house," but whether we are by this to understand that the house was then rebuilt or merely that it was the house into which Mr. John Jackson in that year removed, is not plain. This Mr. Jackson was a well to do tanner: his tannery occupied the site of the present Albion Brewery (see ch. xxi, sec. 35), and he had much property of his own in Brook-side. He was a son of Mr. John Jackson, dyer, of Wrexham, and

6. In the year 1700 "Mr. Lloyd" is charged in the rate books as owner of a house which, if not one of the two houses above named, must have been very near them. He was probably the Rev. Thomas Lloyd, of Plas Power, eldest son of Thos. Lloyd, gent, mentioned under Bryn y ffynnon.

the younger brother of Mr. Joseph Jackson, clothier, who has already been mentioned in this chapter, as well as under No. 43 High Street and elsewhere. He was buried March 1st, 1795. The property afterwards passed into the occupation of two generations of Samuels, who were butchers, and had their slaughter house here.

36. It was obvious from the situation of the last named house before its re-erection, that since it was built the level of the street had been considerably raised. The bridge must have been rebuilt at the same time. At what time this operation took place I do not know.

37. The bridge just named is now always called " The Horns Bridge," but during the 17th century it was commonly known as " The Stone Bridge," a name which seems to imply that the other bridges in the town were of wood.

CHAPTER XXI.

College Street.

1. The older name of the picturesque old street, now always known as " College Street," descending from the south west corner of the churchyard to the bottom of Town Hill, and to the brook was "Camfa'r Cwn," or as it was colloquially called " Camdda'r Cwn," a name which means "The Dogs' Stile," and which continued in use, along with the newer name of College Street, until our own times. This name was doubtless derived from the stile at the top of the street, by which access was obtained to the churchyard, but the question as to how this came to be called " The *Dogs'* Stile" cannot now be answered. For this reason the name got altered during the present century to " Cefn y cwm," that is " Ridge of the hollow," a name which however appropriate, was destitute of any authority, and had no root in the past. There can be no doubt at all that " Camfa'r Cwn " is the correct form of of the old name. " College Street" is itself, however, an old name. It was well established, for example, in the year 1726, and was derived of course from " The College," the name of the house which stands at the top of the street next the stile, and which faces the churchyard,

2. As one descends the street from the churchyard, the houses on the right hand side are all in Wrexham Regis, while those on the left are all in Wrexham Abbot, the line of division between the two townships running along the middle of the street.

3. The houses on the Wrexham Regis side are not important enough to require notice, and I shall therefore only speak of those on the Wrexham Abbot side of the street.

4. As to The College at the top of the street, with its front looking on the churchyard, I will only add to what I have already said about it on page 35 of my *History of the Parish Church of Wrexham*, that it was acquired during the last century by Mr. Samuel Edwards, of the Lichgate House (see pages 37 and 38), and so came with the rest of his property to Mr. John Price, and still belongs to his representatives. It has been largely altered in appearance during the present year (1890). I append a sketch of it before it was altered, copied by my wife from a photograph taken by J. Oswell Bury, Esq.

5. At the top of the street, but below The College, was formerly a tennis court. I find it mentioned in 1692 and again in 1712. It is not absolutely certain on which side of the street it was. If we follow an entry in the parish register under date June 1699, which speaks of "Nathan Hilton, of the tennis Courte house W.A." we must place it on the Wrexham *Abbot* side of the street, but in the rate books Nathan Hilton is rated in Wrexham Regis, and a deed dated 1712, whichincidentally speaks of it, makes me almost certain that it was on the north or Wrexham Regis side.

6. Descending the street, we come on our ieft hand (Wrexham Abbot) side to No 11, The Commercial *Hotel*, which I find called "The Commercial *Inn*", in 1841. But for more than a century before it was known as "The Blue Posts," a name already well established in the year 1724. This house and the two houses adjoining it, belonged at the end of the 17th century, to Hugh Davies, gent. (see under Red House, pages 206 and 207), grandson of the David ap John Robert, who will be mentioned later in the chapter, and after his death became the property of his younger son, the Rev. Stephen Davies, of Banbury (see the Davies pedigree in chap. iii), who sold them in 1723, to Thos. Pownall, flaxdresser, the tenant of one of them, for £261 1 0. Two of Thos. Pownall's sons were engravers (one of them, Thos. Pownall, a seal engraver) in London. Of the other two houses sold by the Rev. Stephen Davies to Thomas Pownall, one below The Blue Posts was known in 1707 and again in 17:2 as "The Ship," but in 1723 as "The Horseshoe," and was assessed at a rather high rate. In 1742 part of "The Blue Posts" was occupied by Mr. Samuel Barber, inn-keeper, who subsequently incorporated the rest of the house, all of which belonged to him. He was buried October 20th, 1761. His successor Adam Roberts, married, June 13th, 1762, Ann Barber, spinster, who was perhaps Mr. Barber's daughter. "The Blue Posts" was bought at the beginning of this century by Mr. Edward Crewe (see later in the chapter), Messrs. Samuel and Watkin Barber (grandsons of the above-named Mr. Samuel Barber) being described as the owners in 1804 (see page 27).

7. Before I leave "The Blue Posts," I may give the following quotation relating to this Inn from Mr. John Jones' *Wrexham and Thereabout Eighty Years Ago*:—"The churchwardens had one peculiar duty. On Sunday morning, during divine service, they used to make an official circuit of the town to see that the public houses were closed. It need not be said that such an exhausting duty required frequent refreshment, and in this they did themselves justice. Their circuit ended at The Blue Posts, in College Street, and here they would sit at their liquor, keeping a man on the look-out at the church door to give them timely notice when the service was approaching its close. They would then walk into the church with the virtuous look of men who deserved well of their country."

8. All the houses between the Commercial Inn and the river (Nos. 9 to 14) are now numbered as belonging to Town Hill, but they were formerly regarded as belonging to College Street, and I shall accordingly describe them under this chapter.

9. The first of these houses (now No. 9 Town Hill), "The Cambrian Vaults," was, until late in the present century, certainly as late as 1857, called "The Miners' Arms." In 1768, Mr. John Jones (see ch. xx, sec. 30), who was also a blacksmith, came to occupy this house, and it eventually passed into his ownership. The house was called "The Miners' Arms" at least as early as 1780. Here Mr. John Jones (see App. iii, sec. 16, August 14th, 1795), remained until his death, in August, 1795. He acquired by purchase the group of cottages called "The Bonc," in "Pentre'r Felin." His wife was Mary Meredith, who, by the tradition of her descendants, was the sister (but as I now know, only a kinswoman) of Edward Meredith, the famous baritone singer. He was the father of Mr. Edward Jones, smith, of Pen y bryn, who afterwards inherited The Miners' Arms, who was the father of the late Mr. Meredith Jones (see pages 126 and 215).

10. Next to The Cambrian Vaults is "The Three Tuns" (No. 11, Town Hill), which was known by that name at least as early as the year 1764. Here lived, from about 1785 until his death in 1803, the Mr. William Edisbury, maltster, whom I have mentioned under Town Hill and Brook Street.

11. There appears to have been originally but one house between what is now called "The Three Tuns" and what is now "The Albion Brewery." This house was occupied at the Restoration, by William Lewis, corvisor, a Quaker, concerning whom I have given some account in my *Hist of the Older Nonconformity of Wrexham*, p. 124), and who was the father of the Mr. Arthur Lewis, also mentioned there. In 1702, it was in the possession of David Parry, and so continued until 1728, when it was owned by Benjamin Parry, who was succeeded, about 1746, by another Benjamin Parry. doubtless his son, who was a glover and skinner, and who married (July 9th, 1750), Elizabeth, daughter of Mr. John Stephenton, of High Street. Here Mr. Parry lived until his death in April, 1802, at the age of 78. Before 1808, the premises had passed into the possession of Mr. John Hughes, whitesmith and bell-hanger, who was perhaps in some way connected with Mr. Parry, and who had one of his sons christened John Parry Hughes. Mr. Hughes had previously (from about 1786), occupied the adjoining premises, part of the site of the present Albion Brewery, so that it must have been in what was then Mr. Parry's, and *afterwards* Mr. Hughes' yard, that the incident I am about to relate, for which tradition vouches, and which is in some measure confirmed by Bradburn's Autobiography, took place. Local tradition connects the name of Mr. John Hughes (who was one of the most

devoted of the early Wesleyans of Wrexham), with the incident, and avers that it was on his premises that Mr. Bradburn preached his first formal sermon, but Mr. Hughes, if the rate books are to be trusted, had no house at all here before 1786, while Mr. Bradburn's sermon was preached in 1773, nor did Mr. Hughes, as I have already said, come to occupy the premises (now Nos. 12 and 13 Town Hill, afterwards so long associated with his name, until after 1802. So that we must conclude that it was in the house or yard at that time belonging to Mr. Benjamin Parry, but *afterwards* to Mr. Hughes, that Mr. Bradburn preached. What confirms this conclusion is that there is some evidence that Mr. Parry himself looked with favour on Mr. Wesley's labours, and even entertained Mr. Wesley, on the occasion of his visit to Wrexham, at this very house. What is certain is that about the time of the opening of the first Wesleyan Chapel at Bryn y ffynnon, one Molly Parry, of Wrexham, was in possession of an arm chair in which, by the tradition of the family, Mr. Wesley sat at tea when he came to Wrexham. Molly Parry's daughter, according to the same tradition, married a Mr. Taylor, and her son, Mr. William Taylor, gave the chair to Mr. Wm. C. Jones, of Chester, who, in his turn, presented it to the Trustees of the Wesleyan Chapel, Wrexham, about 1852 or 1853. Now it is time to relate the local tradition. Towards the end of last century, Samuel Bradburn being then a cobbler in Wrexham, and living at The Dog Kennel, it was announced a stranger would preach in Hughes' yard. A congregation assembled, but the stranger did not come, and Samuel Bradburn, who had exhorted occasionally, but who had never yet preached a formal sermon, was with great difficulty prevailed upon to take the stranger's place, which he did with much acceptance. His fingers were covered with cobler's wax, which, through the perspiration engendered by his excited state of mind, stuck to the hymn book and bible he used. Mr. Bradburn's own statement of his connection with Wrexham and of his first sermon, I have quoted in my account of Early Wesleyanism in Wrexham (see pages 163 to 165). Of course, it is well known that Mr. Bradburn afterwards became a regular Wesleyan minister, famous for his vigorous and persuasive eloquence, and President of the Conference in 1799.

12. Now I return to Mr. John Hughes' business, carried on in in the premises so long occupied by the Parrys. After Mr. Hughes' death the business was carried on by his two sons, Messrs. John Parry Hughes and Robert Hughes, the latter of which died a few years ago, May 22nd, 1881, at the age of 85. Messrs. J. P. and R. Hughes rebuilt the front of the premises (No. 12), the back of which extended along the south side of the churchyard as far as Yorkshire Square.

13. The ground between the messuage last described and the brook, now the site of The Albion Brewery, was occupied at the

beginning of the 17th century by David ap John Robert, a prosperous glover. He had many children, all of whom adopted the surname of Davies. He was thus the progenitor of a rather notable local family, the Davieses of Wrexham—a pedigree of which I have given in the chapter on Town Hill. I am pretty certain he was the brother of the Thomas ap John Robert, who lived in 1620 at the corner of Town Hill and Church Street (see page 38, sec. 6.)   Mr. Bartholomew Davies, one of the sons of David ap John Robert, occupied, at any rate, in 1637, those several houses, shops, cellars and solars, situate over against the Shire hall, which Thomas ap John Robert occupied at the earlier date.   David ap John Robert bought not only the premises on Town Hill, on which The Greyhound was afterwards built (see page 47), various houses and lands in Wrexham Fechan (see pages 183 to 185), a messuage on the north side of High Street, various quilletts in the common fields of Wrexham Regis, and a barn and orchard in Pen y bryn, but he also purchased (April 1st, 1632), of Thomas Jones, gent, of Aben-bury, the tithes of corn and hay of the townships of Wrexham Regis, Wrexham Abbot, and Wrexham Fechan, which tithes the said Thomas Jones had purchased (November 23rd, 1616) of Lord Wotton (see *History of the Parish Church of Wrexham*, pp. 16-17), and these tithes have continued ever since in the possession of the descendants of David ap John Robert, and of their representatives.

14. David ap John Robert was succeeded in the occupation of his house " near The Stone Bridge," by his eldest son Hugh Davies gent, who married Eleanor Puleston (one of the Pulestons of Emral or Hafod y wern) who died in 1646, his death having been hastened by troubles due to the Civil War.   A brief summary of the relation by his widow of some of these troubles may be interest-ting.   At the breaking out of the war, he suffered much by the quartering of [Royalist] soldiers, and by the contributions he was forced to pay : his horses and cattle were also plundered by the soldiery, and his corn and hay eaten and consumed.   He sent the best part of his goods and household stuff to Denbigh Castle, then held by the Royalists, to be preserved, but the same were by the soldiers rifled there, and much of them taken away by them, and after his death, his widow made several journeys to Denbigh and elsewhere to get such of them as were left, and in the end had to pay nearly as much as they were worth before she could get them out of the castle.   She then proceeds to relate other of her own troubles due to the same cause,   Her husband possessed half of the tithes of Wrexham, subject to a certain rent, which at his death was in arrear, and these arrears of rent his widow had to pay to Daniel Lloyd, gent (see *History of Older Nonconformity of Wrexham*, p, 30) "to the use of the state," that is of the Parliament.   Also, shortly after the death of her husband, the Committees of North Wales

ordered her, while she held the said tithes, to pay unto Edward Thomas (see the same, p. 31, note   ), £10 as the composition for the six (?) and twentieth part of the estate she held, which she accordingly paid, and also paid unto Captain Hugh Prichard (see the same, page 4), fifty three shillings "for a musket and furniture for the State's service," and [Parliamentary] soldiers and officers were at various times quartered upon her. Into her account of her troubled relations with her son, Edward Davies, we need not enter, but we may note her statement that by the custom of North Wales, the wife of every person dying possessed of a personal estate ought to have to her own use the one moiety of such estate, the debts and funeral expenses of the deceased being first paid.[1]

15. About the year 1650, Mr. Edward Davies, eldest son of the above named Hugh Davies, went to live at the house next the river, now being described, but in December 2nd, 1658, he leased the premises to John ffernall, dyer, at £6 a year for 21 years. In the lease to John ffernall, the premises let to him are described as consisting of "all that messuage or dwelling house, two stables, one bay of building, backside and garden in Wrexham, between the now dwelling house of William Lewis, corvisor, and a river there, and late in the holding of John Wynn, innholder." In 1705 John Davies, gent, then the representative of the elder branch of the Davies family, leased the premises, or part thereof, to William Hampton, of Handley, Cheshire, tanner, for 99 years, if the said William Hampton, his wife Martha, and Mary, the daughter of Thomas Garnett, tanner, late tenant of the said premises, should live so long. In Wm. Hampton's lease, the messuage situate by the brook side, the stable and the rest of the out houses in the backside (except the kiln and the room over David Parry's shop), as well as the pits in the yard, are mentioned. I suppose this was the same William Hampton, tanner, who on June 2nd, 1706, married Deborah Hughes, and was buried at Wrexham September 9th, 1733, and that the Mr. William Hampton mentioned under Brook Street was his son. In 1742, Mr. Edward Tomkies, tanner, was occupying the premises, but about 1747 Mr. John Jackson, tanner (son of Mr. John Jackson, dyer), rented them, and continued to do so until his death, March 1795. The property in 1792 still belonged to the Thelwalls (the representatives of the Davieses), but in 1799, Mr. Beardsworth, tanner, is described in the rate books as the owner, and it was occupied together with the kiln, hitherto let separately, by Mr. Edward Thomas, who converted the whole into a brewery, the first brewery not connected with a

1. In an agreement dated December 10th, 1714, between Dame Dorothy Jeffreys, widow of Sir Griffith Jeffreys, knight, of Acton, and her son Robert Jeffreys, Esq, of Acton, I find it also stated that the said Dorothy Jeffreys, *accord ing to the custom of North Wales*, was entitled to a moiety of the personal estate of her late husband, *notwithstanding the disposition thereof in his will.*

public house in Wrexham.   But Mr. Thomas soon after died and on June 23rd, 1805, Martha Thomas, his widow, married Mr. Edward Crewe, widower, who I have been told was one of the Crewes of Marchwiel, and who incorporated with the brewery the messuage adjoining, hitherto in the occupation of John Hughes, whitesmith (see before), which had also belonged to the Thelwalls.   In 1808 he is described as the owner of the whole premises, and here he lived for many years, becoming a very prominent man in the town, and acquiring much property, but ultimately (before 1841), becoming bankrupt [2]   The premises form now the site of The Albion Brewery and of a grocer's shop, and belong to the representatives of the late Mr. John Beirne, brewer and tallow chandler, and mayor of the borough in 1876-7.

2. In the latter part of his life he lived in Mount Street, and there died December 21st, 1850, aged 79.

CHAPTER XXII

𝔅rook 𝔖treet.

1. Until 1881, when the brook was culverted, the Gwenfro ran, as an open stream, through the midst of Brook Street, and was spanned, at the bottom of Pentre'r felin, by a stone bridge, and at the bottom of Vicarage Hill by a wooden footbridge. On the right side of the stream there was no more than a footpath, a narrow carriage way running along the whole of the left side. I have been told that, formerly, this carriage way did not extend further down the stream than the bottom of Vicarage Hill, so that carts and carriages coming from Pentre'r felin had no other way of getting to Town Hill than by Vicarage Hill and Abbot Street, and that this was, in fact, the regular way from Ruthin into the centre of the town. But I have found no evidence to show that this was in fact the case. The only fact which invests the statement with any probability is that this thoroughfare was never formerly called " Brook *Street*," but only " Brook *Side*," or by a still older name, " Glan yr afon" (*Bank of the river*).

2. There was a parapet on the left bank of the stream, but none along the right.

3. The whole of the street on the right-hand side of the river is in Wrexham Abbot, and also that portion on the left-hand side, between Pen y bont and Vicarage Hill, but the remaining portion of the last-named portion is in Wrexham Regis. I shall, however, disregard these divisions, and describe the street as a whole, beginning at the corner of Town Hill, working up stream as far as the old Pentre'r felin bridge, and returning on the other side.

4. The wide low archway a short distance from the bottom of Town Hill marks the site of an old brewing kitchen, or place provided with suitable arrangements, where persons, on payment of a small fee, could brew their ale. This brewing kitchen is mentioned as early as the year 1700. In a house adjoining it, and forming part of the same property, Mr. William Hampton, tanner (see under ch. xxi, sec. 15), came to live in 1730. He was probably the son of the Mr. William Hampton, tanner, mentioned under College Street. He had a kiln and two cottages here, but, between 1765 and 1767, the whole property passed into the possession of John Lewis, butcher, and, ultimately, part of it, including the brewing kitchen, into that of Mr. John Jackson, tanner (see ch. xx, sec. 35). In 1794, the property is described as owned by Robert Benjamin, gent, of Rhosnessney, who sold it by auction, March 10th, 1800, when it is described as consisting of " brewing kitchen, dwelling house and stable in Brook Street," this being, so far as I remember,

the first time I find the street so called.   The purchaser was Mr.
William Edisbury, of The Three Tuns (see under College Street),
who owned a great deal of property in Town Hill, besides other
property, as we shall presently see, in Brook Street.

5. A little higher up the street, where Brook Street House now
stands, were two houses and a kiln, which, like the property last
described, belonged, at the beginning of last century, to a family
called Partyn, and by 1767 had become the property of John Lewis,
butcher.   In 1789 they belonged to Mr. William Edisbury, of The
Three Tuns, and I believe it was one of his sons who, about 1814, built
the present Brook Street House with the kiln behind it.   Another
son, Mr. Thomas Edisbury, from 1812 to about 1824 a currier at
No. 2 Town Hill, ultimately lived at this house, and there died
January 13th, 1846, aged 57.   His daughter, Eliza, became the wife
of the late Mr Edward Rowland, of Bryn Offa.

6. Next to Brook Street House, and beyond it, are Saint Mary's
Roman Catholic Schools, the foundation stone of which was laid,
September 2nd, 1869, by Elizabeth, wife of Watkyn Williams, Esq.,
M.P. for the Denbighshire Boroughs.   The managers of this school
now occupy the old Welsh Wesleyan Chapel adjoining, the con-
gregation of which vacated it in 1883 for the new and graceful
Welsh Chapel in Egerton Street.   A debt of £500 remaining on
St. Mary's Schools was discharged by the munificence of the late
Chevalier Lloyd, of Clochfaen.

7. The Brook Street Chapel was built about the year 1859, by
the Welsh Wesleyan Methodists.   This was the fourth attempt, an
attempt which was successful, to establish a Welsh Wesleyan
Methodist cause in Wrexham.   The first chapel was in Pentre'r
felin, under which (see ch. xxv, sec. 4), an account is given of the
earlier history of Welsh Wesleyan Methodism in this town.
When in 1859 the last attempt was made to root a Welsh cause in
the town the services were at first held in a room in the Temperance Hotel, Bank Street, the first sermons being preached there on
September 19th, 1859, by the Revs. William Morgan and Griffith
Hughes.

8. Wrexham was at that time, as it now is, in the Coedpoeth
Circuit, the stations, other than Coedpoeth and Wrexham, in the
circuit being Brymbo, Minera, Bwlch Gwyn, Bron Offa, and
Rhos Llanerch Rugog.

9. The next house on this side the street of any importance was
that which is now called " The Old Three Tuns," but which was
always formerly called " Pen y bont," a name which means "The
Bridge end."   It is possible to trace this house as far back as the year
1668, and in 1670 it was taxed for three hearths.   In 1719, John
Roberts, innkeeper and glover, was living there, and its occupants
for a long time appear to have followed other trades than that of
an innkeeper.   I first find it called " The Three Tuns " in the year

1806, the other inn (in College Street), bearing the same name, being so called as early as 1764, so that the latter rather than Pen y bont has the better claim to the name of "The *Old* Three Tuns."

10. On the other side of the bridge, on the site of the *old* Pentre'r felin Brewery, opening into Thornley Square, was a very old tan yard. Mr. John Wright, tanner, was established here at least as early as 1724, and was succeeded after his death (December 17th. 1752), by his son of the same name, who died February, 176⅔. Then came Mr. Thomas Evans, skinner and tanner (see *Hist. of the Older Nonconformity of Wrexham*, p. 79, note 24), who, on his death, in 1793, was followed by his son, Mr. Edward Evans, tanner (see under No. 29 Bridge Street). All these were Presbyterians, and all but the last were buried in the Dissenters' Grave Yard. Before 1843 the property had passed into the possession of Mr. Alex. Wylde Thornley (see *Hist. of Older Nonconformity*, p. 116, note 6), and a brewery had been started upon it, which has continued until the last two or three years. Thornley Square takes its name from the Mr. Thornley just mentioned, and he gave a large portion of his croft as a site for the British Schools, which were erected in 1844, the scholars having up to that time been taught in the Town Hall. On December 21st, 1854, the late Mr. Alexander Fyfe, a native of, Corgarff, Aberdeenshire, became master of these schools, and so continued for 29 years. To him their success and prosperity are largely due. He died May 6th. 1884, aged 71. The present head master is Mr. Charles Dodd.

11. Until the Gwenfro in Brook Street was culverted, in the year 1881, and the Pentre'r felin bridge removed, the latter formed the northern end of Brook Street, and there was no exit from it in a northerly direction except by going into Well Square, and along The Walks. But the Corporation, when they culverted the brook, built a street from the site of the old bridge, which curved eastward between The Mitre and the Well House, high above the level of the surrounding property, to meet another new street which ran in a straight line below St. Mark's Church, parallel with Regent Street, and so into Bradley Road, which was constructed at the same time, and was continued beyond into Catherall's Lane. This new street, which obliterated the old Walks, was called St. Mark's Road, and gave direct access to Hill Street, which had hitherto been closed at its western end, and was of great use. But it had only been made a short time, when all of it, except the portion north of Bradley Road, was taken by the Wrexham, Mold, and Connah's Quay Railway, when they extended their line from their old station into the centre of the town. There was an understanding that the direct access from the top of Brook Street to Hill Street should be preserved by means of a subway, but this understanding was never carried out The first train, carrying passengers, left the Central Station in November, 1887.

———

CHAPTER XXIII

Abbot Street.

1. In 1620 I find this street called by its corresponding Welsh name "Stryt yr Abad," but in a deed, dated 1682, I find it called "Abbot Street, alias Butchers' Street." The alternative name, which has long since ceased to be used, was doubtless given to it on account of the butchers' stalls which used to stand in it on market days.

2. Until 1887, when the new street connecting Abbot Street with Priory Lane was laid out through the gardens of the Old Vicarage, there was no exit from the northern end of the street into Hope Street. The high wall which enclosed the Old Vicarage and its garden completely shut in that end of the street, nor was there any exit at all from that end, except down Vicarage Hill to Brookside, and through Well Street to Well Square and The Walks.

3. All Abbot Street, except the two houses between Back Chamber Lane and The Sun Inn are in Wrexham Abbot, the two houses excepted being in Wrexham Regis, but I shall describe these two houses, so as to avoid confusion, with the rest of the street, and shall in fact begin with them.

4. The predecessor of the first of the two houses just named, that one which is at the corner of Back Chamber Street and Abbot Street, I find described in 1682 as being commonly called "The Porch House," It is worthy of notice that in the year 1727 the occupier of this house is called "John Whittle, *kaplin*," "Kaplin" must either refer to John Whittle, or be the name of his house. In the first place it would be "capelan," *a chaplain*, and be John Whittle's nickname ; in the second it would be "capelyn," *a small chapel*. And this latter explanation is very interesting if we bear in mind that in 1620 the site of this house formed part of the same property as The Hand Inn, on the other side of Black Chamber Street, and that The Hand Inn, as I have shown on pages 39 and 40 was originally church property. In 1753 the house came to be occupied by Mr. William Jones, wine merchant. and to be called "The Vaults," a name which long clung to it. This Mr. Jones was of Wrexham Fechan (see under Beechley, ch. xvii. sec. 44 and 45), and carried on here the business of a wine merchant

until about 1766, and it continued to belong to his heirs until
about 1791, when it was sold to one John Jones, cooper.[1]

5. The house between that last described and The Sun Inn, is
called in 1781, and again in 1804, "The Anchor."

6. The Sun Inn, now No.21, has been called by that name at least
as early as 1703, and it must, judging from the figure at which it is
assessed in the rate books, always have been a large house.   Thus
in 1715 the house and kiln were charged 13s, while The Golden Lion
in High Street was only charged 10s.   Spite of this, many of its
tenants in succession carried on other trades.   Thus the Thomas
Phillips who occupied it in 1703 was a mason, the Richard Jones
who lived there in 1713 was a tailor, and his successor, also named
Richard Jones, who was buried May 7th, 1774. was a dyer.   In
1724 it belonged to John Puleston, Esq., of Hafod y wern, and it
was sold in 1799 by Bryan Cooke, Esq., the representative of the
the Pulestons, being then described as consisting of house, beer-
house, malthouse, kiln, fold and yard.   Although The Sun, with
its stuccoed front, looks very new from the street, it is easy to see,
when one goes up the side entry, that the house, which is of half
timber and brick, is very old.

7. The whole block of buildings between The Sun and The Bull
which comprises The Cannon (No. 20a), and The Welsh Harp (20)
as well as a house up the side entry, belonged in the middle part of
last century to William Jones, Esq , of Wrexham Fechan (see under
Beechley, ch. xvii), and continued until nearly the end of it, to
belong to his heirs.   Then the house up the entry was bought by
Mr. John Harrison, glazier, father of Mr. John Harrison, Plas
Coch, and grandfather of the present Mr. Robert Harrison, of the
same place.   He died February 6th, 1842, aged 82.   The Cannon,
which is next The Sun, was bought by Mr. John Jones, cooper.   I
do not find it called by its present name before the year 1808.   A
little after the battle of Waterloo, its name was changed, and it
came to be called " The Duke of Wellington," but by 1843 it had
resumed its former name, which it still retains.

8. What is now called "The Welsh Harp" seems to have been
formerly known as "The Fox and Goose.   I find it so called in
1754 and again in 1828.

9. The Bull (No. 19) or Bull's Head, I cannot with certainty
trace back earlier than 1777.   But there is a very old kiln in the
yard, and there are other half timber half brick buildings at the
back.   Some roysterers once during the night took down the sign
of The Brown Cow, and placed it against the wall of The Bull in
Abbot Street, where it was found next morning.

---

1. This house is thus described in 1777 : A dwelling house . . . . . containing a
large dining room, two parlours, a kitchen, scullery. pantry, larder, and brewhouse,
six good lodging rooms, a vault 31 feet long by 16 wide, very convenient for carrying on the wine business."

10. "The Cross Foxes" (No. 17) I first find mentioned under that name in the year 1775.

11. Next to the inn last named, where the court called "Broughton Buildings" now is, was a house of some pretensions with a kiln attached. There from before 1699 until 1742 lived Mr. Charles Roberts, a gentleman who owned a good deal of land in the town, all of which, together with the house now being described and The Cross Foxes, passed before 1780 into the possession of a Mr. Williamson, of Liverpool. In the house which Mr. Charles Roberts had occupied lived from 1751 to 1763 the Mr. Hugh Evans of whom I have given an account under The King's Head, Pen y bryn, and who is strangely described in 1746 as "Doctr and Victr." The old house was pulled down about 1826 by Mr. John Harrison, glazier (see before), and two houses built in its place, which, in their turn, have given way to Broughton Buildings.

12. The last house on this side of the street, next to Broughton Buildings (No. 15), was also formerly a good one, and its noithern gable of red brick, which overlooked the Old Vicarage garden, and is very picturesque, still remains. I can trace it in the rate books as far back as 1726 when it belonged to John Clubb (see *Hist. of Older Nonconformity of Wrexham*, p. 144, note 60), and so passed into the ownership of Mr. Benjamin Jones (see the same, p. 100, note 12). Certainly as early as 1756, a Mr. Braudy occupied it as tenant, and in this connection the four following entries from the Bangor is y coed and Wrexham registers may be quoted :—

Bangor, Sept. 11, 1744, Richard Broady, buried.
 ,,   Dec. 14, 1747, Richard, son of Mr. Joseph Broadie, baptized.
Wrexham, June 3,1773, Richd. Braudy of the Abbot Street, Gent, buried.
 ,,   Nov. 18, 1774, Joseph Braudy, of the Abbot Street, Gent, buried.

13. We now return to the other end of the street, and walk along its western side in the direction of Vicarage Hill.

14. The first house on this side of the street to which I need refer is No. 5 " The Crown," which I first find mentioned under that name in the year 1808, though it can be traced in the rate books as far back as 1715, when it belonged to Mrs. Elizabeth Phillips.

15. As to The Swan (No. 6), I first find it called by that name in 1764, and when The Swan in Pen y bryn was established, it came to be known as "The *Old* Swan. In 1812, Mr. Richard Lovatt, afterwards parish clerk, came to occupy the house, and after his death in 1853, was succeeded by his son, the late Mr. Edward Lovatt, also parish clerk. The Old Swan has been an inn of some reputation, and here the courts leet for the manors of Wrexham Abbot and Stansty Isaf have long been held.

16. Next to the Swan is a wide passage above which is a room belonging to the house adjoining The Butchers' Arms. This

passage afforded access to the old Chapel of the Welsh Calvinistic Methodists, which was abandoned when the new chapel was built in Regent Street in the year 1867. The Abbot Street Chapel was the second chapel of the Calvinistic Methodists in this town, the first chapel being in Pentre'r felin, for an account of which I refer the reader to Chapter xxv, hereafter. The Abbot Street chapel was built in the year 1821, the first baptism which took place in it having been celebrated at the end of that year, and being performed upon the first born child of the Rev. John Hughes, of Fairfield House, by his first wife. The cost of the land and of the chapel on which it was built amounted to about £1100, of which something like two-thirds were contributed, as a loan, by Mrs. Jones, widow of Richard Jones, ironmonger, of High Street. At the end of fourteen years from the building of the chapel, by reason of only partial payment of the interest, the debt on the chapel had risen to £1260. Mr. Richard Hughes and the Rev. Thomas Francis then waited upon Mrs. Jones, who I believe, was then living at The Talwrn, in the parish of Bangor is y coed, and placed before her the unfortunate state of things in connection with the chapel. That lady, thereupon, not merely agreed to accept 4 per cent interest instead of 5 per cent for the money due to her, but at the same time forgave the amount represented by one per cent on the principal from the first time she lent it. The friends of the cause then bound themselves henceforth to repay the interest still due and to wipe off what remained of the debt, and by the year 1854, after many efforts, this work was at last successfully accomplished, although in the meantime much money had been expended in the restoration of the chapel, so that altogether a sum of more than £2000 had been raised.

17, In 1832 the number of communicants was 50, of scholars in the Sunday School between 50 and 60, and of the congregation between 100 and 120.

18. It was from Wrexham in connection with Adwy'r clawdd that the after named churches were begun :—The Tabernacle at Rhostyllen (originally started in the house of an old woman in Bersham, called "Bodo Rolant o'r Ddol") ; Crabtree Green ; Bowling Bank ; Glan y pwll ; Holt ; Zion Chapel, Hope.

19. The chief persons belonging to the old Abbot Street Chapel, were Mr. Daniel Jones[1]; Mr. Thomas Edwards ; Mr. Isaac Kerkham[2]; and Mr. Richard Hughes, stationer (see under No. 56 High

1. Daniel Jones, grocer, of No. 3 Bridge Street, brother of Mr. Thomas Glyn Jones, of Ffynnon groew.

2. Isaac Kerkham, bootmaker, of No. 1 Church Street, came to Wrexham about the year 1818 from Caergwrle, where he had also been a deacon among the Calvinistic Methodists. Of his wife's two sisters, the elder, Elizabeth Jones, married the above named Mr. Wm. Pearce and the other, Anne Jones, married the above named Mr. Richard Hughes. Mr. Kirkham led the singing at Abbot Street : he died July 23rd, 1838 in the 54th year of his age, and was buried in the Rhosddu Road graveyard.

Street), all of whom were deacons (*blaenoriaid*), and Mr. William
Pearce, tanner (see under Beast Market). Now as to the preachers
—these were the Rev. John Hughes, of Fairfield House (see note 6,
ch. xvii); the Rev. Ellis Phillips[3]; the Rev. John Jones[4]; the Rev.
Wm. Edwards[5]; the Rev. William Hughes[6]; and the Rev. Thomas
Francis.[7]

20. The Butchers' Arms (No. 8) I find first so called in 1824,
but it was probably known as such for some time before. This
and the adjoining house belonged until after 1824 to Richard
Croxon, Esq., and before that to his father John Croxon, Esq.,
mayor of Oswestry in 1778, who died March 21st, 1803. Several
of the Croxons lived in one or other of these houses. Between
1743 and the time of his death (January 1747-8), John Croxon,
butcher, occupied the house now represented by the Butchers'
Arms, and at the beginning of the century John and Edward
Croxon, both dyers, lived in the two houses. For notices of the
Croxons consult the Index.

21. It will have been noted what a large number of public
houses are situate in this short street.

22. In the report on the sanitary condition of Wrexham in the
year 1849, the following paragraph relating to Abbot Street occurs:
"Abbot Street is the most unhealthy street in the town, the
annual mortality being 56.2 in the thousand. In one place a
privy and cowhouse are placed in a dark room beneath a dwelling
room with a common boarded floor. Opposite, Harrison's yard is
in a dirty condition with privies and six pigstyes . . . . . Butchers'
yard contains a large cesspool filled with offal and soil, and there

3. Rev. Ellis Phillips, of Bryn Castle, Pen y bryn ; he was of independent
means ; Mr. Edward Francis says that "a pipe was almost always in his lips," and
that he smoked "like an old kiln."

4. Rev. John Jones I find described in 1841 and 1843 as an ironmonger, of
No. 6 Town Hill. His sister married Mr. Evan Powell, to whom he surrendered
his business, giving up thenceforth all his time to the work of the ministry, and
going to live at Bryn Issa, Pen y bryn. He died September 3rd, 1856, in the 48th
year of his age. His only surviving son is Robert Albert Jones, Esq.,of Liverpool,
barrister at law.

5. Rev. William Edwards, draper, of No. 21 and 22 Town Hill, died April 29th,
1852, aged 40.

6. Rev. Wm. Hughes lodged, in the latter part of his life, at No. 39 Chester
Street ; died September 1st, 1865, in his 86th year, and was buried in the Dissenters' graveyard.

7. Rev. Thomas Francis was born February 12th,1800,at a small farm near Llanfair Caer Einion, and when 22 years of age joined the Methodists. In his 27th year he
began to preach, and in 1832 came to the Rev. John Hughes' Academy in Wrexham.
About 1834 he settled down as a grocer at 11 and 12 Hope Street, and in 1846 was
ordained, still remaining for many years in business. He was twice married but
had no children. In his later years he lived in retirement at Bryn Edwyn,
Wrexham, where he died December 20th, 1883. He joined the English cause when
the Hill Street Chapel was built.

are other nuisances about the Welsh Calvinistic Chapel." .... But enough of these horrors.

23. We now turn sharp to our left down Vicarage Hill. It may be interesting to say that the corner of Abbot Street and Vicarage Hill used to be called " Cuckoo's Corner," why I know not.

24. None of the houses in Vicarage Hill call for notice, and though it is undoubtedly an ancient street, I have not hitherto met with the name "Vicarage Hill" applied to it earlier than the present century, and in the rate books it is always treated as though it were a part of Abbot Street.

25. From Vicarage Hill we pass through Well Street into Well Square, which we shall deal with in the last chapter.

Chapter XXIV.

——

The Walks.

1. The Walks now belong to the past, and for this reason an inspection of the large map given in chapter xxvii, in which they are shown, will doubtless be interesting. Although this thoroughfare is, doubtless, very ancient, the first time that I have met with " The Walks," as a name for it, is in the year 1786. At the end of the 17th and until about the middle of the 18th century, the area on both banks of the brook above Pentre'r felin bridge was called " Ireland," or "Ireland Green." Thus, in 1717, the house, afterwards The Mitre, is described as in Ireland, and several houses and yards in The Walks are also said to be in Ireland. As this name, in ignorance of its origin, seemed an absurd one, and as a part of the district so designated was really an island, being situate between the mill-dam and the brook, it was changed, about the middle or towards the end of last century, from "Ireland" to " Island Green," and restricted to the well-known house still so called, and to the land belonging to it. But how came this area to be called "Ireland?" For there is no doubt that " Ireland " and not " Island Green" is the older and more correct name. The late Mr. Hugh Davies, surveyor, once told me that an old inhabitant of Wrexham, many years before, had informed him that a house in The Walks was once called " Gwerddon." *If this information can be trusted*, we get at once a solution of the mystery. For " Gwerddon " means a green spot, and may have been given to the district because of the rich green sward that clothed the meadows on the river banks. But " Gwerddon," or rather the definite form of the name—" Y Werddon"— is also the name by which the sister island is known, and so it may have come to be Englished as " Ireland." But if " Gwerddon" was a translation into Welsh of the English name of the district in which the house stood, this explanation will not apply.

2. Even ten years ago, after the cottages and brewery were passed, The Walks were very pleasant, the path wandering on through green meadows, within sight and sound of the brook until Catherall's Lane was reached.

3. The entries in the rate books relating to The Walks are so intermixed with those relating to Pentre'r felin and the Brook Side, and are so irregular in their arrangement, that it is impossible to get much trustworthy information from them.   In 1808, however, there were three tanneries along The Walks, of which one was on the Island Green property, and belonged to Mrs. Edwards, and the other two were occupied by the brothers Mr. Thomas Evans and Mr. Edward Evans.   These two tanneries, or one of them, as late as 1844, belonged to Benjamin and Edward Evans (see *Hist. of Older Nonconformity of Wrexham*, p. 79, note 24), and formed still a tanyard, the property being marked on the map by Nos. 32-34.   Here now stand the Island Green Brewery.   The "tanyard and garden" which, in 1808, was occupied by Mr. Edward Evans, was, in 1779 and 1786, and I believe at an earlier date still, in the occupation of his brother Mr. Thomas Evans, and belonged to the Evans family, but in 1782 belonged to Thomas Panton, Esq. In 1768, 1771, and for some time after, it was the yard of William Icke, tanner, whose predecessor was Charles Jones, tanner, who was established here at least as early as the year 1742.   As to the tanyard adjoining, which, in 1808, was in the occupation of Mr. Thomas Evans, this comprised a house evidently of some pretension, and belonged to Mrs. Evans.   In 1788, it belonged to Mr. Thos. Evans, senior.   Later than 1781, and earlier than 1742, it had been occupied (and, I believe, owned also), by Mr. Charles Jones, tanner, whose predecessor was Mr. Wm. Poynton, tanner (see under Beast Market).

4. It is evident from the parish registers that as early as the 17th century, what has since been called "The Walks" contained various tanneries and skinyards, but as it is impossible for me to allocate them, I shall say nothing about them, and reserve what I have to say as to the house and estate in later times called "Island Green" to the chapter on Pentre'r felin, which comes next.

CHAPTER XXV.

Pentre'r Felin.

1. "Pentre'r felin," which means "Hamlet of the mill," was formerly the name of an area rather than a street, and had a wider application than it has now. Moreover, there were, at one time, two areas designated Pentre'r felin in Wrexham, so that, for distinction, the one about be described was called "Pentre'r felin Abad" (*The Hamlet of the Abbot's Mill*), the other at King's Mills being called "Pentre'r felin newydd." The last mention of the name "Pentre'r felin Abad" that I have found occurs in the year 1705. The Abbot's Mill will be mentioned in sec. 16.

2. The Pentre'r felin bridge, which was hidden from sight when the brook was culverted in 1881, and was then of stone, was originally of wood. I find it mentioned in 1648 under the name of "Pont Pentre Velin Abbott."

3. Near this wooden bridge was formerly a lane or alley called "Rosemary Lane." Thus (May 27th, 1651), Edward Taylor, gent, of Wrexham (afterwards Captain Taylor, of The Parcau, Pickhill), sold for £50, to Margaret Presland, widow, of Iscoed (his mother-in-law), a property which is thus described in the indentures of sale :—"All those sixteene small dwelling houses or cottages erected in a little Alley or lane called Rosemarie Lane, nere to the end of a wooden Bridge in Wrexham Abbot aforesaid, containing about five and Twenty bayes of building, with seu'all gardens thereunto belonging, and alsoe all that Croft or p'cell of land thereunto belonging and adjoineing, lying in Wrexha Abbot aforesaid, commonlie called and knowen by the name of Errowe Mowre [Erw fawr], bounded upon the North end with the lane leading up into the said Wrexham Abbot, on the South with the lands of Robt. Evans, gent, on the East with a croft of William ap Robert, late of Wrexham Abbot aforesaid, Tanner, on the West with the lands of Edmund Heawood, shopkeep', deceased." What was the exact situation of Rosemary Lane I cannot make out, but it seems quite clear that Erw fawr was no other than what was afterwards called "The Tenters' Field," and which is numbered 87 on the map. It came into the possession of the Thelwalls, of Blaen Ial, and still belonged, in 1844, to their representative, John Lloyd Salusbury, Esq, and contained a little over one acre. It

became, in the early part of last century, the site of a dye-house, in the croft attached to which was a series of tenter rails, on which the dyed stuff was stretched to dry. It is this "Tenters' Field" which gives its name to Tenters' Lane and Tenters' Square.

4. Within Tenters' Field (No. 87), with its front facing Pentre'r felin, was the first Welsh Wesleyan Chapel. It was nearly opposite the old Welsh Independent Chapel, and is marked in Wood's map of Wrexham, which is dated 1833. When it was built I do not know, but the cause of the Welsh Wesleyans was first started in Wrexham by the Rev. Owen Davies (see note 5, ch. xx) and the Rev. John Hughes, who visited the town in 1800. This cause was, for a time, rather flourishing, but eventually (probably soon after 1833), died out, and the chapel was swept away. Two subsequent attempts, which both failed, were made to establish Welsh Wesleyan Methodism in Wrexham, until, in 1859, a fresh and successful attempt was made, and the Brook Street Chapel was taken.

5. The house which is now called "The Castle" was occupied in 1699, and until his death, by Ambrose Lewis, junior, gent. It is pretty certain that he was the son and heir of Mr. Ambose Lewis, schoolmaster, of whom I have said a great deal in *The Hist of the Older Nonconformity of Wrexham* (see p. 36, sec. 71, and p. 54, sec. 31). At any rate the latter is called in the parish registers Mr. Ambrose Lewis, *senior*, while the former is called Mr. Ambrose Lewis, *junior*. Mr. Ambrose Lewis, *the second*, had, besides his house in Pentre'r felin, all the land between Belle Vue Road, Watery Lane, and Wat's Dyke, including The Bonc, the Red House, a field called "Cae Dicas" (*Field of Dicas*, or *Deicws*), and apparently, another field "Sign y bedol," that is "Sugn y bedol" (*The marsh of the horse-shoe*). He had also Cae'r cleifion, described under Pen y bryn, and the estate called "Pwll yr uwd" or "Spring Lodge." He was buried at Wrexham, September 6th, 1714, and his widow, Eleanor, married there (March 23rd, 1722¾), Major John Lloyd (I believe one of the Lloyds of Gwrych), which last was buried at Wrexham, January 3rd, 1737-8. His son-in-law, Mr. Ambrose Lewis the third, died before him and was buried at Wrexham, November 28th, 1728. He was the last in the male line of this branch of the Lewis family, but he left two daughters who grew to womanhood, of whom the younger, Martha, died unmarried, and the elder, Eleanor (baptized May 26th, 1722), married at Wrexham (September 24th, 1748), the Rev. John Lloyd, of Gwyrch, curate of Wrexham, afterwards vicar of Llanasa. After this event until he left the town for Llanasa, Mr. Lloyd appears to have himself occupied the property in Pentre'r felin, which is described in 1753 as consisting of "house, barn, and land." He and his sister-in-law, Miss Martha Lewis, ultimately sold all the Ambrose Lewis property in Wrexham, except

Pwll yr uwd and Cae'r cleifion. The Pentre'r felin house was sold to Mr. John Price, who appears to have been of the family of Price, of Lower Berse. He was a maltster, if not an innkeeper, and he called the house in Pentre'r felin "The Carnarvon Castle," a name which was retained as late as 1824. He probably built the old maltkiln adjoining the Castle yard. He died. December 17th, 1775, aged 55, the property passing to Mr. John Price, draper (see under Church Street), who was, doubtless, a relation, but could not have been a son of his. After the death of Mr. John Price, the elder, John Jones, gent, of Coed y glyn, rented the Carnarvon Castle as a private house, and there lived for many years. Soon after the beginning of the present century, Mr. John Price, the younger, having retired from business, came to live at The Castle, and there died, February 15th, 1813, aged 52. Who built the existing house (which is an exceedingly good one and strangely placed in so poor a neighbourhood), I do not know.

6. In the Castle Yard, in a whitewashed room, the first Calvinistic Methodists of the town of Wrexham were accustomed to meet. At what time this room was first taken it is not possible to say, probably soon after the settlement in the town of Mr. Richard Jones, ironmonger (see page 18), who is known to have been, with his first wife, the means of establishing Calvinistic Methodism in this town. It appears that the Wrexham Methodists, who numbered at first only about a dozen, were in connection with the church at Adwy'r clawdd, and Mr. Edward Francis has shown that, even till the beginning of the present century, they were accustomed to go up to the Adwy to the "seiat" there. In 1797, some buildings immediately opposite the Abbot's Mill in Pentre'r felin were leased for 21 years, from Mr. Edward Jackson, dyer, and converted into a chapel. The lease is dated February 1st, 1797, and the trustees named were :—Mr. Richard Jones, ironmonger, Wrexham ; the Rev. Thos. Charles, of Bala ; the Rev. Thomas Jones, of Mold ; the Rev. Robert Ellis, of Cymau, in Hope, and the Rev. John Edwards, of Gelli Gynan, in Yale. The chapel was at the back in Nailors' yard, while in front facing Pentre'r felin, separated from the chapel by a space of fifteen yards, was a small house were " the old preachers used to rest awhile, smoke, and refresh themselves." This house was also used as a shop, and tenanted by " Mrs. Jones, Y Siop," one of the members.

7. In connection with the early history of Calvinistic Methodism in Wrexham may be mentioned a visit of the famous Rev. Rowland Hill to the town, an account of which is thus recorded in the life of that genial divine : " Some years since an aged lady called upon Mr. Hill, and in the course of conversation enquired, " Do you remember peaching at Wrexham, sir, about fifty years ago, in a field not far from Penybryn ? " " Oh, yes, I remember the time

very well." Both parties smiled when the lady remarked " I see
you remember the pig, sir." " Indeed I do, and never shall forget
it." After the aged couple had enjoyed a hearty laugh, the lady
said, " I was then very young, and was led by curiosity to hear you
preach." Mr. Hill afterwards described the scene which had
impressed the service on his mind. Near the spot where he
preached there was a Tenter field, on which a kind of thread or
yarn was exposed to the air. Several women were taking care of it.
They observed a number of persons assembling to hear a sermon,
and were tempted to quit their employ for a short season. The
gate of the field was left open, when several large pigs walked in.
In a few minutes the intruders got the iron pierced through their
noses entangled in the twine, and the more they shook the more
they found themselves imprisoned. The loud cries of the pigs
alarmed the women, who soon found out the mischief which had
been done. They ran to the spot and a general pursuit took place.
Mr. Hill, while preaching, observed several of the women falling
upon the poor animals, turning them on their backs, and then
endeavouring to disentangle their heads from the twine. This
trifling event produced considerable amusement, and for a time
interfered with the service."

8. The yearly meetings during the early part of this century
were held in the open air. in Jones' Square in Queen Street, were
known by the name of " Sasiwn y dref," and much resorted to by
the people of the neighbourhood. Among the preachers who were
present at these yearly meetings were the famous John Elias and
Thomas Charles, of Bala.

9. For many years Wrexham, Adwy, and Rhosllanerchrugog,
formed what was called a " Taith Sabbothol," or *Sabbath day's
journey*. the same preacher officiating at one of these places in the
morning, in another in the afternoon, and in the third at night.

10. Wrexham has always belonged to the " Cyfarfod misol Sir
Fflint," or *Flintshire monthly meeting* or *presbytery*

11. In 1821, in consequence of the erection of the Abbot Street
Chapel (see ch. xxiii), the chapel in Pentre'r felin was abandoned.

12. There is no other house on the same side of the street of
which I need speak, so we will return to Pentre'r felin bridge, and
deal with the other side.

13. First of all, something must be said as to The Mitre. This
seems to have been built in 1715 by Robert Arthur, tanner, and
the property is described as consisting of house and tanhouse and
as being in " Ireland." It was originally a house of some importance, and marks of its former dignity were manifest about it until
it was pulled down in 1889. After 1718 I cannot trace it in the
rate books before 1742, when it belonged to the Joneses of Croes
Eneurys in Acton, in the possession of which family it long
remained. About the middle of last century Robert Lewis came

to occupy it as a tenant, and there he remained until his death January 30th, 1806, aged 96. I believe he was a dyer, but he appears also to have converted the house into a tavern, and it is certain that in his time it came to be called " The Mitre." It forms now the site of The Mitre Brewery, recently built.

14. A little beyond The Mitre, at the entrance to Brewery Place, a kiln being on the opposite side of the entrance, still stands the old Welsh Independent Chapel, now converted into a warehouse. According to *Hanes Eglwysi Annibynol Cymru*, the first Welsh Independent cause in Wrexham was started in a hired room in Queen Street on the site of the present chapel there, by Mr. Hugh Price, who was a smith by trade, and connected with some branch of the Wesleyans, but who ultimately transferred himself and his congregation to the Independents, Mr. Price being ordained the first minister. After worshipping in this room for nearly 24 years, the congregation, helped by Mr John Jones, of Morton, and Mr. Samuel Moss, erected the Pentre'r felin Chapel, which cost about £200, and was opened Sept. 1st and 2nd, 1844. The ground floor formed a dwelling house, and the chapel was on the first floor. Mr. Price was minister until his death, which is believed to have taken place in the year 1854. The congregation during all this period was small. After a space of time, during which the chapel had no regular minister, the congregation gave a call to the Rev. Roland Williams (Hwfa Mòn), then of Brymbo, who accepted the invitation. After this, the cause began to be more flourishing, and, ultimately, arrangements were made for building a new and larger chapel in Queen Street. In chapter vi, a short account of the later history of Welsh Congregationalism in Wrexham will be found.

15. The cartway that dips down to the back entrance of the Zoedone Works gave access, formerly, to a district covered with squalid cottages, from which fever was seldom absent, called " The Isle of Man. I first meet with this name, which I cannot explain, in the year 1726. In 1699, and again in 1701, this area was called simply " The Isle," and the miller's house stood in it. It was bought in 1881 by the Zoedone Company, and nearly all the old cottages cleared way.

16. We come now to the building which, since 1880, has been the property of the Zoedone Company, which, aforetime, was the Town Mill of Wrexham Abbot, often called "The Abbot's Mill," and from which Pentre'r felin took its name. Just as at the King's Mills in Pentre'r felin newydd, all the inhabitants of Wrexham Regis were compelled to grind their corn, so had the inhabitants of Wrexham Abbot to grind their corn at the Abbot's Mill in Pentre'r felin Abad. Thus, in a deed dated June 15th, 1607, whereby Edward Lord Wotton, and the Lady Margaret, his wife, lease a tenement and garden in Wrexham, to John David, weaver, the following clause occurs : " And further that the John David

shall and will not onely well and ... kepe and observe the custome of grinding his .... corne at the mylls of the said Lord Wotton and Lady Wotton in Wrexham aforesaid, But also, etc." So again by a deed dated October 16th, 1616, by which the said Edward, Lord Wotton, lord of Wrexham Abbot, sells The Court, Wrexham Abbot, unto Hugh Meredith, gent, and others, it is provided that the vendees " shall grynde all there and every of their gryst and mulctvre and all kynde of corne and grayne at the mill or mills now of the said Edward Lord Wotton at Wrexham aforesaid." Finally, by a deed, dated November 30th, 1614, whereby the said Edward, Lord Wotton sells unto Thomas Buckley, gent, of Wrexham, six cottages, the said Thomas Buckley undertakes for himself, his heirs etc., that he and they " shall aisoe from tyme to tyme grynde all his and their gryst and mulcture of all kinde of Corn and Graine at the Mills called Wrexham Mills." In 1768 Sir Watkin Williams Wynn, who was Lord Wotton's ultimate successor, as lord of Wrexham Abbot, is returned in the rate books as owner of the mill in Pentre'r felin, but before 1781, that mill had been sold. The latter has been used as a water corn mill until quite recent years, but within the memory of men no claim has been made upon the inhabitants of Wrexham Abbot to grind their corn there. The pool and race of the old mill are shown in the map given in this chapter.

17. The Island Green house and lands, now solely so called, sadly fallen from their former dignity, must now be dealt with. In 1844 the property consisted of a good house, garden well stocked with fruit trees, drive, plantation, and lawn (No. 28-31 in the map), containing in all nearly 4½ acres, and was both occupied and owned by John Bennion, Esq (see note 2, page 177). Mr. Bennion, in fact, rebuilt Island Green. He had lived previously, at least as early as 1824, at 20 Chester Street, as a solicitor, where he remained for many years. He married Hannah, daughter of William Rowe, Esq., of Sibbesfield, Cheshire. His daughters, Mary Jane, and Hannah Rowe were baptized at Wrexham, on June 12th, 1824, and December 14th, 1827, respectively. The former of these married at Wrexham (November 1st, 1848), Mr. Francis Salter, surgeon, of Oswestry, son of Edward Salter, gent. He had also a son, afterwards John Rowe Bennion, Esq., of Nurstead House, Hants. Mr. John Bennion died September 27th, 1850.

18. When I first find, in 1715, the Island Green property spoken of, no house is mentioned as standing upon it, and in 1742 it is still merely described as consisting of " barn and meadow." It will be remembered also that it was then, and for a long time after called "Ireland Green," not "Island Green," a name which in the chapter on "The Walks" I have attempted to explain. A house is first mentioned in the rate books for 1762, and this and

*

the rest of the property then belonged to Mr. Edward Tomkies, tanner, son of Mr. John Tomkies, tanner, and it is clear that Ireland Green was then the site of a tannery. By whom or when the original house was built I do not know. On April 9th, 1779, " Edward Tomkies, of W.A., junior, tanner," was buried, and three or four years afterwards, I find the Island Green property in the possession of Mr. William Edwards, tanner, of Pen y bryn, and here his son, Mr. Watkin Edwards, died September 1819, aged 37, and Mr. Robert Edwards, probably another son, in 1821, aged 42. After the death of the widow of Mr. William Edwards in 1825, a Mrs. Thompson occupied Island Green, and on July 27th, 1827, Mr. George Mort Thompson, aged 31, was buried from there.   As I have already said, there was still a tan yard upon the premises in the year 1844.

19. In Pentre'r felin were the premises of various tanners, skinners, curriers, and dyers, some of them important men in their day, but the entries relating to them in the rate books are so irregularly arranged, that it is impossible to say anything with confidence about them.

20. As to Watery Lane, the mill race until recent years ran along the whole of the roadway of this lane, the raised footpath on the south side being the only permanently dry part of it. It was culverted in August 1872.

21. I have already said that all the land and houses between Watery Lane and Bellevue Road belonged formerly to the Ambrose Lewis family, represented, after the marriage of Miss Eleanor Lewis, by the Rev. John Lloyd, of Gwrych, and his sister-in-law Miss Martha Lewis. They sold, October 12th, 1764, the group of cottages popularly called " The Bonc," but now " Butler Square," to Mr. John Jones, of The Miners' Arms, College Street, from whom it passed to his grand-daughter Mrs. Butler, who gave to the group its present name.

22. The house now called " Bellevue," with the field numbered 323 on the map, containing in all a little over three acres, were sold with Pentre'r felin House (Carnarvon Castle) to Mr. John Price.   Either Bellevue or the Red House probably represents the house in which the third Mr. Ambrose Lewis lived, but I cannot find the former of these specifically described before the year 1808, when, and for many years afterwards, a foundry was attached to it, and in 1826 I find the kiln mentioned which is still there.   At that time the property had passed into the ownership of Mr. Humphreys, and John Humphreys, Esq., is returned as the owner in 1844. " Bellevue Road," is quite a modern name, and some ingenious person once asked me whether it came to be so called because one gets from this road so excellent a *view* of the *bell* tower of the parish church.

23. On the other side of Belle Vue Road is a group of lands called " The Parkey," that is " Y Parcau"—*The Parks*, all belonging to Sir Watkin Williams Wynn, and comprising the fields numbered 81, 82, 83, 328, and 329. It formerly included the *Old* Cemetery, and, I believe, much land besides. The present area of the fields named, along with that of the Old Cemetery, is about 20 acres. Now, although in 1844 The Parkey is returned as belonging to Wrexham Abbot (by which it is surrounded), from the earliest time at which I find this group especially mentioned until 1829, it is returned as belonging to Wrexham Regis. It may also be said that in 1620 an area of land is described in Norden's Survey of Wrexham Regis as containing 24 customary (that is 50¾ statute) acres, and as called " Parke y llis," that is " Parc y llys," or *Park of the Court*. Now, I believe, the present Parkey forms what remains of the old Park y llys, and in view of its name, and its attachment to Wrexham Regis, the suggestion has often occurred to me that Parc y llys included the old " llys" or court house of the undivided township of Wrexham, and that when, in 1200, a part of Wrexham was assigned to the monks of Valle Crucis, to form the new township of Wrexham Abbot, the court house and park, which stood within that part, were reserved, and attached to Wrexham Regis.

24. Continuing our walk along Belle Vue Road, we come to the Red House, a small farm of about 12 acres, which, in 1842, and for some time before, belonged to John Sparrow, Esq., of Chester Street (who died September 19th, 1847), and included the fields numbered 330 and 334 on the map. One of these fields was called " Cae Dicas," *The field of Dicas*, " Dicas" or " Deicws," being an old Welsh personal name. Across these fields Bradley Road was extended in 1891.

25. Turning now on our left, along the west end of the Old Cemetery, towards Ruabon Road, the first field on our right, numbered 327 on the map, is called " Plas Iolyn," or " Iolyn's Hall." This field once contained a cottage, also called " Plas Iolyn," which, in 1670, is returned as containing two hearths, which was in existence after 1780, but had been swept away before 1826. From the beginning of the last century, the Plas Iolyn property belonged to the Lloyds, afterwards of Plas Power, and in 1844 it still belonged to Richard Myddelton Lloyd, Esq.

26. The field next to Plas Iolyn, numbered 326 on the map, was called " Cae march du" (*Black horse-field*), at least as early as 1661. Both these fields are now being covered with houses.

27. The large map given in chapter xxvii should be consulted, as it affords much information as to Pentre'r felin, The Walks, and the adjoining districts, in the year 1844.

28. A correspondent gave in "The Wrexham Advertiser" of January 14th, 1882, an interesting account of a curious old custom, now disused, of choosing for a definite district of Wrexham a "mock mayor." This district, I may add, was that immediately adjoining the Abbot's Mill in Pentre'r felin. I will give the account in the writer's own words:—

"In those days [about 50 years before], Brookside, The Walks, and Pentre felin, had a kind of confederate local government, which entailed upon the inhabitants of those classic regions the solemn duty of annually electing a mayor. As far as my memory serves me I don't think there were ever more than two rivals for this distinguished honour. These were Tom Ben and "My Lord." The latter, I remember, lived in a kind of mud hut, with a straw thatch and wooden chimney, situate on the Vicarage Hill, which has long ago disappeared, as the buildings which succeeded it are shortly destined to do, in order to make room for a new railway station. Whether Tom stood on a broader platform, as the Yankees would say, than his rival, or whether bribery had begun to bubble forth in those days, I am unable to state, but of this fact I am certain, that for several successive years Tom Ben was elected mayor of Brookside and its environs, while his rival, "My Lord," was left out in the cold. The chairing always took place on Whit Monday, the starting point being the Horns Inn, where all parties directly interested met and drank deep before setting out on their triumphal progress through the Mayor's electoral domains. Four 'good men and true' were selected from the company to bear the Mayor in his decorated chair on their brawny shoulders. The process of elevating a chair containing a chief magistrate to its proper position proved as a rule a very perplexing one, the perplexity being attributable mainly to the elevated position of those who supplied the motive power. The operation generally commenced by one or two of the bearers crying out in an interrogative tone, 'ready,' when, all at once, the whole four would cry out in chorus, 'steady,' whereupon the initial letters of these words would become slightly liquified. Then they would commingle, and each one would shout out at the top of his voice, 'shready,' 'shteady.' The Mayor, meanwhile, might be seen vainly endeavouring to regulate the ballast by leaning backward, then forward, or rolling over from the right hand to the left, and *vice versà*. Of course, after all parties had been engaged in 'levelling up' so long, with the aid of a spirit level, any attempts to do so by means of the naked eye were somewhat likely to prove abortive. But the start once made, the pace all at once became really marvellous. Four more public houses were called at *en route*, The Steps (see ch. xxvii, sec. 2), Old Mitre (see sec. 13), the Old Three Tuns (see page 226), and the New Mitre (see ch. xxvii, sec. 5), two of which have ceased to exist, and the new railway will probably put an end to a third. At the mill pool, where the Zoedone Works now stand, a grand halt was made, and after the newly-elected mayor had exhausted his supply of tin sixpences, he was pitched overhead into the pool, on emerging from which, wet within and wet without, he scampered off home as fast as his legs would carry him . . . . I may as well state here that Tom Ben ended his Wrexham career by being transported for sheep stealing. "My Lord" died a natural death in his hovel on Vicarage Hill, leaving behind him male issue in shape of one son, known by the cognomen of "The Chicken.""

Such a custom as that just described would seem hardly worth recording in a serious history if it were not for the fact that similar customs are, or have been, in existence in other towns in the country, and, indeed, in other countries also.   Mr. Gomme in his *Village Community* (pp. 107-112), finds in them a survival of the licence allowed to the servile non-Aryan part of the population on one day of the year.

CHAPTER XXVI

Wrexham Abbot Detached.

1. The large detached portion of Wrexham Abbot which lies on the eastern side of the borough, and contains a little over 123 acres, represents, I believe, that portion of the old common pasture of Wrexham, which, when Wrexham Abbot was formed, was allotted to that township.

2. The chief house in this area is that which was formerly called "Pwll yr uwd," but now "Spring Lodge." The latter name I first find mentioned in the year 1804, though the older name has continued to be popularly used down to our own times. "Pwll yr uwd" means "Porridge Pool," and the house got to be so called from the pool of the same name, which appears to have formerly existed where the Borough Depôt now is (see page 133, sec. 25). Pwll yr uwd *house* is large and ancient, approached by an avenue from Holt Road, and was the head of a small estate which, in 1844, contained nearly 70 acres, and comprised the fields numbered in the map 426-438. This estate was formerly possessed by a branch of the Pulestons of Hafod y wern, a pedigree of whom is possessed by R. B. Davies-Cooke, Esq., of Gwysaney. This pedigree I have been permitted to copy, and herewith give. Unfortunately, it does not come down later than the year 1665, but the church rate books and church registers enable me in some measure to supplement it. I find, for example, that in 1661 Pwll yr uwd was occupied by Hugh Puleston, gent, and that, after his death[1] in 1666, it was occupied by his widow, Mrs. Jane Puleston, until her own death in 1671. Then, after an interval, during which it was in the tenancy of a farmer, Robert Puleston, gent (probably a son of Mr. John Puleston, second son of the before-named Hugh Puleston), came to occupy it, and married (June 14th, 1686, at Wrexham), "Mrs. Mary Lewis," almost certainly a daughter of the first Mr. Ambrose Lewis, of Wrexham (see page 237).

1. Extracts from the registers relating to several of the first Mr. Hugh Puleston's children will be found on p. 141.
The following extracts relate also to connections of the wife of his eldest son, Edward:
"Anne Bould, sister to Mris. Jane Puleston, was buried ye 11th April, 1669."
"July 8th, 1680, Margaret Bold, of Wrexham, spinster, Buryed."

PULESTONS OF PWLL YR UWD.

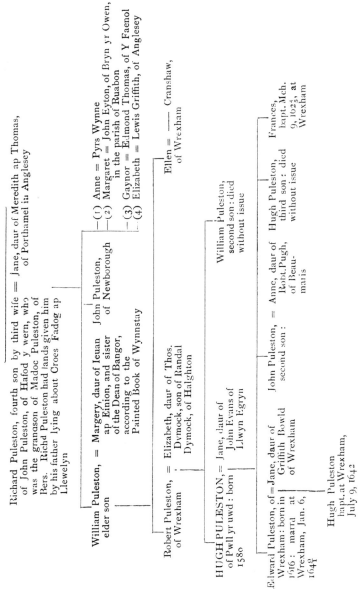

Richard Puleston, fourth son by third wife = Jane, daur of Meredith ap Thomas, of John Puleston, of Hafod y wern, who of Porthamel in Anglesey was the grandson of Madoc Puleston, of Bers. Rich'd Puleston had lands given him by his father lying about Croes Fadog ap Llewelyn

William Puleston, = Margery, daur of Ieuan   John Puleston,   — (1) Anne = Pyrs Wynne
elder son   ap Einion, and sister   of Newborough   — (2) Margaret = John Eyton, of Bryn yr Owen,
    of the Dean of Bangor,   in the parish of Ruabon
    according to the   — (3) Gaynor = Edmond Thomas, of Y Faenol
    Painted Book of Wynnstay   — (4) Elizabeth = Lewis Griffith, of Anglesey

Ellen = —— Cranshaw, of Wrexham

Robert Puleston, = Elizabeth, daur of Thos. of Wrexham   Dymock, son of Randal Dymock, of Halghton

William Puleston, second son : died without issue

HUGH PULESTON, = Jane, daur of of Pwll yr uwd : born   John Evans of 1580   Llwyn Egryn

John Puleston, = Anne, daur of   Hugh Puleston,   Frances, second son :   Robt. Pugh,   third son : died   bapt. Mch.   of Beau-   without issue   9, 162⁴⁄₅, at   maris   Wrexham

Edward Puleston, of = Jane, daur of Wrexham : born in   Griffith Bowld 1616 : marr'd   of Wrexham at Wrexham, Jan. 6, 164⁶⁄₇

Hugh Puleston bapt. at Wrexham, July 9, 1642

The following entries in the parish registers relating to the Pwll yr uwd family may here be given :—

Aug. 28th, 1689, Ambrose, son of Mr. Robert Puleston, buryed.

Nov. 28th, 1704, Peter, son of Mr. Robert Puleston, of pwll yr ywd, w.a., died at Mr. Ambrose Lewis' house, buryed.

Sept. 24th, 1698, Mary, wife of Mr. Robert Puleston, of pwll yr ywd, was Buryed.

4. I cannot find the date of the death of this Mr. Robert Puleston, but he had ceased to live at Pwll yr uwd before the year 1724. In 1755, and again in 1781, Mrs. Potter is returned in the rate books as the owner of the estate. Light is thrown on this fact by the following entry which I have found in the Holt parish register :—

Oct. 11th, 1714, Mr. Peter Potter, of Chester, Bookbinder, and Mrs. Mary Puleston, of Wrexham, spinster, married.

5. Afterwards the estate reverted to the representatives of the Ambrose Lewis family, and in 1811, and for many years after, it was owned by Edward Holt, Esq , of Chester, who married Anne Maria, a daughter of the Rev. John Lloyd, of Gwrych, and grand-duaghter of the third Ambrose Lewis, gent, of Wrexham.

6. In 1768, Mr. John Hughes was tenant of Pwll yr uwd, and was buried at Wrexham, August 8th, 1775, and was followed by another Mr John Hughes, who was still there in 1788. I am convinced, from a memorandum I have seen, that these two last-named were somehow connected with the late Dr. Francis T. Hughes, of Acton House and Horsley Hall.

7. The Pwll yr uwd estate contained in 1844 about 70 acres ; nearly all the rest of the detached portion of Wrexham Abbot in which it is situated belongs to the Acton Hall estate, and was formerly called " Cae mawr" *(Big field)*, being then undivided.

8. Edward Lhuyd in his *Itinerary*, written at the end of the 17th century, mentions a cross here called " Croes pwll yr ywd." The field lying between the Holt Road and that leading there-from t) Rhosnessney, was, in 1844, still called " The Cross Field."

Croes pwll yr uwd probably stood at the apex of this field, where the turnpike gate afterwards was.

CHAPTER XXVII

Esclusham Detached.

1. That portion of the township of Esclusham Below which lies detached in the very heart of the town of Wrexham and which included the Old Vicarage and its garden, and the whole of Well Street and of Well Square, contains one acre and a half, and belonged formerly wholly to the vicar of the parish. Of the explanation of this detachment and of the early history of the Old Vicarage itself, I have already said enough in *The History of the Parish Church of Wrexham*, pp. 8 and 57. The Old Vicarage[1] forms now the offices of the Wrexham, Mold, and Connah's Quay Railway Company, while through the Old Vicarage garden was constructed, about 1887, a new street, which connects Abbot Street with Priory Lane. All this area has been so much altered by the extension of the Railway into the town that I attach a map of it on a large scale as it existed in 1844, which map I have extended so as to show The Walks, now wholly obliterated, and also the old mill pool in Pentre'r felin, and the mill race in Watery Lane, both now filled up.

2. As to Well Street, all that needs be said as to this is that on the south side of it was an inn called The Steps, and on the north side of it, at the point where Bryn y ffynnon Lane entered Well Square, were two cottages, one of which was called " The Fox and Goose," pulled down when the new Railway station was built, in the front of which was an inscription, of which the following is a copy :—

	W.		I.	
E.	M.	R.		P.

Blessed are
they that tr
ust in God.
1693.

1. The Old Vicarage is described in the terrier of 1870 as a mansion house, consisting of a kitchen about 5 yards square, with a small porch and scullery, a passage or hall, a laundry about 15 feet long by 10 broad, a sitting room built as a lean to, with no room over, two parlours, the larger . . . . . square, the smaller 15 feet long by 10 broad, with lodging rooms and garrets and two cellars ; also a brewing kitchen, a stable bay and coach house, and large garden fenced in with a stone and brick wall, the whole containing with the two cottages on north side of Well Street, 2 roods 19½ perches. It is also stated that an acknowledgement of 2/6 a year was claimed for the gable of the last house in Abbot Street which overlooked the Vicarage garden.

PHOTO.-LITH^{O?} BY WOODALL, MINSHALL & THOMAS, WREXHAM.

WELL SQUARE, from bottom of Hill Street, looking south-eastwards.
Before the first Railway Extension.
Gable of Well House on the right, and entrance from Priory Lane to Well Square on left,
enclosure of old well in the middle.

From a Photograph.

3. We come now to Well Square. In the middle of this is the old Town Well, or Ffynnon, of Wrexham, surrounded on three sides by a stone wall, while on the open or east side are steps leading down to the spring[1a]. The water of this spring, which is very cold, is said to yield 2000 gallons an hour. I have myself twice analysed it, and found it, although very hard, of considerable organic purity. Before the establishment of the Water Works, it was much resorted to by persons from all parts of the town. The Rev Geo. Cunliffe, the vicar of the parish, thus wrote of the Town Well in the year 1849 :—"Here numbers of women and children resort hourly, even from the more distant parts of the town, for the purpose of fetching water, and also of carrying away all the gossip they can collect. Here the events of the day are discussed, magnified, and distorted. Here many a frail pitcher is broken, and it had been far happier for some had they daily dipped their pail in the filthy brook than have sought the pure waters of the Ffynnon. About 30 feet below the well (on the south side of Well Square) there exists an old bath significantly called "The Cold Bath," so cold indeed that few submit to the petrifying shock a second time. The refuse water of the well flows into this, and so passes off to the river. The bath is about 14 feet long, 10 feet wide and 5 feet deep. It is now in a dilapidated and dirty state, though full of water."

4. Although all Well Square formed a part of Esclusham, all the houses on its western side were in Wrexham Abbot. But to avoid confusion, I shall describe them here. Among these was Well House, now removed for the new Railway, the front garden of which was in Esclusham, while the house itself was in Wrexham Abbot. Spite of its late woe-begone appearance, it was at one time one of the principal houses in the town. I cannot trace it back with certainty in the rate books earlier than the year 1742. About 1744 Mr. Edward James. currier, came to occupy it. He became the owner of it, and lived therein until his death (October 21st, 1772, aged 66). About 1815 Mr. Thomas Evans, skinner, from Brookside (see *Hist of the Older Nonconformity of Wrexham*, p. 79, note 24), came to live here, and after his death the house was occupied by Mr. John Edwards, currier, a very important man in his time (son of Mr. William Edwards, tanner, af Pen y bryn), and commonly called "The Duke," his elder brother, Mr. Thomas Evans, of Pen y bryn, being called "The King." I believe he died between the years 1814 and 1817.

5. Between Well House and Pen y bont, partly in Bath Street, (which leads from Well Square to Brook Side) was an old thatched house, which I find called in 1817 and in 1828 "The Queen's

1a. On the flat stone which protects the spring are inscribed these words :—
"Iohn Jones erected these steps, 1834."

Head," but which, by 1833 had got to be known as "The New Mitre," a name it long retained.

6. Between Well House and the back buildings of Bryn y ffynnon House was the entrance to The Walks, which has been described in chapter xxiv.

7. There is another detached portion of Esclusham Below which is shown in the map appended to this chapter. It is situate in Pentre'r felin, and contains only about 13 square perches.

[I allow the above to remain as it was written to show how matters stood with Well Square in 1890, but Well House has since been pulled down, the New Mitre has fallen, the Old Vicarage is threatened, and the new Railway is being extended across the square. What will be the fate of the Town Well is not yet clear, but in digging for the railway an old pipe for carrying the overflow of water from the well to the bath or to the river has been discovered. This pipe consisted of the stem of an oak tree which had been cut in two along its length, hollowed out, and the one piece put in the ground upon the other without clasps or couplings of any kind.]

APPENDIX I

Mayors of Wrexham since the Incorporation of the Borough.

L 1857-8, Thomas Edgworth (see pp. 194-196).
L 1858-9, Thomas Edgworth.
C 1859-61, Thomas Painter[1].
C 1860-1, John Clark (see page 70)
C 1861-2, John Dickinson, surgeon (see p. 128).
C 1862-3, John Lewis, solicitor (now of Beechley, then of Rhosddu Lodge).
C 1863-4, John Lewis.
C 1864-5, Joseph Clark, brewer (of the firm of Clark and Orford, see pp. 70, 71, and 210.
C 1865-6, William Overton (son of Mr. William Overton the elder, see p. 27).
C 1866-7, Peter Walker (see pp. 188 and 192).
C 1867-8, Peter Walker.
C 1868-9, Thomas Rowland[2].
L 1169-70, William Rowland[3].
C 1870-1, John Beale (see p. 71).
C 1871-2, John Barnard Murless[4].

1. Thomas Painter, second son of Mr. John Painter, bookseller, stationer, and printer (see under Nos. 18 and 19 High Street), succeeded to the business in High Street of his elder brother (see *History of Older Nonconformity*, p. 86, note 33); married (October 22nd, 1839) Ann, daughter of William Overton, the elder, of No. 30 High Street; built Bodlondeb, Grove Road; first chairman of Gas Company and Market Hall Company; on the commission of the peace; one of the tallest and handsomest men in the town; died at Ilar Villa, January 16th, 1889, aged 82; left no children

2. Thomas Rowland, son of Mr. William Rowland, of the Nag's Head Brewery; his eldest daughter became the wife of Evan Morris, Esq. (afterwards Sir Evan Morris); died at Oaklawn, Fairy Road, January 15th, 1889, aged 68.

3. William Rowland, druggist, of No. 9 High Street : died November 25th, 1878, aged 56, at his residence, Wrexham Fechan; brother of the late Mr. Edward Rowland, and father of the present Messrs. Rowland, of No. 9 High Street.

4. John Barnard Murless. of Wynnstay Arms: a native of Taunton ; came to the Wynnstay Arms from Fermoy, County Cork, in 1864, from the tenancy of which he retired in May 1888; died at Bryn Offa, December 18th, 1888, aged 60 father of the present Mr. Charles Murless, of Wynnstay Arms.

c 1872-3, Jas. Charles Owen[4a].

  1873-4, Robert Lloyd (see p. 19).

  1874-5, Robert Lloyd.

c 1875-6, Thos. Eyton Jones, M.D.

c 1876-7, John Beirne (see p. 224).

c 1877-8, Jas. Charles Owen[4a].

L 1878-9, Isaac Shone, civil engineer (of Pentre'r felin House).

c 1879-80. Edward Smith, draper (of No. 26 High Street).

L. 1880-1, George Bradley[5].

c 1881-2. Thomas Rowland[2].

c 1882-3, Yeaman Strachan (died Dec. 2nd, 1891, aged 61, at
            Roslyn Villa, Grosvenor Road).

c 1883-4, John Barnard Murless[4].

L 1884-5, Samuel Thomas Baugh (see Appendix iii, note 110).

c 1885-6, William Edge Samuel.

L. 1886-7. John Prichard.

L 1887-8, John Jones, solicitor (of St. John's. died April 3rd, 1892,
        aged 70).

c 1888-9, Evan Morris[6].

c 1889-90, Henry Venables Palin, M.B.

c 1890-1, Henry Venables Palin, M.B.

c 1891-2, Frederick W. Soames.

    4a James Charles Owen, J P , solicitor, of Madeira Hill : in 1847 taken into
partnership by the late Mr. John James, a partnership which was ultimately
dissolved; died August 15th, 1887, aged 71.

    5. George Bradley, a native of Cefn : became in 1863 editor and part proprietor
of *The Wrexham Advertiser*, and so continued until his death ; put on the
commission of the peace for the borough in 1881; died at Grove Park, April 25th,
1890, aged 64 ; Mr. Ashton Bradley, solicitor, of Wrexham, and Mr. G. H.
Bradley, of Mold, are his sons.

    6. Evan Morris, son of Joseph Morris, and grandson (not nephew) of the Mr.
Evan Morris mentioned in note 28, p. 112 of *The History of the Older Noncon-
formity of Wrexham*. He was born July 25th, 1842, was articled to Mr. J.
Devereux Pugh, of Wrexham, admitted a solicitor in 1872, and soon after set
up in practice first in Temple Row, and afterwards at The Priory. He married
September 17th, 1872, Fannie Elizabeth, eldest daughter of the late Mr. Thomas
Rowland, by whom he had six daughters and one son. He lived first at Highfield,
Stansty, and afterwards at Roseneath, Wrexham. He was engaged in innumerable
public undertakings, but came before the public most in his connection with the new
railway schemes. He was elected mayor from outside the council and was knighted
by the Queen, August 27th, 1889, during his year of office on the occasion of her
visit to the town. He soon after became ill, and died April 18th, 1890, at Eastbourne, aged 48. He was at the time of his death hon. major of 1st Volunteer
Battalion Royal Welsh Fusiliers.

Early Books Printed at Wrexham.

1. As I have elsewhere said (see *Hist. of the Parish Church of Wrexham*, p. 152, note 63), the book—*Holl Ddyledswydd Dyn*)—said to have been printed in 1718 by Edward Wickstead. of Wrexham, was not printed at Wrexham at all, but at Shrewsbury.

2. The following is as accurate a list as I can make of books printed at Wrexham up to 1805. The list is not complete, for there are two books printed at Wrexham which I saw many years ago, and which, as I made no note of them, do not appear in it. Several, also, of the books noted in the list I have not myself seen, and are given at second hand. Those marked with an asterisk will be found in the Local Department of the Wrexham Free Library. Of all the printers an account is given in the chapter on High Street.

(a) *Histori Nicodemus*, gan Dafydd Jones. Printed at Wrexham in 1745, by Richard Marsh. The author was afterwards a well-known printer in Trefriw.

(b) *Porthor Ysprydol, sef Galwad i bawb i ymgeisio Duw.* Gwedi ei osod allan gan John Prys [Philomath]. Said to have been printed at Wrexham in 1760. John Price lived at Ty'n llan Isaf, Bryn Eglwys; he died 1795, aged 91, and was buried in Bryn Eglwys churchyard.

(c) " *Pregeth ar Achlysur o Chwythiad arsywdus Powdwr-gwn in Nghaerlleon Gawr.*" Printed by Richard Marsh in 1772. This pamphlet was a translation into Welsh by the Rev. Benjamin Evans, of Llanuwchllyn, of a sermon preached at Chester by the Rev. Joseph Jenkins, M.A., afterwards minister of the Baptist Chapel, Wrexham.

(d) *Patrwn y Gwir Gristion, neu Ddylyniad Jesu Christ.* A translation of The Imitation of Christ by Thomas a Kempis. Printed at Wrexham in 1775, by Richard Marsh.

(e) *Duwdod Jesu Grist, neu Atteb i'r Gofyniad a welir yn Matt. xvii, 13, 14, and 15, a gynnwysir mewn Pregeth ar y geiriau hyny, o waith y Parch. Evan Hughes, curad Llanfihangel y Pennant.* Said to have been printed at Wrexham in 1777.

(f) " *Llyfyr y tri Aderyn, neu Ddirgelwch i rai i'w ddeall, ac eraili i'w watwar, sef, Tri Aderyn yn ymddiddan, sef yr Eryr, y Golomen, a'r Gigfran, neu Arwydd i annerch y Cymry am y Flwyddyn,* 666." (see *Hist. of Older Nonconformity of Wrexham,* p. 17). By Morgan Llwyd o Wvnedd. Fourth Edition. Printed by Richard Marsh, 1778 (see *Hist. of Older Nonconformity of Wrexham,* pp. 10-35).

(*g) *Cyfarwyddiad i Fesurwyr.* Argraphiad newydd gyda Chwanegiadau. Printed by Richard Marsh in 1784.

(*h) *Practical Treatise on Farriery,* by William Griffiths, with frontispiece drawn by Henry Bunbury, Esq. Printed by Richard Marsh. Preface dated 1784.

(*i) *Toxophilus,* by Roger Ascham. Edited by the Rev. John Walters, master of Ruthin Grammar School. Printed in 1788 by Richard Marsh.

(j) " *Ode io the Immortality of the Soul, an Elegy,* by the Rev. John Walters, master of Ruthin Grammar School. Printed at Wrexham by Richard Marsh, in 1788.

(k) *A Week well spent, or Serious Reflections for every Day in the Week.* By the Rev. Joseph Jenkins, M.A. [see above]. Printed in 1791.

(l) *Undeb Crefyddol neu Rhybudd yn erbyn Schism.* Printed at Wrexham, in 1792, by John Marsh.

(*m) "*Essays and Reflections, Religious and Moral.*" By Thomas Apperley, Esq. [see pages 97, 111, and 112]. Printed, in 1793, by John Marsh.

(n) "*Natural Evil from God; being the substance of a Discourse delivered at Pen y bryn Meeting House, on the General Fast Day,* April 19th, 1793, by Jenkin Lewis (see *Hist. of Older Nonconformity of Wrexham,* pp 115-117. Printed by John Marsh, 1793.

(o) *Cywydd y Duwdod,* gan Dafydd Ionawr (David Richards, see page 108). First Edition printed at Wrexham in 1793, by Anna Tye.

(p) *Sylwedd dwy Bregeth.* The two sermons were preached at Glynceiriog, and the substance of them printed in Wrexham in 1794, by Joseph Tye.

(q) *Survey of the Diocese of St. Asaph,* by Browne Willis. New Edition by the Rev. Edward Edwards (see *Hist. of Par. Church of Wrexham,* p. 82), 2 vols. Printed, in 1801, by John Painter.

(r) *Sententiæ, or Moral and Religious Instruction Epitomized,* by John Bowden. Printed by Anna Tye in 1805.

3. I copy also from the advertisement sheet of a book printed by Richard Marsh, 1778, the following list of other works printed by him :—

(a) *Llyfr Testament Newydd yn Gymraeg gyda'r cynhwysiad o flaen y Pennodau.*

(b) *Llyfr Gweddi Gyffredin yn gymmwys i'r Llogell neu'r Bocced.*

(c) *Llyfr Hunan ymholiad.*

(d) *Llyfr Cydymmaith yr Eglwyswr, yn ymweled a'i Claf.*

(e) *Llyfr Cydymmaith i'r Allor.*
(f) *Llyfr Mesur Coed, etc.* (see sec. 2, g).
(g) *Pattrwn y Gwir Gristion, neu Ddylyniad Jesu Grist* (see sec. 2, d).
(h) *Llyfr Saith o Bregethau,* gan Robert Russell.
(i) *Y Llyfr Plygain, neu'r Primer Cymraeg.*
(j) *Llyfr Taith y Pererin,* gan John Bunyan.
(k) *Llyfr Taith y Christianes, neu'r ail rhann o Daith y Pererin,* gan John
    Bunyan.
(l) *Geir Llyfr, neu Ddictionary Cymraeg a Saesoneg, sef Cymraeg o flaen y
    Saesoneg.*
(m) *Llyfr Ficcar Llanddyfri—y Chweched Ran.*
(n) *Llyfr A B C, neu Gatechism yr Eglwys.*
(o) *Llyfr Hanes o fywyd a marwolaeth Judas Iscariot.*
(p) *Llyfr Histori Nicodemus, etc.* (see sec. 2, a).
(q) *Llyfr Hanes Tair Sir ar ddeg Cymru.*
(r) *Llyfr Bardd Cwsg.*
(s) *Llyfr Meddyginiaeth a Physygwriaeth i'r anafus a'r clwyfus.*
(t) *Llyfr Myfrdodau Bucheddol ar y Pedwar Beth Diweddaf.*
(u) *Llyfr Histori'r Geiniogwerth Synnwyr*
(v) *Llyfr o Weddiau Duwiol.*
(w) *Llyfr y Tri Aderyn* (see sec. 2, f).

Extracts from Parish Registers.

1. In this appendix no extracts will, as a rule, be given which have already been incorporated in this volume, or in any of the earlier volumes of the present series, nor will any extracts be given relating to the country townships of the parish, as these will appear in the next and final volume. And of those that remain, only the most interesting will here be found, otherwise, this book would be swollen to at least twenty times its present size, and a heavy pecuniary loss be sustained. When the letter " W " occurs in the entries, this stands for " Wrexham." In like manner " W.R.," " W.V.," and " W.A.," stand for " Wrexham Regis," " Wrexham Vechan," and " Wrexham Abbot."

2. Large portions of the first register are atrociously written, nor are other portions of the later registers much better in this respect, so that, though I have collated the greater part of the extracts here given, I cannot feel quite sure that every extract is exactly copied. I should have compared the whole of the extracts a second time with the entries in the registers, as well as collated them with the copies at St. Asaph, if my state of health had permitted.

First Register.

The first register, *in the original handwriting*, begins in June, 1618, and ends in March, 164$\frac{4}{5}$, there being two or three entries which were subsequently made, in an irregular way, in it. At the top of the first page is written the name "Edward Owen." Several pages, or portions of pages, are wanting. I give, first, some selected entries of baptisms, then of marriages, and, finally, of burials.

BAPTISMS.

Lewis, the sonne of Godfrey Kyffin, was baptized the viith daie   Dec. 1618
Amie [or Ann] the daughter of Thomas Bulkeley, was baptized the xvi
    [or xxit] daie   Dec. 1618
Edward, the sonne of Edward Crewe, was baptized the xxiith daie   „   „
Jon, the sonne of William Jones, Mr of Arts, was baptized the xxiith daie
    Mch. 1619-20

James, the sonne of Edward Crewe, was baptized the xxv_{th} daie July 1621

Margaret, the daughter of Edward Lloyd, gentleman, was baptized the xiii_{th} daie   October 1621

Jane, the supposed daughter of Thomas ap Jn. ap Hughe, of Llanvihangell, in the countie of Merionyth, was baptized the same daie [Dec. 3,1621]

Geoffrey ap Arthur, Suretie [other entries of the same kind]

Roger, the sonne of Edward Sonlley, was baptized the same daie, Mch. 26, 1622

Richard, the sonne of John Sonlley, was baptized the 28th daie   May, 1622

Jn. the sonne of Jn. Sonlley, was baptized the xviiith daie   Sept. 1624

Ffrances, the danghter of Edward Lloyd, gent, was baptized the iiiith daie Nov. 1624

Sarah, the daughter of Sydney Ellis,[6] was baptized the xxiii_{th} daie, July 1625

George the [sonne] of David Ll'en, of Eyton Park, was baptized the same daie Aug. 23, 1625

'Marie, the daughter of Edward Sonlley, was baptized the   daie, Dec. 1625

Ffrances, the daughter of Roger Decka, was baptized the first daie, Jan^r. 1625-6

Roger, the sonne of John Sonlley, was bap. the v_{ij}i_{th} daie   Dec. 1626

Roger, the sonne of Jn. Sonlley, was bapt. the xv_{th} daie   Jan_r 1626-7

Ellis the sonne of Roger Decka, was bap^d. the xx_{th} daie   Dec. 1630

Catherine, the daughter of Sydney Ellis,[6] was bap^d. the xxiii_{th} daie, Jan^r 1630-1

Robert, the sonne of Roger Sonlley, was baptized the xv_{th} daie, Sep. 1632

Arthur [or Andrew], the sonne of Edward Crue, was bap. the xx_{th} daie Dec. 1633

Robert, the sonne of Robert Sonlley, was bapt. the xx_{th} daie   Mch. 1634-5

George, the sonne of Edward Crue, was baptized the xth daie   May 1635

Thomas filius Rodolphi Crichley,[7] bapt. fuit 17o die January,   1635

Jana filia Edwardi Gwalgmai   ,,   18o   ,,   ,,

Maria fili Ambrosii Kinaston et Margarettæ ux eius bapt. fuit 2o die Junii 1636

Johannes filius Thomœ Decka Johannœque ux eius bapt. fuit 9o die Junii 1637

Josephus[8] filius Rodolphi Chrichley Aliciœque ux eius bapt. fuit 10o die Funii 1637

Eduardus filius Thomœ Tilston Aliceœque ux eius bapt. fuii 14o die Junii 1640 '

Alicia filia Gulielmi Sontley Elizabethœque ux eius bapt. fuit 19o die Decembris, 1640

Anna filia Thomœ Baker Dorotheœque ux eius bapt. fuit 31o die Martii 1641

Eduardus filius Johannis Hanmer Elinæque ux eius bapt. fuit 7o die Octobris 1641

Eduardus filius Humfredi Kinaston Luciœque ux eius bapt. fuit 8o die Decembris. 1641

6. Sydney Ellis, gent, undoubtedly one of the family of Elise of Alrhey, in the parish of Bangor is y coed.

7. Ralph Critchley, see *Hist. of Older Nonconformity of Wrexham*, p. 4.

8. Joseph Critchley, see *Hist. of Par. Church of Wrexham*, p. 90, note 55.

Hugo filius Hugonis Middleton9 Mariœque ux eius bapt. fuit 9º die July
1642
Dorothea filia Francisci Manley10 Elizabethœque ux eius bapt. fuit 4º dei
Januarii 1642-3
Faulco filuis Thomœ Baker Elinorisque ux eius bapt. fuit 29º Januarii,
1642-3
Robertus filius Gulielmi Sontley Elizabethœque ux eius bapt. fuit 8º
Februarii, 1642-3
Margaretta filia Rogeri Sontley Margarettœque ux eius bapt. fuit 28º
Martii 1644

MARRIAGES.

Thomas Decka et Johanna Thomas mariti sunt 26 die Aprilis,   1637
Petrus Wells [Weld]et Maria Critchley mariti sunt 30 die Aprilis,   1638
Gulielmus Sontley et Elizabetha Sontley mariti sunt 26 die Novembris
1640
Rogerus Decka et Gwenna John mariti sunt 29 die Maii,   1641

BURIALS.

Allis, the daughter of Edward Soulley was buried xxiiith daie, Apl.   1621
John Price, gent, the xiith daie   Oct. 1632
Edward Sonlley was buried the xxiii   June 1633
Roger Decka [Decka] was buried the second daie.   October 1633
Jon Sonlley, tholdr, was buried the xixth daie,   Feb. 1633-4
Ann, the wief of Roger Sontley was buried the xxiii daie   May 1634
Eduardus Crew, sepult fuit 29 die Januarii,   1638-9
Catherine Sontley, sepult fuit 7 die Febuarii,   1638-9
Jana Sontley,   „   7 „   „   „
Valentinus Tilston „   31 „ Martii,   1639
Eduardus Sontley   „   2 „ Junii,   1639
Johannes Caluely,   „   26 „   „   1639
Robertus Sontley,   „   19 „ Januarii,   1640-1
Dorothea Decka   „   7 „ Martii   „
Anna Sontley   „   1 „ Aprilis,   1641
Eduardus Meredith, Ar.11 sepult fuit 2 die Junii,   1643
Sara Critchley, alias Thomas, sepult fuit 19 die Octobris,   1644

4. As the chief families of Wrexham had, at the beginning of
the 17th century, adopted surnames, and the foregoing extracts
relate to those families (many of whom were English), no one reading them can participate in the profound impression which the
study of this first register suggests as to the predominantly Welsh
character of the town, or at least of the parish, at that time.   An
enormous proportion of the persons mentioned in the register had
no surnames at all, while among the female christian names that
occur in it are such as Gwenhwyfar, Deuli, Marsli, Gwen, and
Morfydd, and, at a later date, Eurlliw and Sina.

9. Mr. W. M. Myddelton believes this Hugh Myddelton to be the Capt. Hugh
Myddelton, of Flint, who petitioned the Justices at the Quarter Sessions, after the
Restoration, and obtained a pension from "the maimed soldiers' mize."
10. Francis Manley, Esq., of Erbistock, who fought on the Royal side during
the Civil War, and received the honour of knighthood after the Restoration.
11. Edward Meredith, Esq., a brother of Sir William Meredith, and Hugh
Meredith, Esq. (see p. 201).

Second Register.

5. The second register, in the original handwriting, begins on March 27th, 1662, and ends on November 16th, 1666, but includes many blank pages, there being several periods during which no entries were made. Baptisms, marriages, and burials, are grouped together.

May 11, 1662, Thomas Owen,[12] the Curat of Flint, and schoolmaster at
    Mould   Buryed

June 15, 1663, Anne Hanmer, of Wrexham Abbot, the daughter of Thomas
    Hanmer, of Maesgwaelod, in the p'ish of Overton   Buried

Margaret, daughter of Robert Lloyd, by Elizabeth, his wife, was borne
    half an ower after eleven of the clock of the evanig in the yeare of our
    Lord 1663, And be it remembered that the signe then was in the
    Knee. The said Margaret was christened the 26th day of June

Janry. 15, 1662-3, Thomas Baker,[14] of Wrexham, and Jane Edwards of
    Stanstie, married

February 9, 1662-3, John, the son of Joseph Chrichley, of Wrexham Regis,
    Bapt.

Dec. 11, 1663, Margaret, the daughter of Thomas Baker,[14] of Wrexham
    Regis, Bapt.

Mch. 25, 1664, Grace, daughter of Mr. Ambrose Lewis (see ch. xxv, sec. 5)

June 15, 1664, Elizabeth, the daughter of John Matthews, Esq., of
    Wrexham Abbot, Bapt.

Mch. 28, 1665, Mary, the daughter of Mr. Richard Dutton,[15] of Wrexham
    Abbot, Bapt.

Mch. 31, 1665, Mrs. Elizabeth Lloyd, of Plas Enion   Buried

Apl. 11, 1665, John Bell, of W.R., apothecary[16]   Buried

Aug. 8, 1665, Elizabeth ye daughter of Edward Greene, cle.,[17] by Margaret
    his wife, was borne between eleven and twelve att night on ye 26th of
    July, 1665

Jany. 27, 1665-6, Thomas, the sonn of Thomas Baker, grocer, was   Bpd.

Mch. 14, 1665-6, Elizabeth ych Richard, of Wrexham Abbot, vid,   burd.

June 9, 1666, John Matthews, Esq. was buried

---

12. The name of "—— Owens" appears under date 1650 as one of the perpetua curates of Flint.

13. I think this Margaret was the youngest daughter of Robert Lloyd, Esq., of Plas Badi (now New Hall), in the parish of Ruabon.

14. The Bakers were a very important local family in Wrexham, during the 17th century. At the time of the Civil War there was a Captain Thomas Baker, of Wrexham (see *Hist. of Older Nonconformity of Wrexham*, p. 8, note 9). A little later a Mr. Thomas Baker, mercer and grocer, was settled in the town, and between 1697 and 1702, the Rev. Thomas Baker, a member of the same family, was vicar of Llanrwst, and between 1702 and 1732, rector of Manafon, his wife's christian name being "Lumley."

15. Richard Dutton, Esq., was one of the chief men of Wrexham in his time. He saved his estates by the payment of £185 to the Parliamentary sequestrators.

16. Mr. Bell's wife, Dorothy, was a daughter of Matthew Trevor, Esq., of Trevor.

17. The Rev. Edward Greene, curate of Wrexham.

June 15, 1666, John, the sonn of John Matthews, Esq. was buried

Aug. 6, 1666, Rondle Stronge in the Arme was buried

Aug. 6, 1666, John, the son of Mr. Ambrose Lewis, of W.R., was Bpd (see page 237)

Aug 14, 1666, Elizabeth Crue was buried

Third Register.

6. This register, in the original handwriting, begins on March 25th, 1668, and concludes on October 31st, 1682, but contains on the fly-leaf a few entries relating to the years 1666 and 1667. There are many gaps in it, and sometimes a whole page is left to be afterwards filled up.

Mch. 1, 1668, Douse, daughter of Mr. Ambrose Lewis (see page 237), buried

July 12, 1669, Mr. Henry Davies, and Mrs. Margaret Manley, of ye Lach were married

Aug. 13, 1669, Martha, the wife of Charles Bratchaw,   Buryed

Dec. 31, 1669, Robert, ye sonne of Edward Greene, by Margaret, his wife, was borne between 6 and seaven of ye clock at noon ye 24th [so!]

July 27, 1670, Mrs. Mary Goodin, wife of Mr. James Goodin, Appo., Buried

Dec. 12, 1670, Capt. Naney Lloyd[21]   Buried

Sept. 9, 1671, Mrs. Magdalen Platt, wife of Thomas Platt, mercer[22] Buryed

Sept. 19, 1671, Jane Platt, wife of Mr. Ffrancis Platt   Buryed

Dec. 2, 1671, Mrs. Mary, ye wife of Mr. John Chambers[23]   ,,

Dec. 15, 1671, Joseph, the sonn of Joseph Crichley (see page 33),   Bapt.

Janr. 13, 1671-2, Mrs. Barbara Hughes   Buryed

Feb. 16, 1671-2, Grace, ye daughter of Mr. Ambrose Lewis (see page 237) Buryed

Mch. 24, 1671-2, Katherine, ye daughter of Jon Trevor   Bapt.

Apl. 6, 1672, Mr. Thomas Platt, ye younger   Buryed

Apl. 27, 1672, Mr. Phillip Roberts   Buryed

May 26, 1672, Sarah a daughter of Edd. Lewis, Gentleman   Bapt.

June 4, 1672, Thomas Baker, junior (see note 14)   Buried

June 23, 1672, Grace, ye daughter of Mr. Joseph Critchley (see page 33), Buried

18. Mr. Henry Davies, of Ashton, Cheshire, and Mrs. Margaret Manley, of the same county.

19. Charles Bradshaw, Esq., of Plas Gwern, Wrexham, afterwards of Holt.

20. Mr. Jas. Goodwin, see *Hist. of Older Nonconformity of Wrexham*, p. 132.

21. Capt. Nanney Lloyd, see *Hist. of Par. Church of Wrexham*, p. 88, note 22. He was almost certainly a younger son of Robert Lloyd, Esq., of Rhiw Goch; his wife's name was Alice.

22. Thomas Platt, who, I believe, lived on Town Hill, was a prosperous tradesman, and issued a token of which the obverse was :—THOMAS PLATT, HIS HALF PENY, and the reverse was :—IN WREXHAM, 1666, T.M.P.

23. Mary, wife of John Chambres, of Plas Chambres, near Denbigh, to whom she had been married, at Wrexham, Jan. 14th, 1670-1.

June 30, 1673, Edward Greene, curate, was   Buried
Oct. 13, 1673, Ellis Hughes and Mary Trevor were married
Nov. 9, 1673, Mary, the wife of Mr. Edward Crew,[24] of Wrexham, was
    Buried
Janr. 6, 1673-4, Roger, the son of Mr. Roger Roberts, of Pentrefelin,[24a] was
    Buried
Feb, 3, 1673-4, Mary, the daughter of John Dolben, Esq.,[25] was   Baptized
Feb. 13, 1674-5, Lewis, commonly called Lewis y Bais[26]   buried
May 20, 1675, Elinor Critchley, of ye Black Boy, was   buried
Jnne 18, 1675, Anna Lewis, wife to Williä Quaker was (see *Hist. of Older*
    Nonconformity of Wrexham, pages 23 and 24) buried
Aug. 9, 1675, Bridgett, wife to John Lloyd, curate,   buried
Aug. 9, 1675, Rowland, son to the aforesaid Jon. Lloyd, was Bap.
Aug. 18, Richard, son to John Evans, of Bryn y grog, gentle,   Buried
Sept. 7, 1675, Peter Lloyd of Black Lion, gent, was Buried
Oct. 27, 1675, Ffrancis Skewm, gent,[27] was buried
Oct, 29, 1675, John Povah, gent, was buried
Feb. 29, 1675-6, John, son to John Baker, Ironmonger, was bapt.
Apl. 20, 1676, John, son to William Owens, gent, Bapt.
June 20, 1676, Richard Dutton, Esq. (see note 15), Buryed
Oct. 16, 1676, William, son to John Doleben, Esq., Bapt. [Buried on 24th]
Nov. 10, 1676, Samuel sonne of Ambrose Lewis, schoolmr., Bapt.
Dec. 2, 1676, John, son to Ffrancis Edisbury, gent, Bapt.
Feb. 7, 1676-7, John Perry, of Wrexham, gent,[28] Buryed
July 20, 1677, Rebecca, daughter to William Owens, gent, Bapt.
Dec. 28, 1677, Jane Hanmer, spinster, Burd.
May 29, 1678, John, son to Mr. Thomas Lloyd, Attorney att Lawe, Bapt.
Aug. 15, 1678, David Lloyd, gent, son to Mr Morgan Lloyd, was Buried
Oct. 14, 16, 1678, Katherine, wife of Mr. Ralph Weld, Buried
Nov. 1, 1678, Jane, Da: to John Dolben, Esq.,[29] Bapt.
Janr. 27, 1678 9, John Davies, of Wrexham, mercer, Buryed
Mch. 7, 1678-9, John Weld, of Wrexham, gent, Buryed
May 9, 1679, John Baker, of Wrexham, Ironmonger, Buryed
June 10, 1679, Roger Roberts, of Wrexham, gent,[24a] Buryed
Sept. 2, 1679, Dorythy, daur. of John Baker, of Wrixham, Ironmonger,
    Buryed (see note 14)

24. Mr. Edward Crue was a brother of Mr. Silvanus Crue (see p, 25).

24a. At the Quarter Sessions held at Wrexham, Oct. 1663, Mr. Roger Roberts, was "presented" for not going to church, being, apparently, a nonconformist.

25. John Dolben, Esq., of Segrwyd and Wrexham (see Index), the last of that name.

26. Lewis y Bais, that is *Lewis of the petticoat.*

27. On the history of this Mr. Francis Scawen (or whatever was his name), some light is thrown by the following entry in the Ruabon register, under the heading of baptisms :—Elias, fil. Elenor David ut dicitur & quendam ffrancisci Escawen, Comonly called Captayne Escawen de Marchwiel 9 bris ye 9, 1673." The burial of " Madam Mary Scawen, widdow of Wrexham" is also recorded in the parish registers of Wrexham.

28. The daughter of this Mr. Perry was wife to John Dolben, Esq., of Segrwyd and Wrexham.

29. This Jane Dolben was afterwards the wife of John Mostyn, Esq., of Gwyddelwern and Segrwyd.

Oct. 30, 1679, Geo. Buttall, of the Lampint,[30] Buryed

Apl. 33, 1680, Katherine, ye suposed daugh. of Sʳ. John Winne, of Watt Stay, was Baptized

May 4, 1680, Thomas, son of John Taylor, gent,　　　　　　　Buryed

Sept. 17, 1680, Shusan, daugh. of Thomas Broughton, gent,　Baptized

Nov. 2, 1680, Thomas Manley and Anne Hunt, of Bunbury, maryed

Apl. 28, 1681, Silvanus Crue, goldsmith　　　　　　　　　　Buryed

Richard, the suposed son of Thomas Lloyd, of ye parish of Llan Badarn ffaur, in the county of Cardigan, by Jane Humphries, of the same County. John Moris and Oliver Owens are Bound in fforty Pounds to Keepe the Parish of Wrexham Harmless from this Child, and this Child was baptized on the 20th day of August, 1681

Aug. 28, 1681, Ralph Weld, of Wrexham Regis, gent (see note 36), Buryed

Oct. 20, 1681, John, son of Thomas Broughton, gent,　　　Baptized

Dec. 2, 1681, Edd. Davies, of Wrexham, Mercer, was　　　Buryed

Janr. 29, 1681-2, Ellinor Hanmer, of ye Beast Market, was　Buried

Apl. 11, 1682, Ould Mrs. Elizabeth Wright, of the Lampint.　Buryed

May 16, 1682, Margarett, da. of John Matthews, of Pen y bryn, gent, Buryed

Oct. 23, 1682, Mary, daughter of Gilbert Fownes, gent, of Wrexham Regis Bapt.

ffourth Register.

7. This register, written on paper, deals with a period which is covered by the third and fifth registers. It is quite independent of them, and gives often information which they do not contain. I shall therefore copy a few extracts from it. It covers the period from August 27th, 1678 to August 1686. Professing to be a record of all baptisms, marriages, and burials, it, in fact, records burials only.

Mr. Thomas Platt was buried in woolen the eight and twentieth day of April, 1679

John Roberts, of Bersham, Welsh poet, was buried in woollen the 16th day of June, 1679

ffrancis Decka of Wrexham was b. in w. the 4th day of October, 1679

Susan, daughter to Thomas Broughton, exciseman, was b. in w. the 17th of October, 1679

Jane Royden, of the Abbott Land was buried the .... day of January, 1682 [1682-3]

Mr. Thomas Davies, then High Constable, buried the 5th of February, 1682 [1682-3]

John Trevor, of Trevor, Esq., was buried on the 16th of March, 1682 [1882-3]

Judith Eyton, of Ruabone parish, was Buryed on ye first of December, 1682

30. George Buttall issued a token of which the obverse was :—GEORG. BUTTALL HIS HALFPENNY, G.G.B. and the reverse : IN WRIXHAM 1664, The Ironmonger's Arms." His wife's name was Grace. Of the Buttall family I have said a good deal in my *History of the Older Nonconformity of Wrexham.* To this family belonged Gainsborough's " Blue Boy."

Fifth Register.

8. The fifth register, in the original handwriting, begins on the 1st of November, 1682, and comes to an end on the 24th March, 1702.

Nov. 13, 1682, John, sonn of Edd. Croxon, dyer, of Wrexh. Abbot (see ch. xxiii, sec 20), Bapt

Nov. 15, 1682, Captin William Eyton,   came from berbadus, was in the quier of Wrexh. Buryed

Nov. 30, 1682, Ellinor Crue   Buryed
Feb. 1682-3, Anne Critchley, widow, of ye Black Boy,   Buryed
Mch. 30. 1683, Howell, son of Mr, Thos. Vaughan, m: rcer, w.r.   Buryed
May 22, 1683, Anne, da. of Phill. Hughes, gent, of W exh.   ,,
June 20, 1683, Mrs Elizabetn Hill, widdow, of Wrexh Regis,[33]   ,,
Sept. 5, 1683, Elizabeth, da. of Robert Lloyd, gent   ,,
Dec. 8, 1683, Madam Mary Scawen, widow, of Wrexham   ,,
Janr. 26, 1683-4, John, son of Edward Lloyd, gent, of Wrexham Regis, bapt

Janr. 29, 1683-4, Eurlluw Tuddir, of Wrexh. Abbot   Buryed
Apl. 24, 1684, Shusan, da : of Mr Thos Vaughan, mercer   Bapt.
July 18, 1684, Andrew, son of Mr. Thomas Lloyd, Attorney at Law, Bapt
   [Buried Mch. 17]
Feb. 19, 1684-5, Mr Edward Nanney, Ironmonger, of Wrexham,   Buryed
Mch. 18, 1684-5, John Hughes, of wrexham Abbot, Gent   ,,
Mch. 27, 1684, John Spursto Barbour, of Wrexham, Gentleman   ,,
Apl. 22, 1685, Mrs. Mary Griffiths, widdow, of Wrexham Regis   ,,
Apl. 24, 1685, Mary, da : of Mr. Edward Nanney, Ironmonger   Bapt
June 3, 1685, Robert, son of Mr. Tho. Vaughan, mercer, of Wrexham   ,,
July 26, 1685, Humphrey Hanmer, of Elsmare parish, and Elinor Ryce, of
   of wrexham parish, maryed
Aug. 22, 1685, John, son of Mr. John Baker, Ironmonger   Buryed
Nov. 28, 1685, Thomas, son of Mr Samuel Platt, born the 10th of November
   and was baptized the 20th
Dec. 28, 1685, Samuel Hughes and Rebecca Sontley   Maryed
Dec. 28, 1685, Thomas Rogers, Recorder of Wrexham   Buryed
Janr. 23, 1685-6, Thomas Lloyd, an Attorney at Law was   ,,
Feb. 26, 1685-6, John Maddocks, of place Gwern, Gent   ,,
Elizabeth, da : of John Wynne, Gent, Bryn y funnon, born the 21st of
   January and baptized the 3rd of feb., [1685-6][34]
June 10th, 1686, Mr. Thomas Vaughan, mercer, of Wrexh. Regis was
   Buried
June 11th, 1686, Mrs Dorothy Smyth, widd. of wrex. Abbot   Buried
June 15, 1686, Mr Thomas Vaughan Att att Law was buried

31. Probably the fourth son of Sir Gerard Eyton, knt., of Eyton Isaf

32. Widow of Joseph Critchley, of the Black Boy (see page 33)

33. The last of the Sontleys of Old Sontley—Miss Anne Sontley—married John Hill, Esq.' of Rowley's Mansin, Shrewsbury, and I suppose Mrs Anne Hill was one of the last-named family.

34. John Wynne, gent, see *History of Older Nonconfoi mity*, p. 59

July 10, 1686, The Lady Doro manley, of W.R. was buried[25]

Margaret, da. of Mr. Tho Vaughan, mer, was borne the 6th day of November, baptized 19th day, 1686

Feb. 14, 1686-7, Roger, son of Mr Thos Lloyd, attor. att Law   Buried

May 17, 1687, Mr Samuel Platt, of wrex. Abbot, Gentleman   buried

Aug. 28, 1687, John Middleton from Nanklin, buried

Sept. 15, 1687, William Edisbury and Dorothy Decka, of Marchwiel parish, married

Sept. 23, 1687, Elizabeth, daughter of Mr Samuel Platt   buried

Elinor, da : of Mr Humphrey Powell, Viccer of fflint,[37] born 29 October, baptized 21 day [so !], 1687

Oct. 31, 1687, Mrs Elizabeth Eyton of W. R.   Buryed

Simon, son of Simon Pennant, of w., born ye 28 of November, bapt. 30 day 1687

May 1, 1688, Mr Wm Jorden   minister of Llanroost   Buried

July 16, 1688, Mr Peter Weld, of w.r. buryed

Aug. 1688, Mr Edward Lloyd, and Mrs Barbarah Ellis, marryed

Apl. 16, 1689, Mr John Parry, of Bagillt and Mrs Mary Ellis of Cornist, of Holywell parish in com. fflint, Maryed

May 3, 1689, Mr Gabriel Platt of wrexha., buryed

Roger, son of Cornelius Manley [of Erbistock] borne the 23 of Aprill, bapt the 7th of May [1689]

Dorothy, da of William Lloyd, Dean in Ireland, borne the 8th of May, bapt the 9th, 1689

July 23, 1689,   the son of Mr. Richard Mostyn of London, was buried in the chancell

Janr. 12, 1690-1, Margaret Crue, Spinster of W.R. Buried

June 19, 1691, Robert Powell [Apothecary] and Mary Weld Maried (see page 110)

John, son of William Lloyd, Lord Bishop of Killalah [Killaloe] Born the 24th of ffebr, Bapt the 25th (March 1691-2)

35. Dorothy, Lady Manley, probably widow of Sir Francis Manley, of Erbistock, a daughter of Sir Gerard Eyton, knt., of Eyton Isaf

36. Probably one of the Myddeltons of Nantglyn

37. Rev. Humphrey Powell. Mr Powell's name does not occur in Archdeacon Thomas' list of the perpetual curates of Flint, but in Henry Taylor's *Historic Notices of Flint* the name of Humphrey *Howell* is given under date 1707, as one of the *rectors*.

38. The name of Jordan occurs neither in Archdeacon Thomas' list of the Vicars nor in his list of the rectors of Llanrwst. Perhaps he was curate.

39. The Welds of Wrexham were a very important local family. In the year 1678 Peter Weld, of Wrexham, is mentioned as nephew of Thomas Weld, Richmond, " citizen and grocer of London," who was born at Wistaston.

Mch. 28, 1692, Mr John Hayle and Mrs Anne Middleton, Maried[40]
July 19, 1692, Mr Jasper Peck and Madam Amy Eyton Maried[41]
Samuell, son of Gypson Saint Leger, of London, Esq., Born the 6th, Bapt.
    the 8th [Oct.]
Oct. 26, 1692, Mr Eubule Lloyd, of Glewsig, Buried[42]
Shusannah, daughter William Lloyd Lord Bishop Gillalah [Killaloe],
    born the 18th, bapt 20th (Sept. 1693)
Nov. 29, 1693, Anne, da of Mrs Susannah Edwards, of Cnolton, was
    buryed
July 4, 1694, Captain Joseph Massey and Dorothy Langford, of Gramore,
    in Cheshire, was Maryed
Oct. 12, 1694, Mrs Alice Lloyd, widdow, of The Beastmarket, Buryed
    (probably widow of Captain Nanney Lloyd, see note 21)
Oct. 23, 1694, Mr John Stoddart and Mrs Christian Andrews, were Maryed
Dec. 4, 1694, Richard Middelton, gent,[43] and Mrs Barbarah Wynne were
    Maryed
Amy, daughter of Jasper Peck, Esq,, of Cornish, Born 30th of November,
    Bapt the 7th of December[41]
Dec. 27, 1694, Mr Philip Hughes, of wrexham vechan, was Buryed
Feb. 23, 1694-5, Mr Owen Wynne, Chirurgion, of w.r,, was Buryed
Jasper, son of Jasper Pecke, of Cornish, Esq., born the 8tn of February,
    Bapt ye 19th, 1695-6[41]
July 20, 1696, Margaret Ellis alies wich, of Esclusham, Buryed
Nov. 27, 1696, Mrs Elizabeth ffownes, of Wrexham Regis, Buryed[44]
Apl. 17, 1697, Mr John Matthews, of Trenanney, was Buryed
May 5, 1697, Katherin, Da of Mr Jonathan Lloyd, late schoolmaster of
    Wrexham, born 27th of April, bapt . . . 1697

40a. Miss Margaret Jeffreys of Acton married Robert Betton, gent, of Shrewsbury. (The above entry has become accidently misplaced).

40. This Mr Hale, Mr W. M. Myddelton believes to have been of Hough,
Cheshire. A Miss Hale was living, as a friend, in 1720, with Miss Mary Myddelton at Croes Newydd, and she was a daughter of Mr Johr. Hale, of Clough.

41. This Jasper Peck, Esq., of Cornish, in the parish of Holt, was the son of
Jasper Peck, Esq., of Cornish, and grandson of the John Peck, Esq., mentioned on
page 8 of my *History of the Older Nonconformity of Wrexham*. He was succeeded
by another Jasper Peck, of Cornish and Drayton in Hales. The above named
Jasper Peck married Amy, youngest daughter of Sir Kendrick Eyton, kt., of Eyton
Isaf.

42. I have wondered whether this was the Eubule Lloyd, gent, of Eglwysegl,
who was one of the sons of the Rev. Edward Lloyd, of Llangower, and
one of the brothers of the Rev. Dr. Wm. Lloyd, Bishop of Norwich. His daughter
Mary married William Williams, gent, and their descendants were the Lloyds and
Williamses of Pen y lan.

43. The third Richard Myddelton, gent, of Plas Newydd, Llansilin. Barbara
Wynne was the third daughter of William Wynne, Esq., of Melai, and was her
husband's cousin. They had no issue.

44. Mrs Elizabeth Fownes was the wife of Mr Gilbert Fownes, formerly a
draper of London. She was a daughter of Sir Kenrick Eyton, knt., of Eyton Isaf.
Mr and Mrs Fownes had a son, afterwards Sir William Fownes, of Plas Power (see
Index).

19

September 13, 1697, Mr John Lloyd, Corvizer and Recorder of w.a., was
     Buryed

Dec. 27, 1697, Elizabeth, Da of Mr Thomas Lloyd, minister, of W.R., born
     the 19th, Bapt the 27th

Mch. 18, 1697-8, William, son of Mr William Williams, of havod y boch,
     born the 3rd of March, bapt the 18th[42]

Apl. 3, 1698, Mrs Dorothy Kyffin, of Wrexham Abbot, was Buryed

Aug. 15, 1698, Hester Middelton, gent, of Wrexham Abbot, Buryed

Oct. 29, 1698, Arthur Newcomb, of the City of Chester, gent, and
     Elizabeth Kendricke, of the same, Mr J. Wynne,[31] to pay the King

Dec. 1, 1698, Mary, daughter of Mr Ambrose Lewis, junior, of w.a., born
     28th of November, Bapt the first of December, 98 (see page 237)

Dec. 12, 1698, Mary Thomas, of the Green, alias Gamtha (i. e y Gamfa
     " The Stile ") Poor Buryed

Feb. 14, 1698-9, Anne, the daughter of Mr Thomas Lloyd, minister of w.r.
     born the 4th of ffebruary, Baptized the 14th

June 17, 1699, Anne Crue, of hoult, died at Eustas Crewe of w.r., was
     Buryed

Aug. 26, 1699, Mr John Lloyd, of Trawsfynydd, minister, died at Wrexham
     Regis, and was Buryed

Aug. 27, 1699, Elinor Pierce, widdow, of Beastmarket, her son Charles
     Roberts, Tanner, is to pay the King's tax, and was Buryed

Dec. 30, 1699, Mr ffoulke Vaughan, of Bron highlock [heulog] and Mrs
     Joyce Ellis, of Croes Newydd, were Maryed

Feb. 10, 1699-1700, Stephen Stephenton, Dyer, and Mary Jones, of Wrex-
     ham Regis, were Maryed

Feb. 13, 1699 1700, Ambrose, son of Ambrose Lewis, of Wrexham Abbot,
     born 25th of January, and Baptized the 13th of february

Feb. 13, 1669-1700, John ap Edward, of Pentre velinnewidd, w.r. (see page
     182), Buryed

Apl. 24, 1700, Anne,[46] wife of John Matthews, late Coroner, was buryed
     in Ruabon Churchyard

May 8, 1700, John, son of Ellis Jones, of hene place [Henb]as] born 2nd of
     May, Bapt 8th, Steward of Esq. Robinson now

May 14, 1700, Martha, da of Edward Moris, of Park Eyton,[17] Buryed

May 30, 1700, Mr Phillip Roberts, of Abbot Street,[48] Buryed

July 29, 1700, Margaret, the wife of John Dolben, of Wrexham Regis, was
     Buryed

Aug. 23, 1700, Richard Middleton, gent, of Llansillan, Buryed[49]

45. Miss Hester Myddelton was probably the youngest daughter of Captain
Roger Myddelton, of Plas Cadwgan.   From 1672 until her death she lived in the
house now represented by 31 Bridge Street (see page 216)

46. Mrs Ann Matthews, wife of John Matthews, gent, coroner, of Coedleoedd.
in the parish of Ruabon.

47. See page 66, sec. 38

48. Perhaps came from the house of Mr Charles Roberts in Abbot Street (see
p. 70, sec. 63 and page 230)

49. The third and last Richard Myddelton, Esq., of Llansilin (see note 43)

Oct. 1, 1700, Thomas Ragge [Wragg, see page 35, note 14], and Mary Cleveley, of W. R., Maryed

Mch. 23, 1700-1, Thomas, son of Mr. Samuel Platt, of w.r. was Buryed

Apl. 27, 1701, Edward Jones, the Baylive of this town, was Buryed

May 27, 1701, Mr Roger Damport, of haulewell, died at Widow Jenkins, and was buried at Hawlewell

May 28, 1701, Mr. John Lloyd, Register of St Asaph, was Buryed

July 29, 1701, John, son of Stephen Stephenton, Dyer, of W.R., born 19th of July, baptized 29th

Oct. 9, 1701, Mrs Elizabeth Lloyd, widdow, of the Lampint, was Buryed

June 2, 1702, Chas. Sutton[50] and Katherine Pryce, of w.a., were Maryed

Nov. 12, 1702, Martha, daughter of Mr Ambrose Lewis, of Wrexham Abbot Born 12th of November, Baptized 19th

Nov. 30, 1702, Elizabeth, wife of John Lloyd, late Register of St Asaph, who came from ffint Town, was Buryed

Dec, 4, 1702, Mrs Ann Lloyd, Spinster, of the Lampitt, Buryed

Dec. 11, 1702, Elis Alington, yeoman, and Mary Humphreys, of Hope Street, Maryed

Sixth Register.

9. This register in the original handwriting (except perhaps the last few pages), begins on March 24, 1702-3, and ends on March 23rd, 1729-30.

Apl. 23, 1703, Barbarah, Da of Richard Speed, Ironmonger, born the 12th of Aprill, baptized 23rd [see page 58, sec. 23]

Apl. 27, 1703, Mr Gilbert ffownes, gent, of Chester Street, was buryed [see note 44]

May 28, 1703, Aqualah Wickes, gent, of W.R., Buryed[51]

Sept. 2, 1703, Owen Bould, Esq., of Llangwifine in Anglesea, was Buryed

Sept. 17, 1703, Richard, son of Mr Thomas Bradshaw, junior, of w.r.,born the 2nd of September, Baptized

Mch. 20, 1703-4, Mr Edward Cleaton, died [at] Mrs Sara Davies, w.a., was Buryed

Mch. 24, 1703-4, Thomas, son of Thomas Wragg, exciseman, of w.r., born 19th of March, baptized 24th

May 19, 1704, Elinor Clubb, a wich of Broughton, was Buryed

Sept. 20, 1704, Edward, son of Mr Ambrose Lewis, of Wrexham Abbot, born 19th. Baptized the 20th

---

50. I wonder whether this was not one of the family of Captain Ellis Sutton,who during the Civil War ruined himself in the royal cause, and after selling his estate of Gwersyllt Issa to Colonel Geoffrey Shackerley, came to live in Wrexham. His house was in or near Abbot Street. He was buried at Gresford, May 2nd. 1712, (see Index)

51. Aquila Wyke, gent, second son of Lady Broughton (wife of the last Sir Edward Broughton, of Marchwiel Hall), by her first husband, Aquila Wyke, of Westminster. The above named Aquila Wyke had a nephew of the same name, son of his elder brother Edward Wyke, who, after the death of Lady Broughton, became owner of the Marchwiel estate

Mch. 10, 1704-5, Uzebius, son of John Watson, smelter of lead, in Pentre velin newydd, R., was Buryed

May 20, 1705, John Jones, Walker, of w.a., was scalded to death, Buryed

Oct. 3, 1705, Robert Lloyd, Apothecary, of Wrexham Regis, was buryed (see p, 90)

Dec. 3, 1705, Hugh Davies, Recorder of Abbot Land, died in W.R., Buried[52]

Dec. 19, 1705, Edward Wynne, ale Draper,[53] of Abbott Street (mentioned)

Mch. 8, 1705-6, Evastus Crue, pothecary, of R., Buryed (see page 35)

Apl. 5, 1706, Ralph, son of Thomas Wragg, surveyor, of Wrexham Regis, born 20th of March, bapt (see page 35, note 14)

Apl. 24, 1706, Samuel Platt, of W.R., was buryed

June 2, 1706, William Hamton, tanner, and Deborah Hughes of w.a. were Buryed

Oct. 5, 1706, William Parry, quaker, and Dorothy Davis, of w.a., Maryed

Nov. 13, 1706, Eleazer Owens, gentleman, Dyed at the George, R., buryed

Dec. 27, 1706, Mrs Martha Roberts, widdow, of Chester [Street?] W. Regis, was buryed

Jan. 22, 1706-7, Elizabeth, Da of Ambrose Lewis, gent, of w.a., born 7 of January, Baptized 22

May 5, 1707, Thomas Crue, Apothecary, of high street, Buryed (see page 25)

June 19, 1707, Mr John Bulkely and Mrs Mary Lee of Ruabon, Maryed

July 11, 1708, Thomas Whithead, Stone Carver, of w.a., Buryed (see page 213)

Nov. 7, 1708, Thomas Wragge, Surveyor of Wrexham Regis, was Buryed (see page 35, note 14)

Jan. 5, 1708-9, John Dolben, gent, of Bryn y ffonen, W. R., was Buyred

Feb. 11, 1708-9, Mr Thomas Bradshaw, junior, of W.R., was Buryed (see page 214)

Mch. 3, 1708-9, Margaret Brerton, widdow, of w.a., was Buryed

Dec. 12, 1709, Mary Hughes, alias Scould, of w.a., Buryed

Janr. 4, 1709-10, Madam Katherin Fowell, Docter Rawsendale Aunt, Buryed[64]

Janr, 5, 1709-10, Madam Amy Beale, Dyed at Mr Jarrard Eyton house, Buryed

Janr. 4, 1709-10, Mrs Jane Neale, widdow, of Wrexham Vechan, was Buryed[55]

52. See Davies pedigree in ch. iii.

53. Another " ale diaper."—" John Phillips of the bear head, w.r."—is mentioned in the parish registers under date September 2nd, 1696. In Dr Murray's New Dictionary the name is supposed to have been originally "jocular" in allusion to linen draper, and the following quotation from R. Young's *Charge against Drunkenness*, given :—" These godless ale drapers and other sellers of drink."

54. See the Rosindale pedigree in ch. vii

55. In the rate books Mrs Neale's house is described alternately as hers and as Lady Wake's. I do not know which house it was. In 1670, Sir William Neale, who defended Hawarden Castle against the Parliamentary troops, was living at Llai Hall.

May 9, 1710, Mrs Elizabeth Lloyd, of Pen y bryn, was Buryed

June 4, 1710, Charles Jones, tanner, and Sarah Croxson, of w.a., were Marryed (see page 230)

June 20, 1710, Hugh Hughes, baylive, of Beast Market [mentioned]

July 5, 1710, Ellis, son of Mr Charles Sutton, of w.a., born 28 of June Bapt 5 of July (see note 50)

Sept. 9, 1710, Robert Thomas, baylive, of w.r. [mentioned]

Feb. 9, 1710-1. Alice, widdow of Mr Thomas Lewis, Postmaster of w.r., was Buryed

May 9, 1711, Rich. Powell, Chirurgeon, of Chester Street, Buryed

May 9, 1711, William Jones, Slater, of the Teniscourt, Buryed

Oct. 24, 1711, John, son of John Croxson, Dyer, of w.a., born ye 22nd, Bapt (see Index)

Feb. 1, 1711-2, Thomas Beech, Ironmonger, of Beast Market, w.r. Buryed[56]

Feb. 5, 1711-2, Captin John Lloyd, of White Horse, Buryed

Apl. 9, 1712, James Cawley, Esq., from Gwersyllt, Buryed (see page 54, note 3)

Apl. 30, 1712, Martha, da. of Mr Thomas Atcherley, Ironmonger, w.r, Buryed[57]

July 15, 1712, Robt. Corbet, of Cnockin, gent, and Mrs Elizabeth Parry, of Osbaston, Salop, married

Sept. 5, 1712, Anne, wife of John Croxon, dyer, of Abbott Street, was Buryed[58]

Nov. 1, 1712, Roger, son of Thomas Atcherley, Ironmonger, of w.r., born 2 October, Bapt[57]

Nov. 19, 1712, Mr Woods, of Bryn y funnon, was Buryed

Feb. 8, 1712-3, Thomas Baker, gent, and Mrs Elizabeth Lloyd, Pentre-hobin, maryd

Mch. 20, 1712-13, Mrs Anne Weld, Spinster, of w.r., was Buryed

Apl. 22, 1713, William Phillips, Scrivener, of Nea [Nef], w.r., was Buryed

Aug. 4, 1713, Thomas Swetnall, gent, and Mrs Penelope Warburton, of Chester, maryed

Aug. 26, 1713, Richard Lachbrock, Doctor, of Hope Street, was Buryed

Aug. 31, 1714, Mr John Eyton, Place usa, Corwen Parish, died at Hafod y wern, was buryed[59]

Sept. 24, 1714, Edward, son of John Dacomb, gent,[60] of w.a., was born 19, Bapt 24 [buried Sept. 27, 1715]

56. Thomas Beech, an old inhabitant of Wrexham, father perhaps of the Mr. Thomas Beech, wine merchant, of Hope Street, mentioned on page 55

57 See p. 51, sec. 3

58. See page 232

59. Probably the youngest son of the Rev Owen Eyton, Rector and Vicar of Corwen, and of Plas Isaf yn Edeyrnion   The Rev Owen Eyton was the youngest son of Sir Gerard Eyton, of Eyton Isaf, in the parish of Bangor Isycoed.

60. Mr John Dycomb is often referred to in the registers (see Index): his house was in the lower part of Pen y bryn, now called Bridge Street, and next but one to The Horns. The Dycombs appear to have been related to the Wykes of Marchwiel Hall.

Sept. 19, 1714, Robert, son of Mr Edward Jones, of w.a., borne ye 15th, bapt ye 19th,

Dec. 21, 1713, William, son of William Hampton, of w.a. . . . bat.

Oct 12, 1714, Madam Ann Parry, Dyed at Mr Jarrard Eyton House, ye 12th of October, Buryed

Nov. 14, 1714, Katharine, wife of John Daxton [Dycomb, see note 60], gent of Penybrinn, was Buryed

Dec. 14, 1714, Mrs. Shusan Acherley, widdow, of w.r., was Buryed (see page 51)

Dec. 25, 1714, Richard Hughes, Balive, of w.a., was Buryed

Apl. 2, 1715, Arabella, da. of Mr Ed. Jones, of w.a., born ye 1st, Bapt. ye 2nd

Apl. 4, 1715, Mr Thomas Bradshaw, Scrivener, of w.r., was Buryed (see Index)

July 22, 1715, Elizabeth da of Mr Thomas Atcherley, Ironmonger, of w.r., born ye 2nd, Bapt

Nov. 12, 1715, Mrs Gainor Pugh, Spinster, of Love Lane, was Buryed[62]

Feb. 25, 1715-16, Jane, da of Mr John Jones, Atturney of W.R., Bapt

Oct. 31, 1716, John, son of Captain Maxwell, Cockman, born ye 20th, Bapt

June 17, 1717, Mary, da. of Mr Roger Middelton,[61] Apothecary, of w.r., was Buryed

Sept. 20, 1717, Robt., son of Mr Robert Diçomb, of w.a., Bapt (see note 60)

Dec. 1, 1717, Jon. son of John Jones, atturney at Law, of w.r., Bapt.

Feb. 2, 1717-18, William, son of Dr Rowland Pugh[62] of w.r., born ye 24, Bapt ye 27

July 6, 1718, John Evesson, Attorney at Law, and Mrs Jane Powell, married

Sept. 19, 1718, John Croxon, dyer, (see page 232), and Elizth. Fisher, of w.r., were marryed

Dec. 6, 1718, Thomas Povah, Taylor, then ye Offering began there

Buried

Aug. 19, 1718, Gabriell Wynne, Vicer of Estin Parish, and Margaret Parry, marryd[63]

Sept. 25, 1718, Mrs. Ruth Maddocks, of w.r., was Buryed

June 17, 1720, John Jackson and Sarah Jones, of w.r., Marryed (see page 37)

July 17, 1720, Francis, da of John Jones, Esq., Born 17, Bapt ye 19th of July

Aug, 31, 1720, Walter, son of Walter Griffiths, gent, of Pen y bryn, was Buryed[64]

Apl., 1721, John Croxon, Dyer, of w.a. (see page 232), Buryed

61. Roger is here probably mistakenly written for George Myddelton

62. This was probably Dr Rowland Pugh, of Mathafarn. Gaynor was a female name.

63. The Rev Gabriel Wynne was Vicar of Estyn (that is Hope) during the years 1705-1725.

64. I wonder whether this was Mr Walter Griffiths, of Bron gain yn Mechain. It could hardly be Mr Walter Griffiths, of Rhual.

July 30, 1721, Robert Price, alias ticklemé of w.a, [buried!]

Oct. 21, 1721, John, son of Walter Griffiths, gent, born ye 13th, Bapt ye 20 (see note 64)

Jan. 13, 1721-2, Mr Robert Simon of Ruabon parish and Mrs Jane Griffiths of this, were marryed

Mch. 10, 1721-2, Stephen, son of John Stephenton, w.r., born ye 9th, Bapt

Mch. 30, 1722, John Jones, Stranger, freeholder, Dyed at the Election, Buryed

May 22, 1722, Elinor, da of Mr Ambrose Lewis, born ye 19th, Bapt[65]

July 25, 1722, Mrs Mary Powell, widdow, of w.r.

Oct. 22, 1722, Mrs Joanah Lloyd, of Chester Street, Buryed

Jan. 20 (or 29), 1722-3, Betty, da of Mr Henry Turner, of Pen y bryn, Bapt

Mch. 1, 1722-3, Thomas, son of Mr Thomas Davies, of Tuttle Street, . Bapt

Mch. 3, 1722-3, Joseph, son of John Jackson, dyer, of w.r. . . . . . Bapt (see page 33, sec, 37)

Mch. 9, 1722-3, Eliz., da of John Stephenton . . . Bapt

Aug. 1723, Thos Griffiths, alias Porthman (i.e. Porthmon--" Drover ") mentioned

Aug. 13, 1723, Mr William Dolben, gent, Buryed (see Index)

Oct. 24, 1723, Mrs Elinor Lloyd, of Chester Street, Buryed

Feb. 14, 1723-4, Francis, da of Mr John Jones, Atturney, Bapt

Feb. 21, 1723-4, Eliz. da of Mr Ambrose Lewis, of w.a., born ye 13, Bapt ye 21

Nov. 16, 1724, Old Mrs Anne Crue, of High Street, Buryed (see page 25)

Nov. 23, 1724, Mr Thomas, Master Surgeon, Buryed

Dec, 18, 1724, James Edward Macburney, son of Mr Edward Macburney, Surgeon, born ye 3rd, Bapt

Feb. 2, 1724-5, John, son of John Stephenton, Innkeeper, of w.r., Bapt

Apl. 13, 1755, Mrs Elizabeth Beech, of w.r., Buryed [see note 56]

June 22, 1755, Mrs Ruth Wright, of Chester Street, Buryed

Sept. 11, 1725, John, son of John Jackson, Dyer, of w.r., born ye 5, Bapt (see page 216)

Mch. 19, 1725-6, Philipa, da. of Mr William Henry, Dancing Master, born ye 18, Bapt ye 19th (see Index)

Apl. 9, 1726, Trevour Davies, of W.R., Atturney att Law, Buryed

May 7, 1726, Martha, da. of Mr Ambrose Lewis, born ye 25, Bapt

Oct. 14, 1726, Mr Edward Macburney, Surgeon, Buryed

Dec. 17, 1726, Mrs Cath. Crue, Spinster [Buried?]

Mch. 20, 1726-7, Watkin, son of Robert Samuel of Spotty, Bapt (see p. 90)

Mch. 23, 1726-7, Mr Jonathan Phillips, Buryed

Apl. 16, 1727, Jane, wife of Edward Croxson, Dyer of w.a., Buryed (see page 23, sec. 20)

May 19, 1727, Thomas, son of Mr Edward Mackburney; father dyed before the child was born, Bapt

Sept. 13, 1727, Mrs Anne Moore, Spinster, of Coid y glyn, Buryed

Dec. 12, 1727, Saera, wife of Thomas Davies, gent, Buryed

65. Afterwards wife of Rev John Lloyd, of Grwrych (see page 237)

66. I suppose the wife of the Rev Canon Thos. Evans, one of the Vicars Choral of St Asaph, who was appointed in 1709

Mch. 28, 1728, Grace Hughes, alias Sufficient, Buryed

Apl. 7, 1728, Anne, child of Mr Edw. Mackburney, Surgeon, Buryed

Apl. 27, 1728, Elizabeth, da of Mr Wm. Henry, Dancing Master, Bapt (see Index)

Sept. 21, 1728, Mrs Jane Evans, wife of Mr Evans, Vicar of St Asaph[66] Buryed

Oct. 18, 1728, Anne, da of Mr Ambrose Lewis, born ye 9th, B[apt]

Dec. 17, 1728, Mrs Bridgett Manley, of Erbistock, Buryed

Feb. 1, 1728-9, Mr Thomas Davies, gent, Buryed

Feb. 4, 1728-9, Mr Ellis Williams and Mrs Martha Payn, marryd

Feb. 26, 1728-9, Mary, child of John Stephenton, Buryed

Mch. 7, 1728-9, Mrs Martha Wright, Spinster, of W.R., Buryed

Mch. 19, 1728-9, Thos., son of Mr Ralph Wragg, born ye 9, Bapt (see ch. i, note 14)

Mch. 31, 1728-9, Jane, child of Mr John Jones, Atturney, Buryed

July 25, 1729, James, son of Mr Wm Henry, Dancing Master, of W.R., Bapt. (see ch. 4, sec. 35)

Jan. 19, 1729-30, Mary Stephenton, widow of w.r., Buryed [widow of Stephen Stephenton, see page 26]

Seventh Register.

10. The seventh register which begins on March 25th, 1730, and ends in unbroken order on December 30th, 1756, is not apparently in the original handwriting.

June 18, 1730, Thomas, child of Mrs Anne Mackburney, widow. Buried

July 10, 1730, Robert Pyke, goldsmith from Chester, and Sarah Peeres of this [parish], Marryed

Aug. 29, 1730, Eliz., wife of Mr John Hughes, Brazier, from Chester, Bury'd (see page 88)

Dec. 24, 1730, Madam Ursula Lloyd, of Havodinos, Bury'd

June 5, 1731, Christian, Da. of Mr Robt. Pyke, born ye 27, B[apt]

June 12, 1731, Dan. Wms., als. Bara Howes (i.e. House Bread) mentioned

July 11, 1731, John Cadwalad, Huntsman to Robert Williams, Esq. of Bryn y ffynnon [mentioned]

Nov. 28, 1731, Thos. Wms. Als. Arth (i.e " Bear " mentioned)

Dec. 2, 1731, Little Devil's wife of Pen y bryn, smyth, Bury'd

Janr, 23, 1731-2, John Jones, alias Paice Lace [mentioned]

Feb. 13, 1731-2, David Jones, cobler, als Nig Nag [mentioned]

May 17, 1732, Mr Hanmer Kynaston, was Buryed

Sept. 20, 1732, Mrs Luce Mostyn, Spingter, Buryed

Dec. 6, 1732, John, son of Mr Hanmer Pennant, born ye 4th, Bapt

Apl. 25, 1733, Mr Hanmer Pennant Buryed

67. Lucy, daughter of Thomas Mostyn, Esq., of Rhyd, by Margaret, his wife daughter of Edward Lloyd, Esq., of Halghton.

Sept. 2, 1733, Mr Griffith Wms. of High St., buryed

Nov. 18, 17?.?, Mr Edward Lloyd of Ruabon Psh., and Mrs Margaret Lloyd, of trevour, married[68]

Feb. 21, 1733-4, Charles, son of Mr John Jones, Atturney, buryed (see p. 50)

June 16, 1734, John Croxson, butcher, and Elizabeth Poole marryed (see p. 232)

Oct. 11, 1734, Thos.,[69] son of Wm. Henry,·Dancing Master, of w.a., born ye 28th, Bapt.

Feb. 25, 1734-5, John Samuel, of Angel Street,[70] [mentioned]

Mch. 27, 1735, Fleetwood, son of ye Rev. Wm. Powell, Dean of St Asaph[71] born ye 14, Bapt

May 4, 1735, James, son of Josiah Boydell, a gentleman to Sir John Glynne Buryed

June 7, 1735, Fleetwood, son of Rev. Wm. Powell, of place gronow, buried[71]

Janr. 5, 1735-6, Mrs Margaret Bucknal, a widow, Gentlewoman, Buried

Apl 2, 1736, Mr Dannald, Surgeon, of Wrexham, Buried[72]

Apl. 10, 1736, John, son of Dr Powell, Dean of St Asaph,[71] born ye 27 of Mar. [Bapt]

June 10, 1736, Mrs Elizabeth Griffith (aunt to Mr Griffith of Garn), Buried

Oct. 21, 1736, Edd. son of John Jones, alias Shone Coch,[73] Gardiner [mentioned]

Dec. 5, 1736, Elinr. wife of Mr John Lloyd, buried

Janr. 9, 1736-7, Ion, son of Rev. Dr. Powell, Dean of St Asaph, buried (see note 71)

Mch, 18, 1736-7, Thomas, son of Thos Moyle, gent, born ye 25,[74] Bapt

June 20, 1737, Saml. Wragg, gent, a stranger, Buried

Aug. 12, 1737, Deborah, Da of Robt. Whitney, gent[75] Buried

68 Edward Lloyd, Esq., of Plas Madoc, in the parish of Ruabon, and Margery, second daughter of Thomas Lloyd, Esq., of Trevor. Mr Lloyd was only 17 years old when he married, and died without issue in the following year.

69. This child became afterwards the famous Dr. Thomas Henry, F.R.S., of Manchester, and father of Wm. Henry, Esq., M.P. & F.R.S. He was the friend of Dr Priestley and Dr Franklin ; died June 18, 1816, and was buried in the grave-yard of Cross Street Chapel, Manchester

70, This is the only occasion on which I find Angel Street mentioned, nor do I know where it was

71. Rev Wm. Powell, A.M., D.D., nephew of Bishop Fleetwood, at this time sinecure rector of Hope, afterwards Archdeacon of Chester

72. Mr Dannald, see the Davies pedigree in ch. iii, and *History of Older Nonconformity*, p. 134, note 3.

73. Shone Coch or Shôn Goch, that is John the Red

74. Probably one of the Moyles of Ruthin

75. Probably one of the Whitneys of Hawarden

Oct. 30, 1737, Long Finger'd Bett, a Peddlar, Buried

Dec. 26, 1737, Mrs Barbarah Barker, Spinster, Buried

Janr. 11, 1737-8, The Rev. Robert Evans, of Coddington, Buried

Janr. 13, 1737-8, John Eels, son of James Jones, gent, Buried

July 8, 1731, Augustine, Da of James Jones, gent, born June ye 14, Bapt

July 20, 1738, Thomas, son of Thomas Moyle, of W., gent, born June ye 25 (see note 74), Bapt

Aug 11, 1738, Jane, Da of Henry Roberts, of w.a., gent, born Aug. ye 8, Bapt

Oct 26, 1738, John Foulkes. of Tir Gwynn, in the Pish of Llangwm, Buried

Mch. 26, 1739, Mrs Mary Crue, Apothecary, Spinster, (see page 25, sec.20) Buried

May 19, 1739, Mr Thomas Jones, Apothecary, Buried

July 31, 1739, Brigett, Da of Mr Edd. Lloyd, Attorney at Law, born ye 9, (see note 76), Bap.

Oct 19, 1739, Hugh Hughes, Bailif of Wrexham, Buried

Janr. 12, 1739-40, Mr Pyke, Silversmith, from Chester (see July 2, 1730), Buryed

May 1740, Mrs Cole, of Wrexham, Buried

July 3, 1740, Elizabeth, Dau. of Mr Edd. Lloyd, Attorney at Law, born June ye 11 (see note 76), Bapt

Aug. 10, 1740, Mrs Brereton, widow of Wrexham[77] Buried

July 24, 1741, Elizabeth, Dau. of Mr Foulkes, Curate of Llanufydd, born ye 9th, Bapt

Sept 1, 1741, William, child of Mr Edd Lloyd, Attorney at Law (see note 76), Buried

Nov. 24, 1741, Mary Bedward, Badger[78] Buried

July 16, 1742, William, son of Mr Edward Lloyd, Attorney at Law (see note 76), Buried

Sept 9, 1742, Mr Robert Parry, Buried

76. Edward Lloyd, Attorney, of the Lampint (see page 121), afterwards of Chester Street, married Bridget, one of the daughters of Hugh Davies, *the third* (see the Davies pedigree in ch. iii.)

77. Mrs Jane Brereton (see page 55), wrote several poems, which were published in 1744, after her death, under the title of *Poems on Several Occasions.* She was one of the two daughters of Mr Thomas Hughes of Bryn Griffith, near Mold, and was born in 1685. She married, January 29th, 1711, Mr Thomas Brereton, only son of Major Brereton, of   , Cheshire, who speedily squandered his money, and did not always behave kindly to his wife, who was compelled, taking her children with her, to retire to her friends in Wales. Soon after the drowning of her husband at the mouth of the river Dee, Mrs Brereton, according to the preface to her book, removed to Wrexham "for the benefit of her children's education, and was soon distinguish'd by the most considerable Families in and about that Town, and it must be allowed by all," adds the editor "that that Neighbourhood is remarkable for Politeness, Taste, and Hospitality." She died August 7th, 1740, leaving two daughters, Lucy and Charlotte, her two sons having died young.

78. A "badger" "signifies a person who buys corn or victuals in one place, and carries them to another to sell and make profit by them."— Jacob's *Law Grammar.*

Sept 13, 1742, Mrs Susannah Hughes, Spinster, Buried

Janr. 24, 1742-3, Ellis, son of Mr William Henry, Dancing Master, born ye 8, Bapt (see page 65, sec. 35)

Mch. 11, 1742-3, Mrs Dorothy Hughes, Spinster   Buried

May 5, 1743, Mrs Blackborn, widdow,   Buried

Mch. 24, 1743-4, Mrs Margaret Hartford, widow,   Buried

July 17, 1744, Edward,[79] son of Edward Meredith, of Velin Puleston, smith born 16, Bapt

Dec 1, 1744, Mrs Dorothy Lloyd, of W.R., Spinster   Buried

Feb 19, 1744-5, Mr Stephenton[80] and Mrs Anne Porter, both of this parish. were married by license

May 2, 1745, The Rev Mr John Brown of Melton Mowbray Parish, and Mrs Ann Jones, of this Parish, married

Janr. 21, 1745-6, Charles Edward, son of Mr Stephen Stephenton of W.R., Attorney at Law, born 30, Bapt

May 31, 1745, Mrs Betty Thistlethwaite, of W.R., Spinster, Buried

Janr. 20, 1745-6, Old John Morrice, of W.R., Bodicemr, 102 years old, Buried

Apl. 20, 1746, Mary, Da of Mr Wm. Lewis, of W.A., gent, Buried

May 20, 1746, Sarah, wife of Mr John Jackson, of W.R., dyer, Buried (see p. 31)

June 3, 1746, Jane, Da of Mr Edward Lloyd, Attor. at Law (see note 76) Buried

July 2, 1746, Mrs Berenice Tyrwhitt, of w.a., widow, Buried

Apl. 14, 1747, Miss Elizth. Henry, of W. R., Spinster (see pp. 65 and 121) Buried

Apl. 23, 1747, Miss Phillippa Henry, of W.R., Spinster (see pp. 65 and 121) Buried

July 31, 1747, Mary Clement,[81] da of Robt Samuel of W.R., butcher, born 18 (see ch. xv, sec. 12), bapt

Oct 16, 1747, Charles Allanson,[82] son of Mr Jaques Wighton, of W.R., Supervisor, Bapt

Janr 12, 1747-8, John Croxson, of w.a., butcher, (see page 232) Buried

May 10, 1748, Evan Lewis, from Pentre Halkyn, Minera to pay, Buried

---

79. I have said on page 62, note 13, on the statement of a member of the family, that this Edward Meredith was afterwards the famous baritone singer of whom I have several times spoken (see Index), but I have since discovered that this statement was inaccuaate. The two Edward Merediths were, however, probably related.

80. Stephen Stephenton, attorney (see page 38). His wife was a daughter of John Porter, of the Plume of Feathers.

81. Mary Clementina, afterwards the wife of Edward Ellis, gent, of Tuttle Street (see p. 158)

82. Rev. Charles Allanson Wighton, afterwards (1799-1825) perpetual curate of Holt.

May 7, 1748, Judith, da of Joseph Jackson, of w.r., dyer, born 2nd,[83] Bapt
Aug. 14, 1748, John, son of Edward Meredith, of Velin Puleston, smith,
    born 7 (see page 214), Bapt
Janr. 27, 1748-9, William, son of Mr Edw. Lloyd, Att. at Law (born Oct.
    22, 1748), (see note 76), Buried
Apl. 25, 1749, Mrs Frances Edwards, from Stoke, Buried
June 30, 1749, Mrs Eliz. Foulkes, of W.R., widw., Buried
July 15, 1749, The Rev Mr Edward Jones, Curate of Bryn Eglwys, Buried
Sept. 15, 1749, Mary, da of Mr Edw. Lloyd, Att., born 17 (see note 76) Bapt
Nov. 18, 1749, Robert Samuel, of Plas Coch, yeoman, Buried
Mch. 7, 1749-50, Mrs Anne Price, of W. R., Spinster, Mr Manning's niece,
    Buried
Janr. 24, 1750-1, Madam Hughes, of W.R., widdow. buried at Gresford
    Buried
Janr. 21, 1752, Elizabeth Owens of W.A., Mudaness [female mute], Buried
Mch. 19, 1752, Mrs Frances Robinson of W.R., widow, Buryed
July 9, 1752, Thomas, son of Mr Stephen Stephenton, of W.R., At,. at Law
    Buryed
Janr. 18, 1753, Thomas Griffith ab Tom Tea, Poor, Buryed
Sept 1, 1753, John, son of Mr John Eddowes of Abenbury Vechan, tanner,
    born 10,[84] Bapt
May 18, 18, 1754, Mr John Hughes, of W.R., Att at Law, Buried
Janr. 11, 1755, Mrs Elizabeth Crue, of W.R., Spr. Apoth. (see page 25)
Feb. 10, 1755, Mrs Elizth, Williams, of the Hope Street, W.R., Widr.,
    Died ye 6th, Buried,
Apl. 2, 1756. Thomas, son of Mr Stephenton, of W.R., Buried
Apl. 13, 175\. Anna Maria, dau. of the above Mr Stéphenton, Buried
Nov. 30, 1756, Thomas Roberts, Raiser of Malt for the King's Mill, Buried
Dec. 7, 1756, Mr Thomas Jones, of the Beast Market, in W.R., Buried

Eighth Register.

11. This register which begins on January 2nd, 1757, and ends
oc May 31st, 1776, is not apparently in the original handwriting
during the first few pages of it.

July 13, 1757, Mrs Ruth Walker, of W.R., widow, Buried
Dec 29, 1757, Eleanor, daughter of Mr Stephenton, of W.R., Att., born 26,
    Bapt
Apl. 4, 1758, Miss Humberston, Buryed at Gresford
May 13, 1758, Mrs Gwen Powell, late of Chester, Buried
Sept. 26, 1758, Mr Thomas Pate of ye Lodge, in Gresford Ph., Buried
Janr. 10, 1759, Mrs Christian Pearce, Post Mistris, Buried
Mch. 14, 1759, Mr Josaph Jones Clothier (see page 17), Buried

---

83. Judith Jackson, afterwards wife of John Meller, Esq. (see p. 42 note)

84. John Eddowes the third, who married Elizabeth. daughter of Mr Robert
Taylor, of Llwyn y cnottiè, and the son of John Eddowes the second, who married
Mary Poynton (see page 130)

Nov. 7, 1760 . . . John Ellis, W.R., beliff . . .

Janr. 17, 1762 . . . David ye Cop of W.A., Liberor . . .

Apl. 15, 1762 . . . Robert Bousfield, of W.R., Baliff . . .

Janr. 11, 1762, Elizth. Daur. of Mr David Crew, Apothecary (see pages 52 and 67), born Dec. ye 12th, Bapt

Janr. 29, 1762 . . . John Ellis, of W.R., Baliff . . .

Aug. 6 1763, Mr Thomas Thomson, one of his Majestyes phichisons from London, dyed at the Eagles, Buried

Aug. 9, 1763, Bridget, Da of Mr William Jones, W.R., Wine Merchant (see page 175), Buried

Mch. 13, 1764, Anna Maria, Dau, of Mr David Crue, of W.R., Apothecary (see pages 52 and 67), born Feb. 14, Bapt

Sept. 11, 1764, Frances, dau. of John Colley Humberston, Esq., was born ye 11 of August (see p. 68), Bapt

Dec. 23, 1764, Mary Roberts, elias [alias] Mollwyryon,85 Buried

Mch. 27, 1765, Robert Birchinshaw from Ruthin, gent, Buried

July 2, 1765, Harriet,86 Dau. of Mr David Crue, W.R., Apothecary, born ye 3 June, Bapt

Janr. 28, 1766, Eliz., Dau of Mr David Crue, of W.R., Apothecary, Buried

Mch. 1, 1766, Gilbert,87 son of Benjamin Gimping, of Bersham fur. born feb. 8, Bapt

July 16, 1766, Eliz. Jones, Elias [alias] Gambo, Poor, Buried

Aug. 7, 1766, Belinda, Dau of Mr William Jones, of W. Regis, Wine Merchant (see page 175), Bapt

Mch. 31, 1767, Henry, son of Mr David Crewe, of W.R., Apothecary, was born 17 of feb. (see pages 53 and 67), Bapt

Oct. 6, 1767 . . . Simon Jones, from Pentrevelin Newidd . . .

Oct. 17, 1767, Eliz., dau of Benjamin Gilpin, of Bersham furnist, born 28 of Sept. (see page 38), Bapt

Oct. 28, 1767, Eliz., wife of Mr William Jones, Wine Merchant (see page 175), Buried

Dec. 30, 1765, John, son of Mr John Jones, of Chester Street, born ye 7, Bapt

Dec. 28, 1767 . . . William aBarthur, butcher . . .

Janr, 4, 1768 . . . John Lloyd, of W.R., Bayliffe . . .

May 31, 1768, Eliz., Dau of Mr David Crue, of W.R., Apothecary, was born the 10 (see pages 53 and 67), Bapt

Dec. 26, 1769, Margaret Wynne, Dau of Thos. Parry, Attor. at Law, born 3 Nov., Bapt

85. " Moll Wirion," that is " Daft Moll "

86. Harriet Crewe, afterwards wife of Mr John Johnson Boutflower (see sec 14 under date March 6, 1794): there is a tablet to her memory in Whitford Church, Flintshire, whereon she is described as wife of John Johnson Boutflower of Salford, surgeon, as niece of the Rev Edward Crewe, of Isglan in Whitford parish, and as having been buried at St Mary's, Manchester, August 12th, 1831

87. Afterwards the famous Gilbert Gilpin of Dawley, of whom an account may, perhaps, may be given in another volume,

Dec. 22, 1769, Edward, son of Mr David Crewe, of W.R., Apothecary (see pages 53 and 67), Buried

Mch. 21, 1769, Mary, dau of Richard Skye, of W.R., Attorney at Law, Bapt

Sept 22, 1770, Griffith Williams, of W.A., Mouldywart[88] Catcher, Buried

Dec. 18, 1770, Bridget, Dau of Mr Lloyd, the attorney of Chester Street[76] Buried

May 22, 1771, Mr Thomas Wragg, gent, of W.R. (see Index), Buried

June 4, 1771, Thos Parry, of W.A., that was killed at the Syth Mill, Poor, Buried

June 18, 1771, Catherine Goch,[89] alias Edwards of W.A., Poor, Buried

Nov. 23, 1771, Thos., son of Mr David Crew, of W.R., Apothecary (see pages 52 and 67), Bapt

Janr. 18, 1772, Eliz., wife of Mr David Crew, of W.R., Apothecary, Buried

Aug. 10, 1772, Edw Parry of Stansty, Late Collector of the King's Rents, Buried

Janr. 9, 1773, Nanney Squint, Elis [alias] Pritchard, from the Workhouse, Poor, Buried

Feb 24, 1773, Ursilah, wife of Mr Myers Limner, native of Sardinah, Buried

Mch 16, 1773, Mrs Ann Mackburney, widow, Buried

May 8, 1773, Mr John Parrot of Seven Bridge Lane, Buried

July 13, 1773, John Lewis, of Velin Puleston, Turnpick Man, Buried

Sept 24, 1773, John, son of William Edwards, of W.A., tanner, born the 15 (see page 210], Bapt

Oct 23, 1773, Sarah, wife of William Edwards, of the Pallis in pen abrin, Buried (see page 210)

Janr 4, 1774, Judith, wife of Mr Joseph Jackson, Draper Buried (see p. 33)

Apl 20, 1774, Mr William Henry, of W.R., Dancing Master (see page 65) Buried

June 10, 1774, Dorothy, wife of Mr William Wigley, of London, Buried

Aug 26, 1774, John Robts, of Abbot Street, Blind barber, Poor, Buried

Sept 9, 1775 . . . John Hughes, Elice [alias] Champion,[91] Poor

Oct 18, 1775, Mr John Kirck, gent of W.R., Buryed

Janr 4, 1775, Dorothy Langford, Dau of Mr John Meller, of W.A., gent, born 19 of November, Bapt

Janr 31, 1776, John Jones, Elice [alias], Go bim, Portar, Poor, Buried

88. " Mouldwarp," that is " mould thrower," or *mole*.

89. Catherine Goch, that is *Catherine the Rea*

90. Mentioned also in 1767

91. Probably *champion* prize-fighter, for prize-fighting was formerly an established institution

Ninth Register

12. After April 16th, 1754, no marriages are recorded in the ordinary register, two other special registers being kept, one for marriages by banns, the other for marriages by licence. What I have called the "ninth register" records only marriages by licence, It ends on October 17th, 1768.

Apl 18, 1775, Robert Samuel, with consent of his mother, and Eliz. Wragg (see p. 20)

May 16, 1755, Hugh Evans, widower, and Mary Cocker of par: of Ellesmere Spinster (see pp. 211 and 230)

May 25, 1756, Mr Thos Turner of Selattyn parish, and Miss Mary Lloyd of Wrexham, Spinster, at Minera, by John Eyton, clerk : Witnesses : Thomas Edwards, vicar, and Geo. Ravenscroft

Janr 29, 1761, John Waithman, Batchelor,[92] and Mary Roberts, Spinster, both of the parish of Wrexham

June 23, 1762, Joseph Priestley,[93] of the parish of Warrington, and Mary Wilkinson

Oct 7, 1764, John Croxson of this parish, butcher, and Alice Jones of the parish of Oswestry, Spinster

Apl 1765, Benj. Gilpin, clerk, and Eliz. Davies, both of this par.

Janr 11, 1766, Thomas Stubbs, schoolmaster, and Esther Evans, Spinster, both of this parish

Tenth Register.

13. "The Tenth Register," which records marriages by licence only, begins on October 21st, 1768, and ends on November 11th, 1791.

July 15, 1769 John Lloyd Clerk,[94] Rector of Betws Gwerfel Goch Bachelor, and Ann Thelwal of this parish, Spinster ; Witnesses: Cath Wynne and S. Thelwall

Sept 9, 1770, Richard Manning, Apothecary, and Margaret Pate, Spinster, both of this parish

92. This John Waithman, saddletree maker, of Pen y bryn, was he, one of whose sons was afterwards the well known Alderman Robert Waithman, of London, whose baptism I cannot find recorded in the Wrexham registers, though entries relating to several other of John Waithman's children occur.

93. This was the famous Dr Priestley of Birmingham (in 1762 a tutor at the Dissenting Academy at Warrington). His wife was daughter of Mr Isaac Wilkinson, and brother of the well known John Wilkinson, "the father of the iron trade"

94. This Rev John Lloyd must be, I think, the father of John Salusbury Lloyd Esq. (see page 33)

95 See page 21, sec 13

Aug 5, 1772, Rowland Samuel, Currier, and Mary Thomas, Spinster, both of this parish[93] (see p. 26)

Sept 13, 1776, Thomas Mires, Furnaceman, and Mary Waithman, widow[96]

Sept 23, 1776, Raleigh Coleborne, gent, and Mary Barnes, both of this parish

Feb 2, 1785, Rev David Jenks, rector of Whepsnade, in county of Bedford, and Eliz. Dod[97] of this par.; Witnesses: Frances Puleston, Mary Dod, Robert Dod

Eleventh Register.

14. "The Eleventh Register," which contains entries relating to marriages by licence only, begins on December 12th, 1791, and ends on February 11th, 1813.

Nov 6; 1793, Rev John Williams. Rector of Begelly, Diocese of St David's and Elizabeth Carruthers of this parish[98]

Mch 6, 1794, John Johnson Boutflower, of Manchester, and Harriet Crewe (see note 86); Witnesses: Th. L. Jones and A. M. Crewe

Feb 14, 1797, David Crewe and Dorothy Morrall, both of this parish [see pages 52 and 67],

June 6, 1798, Richd. Stanley, of Rotherham in the diocese of York, and Dorothy Langford Meller, of this parish [see sec 11, under Janr 3rd, 1775]

Feb 23, 1800, Johnson Butler Carruthers[98] and Cath. Price [see page 108, sec 41], both of this parish

Dec 15, 1800, Chas Poiser [the elder, see pages 25 and 31] and Anne Jones both of this parish; witness, Thos Jones

Apl 19, 1804, Robt Wm Wynne of Garthewin in the parish of Llanfair Talhaiarn, in the county of Denbigh, and Letitia Stanley[99] of the parish of Wrexham

Sept 8, 1808, Thos. Hy. Hindley, merchant and a Bachelor of Manchester, and Dorothy Meredith [see note 79 and page 62 note 14] of this parish

Janr 24, 1809, Thos Roberts, Clerk and Bachelor of Hendre, Parish of Aberech, Dioc. of Bangor, and Anna Diana Owen of this parish, Spr.

96. The widow of John Waithman mentioned in note 92

97. Robert Dod, Esq. was at this time tenant of the Mount House

98. Other entries relating to the Carruthers in the Wrexham and Bangor is y-coed registers may here be given :

B June 9, 1805, Thomas Johnson, son of Johnson and Catherine Carruthers, of Parkey, born Feb. 15, 1801, Bapt

B June 9, 1805, Elizabeth, daughter of ditto, born Mch 10, 1803, Bapt

B June 9, 1805, Edwin Montague, son of ditto, born Apl 22, 1805, Bapt

W June 20, 1811, John Robert, a child of Capt Carruthers, Buried

W Mch 3, 1813 ———— son of Mr J. B. Carruthers, W.A., one week, buried

99. Letitia, daughter of Rev John Fleming Stanley : her daughter, Diana Wynne, married Philip Yorke, Esq., of Erddig

Aug 13, 1811, Wm. Overton, Grocer and a Bachelor, and Eliz. Parry a widow[100]

Nov 2, 1812, Mr Chas Poyser, gent and a widower, and Mary Ann Langford, Spinster, both of this parish [see pages 25 and 31]

Twelfth Register.

15. The Twelfth Register contains notices of baptisms and burials, but none of marriages. It begins on June 1st, 1776, and ends on February 1st, 1789, covering at the end, in point of time, the thirteenth register.

Aug 12, 1776, Thos (see page 65), son of William Durack, of W.R., Dancing Master, Bapt

Apl. 24, 1777, Edward Meredith, of Vellin Puleston, Smith, Buried

June 6, 1777, Mr Edward Thomas, gent, of the hope street, Buried

June 18, 1777, Mr George Churchill, gent, Buried

Aug. 8, 1777, William Barnes, son of Mr Ralulph Coleborne, of W.R., Surgeon, bapt

Feb. 21, 1778, Richard,[101] son of John Meller, of W.A., gent (see pages 42 and 43), born the 15 of Dec., bapt

Feb 4, 1778, Miss Peggy Blackburn, Spinster, Buried

Apl. 30, 1778, Mr John Shaw, of W. R., Gentleman, Buried

Nov. 30, 1778, John, son of Mr John Eddowes, of W.R., Tanner,[102] Bapt

Mch. 19, 1779, Mary Ann, dau of Mr John Jones, of W.R., Bapt

May 12, 1779, Old Robert Ellis, the puding woman's husband, Poor, Buried

June 4, 1779, Mary, wife of Mr Th Jones, of W.R., Attorney, Buried

Oct 29, 1779, John Langford, son of Mr John Meller, of W.A., gent, was born the 20 of August (see pages 42 and 43), Bapt

Mch. 13, 1780, Mr Richd Sidebotham, of the Red Lion, Buried

May 25, 1780, John Jones, Belife, of the Beast Market, Buried

Dec. 20, 1780 . . . Robt Jones, of W. R., Bayliffe [mentioned]

Apl. 6, 1781, Henry Woolrich, of W.R., Apothecary, Buried

May 5, 1781, Major John Bell, of W. Vechan, Buried

Oct, 1783, "From the 1st of this month a tax of 3d for registering the burial of each person is impos'd by Act of Parliament, and a Licence granted for yt purpose to ye Vicar from ye Stamp Office instead of Stampt Books."[103]

Apl. 23, 1785, Ruth Speed (widow of Griffith Speed, Esq., see Index), Buried

June 24, 1786, William Owen, son of John and Elizth Eddowes (see p 130 Bapt

Dec., 1788, John Jarrett [Gerrard], W. R., organist, Buried

100. William Overton, the elder (see page 27), and Elizabeth, widow of Mr John Parry. maltster (see page 151)

101. Afterwards Captain Richard Meller, of the Isle of Man

102. John Eddowes, the fourth, see page 130

103. A similiar statement is made with regard to the registration of baptisms

Thirteenth Register.

16. The Thirteenth Register, like the twelfth, contains notices of baptisms and burials, but no mention of weddings. Its first entry is on December 5th, 1788, and its last on November 16th, 1800, the two registers, in point of date, overlapping each other

17. On the first page of this register the two following sentences appear :—" When the word Poor is added to the Name of any Person buried, it signifies that there were no offerings, and the Parish pays one shilling to the Curate for each person, and when it occurs among the Christenings of Base-born Children the Parish pays Two Shillings for each. Offerings at Funerals were introduced in this Parish 19th of August, 1730."

Feb. 4, 1789, Eliz. Dolben, W.A., Buried

Apl. 1, 1789, John Hughes, Chester, Buried

Sept. 21, 1781, Thos Owen, son of Thos and Mary Lee, Captain in ye African Trade, Bapt

May 3, 1792, Dr Pearson Croasdaile, from Dublin, W.A., Buried

Janr. 1, 1793, Harriet, D. of Thos. and Eliz. Edwards, Tanner, W.A., born Janr 1, 1792 (see sec. 20, under Jan. 29, 1815), Bapt

Feb. 9, 1793, Benj. Gilpin [of Bersham], Buried

July 13, 1793, Edward Harrison, a child Bersham. The First Corpse interr'd in the New Burial Ground, Buried

Janr. 3, 1794, Ralph Williamson, Buried

Sept. 21, 1794, John Meredith, of V. Puleston, Smith, Buried

Janr. 17, 1795, Roger Haie, Esq., from Birmingham, Buried

May 20, 1797, Richd. Phillips, S. of Richd and Anne Jones, W.R., Iron-monger,[104] Bapt

Dec. 24, 1797, Meredith Jones, S. of Edward and Eleanor Jones, W. smith, 9 9ᵣ. [i.e. November] Bapt

Sept. 4, 1798, Thos, S. of the Rev Thos and Mary Kemmis, of the Parish of   Kildare Street in Dublin, a Family which came here at the time of the rebellion in Ireland, Bapt

Nov. 1, 1799, Thos Jones, Esq., W.A., who died of a Wound receav'd in a Duel at Whitchurch with Mr Manning, being the only one which happened for upwards of 36 years in this parish, Buried

Dec. 11, 1799, Maria Clementina, Dr of Chas Ed. and Esther Studley,W.A. Bapt

Fourteenth Register.

18. The Fourteenth Register, relating to baptisms and burials only, has for its first entry of baptisms, November 21st, 1800, and for its last December 30, 1812 ; and for its first entry of burials November 21st, 1800, and for its last December 29th, 1812.

---

104. R. P. Jones, afterwards the well known Dr Rd. Phillips Jones, of Chester His sister Mary, also mentioned on next page, is again mentioned in sec. 20, under Oct. 21, 1823

Janr. 8, 1802, John, S of John and Martha Foulkes, Att., W.R. [born] Aug. 19, Bapt

Janr 9, 1802, Mary, da : of Richard and Anne Jones, W.R., Ironmonger [born], 2, 10r [i.e. December]104 Bapt

Sept. 11, 1802, Charles, S. of Ch. and Anne Poyser, W.R., mercer, born Sept. 28, 1801, Bapt

Nov. 19, 1803, Mrs Mary Lloyd, widow, W.R., Buried

Janr. 11, 1804, Thos Stanton (see page 130), S of John and Mary Eddowes W.R., Tanner, | born] May 16, 1803, Bapt

Apl. 3, 1806, AnneFhillips, widow, W.R., aged 102, Poor, Buried

Apl. 23, 1806, Thos., S of Thos and Constantia Jones, Gunsmith, W.R., (see page 48), born 10, Bapt

July 28, 1806, Frances,105 D of John and Mary Eddowes, W.R., Tanner, [born] 12 Janr. Bapt

Oct. 13, 1807, Thomas Oliver Vassal, Esq., Somersetshire, Buried

Nov. 19, 1807, Richard Ayres, Surgeon, Wrex. Regis, Buried

Dec. 30, 1807, Thomas, son of Capt Richard Edwards, of his Majesty's Sixty Second Regiment of Foot, by Arabella, his wife, born Dec, 3, Bapt

Mch 8, 1808, Mary, da: of Charles Watkin Williams Wynne, Esq., and Mary his wife, born at Acton, March 2nd,106 Bapt

Sept. 20, 1808, John Jones, Poet, Esc. Above [Aged] 81, Bapt

June 21, 1809, Edward Humphreys, S of Edward and Mary Dymock, of Penley. in the county of Flint, born May 16,107 Bapt

Sept. 21, 1809, Thos. Davies, a pauper of W.R., in 100[th year of age] made a pair of Shoes within a yr of his Death, Buried

July 24, 1810, Charles Vincent, son of Charles and Mary James, Esq., Spring Lodge [Born], May 29th, Bapt

Aug. 18, 1810, Thos. Henry and Ed. Meredith, twin sons of Thos. Henry Hindley, Esq., by Dorothy his wife, of Manchester, now at Bryn y ffynnon, [Born] June 29, 1809, Bapt

Nov. 10, 1810, Richd Edwards, Esq., of the post office, Buried

Nov. 18, 1810, Catherine Meyrick, of W.A., 101 years, Buried

Mch. 13, 1811, Anne, wife of Mr Charles Poyser, Draper, æt 30,108 Buried

July 19, 1811, Shiplev George, S. of George and Jemima Foster Bullen Captain in H.M. Regiment of the Scots Greys, Bapt

Janr. 7, 1812, Mary, wife of Mr Brassey, Eaton, æt 29, Buried

May 29, 1812, Geo. Frederic, S. of Charles and Mary James, Bersh. [Born] Mch. 27, Bapt

Nov. 6, 1812, James Nesbitt, son of Capt. Robert Evans, R.N., by Isabella Evans, his wife, born Dec. 27, 1811, at Chirk, Bapt

105. Frances Eddowes, see the Eddowes pedigree, page 131

106. Chas. Watkin Williams-Wynn, Esq., of Llangedwyn, younger son of the second Sir Watkin Williams-Wynn of Wynnstay, his wife being Mary, eldest daughter sf Sir Foster Cunliffe, Bart., of Acton

107. Mr Edward Dymock's wife was a daughter of John Jones, gent, of Coed y glyn, Wrexham, see pages 191 and 192

108. Anne, first wife of Mr Charles Poyser, the elder, see pages 25 and 31

Dec. 7, 1812, Rowland Samuel, the first general overseer of this parish in office 27 years, [Aged] 74[109]

Fifteenth Register.

18. The Fifteenth Register, consisting of records of burials only, dates from January 3rd, 1813, to October 17th, 1824.

Feb. 19, 1813, Bernard, son of Moses and Lydia Lewis, Abenbury Fawr, Farmer[10]

May 17, 1816, John Thompson, Willow House, [Aged] 36, Buried

Oct. 18, 1822, Mrs Dorothy Crewe, York St., [Aged] 84 (see page 67), Buried

July 2, 1824, The Reverend James Hastings, Holt Street House, [Aged] 75, Buried

Sixteenth Register

19. The Sixteenth Register, consisting of records of baptisms only, dates from January 2nd, 1813, to July 6th, 1824.

Apl. 3, 1813, William, [111] son of William and Elizabeth Overton, Charles St., Wrexham Regis, grocer

July 8, 1815, Charles,[112] son of John and Mary Edwards, Well House, Currier

Nov. 23, 1815, Samuel Thomas, son of Joseph and Martha Baugh, Wrexham Regis, Shoemaker

Nov. 6, 1816, John,[114] son of Moses and Lydia Lewis, Old Llwyn Onn, farmer

Mch. 3, 1818, Edw., [115] son of Edw. and Mary Rowland, High Street, Druggist

Dec. 8, 1818, Wm. Langford,[116] son of John and Sarah Foulkes, Chester St., W.R., Esquire

109. Rowland Samuel, see *Hist. of Par. Church of Wrexham*, p. 107, note 274

110. The late Mr Bernard Lewis of Spring Lodge, and elsewhere

111. The present William Overton, Esq.

112. Charles Edwards, Esq., of Well House ; buried at Wrexham

114. The present John Lewis, Esq., of Beechley, solicitor; mayor in 1862-3

115. The late Mr Edward Rowland, for many years of Bryn Offa, and afterwards of Fern Bank, Grove Road, where he died March 16th, 1889. He spent many years in Adelaide, and after he returned to Wrexham interested himself in making a fine collection of old books, prints, coins, pottery and bric a brac.

116. Wm. Langford Foulkes, see p. 123, note 3

Seventeenth Register.

20. The Seventeenth Register, consisting of marriages only, dates from February 13th, 1813, to November 14th, 1823.

Nov. 19, 1813, Watkin Edwards (see pages 210 and 242), malster and a widower, and Mary Jones of this parish, spinster

Aug. 22, 1814, Geo. Smith, Esq., a widower of the Parish of All Saints, Northampton, and Anne Roper of this parish ; Witnesses : Wm. Massie, R. M. Lloyd, Charlotte Smith, Elizth. Smith, and Benedicta Massie

Nov. 29, 1814, Richard Eyton Edwards of this parish, Bachelor, and Harriet Edwards of this parish, Spinster (see page 214)

Janr. 29, 1815, Richd Christ^r Mansell, Bach., and Marg^t Jones, Spinster, both of the township of Acton, in this parish

Feb. 20, 1215, Archdale Wilson Taylor of the parish of St Aldates in Oxford, and Catherine Briggs, of the parish of Wrexham, Spinster ; Witnesses : Bridget Strong and Thos Trevor Trevor

May 29, 1817, Rd. Meller Benjamin, Solicitor, Bach., of this parish, and Isabella Chloe Downman of this parish (see " Hist. of Par. Church of Wrexham," page 218, note 34)

Apl. 13, 1819, Joseph Willan, Surgeon, Bach., and Seraphina Jones, Spinster,[117] both of this parish

Oct. 21, 1823, Mr John David Lee, Attorney at Law, Bach. of this parish, and Miss Mary Jones, Spinster, of the parish of Bangor (Talwrn, see under sec. 19, January 9, 1802)

21. I have decided, on grounds which appear to me to be sufficient, to give extracts from none of the registers which begin after the year 1825.

---

117. Seraphina Jones, apparently a daughter of Mr John Jones, surgeon, of Mount Street

APPENDIX

IV.

𝕃ocal 𝕎ills.

1. Among the many local wills which I have perused, the following is in many ways so curious that I have thought it worth while to print it in full. I cannot identify any one of the three " mansion houses " mentioned.

" Uppon Sondaye, tbe Twelfte daye of October, One Thousand Sixe Hundreth ane ffyve, David Handson sente his wife for me aboute Twelve of the Clocke at nighte to make his laste will, and I and John ap Hughe ap Harry and the watchemen appointed for that nighte standinge in the streete, the said David Handson declared his last will, and willed me to sett downe the same in wryting to the effecte followinge (that is to saye), ffirst his will was that Ellen, his wife shold enioye the mansion house where he then dwelled, wᵗʰ the appurtennces and one garden neere the brooke, wᵗʰin the towne of Wrexham duringe her naturall life, And that the same after her deathe shold wholie remaine to Margaret, his eldest daughter, her executors and assignes. And his will further was that Jane, his second daughter should haue and enioy one other mansion house withe the appurtennces latelie purchased of Giles Owen, And one close or pcell of grounde in the towne of Wrexham aforesaid commonlie called yr errowe ym hen y dre to have and to hold the same unto her the said Jane, her heirs and assigns for ever. ffurthermorᵉ he gave and bequeathed unto Marye, his yongeste daughter, the mansion house withe the appurtennces wherein ⟨ riffithe ap Griffithe then did and yet doth dwell, and a piece of grounde to the same adioyneinge commonlie called the Brynne. All the reste of his substance he gave to his said wife and Three daughters wch ffoure he appointed to be his executrices. Being demaunded what money was due vnto him wᵗhout specaltie he declared that John Owens was in his Debte in theis seull somes, viz: Thirteene poundes and sixteene shillinges, and Tenne shillinges, and that Mistres Jane Roberts owed him Three poundes, and that David ap Hughe ap Edwarde and Agnes Verche Madocke owed him Twentie shillinges apeece, whereof he willed⟨ his executors to abate unto either of them Tenne shillinges. His will further was that if any of his said intended executrices shoold then dye that then the surviving executrices should haue the whole benefytte of that his last will. He afterwards willed that his yongest daughter should have a barne in the end of the towne of Wrexham over and besides her formr legacy. Before the puttinge of any word in wrytinge herein the said David Handson became speechles, and instantlie therevpon dyed.

ffoulk Salisburie.

This will was proved in London, May 14, 1606, by the four executrices. Who the Foulk Salusbury, the lawyer who drew up the will, was, I do not know. I suppose he belonged to one of the many branches of the house of Lleweni,

2. An abstract of the will of John Tilston, gent, of Wrexham (dated August 17th, 1613, proved February 17th, 1613-14,) may also be given.

I desire my body "to be conveyed from the place where God shall call for me unto my Cosen Mr Henry Tilston's house in Chester, and from thence to be buried in the minster of Chester in the Ile called the Merchantes Ile." He speaks of his lands and tenements in Wrexham, Morton, Esclushⁿm and Chester; of his son Valentine (see Puleston pedigree in ch. xii, and *Hist of Older Noconformity of Wrexham*, p, 10); of his daughter Ciceley wife of Edward Owen of Wrexham; of his daughter Anne, wife of Edward Brereton; of his son-in law, John Edwards (apparently of Stansty), and of many other kinsfolk. To Ellen, wife of his son Valentine, "if shee and her husband be reconciled and live together at the tyme of his death, and if she survive her said husband," £10 p ann. to be paid her out of his estates. "Having hitherto paid £7 p ann. to Robt Puleston of Hauody Werne and Wm Puliston of Abimbrey, for the use of Ellen, wife of my son Valentine, by reason of variance between my son and his wife, I will that my son pay her that sum yearly after my death." "To my dau Anne £13 6 8 p ann. from the issues of my lands in Estlensham [Esclusham], co. Denbigh, lately purchased by way of mortgage for 200 marks of Roger ap Roberte, gent." To my godson David Edwardes, and Elizabeth Edwards, children of John Edwardes of ^tanstie, £6 between them." To my cousin Henry Tilston of the Inner Temple, London, and my son-in-law John Edwards "my two nutt cupps trymmed and covered with silver." To sd Henry "my ringe wth Deathe's head to weare for a remembrance." To my son Val. my wearing apparel "excepte my best murrey gowne wch I will to be sould and employed as other of my goodes." To my cousin Rich. Primate [innkeeper] of Chester, a silver beer cup. To my cousin Robert Blease, my book ofacts and monuments. To 10 poor men "gownes of black frice" and dinners on the day of my funeral, £5 to be then distributed among the poor. For the maintenance and repair of Wrexham Church 40s, etc.

3. I have reserved the most interesting of the three wills which I have selected for printing to the last. Those who have read my *History of the Older Nonconformity of Wrexham,* (the third volume of this series) will remember how large a part of it I devoted to an account of Morgan Lloyd, a man to be revered not only for his eloquent preaching, unblemished character, and unique personality, but also for his contributions to Welsh literature and his passionate and unfeigned love to his native land. My friend, Mr. W. M. Myddelton of St Alban's, lately discovered Morgan Lloyd's will at Somerset House, and advised me of the fact. I lost no time in having it copied word for word, and now print it. The will was made May 20th, 1658, and proved April 13th, 1660.

The last will and testament of Morgan Lloyd, a servant (through Grace) of Jesus Christ and Preacher of his Everlasteinge Gospell at Wrexham in the Countie of Denbigh in Wales, on the Twentieth Day of the Third Month (called May) in the One Thousand sixe Hundred ffiftie and Eight yeare of our Lord, I committ my Immortall Spiritt and Soule into the Everlasteinge Armes of the wonderful ffather of my Deare Lord Jesus Christ the Messiah (his onelie God and myne in whom my life is hid), and I leave this Outward Bodie to bee interred in the heart of the Earth To rest vntil the Day of Resurrection, Thus I departe having christian love to all rejoyceinge in the good, and hating oneley the Evill one of all, Being most wearied with the Bodie of Death that is about my selfe, Butt I am goeing into Paradize, And for asmuch as the God of Abraham (my ffather) and Possessor of heaven and Earth hath bestowed on mee a wife, and giveinge me Children I bequeath vnto them of the small outward thinges as ffoloweth :—To my ffirst begotten Sonne David Lloyd, I leave all my Landes and hereditaments called Kynvell [Cynfel] in Maentwrog in the Countie of Merioneth with my howses there, and the appurtenances thereof, As also my bookes and Papers ; To my second Sonne Samuell Lloyd, I bequeath my tenement in Treff Allen [Trefalyn, or Allington] in Denbighshire, lately called Sinedales,?) Tenement and now leased for ffowerteene yeares to Thomas ffoster, To my third Sonne Caleb Lloyd, To my ffourth Sonne Joshua Lloyd, To my daughters Anne and Elizabeth, I leave and bequeath (a small portion) in gold, silver, plate, household stuffe and Cattell to be Equally divided betweene them ffower. Moreover my will is that in case my sonne David Lloyd Dye without lawfull Issue, That then Kynfell bee the Inheritance of my sonne Samuell, And that the Tenement of Treff Allen aforesaid descend, descend (sic!) to my Sonne Caleb, and that the heyre of Kynvell may not enioye or retaine the Tenement of Treff Allen, while any younger brother or sister of his be alive, and that if Samuell dyeth without lawful Issue, my Will is, that the Tenement of Treff Allen descend to the next younger Sonne or Daughter of myne. Also for the Removeall of worldie cares from my wife after my departure, I desire and appointe my ffaithfull freinds, Ambrose Moston (minister of God's word), and John Pugh of Glynceiriog to be the executors of this my last Will in the sight of God. I appointe also my lyvinge wife Anne Lloyd, Overseer to see this my Will performed, Moreover I appoint the above named Executors to see my wife's joynture of Twentie Poundes yearely paid her, And lest Kynvell should not afford my mother her full thirds, and my wife her full joynture, I doe bequeath to my wife the meadowe in the Tenement of Tref Allen, Dureinge her naturall life ; and after to retorne as aforesaid, Also my will is that Ten Poundes to my mother, Mary Lloyd (in case shee survive mee), be paid to her within one month after my decease, and finally my appointment is That the proffitte of the above menc'oned be Equally and Conscientiously and discretly disposed of for the educac'on of all and every one of my children till they come to age, and that when any of them shall arrive to one Twentie yeares, his or her Inheritance or porc'on be disposs-able by himselfe or her selfe as (I know) the Provident Wisdome of Jehovah (my God) who ordereth all thinges will certainly appoint for good. In Witnes also that this is my last Will and Testament, and that I doe hereby revoake and make voyd all my former Wills in theise matters, I putt my hand and Seale the Day and yeare above written

Mor: Lloyd.

Proved at London, 18 Apr., 1660, and adm'on granted to Ambrose Moston (see *Hist of Older Nonconformity of Wrexham*, pp.35, 36 and 39) and John Pugh, ex'ors

---

V.

The Yales of Yale.

The parish registers of Wrexham contain many references to the Yales of Plas yn Iâl (Hall in Yale), all of which are embodied in the following pedigree. Mr Humphrey Yale is described in 1698 as of Wrexham Abbot, and his son Mr David Yale, as of Penybryn, Wrexham. Mr David Yale's son, the Rev. John Yale, senior, lived also from 1742 to 1754, within the parish of Wrexham, being during that period the resident curate of Berse, though he was at the same time and until a later date (1742-1760) rector of Gwaunysgor. From 1760 until the end of his life he was both rector of Llandegla and perpetual curate of Bryn Eglwys—the parish in which Plas yn Iâl is situate. But he still lived for many years in this town, for he is charged in the Church rate book from 1764 to 1769 for part of Ty Meredith (see page 94) in Chester Street; from 1770 to 1789 for The Office (see page 147); and from 1781 until after 1793 for Mount Street House in the same street, I expect his son the Rev. John Yale, junior, helped him in his duties, and he evidently lived for a while at Mount Street House after his father's death, and perhaps in some of the other houses named. Miss Margaret Yale, sister of the Rev. John Yale, senior, lived from 1768 until about the end of the century at the house in Chester Street which is now "The Rose and Crown."

The Yales of Yale are now extinct, and those who now possess their estates and bear their name are descended from the family of Jones of Llwyn onn, and inherit under the will of Miss Sarah Yale, the last of the race.

I cannot make out who the George Yale was, who, according to the Holt register, died at Plas Jenkin (in township of Dutton Diffaeth and Abenbury), and was buried at Holt, April 22nd, 1704.

YALES OF YALE.

Humphrey Yale, of Plas yn Ial.

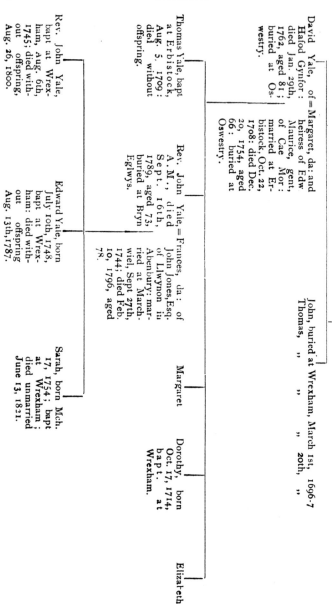

David Yale, of = Margaret, da: and
Halod Gynfor : heiress of Edw
died Jan. 29th, Maurice, gent,
1762, aged 81; of Cae Mor:
buried at Os- married at Er-
westry. bistock, Oct. 22,
1708: died Dec.
20, 1754, aged
66 : buried at
Oswestry.

John, buried at Wrexham, March 1st, 1696-7
Thomas, ,, ,, ,, 20th, ,,

Thomas Yale, bapt
at Erbistock,
Aug. 5. 1709 :
died without
offspring.

Rev. John Yale,
A. M., died
Sept. 16th,
1789, aged 73:
buried at Bryn
Eglwys.

Rev. John Yale = Frances, da: of
of Llwynon in John Jones, Esq.
Abenbury: mar- of Llwynon in
ried at March- Abenbury: mar-
wiel, Sept 27th, ried at March-
1744; died Feb.
10, 1796, aged
78.

Margaret

Dorothy, born
Oct. 17, 1714,
bapt. at
Wrexham.

Elizabeth

Rev. John Yale,
bapt at Wrex-
ham, Aug. 6th.
1745; died with-
out offspring,
Aug. 26, 1800.

Edward Yale, born
July 10th, 1748,
bapt at Wrex-
ham : died with-
out offspring
Aug. 13th, 1787.

Sarah, born Mch.
17, 1754; bapt
at Wrexham ;
died unmarried
June 13, 1821.

Corrections

IN THE

HISTORY OF THE PARISH CHURCH OF WREXHAM.

P. 15, top line, for " fsesionum," read " fessionum "

P. 46, line 25 from top, for " nearly three acres," read "a little over two acres "

P. 56, line 3 from top, for " Thos," read " Townshend "

P. 68, line 4 from top, for " Tegengl," read " Tegeingl "

P. 86, note 4 : Instead of the sentence, " He married Jane, daughter of Edward
Puleston, of Llwyn y cnottiau, Esq., and widow of Thomas Goldsmith,
gentleman," read " He married Jane, fourth daughter of the Rev.
Edward Puleston, M.A., of Llwyn y cnottie (parson of Llanynys), and
relict of Thos. Gouldsmith, gent, second son of Thos. Gouldsmith,
mercer, of Wrexham,"

P. 87, note 12, line 3, for " Helen," read " Eleanor "

P. 99, note 163 : Erase the words "a kinsman of Dr. Daniel Williams." The
Hugh Edwards whom the Doctorr names as his kinsman was, I now
believe, another person of the same name.

P. 111, note 294, last line : Between " Liverpool " and " died " insert the word
" He."

P. 113, note 315, last line, for " 32," read " 35 "

P. 143. line 3 from top, for " Lane, Wrexham," read " now The Grange Farm "

P. 146, note 46, 1st line, for " the son of Thomas Yale, one of the pilgrim fathers,"
read " the son of David Yale, senr," see p. 214 (53)

P. 151, note 62, for " Gathewsin," read " Garthewin "

P. 207, (6), after inscription to Mrs. Myddelton, write : She died April 8th, 1747,
aged 59

P. 218 (11b) last line: For " 1853 " read " 1850."

P. 219, line 13 from top, for "second-named," read " first-named "

Also consult pages 222-225 of the *History of the Parish Church of Wrexham*, the
errata attached to the first page of that book, and pages 166-167 of the *History of
the Older Nonconformity of Wrexham.*

Corrections

IN

"HISTORY OF OLDER NONCONFORMITY OF WREXHAM."

P. 35, line 9 from bottom, for ."her son," read "her grandson, second son of
Morgan Lloyd "

P. 53, line 5 from bottom : For " 1669 " read " 1699 "

P. 58, line 22 fram top : For " Prospect House " read " Red House "

P. 76, lines 21 and 26 from top : For " Bewdley " read " West Bromwich "
„   Line 8 from bottom : For " 1883 " read " 1833 "

Page 83. bottom line : For " sister in law Mrs Ellen Boult (see sec 34)" read
"nephew, Mr William Boult "

P. 86, note 33, 4th line from top : For " June 29th, 1816 " read " June 16th,
1829 "

P. 87, 8th line from top : For "William" read "J"

P. 103, sec 20 : The Rev. Dafydd Jones of Adwy'r clawd, who was buried in the Dissenters' Grave Yard, Wrexham, on March 1774, was, I now learn, a Calvinistic Methodist preacher, and not the pastor of the Baptist Chapel, Wrexham. The latter went not to Adwy, but to Liverpool. and there died, July 20th, 1779, aged 72, and was buried in the old Baptist Cemetery, Everton Road, where also was buried his wife, Mary, who died February 1780, aged 78. Erase in the text whatever is contrary to these facts.

P. 104, lines 1-3 from top: erase the whole sentence beginning " I always fancy " etc

P. 112, note 28 : For "Uncle" read "Grandfather"

P. 113, note 32, 2nd line : for "1757," read "1857 "

P. 116, note 4, last line ; For " 1826 " read " 1836 "

P. 121, note 19 : For " 1863 " read " 1883 "

P. 133, note 2, 4th line : for " December 11th," read " December " erasing 11th

P. 149 under April 21st, 1766 and in note 78 : For " Hall " read " Holt "

Corrections

IN THE

"HISTORY OF THE TOWN OF WREXHAM, ITS HOUSES STREETS, FIELDS, AND OLD FAMILIES,"

(THE PRESENT VOLUME).

P. 2, line 22 from bottom : for " Magaret," read "Margaret '

P. 3, line 4 from bottom: for "existance," read " existence "

P. 5 note, line 2 from bottom: for "Trever," read " Trevor "

P. 9 note, first line : for " felling," read " felting "

P. 9 note, fourth line : for " form," read " from "

P. 11, 6th line from bottom: for " forget " read " forgot "

P. 17, line 13 from top : for " 1757," read "1759 "

P. 18, line 10 from top : for " Llanddyn," read " Llandin "

P. 29, line 22 from top : erase all the sentence beginning thus " I think there is little doubt " etc. Since this sentence was written I have come across a document dated December 1789, in which Wm. Lloyd of Wrexham, *surgeon*, and William Lloyd, *the younger of Flaspower*, Esq., are both mentioned, so that they were evidently different persons. I suppose it was Mr Wm. Lloyd, the surgeon, who married Miss Mary Jones, of Apothecary's Hall (see page 30, sec. 29).

P. 32, line 3 from bottom : for "country," read " county "

P. 33, line 10 from top : for " Betwys," read " Bettws "

P. 37, line 18 from bottom : for " aferrwards," read "afterwards "

P. 38, line 4 from bottom : for " Cefn y Cwn," read "Camfa'r Cwn "

P 40, note, last line : for " of heir," read " heir of "

P. 42, line 18 from top : insert between " was " and "entirely," the word "an

P. 47, line 14 from top : for " representation," read " representative "

P. 49, line 11 from bottom: for " Wrexhem," read " Wrexham "

P. 50, line 5 from top: for "mainhood," read " manhood "

P. 50, last line of note : erase stop between "ynghafell," and "y eglwys "

P. 52, line 4 from top : for " Crue," read "Crewe "

P. 54, note 3, 4th line: for " John," read " James "

P. 62, note 13: The statement here made that Edward Meredith, *the singer*, was a *son* of Edward Meredith, smith, of Felin Puleston, which rested on the statement of one of the latter's descendants, I have since discovered to be inaccurate

P. 66, line 26 from top : for "*in* Hafod Gynfor," read "*and* Hafod Gynfor, etc."

P. 73, line 16 from bottom : for "is" read "are"

P. 79, note, 6th line : for "Esclustr," read "Esclushä"

P. 81, line 9 from top : for "Methodistiaith yn Ngwrescam," read " Methodistiaid Calfinaidd yn Ngwrecsam "

P. 88, line 16 from top: for "Cefn y Cron," read "Camfa'r Cwn "

P. 94, line 8 from bottom: for "by Chester, whom," read "Chester, by whom

P. 122, line 10 from bottom: for "Cai," read "Cae"

P. 131 : for Sir John Gladstone, *knight*," read "Sir John Gladstone, Bart."

P. 132, line 10 from bottom : for "important," read "unimportant"

P. 133, lines 19 and 21 from top: for "Aerau," read "Acre "

P. 134, line 14 from bottom: for "1623," read "1620"

P. 171, lines 2 and 8 from top : for "Brynyffnnon," read "Brynyffynnon "

P. 172, year 1847: for "Coullas " read "Coultas"

P. 190, note, last line but two . for "Bnchdraeth," read "Buchdraeth "

P. 211 and 212: As to the Latin quotations from Coleridge's letter "afflictum " on page 211 is certainly wrong : one would expect "afflicte," but I have followed the copyist. As to the lines on page 212, "mala fide " should be "male fida," as in the copy

P. 234, lines 9 and 10 from bottom : for "the definite form of the name, Y Werddon," read "what was taken to be the definite form," etc., The actual Welsh name of Ireland is "Iwerddon," not "Y Werddon"

P. 240, 12th line from bottom : for "way," read "away "

P. 240, bottom line : for "the John David," read "the said John David "

P. 254, 14th line from bottom: for "Duwdod " read "Druidod "

P. 254, 12th line from bottom : for "Anna Tye " read "A. Hughes "

P. 265 : The entry corresponding to note 40a has been omitted. It is as follows

P.   Aug. 22, 1689, Mr. Robert Betton, junr., buryed

P. 265, last line of note 40 : for "Clough " read "Hough "

P. 272, third line from bottom : for "Spingter " read "Spinster," and insert the note reference 67

ADDENDA.

In the list of "Early Books printed in Wrexham " on pages 252-255, the two after-named were unaccountably omitted :—*The Tracts of Powys*, 1795, printed by J. Marsh "at the Druid Press, Wrexham, a thin quarto volume by Philip Yorke, Esq," the groundwork of his later and more important work, *The Royal Tribes of Wales*, R. Williams.

The Royal Tribes of Wales by Philip Yorke, Esq., of Erddig, printed by John Painter, 1799.

LIST OF SUBSCRIBERS.

Acton, T. Arthur, Grove Road, Wrexham
Alexander, Wm., 6 Hill Street, Wrexham
Allmand, Ernest, Hope Street, Wrexham
Allmand, Frank, Chester Street, Wrexham
Ashley, W. J., University of Toronto, Canada

Bethell, Wm., Derwent Bank, Malton
Barnes, Lieut.-Col. J. R., The Quinta, Chirk
Barton, Thos. B., 3 Grove Park, Wrexham
Bate, George, White House, Bersham, near Wrexham
Bates, Thomas, 1 Tenter's Square, Wrexham
Beirne, John, Albion Brewery, Wrexham
Beirne, Wm., Charles Street, Wrexham
Bennett, Edgar, 2 Court Ash, Yeovil
Berkeley, Arthur W., Witton Terrace, Wrexham
Bewsher, Mrs. Anne, Homestead, Wrexham
Brown, F. B. (Rev.), Coed Efa, near Wrexham
Burton, John, The Old Parsonage, Gresford
Bury, John, 10 Temple Row, Wrexham (4 copies)
Bury, J. Oswell, Derby Villa, Wrexham (2 copies)
Bury, Thomas, Town Clerk, Wrexham

Caldecott, Geoffrey. 12 Regent Street, Wrexham
Chadwick, J. A., Burton Brewery, Wrexham
Clarke, Edwin S., Oak Alyn, near Wrexham
Cooper, F., Regent Street, Wrexham
Cudworth, James, 5 Wrexham Fechan, Wrexham

Darby, John H., Brymbo Hall, near Wrexham
Davenport, John L., Foster Street, Wrexham
Davies, Charles, Tailor, Wrexham
Davies, Edward, M.D., Plas Darland, Wrexham
Davies, Howel, Bôdhowel, Wrexham
Davies, Llewelyn, Eirianfa, Wrexham
Davies, Meredith, 1 St James's Terrace, Rhosddu
Davies-Cooke, Philip B., Gwysàney, Mold (3 copies)
Davies, Rev. D. Stanley, St James' Vicarage, Rhosddu

Davies, Wm., 13 Queen Street, Wrexham
Dobie, Alexander, Regent Street. Wrexham
Dodd, Chas., Clovelly Cottage. Wrexham
Done, Robert Henry, Town Hall, Wrexham
Edgar, James, Milton Villa, Wrexham
Edwards, David, Brynawel, Wrexham
Edwards, Edward, Grove Park. Wrexham
Egerton. Sir R. E., Coedyglyn, Wrexham
Evans, E. D., 31 Regent Street, Wrexham
Evans. Edward, J.P., Bronwylfa, near Wrexham
Evans Rev. M. O., Avilion, Wrexham
Evans, W, R., 29 Chester Street, Wrexham
Evans, R. W., Old Vaults, Chester Street, Wrexham

Findlay, G. J., Plaspower Colliery, Wrexham
Fitzhugh, T. Ll., Plaspower. near Wrexham (5 copies)
Fletcher, Rev. Canon W. H., The Vicarage, Wrexham
Francis, Jno., Nythfa, Wrexham
Fraser, James, 18 Queen Street. Wrexham
Fraser, W. Angus, 7 Hill Street, Wrexham
Frater, George, Williams' Bank, Wrexham

Giles, E., Brymbo House, Nr Wrexham
Green, T. E., Parr's Bank, Wrexham
Griffith, N. R., The Elms, Wrexham
Griffith, Rev. T. Ll., Deal Rectory, Kent
Gummow, M. J., Regent Street, Wrexham

Harrop, John, 14 King Street, Wrexham
Hawkins, F. H., The Priory, Wrexham
Heyward, Wm., 30 Chester Street, Wrexham
Hodgson, T., Inglenook, Bowdon, Cheshire
Howell, Ven. Archdeacon, Vicarage, Gresford
Hughes, J. Allington, Solicitor, Wrexham
Hughes, Edward, 27 Wrexham Fechan, Wrexham
Hugh- Jones, Ll., The Priory, Wrexham
Huxley, Charles, Builder, 11 Smithfield Road

James, T. Reginald, Brynyffynnon Offices, Wrexham
Jerman, Rev. E., Bersham Road, Wrexham
Jones, David, 1 Arybryn Terrace, Wrexham
Jones, E. Bryn Menai, Wrexham
Jones, Edwin, 12 King Street, Wrexham
Jones, E. Meredith, Charles Street, Wrexham
Jones, F. Meredith, St John's, Wrexham

Jones, R. Meredith, Rockland, New Brighton (2 copies)
Jones, Henry, 7 Cunliffe Street, Rhosddu
Jones, Hugh, Lion Stores, Wrexham
Jones, John, Grove Lodge, Wrexham
Jones, Peleg I., Eirianfa, Broughton, Nr Wrexham
Jones, Robert, 25 Gwynfa Terrace, Wrexham
Jones, A. Seymour, Pendower, Wrexham (2 copies)
Jones, Thomas, Lion Stores, Wrexham
Jones, T. O., F.R. Hist. S., Llandudno
Jones, Rev. W. V., M.A., 7 Stanley Street, Wrexham

Kenrick, J., The Lodge, Rhosddu
Kyrke, R. V., Penywern, near Mold

Lerry, C. D., 8 Albert Street, Wrexham
Lewis, J., Beechley, Wrexham
Lloyd, Edward, Regent Buildings, Wrexham

Mainwaring, Chas. S., Galltfaenan, Trefnant R.S.O.
Manchester Public Free Reference Library, King Street
Martin, William, 52 Hope Street, Wrexham
Mason, Edmund, Beaconsfield, Wrexham
Mason, Job, Percy Lodge, Wrexham
Meredith, Lieut.-Col. H. W., Pentrebychan, near Wrexham
Murless, Charles, Wynnstay Hotel, Wrexham
Myddelton, W. M., Holywell Hill, St Albans

Nicholson, A. C., Salop House, Oswestry

Oliver, John, 16 Talbot Road, Wrexham
Overton, Wm., Irvon House, Wrexham
Owen, Alfred, Woodhey, Wrexham
Owen, Benjamin, Victoria Road, Wrexham
Owen, Edward, India Office, London, S.W.

Parry, J. W., 23 High Street, Wrexham
Parry-Jones, W. R., Plasyfron, Wrexham
Pierce, D. D., 16 Hope Street, Wrexham
Pierce, Mrs Jane, Sherbourne House, Leamington
Pierce, J. Hopley, Solicitor, Wrexham
Pierce, Wm., 31 Bridge Street, Wrexham
Piercy, Robert, Island Green House, Wrexham
Phennah, James, 4 Temple Row, Wrexham
Phennah, Richard, Woodlands, Chester Road, Wrexham

Potter, W., High Street, Wrexham
Powell, Benjamin, 14 Queen Street, Wrexham
Powell, Ellison, Constitutional Club, Northumberland Avenue, London
Powell, J. E., 6 Town Hill, Wrexham
Powell, Mrs. Mary, Irvon Villa, Wrexham
Preston, A. C., Wrexham
Prichard, John, Longfields, Wrexham
Prichard, Wm., Highfield, Wrexham

Rawlins, F. L., Dyserth Road, Rhyl
Rees, Rev. W., Berse Drelincourt, Wrexham
Richards, Evan, Brynyffynnon, Wrexham
Roberts, Rev. D., D.D., Greenfield, Wrexham
Roberts R., M.R.C.V.S., 30 Bridge Street, Wrexham
Roberts, John, M.R.C.V.S., 46 Chester Street, Wrexham
Rocke, George, 60 Weston Street, Bermondsey, London
Rogers, John Tudor, Bryn Tudur, Penygelli
Rogers, M., 12 Henblas Street, Wrexham
Rogers, J. Williams, 2 Chapel Street, Wrexham
Russell, W. J., B.A., Grove Park School, Wrexham

Samuel, Thos. M., 3 Holt Street Terrace, Wrexham
Samuel, W. E., Builder, Wrexham
Sauvage, Thos., Golden Eagle, Wrexham
Seebohm, F., The Hermitage, Hitchen
Scott, Thomas, Ash Grove, Wrexham
Sephton, Jno., The Gables, Percy Road, Wrexham
Shrubshole, George W., Chester
Smallwood, John, 7 Charles Street, Wrexham
Smallwood, R, H., Regent Street, Wrexham
Smith, Edwin, 33 Wheeley Road, Birmingham
Soames, F. W., Llwyn Onn Hall, near Wrexham
Stobo, Robert, 27 Lambpit Street, Wrexham
Storr, F., Egerton Street, Wrexham
Sturge, F. A., Coed Efa, Nr Wrexham (2 copies)

Taylor, Henry, F.S.A., Curzon Park, Chester
Taylor, Wm., 24 Abbot Street, Wrexham
Thomas, John Lewis, Arybryn Terrace, Wrexham
Thomas, John E., C. Engineer, Wrexham
Thomas, Wm., Bron Llwyn, Wrexham

Underwood, J. 30 Hope Street, Wrexham

The Atlas of Wrexham, 1872

Bridge Books are publishing in a large page format (A3) a reprint of the 1872 Ordnance Survey map of Wrexham at a scale of 10 feet=1 mile.

This is the most detailed survey ever carried out of the town and shows every street in detail e.g. all buildings, pavements, garden paths, sheds, greenhouses, ponds, driveways, railway tracks, turntables, lamp-posts, even outside toilets as well as naming every church, chapel, public house, public building (many with room plans), street, road, court, alleyway, notable houses, breweries, banks and post offices.

This atlas is the ideal companion volume to *The History of the Town of Wrexham* by A N Palmer and will be an essential reference source for anyone with an interest in the town in the second half of the 19th century.

The edition will be limited. Available early 1998.

64pp, 420mm x 295mm, softback, £14.95.

To reserve your copy of *The Atlas of Wrexham, 1872*, or to order a copy of our current catalogue, please contact Bridge Books now on 01978-358661.